2D
iOS & tvOS
Games
by Tutorials

By the raywenderlich.com Tutorial Team

Mike Berg, Michael Briscoe, Ali Hafizji, Neil North,
Toby Stephens, Rod Strougo, Marin Todorov and Ray Wenderlich

2D iOS & tvOS Games by Tutorials

Mike Berg, Michael Briscoe, Ali Hafizji, Neil North, Toby Stephens, Rod Strougo, Marin Todorov and Ray Wenderlich

ISBN: 978-1-942878-14-8

Dedications

"To my wonderful wife and family, who make it possible to do what I do."

—*Mike Berg*

"To what's really important in life - family. To my mom Barbara,
sister Kimberly, friend Kelli, daughters Mcghan and Brynne,
and all six of my grandchildren; thanks for the love and support.
And to my dad who has moved on; I miss you Pops."

—*Michael Briscoe*

"To my beautiful wife Batul and my parents - Thanks for
supporting and believing in me."

—*Kauserali Hafizji*

"To my family and loved ones who always support me and my ambitions."

—*Neil North*

"To Caroline, Nina and Lucy – for your endless encouragement and support."

—*Toby Stephens*

"To my always supportive and understanding wife Agata, and my family.
I love you very much."

—*Rod Strougo*

"To my parents - ever so supportive and loving. To Mirjam."

—*Marin Torodov*

"To the editors, authors, and translators at raywenderlich.com.
Teamwork lets you dream bigger!"

—*Ray Wenderlich*

About the authors

Mike Berg is a full-time game artist who is fortunate enough to work with many indie game developers from all over the world. When he's not manipulating pixel colors, he loves to eat good food, spend time with his family, play games and be happy. You can check out his work at: www.weheartgames.com

Michael Briscoe is an Independent Software Developer with over 30 years of programming experience. His platforms of choice are anything Apple, from the Macintosh, to iPhone, iPad, and Apple TV. His specialty is entertainment software, like games, and simulations. Visit his website at: skyrocketsoftware.wordpress.com

Kauserali Hafizji (a.k.a. Ali) is a developer at heart. He is an avid programmer and loves writing code, even over the weekend. A good read, cool dip in the pool and a hot cheesy meal would be the perfect end to his weekend. You can find Ali on Twitter as @Ali_hafizji.

Neil North is an Asset Management, Software Development and Business Automation Professional who also enjoys creating indie games, audio engineering and helping other people to achieve their creative goals. He also teaches iOS game and app development and has courses on Udemy and CartoonSmart. Neil is proudly based in Australia. Visit his web site: apptlycreative.com

Toby Stephens has over twenty years of software development experience, and is currently Head of Mobile Development at inplaymaker in London. Toby has a passion for gaming and game writing. He also writes music and enjoys a spot of bread baking. You can find him on Twitter: as @TJShae and on his website: tjshae.com

Rod Strougo began his journey in physics and games way back with an Apple][, writing games in Basic. Rod's career took a diversion, spending 15 years writing software for IBM and AT&T. These days he follows his passion in game development and teaching, providing iOS Training at Big Nerd Ranch and cool secret projects. Originally from Rio de Janeiro, Brazil, he lives in Atlanta, GA with his wife and sons.

Marin Todorov is is an independent iOS developer and author. He started developing on an Apple][more than 20 years ago and keeps rocking till today. Besides crafting code, Marin also enjoys blogging, writing books, teaching, and speaking. He sometimes open sources his code. He walked the way to Santiago. Visit his web site: www.underplot.com

Ray Wenderlich is an iPhone developer, gamer and the founder of Razeware LLC. Ray is passionate about both making apps and teaching others the techniques to make them. He and the Tutorial Team have written a bunch of tutorials about iOS development available at: www.raywenderlich.com

Harken all genders! You may or may not have noticed that all of this book's authors are men. This is unfortunate, and not by design. If you are a woman developing for iOS and are interested in joining the Tutorial Team to write about gaming topics, we'd love to hear from you! ☺

About the editors

Tammy Coron was the tech editor of this book. She is a writer, musician, artist, and software engineer. As an independent creative professional, Tammy spends her time developing software, writing, illustrating, and reminding others that The Impossible Just Takes A Little Longer. She also hosts the Roundabout: Creative Chaos podcast.

Bradley C. Phillips was the editor of this book. He was the first editor to come aboard at raywenderlich.com, and has worked as a journalist and previously directed the intelligence department of an investigative firm in New York City. Right now, Bradley works freelance and pursues his own projects. Contact him if you need a skilled and experienced editor for your blog, books or anything else.

Ray Wenderlich was the final pass editor of this book. He is an iPhone developer, gamer and the founder of Razeware LLC. Ray is passionate about both making apps and teaching others the techniques to make them. He and the Tutorial Team have written a bunch of tutorials about iOS development available at: www.raywenderlich.com

About the artists

Mike Berg created the artwork for most of the games for this book. Mike is a full-time game artist who is fortunate enough to work with many indie game developers from all over the world. When he's not manipulating pixel colors, he loves to eat good food, spend time with his family, play games and be happy. You can check out his work: www.weheartgames.com

Vinnie Prabhu created all of the music and sounds for the games in this book. Vinnie is a music composer/software engineer from Northern Virginia who has done music and sound work for concerts, plays and video games. He's also a staff member on OverClocked ReMix, an online community for music and video game fans. You can find Vinnie on Twitter as @palpablevt.

Vicki Wenderlich created many of the illustrations in this book, and the artwork for Drop Charge. Vicki discovered a love of digital art several years ago, and has been making app art and digital illustrations ever since. She is passionate about helping people pursue their dreams and makes app art for developers available on her website: gameartguppy.com

Table of Contents:

Introduction

In this book, you will learn how to make iOS and tvOS games in Swift using Apple's built-in 2D game framework: Sprite Kit. However, this raises a number of questions:

- **Why Sprite Kit?** Sprite Kit is Apple's built-in framework for making 2D games on iOS. It's easy to learn, especially if you already have some Swift or iOS experience.

- **Why iOS?** For a game developer, there's no better platform. The development tools are well-designed and easy to learn, and the App Store makes it incredibly simple to distribute your game to a massive audience – and get paid for it!

- **Why tvOS?** Just recently Apple released a new Apple TV, along with the ability for developers to write their own games for it. And one of the great things about Sprite Kit is it's cross-platform on iOS, OS X, and tvOS. If you get your game running on iOS it's incredibly easy to get it working on the other platforms as well. And it's super exciting to get your games to run on the big screen!

- **Why Swift?** Swift is an easy language to get started with, especially if you are a beginner to the iOS platform. In addition, we believe Swift is the way of the future for iOS development, so take this as an opportunity to develop your Swift skills early!

- **Why 2D?** As impressive as 3D games may be, 2D games are a lot easier to make. The artwork is far less complicated, and programming is faster and doesn't require as much math. All of this allows you as a developer to focus on creating killer gameplay.

If you're a beginner, making 2D games is definitely the best way to get started.

If you're an advanced developer, you can still make a 2D game much faster than a 3D game. Since it's not necessarily the case that you earn more money with 3D games, why not go for the easier win? Plus, some people (like myself) prefer 2D games anyway!

So rest easy – with iOS, tvOS, 2D games and Sprite Kit, you're making great choices!

History of this book

Two years ago, we wrote a book called *iOS Games by Tutorials*, covering how to make 2D games with Sprite Kit. One year later, we released a second edition fully ported to Swift, as a free update for existing customers.

This year at WWDC, Apple announced a brand new set of APIs called **GameplayKit**. These are a set of APIs that make it easy to add pathfinding, AI, and other cool features into your games.

Then there's the elephant in the room - **tvOS**, which now allows us to create games for the living room!

These changes were so significant that rather than trying to give them a token coverage in an update to iOS Games by Tutorials, we decided it would be better to revamp the book completely. Hence this book!

If you have already read *iOS Games by Tutorials* and you're wondering what's new in this book, here are the highlights:

- **Zombie Conga**: Chapters 1-4 are mostly the same as in *iOS Games by Tutorials*. Chapter 5, "Camera" is completely new, covering the new SKCamera class introduced in iOS 9. We also moved coverage of Labels to this game in Chapter 6, "Labels". Finally, we added a new chapter on porting the game to tvOS in Chapter 7, "Beginning tvOS".

- **Cat Nap**: These chapters have been heavily refactored to make use of new features introduced in the Sprite Kit Scene Editor in iOS 9, such as reference nodes. Chapter 12, "Crop, Video, and Shape Nodes" is completely rewritten to cover the topic more effectively. Finally, we added a new chapter on some more advance tvOS porting techniques in Chapter 13, "Intermediate tvOS".

- **Drop Charge**: This is a new game and new set of chapters (Chapters 14-17). In these chapters, you'll review previous material in the book and learn about GameplayKit state machines, particle systems, and juice.

- **Dino Defense**: This is a second new game and new set of chapters (Chapters 18-20). In these chapters, you'll take a deep dive into GameplayKit and learn about its Entity-Component System, Pathfinding, and Agents, Goals, and Behaviors features.

- **Delve**: This is a third brand new game and new set of chapters (Chapters 21-24). In these chapters, you'll dive into more advanced concepts like tile map games, procedural levels, and GameplayKit randomization.

- **CircuitRacer**: Chapters 24-25 are mostly the same as in *iOS Games by Tutorials*. There are also two brand new chapters covering the new ReplayKit API and iAd integration (Chapters 27 and 28).

As you can see, it's a major overhaul. If you've read the book before and have limited time, the best thing to do would be to focus on the new games, or the chapters that interest you most.

About this book

If I may say so, this book is something special. Our goal at raywenderlich.com is for this to be the best book on game programming you've ever read.

There are a lot of game programming books out there, and many of them are quite good, so this is a lofty goal! Here's what we've done to try to accomplish it:

- **Learn by making games**: All the books teach the high-level concepts and show code snippets, but many leave you on your own to put together a complete, functioning game. In this book, you will learn by making five games in a variety of genres – games that are actually fun. Our hope is that you can and will reuse techniques or code from these games to make your own games.

- **Learn by challenges**: Every chapter in this book includes some challenges at the end that are designed to help you practice what you've learned. Following a tutorial is one thing, but applying it yourself is quite another. The challenges in this book take off the training wheels and push you to solidify your knowledge by grappling with a problem on your own. (We also provide the answers, of course.) You'll have a blast doing them, too!

- **Focus on polish**: The key to making a hit game is polish – adding loads of well-considered details that set your game apart. Because of this, we've put our money where our mouths are and invested in a top-notch artist and sound designer to create resources for the games in this book. We've also included a chapter all about polishing your game with special effects – otherwise known as adding "Juice" – which we think you will love.

- **High-quality tutorials**: Our site is known for its high-quality programming tutorials, and we've put a lot of time and care into the tutorials in this book to make them equally valuable, if not more so. Each chapter has been put through a rigorous multi-stage editing process – resulting in some chapters being rewritten several times! We've strived to ensure that each chapter contains great technical content while also being fun and easy to follow.

After you finish reading this book, please let me know if you think we were successful in meeting these goals. You can email me anytime at ray@raywenderlich.com.

We hope you enjoy the book, and we can't wait to see what games you come up with!

iOS game development: a history

As you will see, it's easy to make games for iOS with SpriteKit – but it wasn't always so. In the early days of iOS, your only option was to make your game with OpenGL ES, which (along with Metal) is the lowest-level graphics API available on the platform. OpenGL ES is notoriously difficult to learn, and it was a big barrier to entry for many beginning game developers.

After a while, third-party developers released some game frameworks on top of OpenGL, the most popular of which was called Cocos2D – in fact, several of us wrote a book on the subject! Many of the games at the top of the App Store charts were made with Cocos2D, and many developers can say that Cocos2D was their entry point into the world of game development.

Cocos2D was a great framework, but it wasn't written or supported by Apple. Because of this, there were often problems when new versions of iOS were released, or with integrating other Apple APIs into the system.

To resolve this, with iOS 7 Apple released a new framework for making 2D games: Sprite Kit. Its API is very similar to Cocos2D, with similar types for the sprites, actions and scenes that Cocos2D developers know and love, so fans of the older framework will have no trouble getting up to speed. Sprite Kit also has a few extra bells and whistles, like support for playing videos, making shapes and applying special image effects.

The Sprite Kit API is well-designed and easy to use, especially for beginners. Best of all, you can use it knowing that it's fully supported by Apple and heavily optimized to make 2D games on iOS.

From here on out, if you want to make a 2D game on iOS, tvOS, or MacOS X, we definitely recommend you use Sprite Kit rather than other game frameworks. There's one big exception: if you want to make a cross platform game (i.e. for Android, Windows, etc). Sprite Kit is an Apple-only API so it will be more challenging to port your game from Sprite Kit to other platforms than using other options such as Unity.

If you just want to make something simple for Apple platforms only, Sprite Kit is the way to go. So let's get you up to speed with Sprite Kit!

What you need

To follow along with the tutorials in this book, you need the following:

- **A Mac running OS X Mountain Lion or later**. This is so you can install the latest version of the required development tool: Xcode.

- **Xcode 7.1 or later**. Xcode is the main development tool for iOS. You need to use Xcode 7.1 or later in this book, because Xcode 7.1 is the first version of Xcode that supports tvOS development. You can download the latest version of Xcode for free from the Apple developer site here: https://developer.apple.com/xcode/download/

- **An iPhone or iPod Touch running iOS 9 or later, and a paid membership to the iOS development program [optional]**. For most of the chapters in the book, you can run your code on the iOS 9 Simulator that comes with Xcode. However, there are a few chapters later in the book that require a device for testing. Also note that Sprite Kit performs better on devices than it does in the Simulator, so your frame rates will appear lower than expected when running your game in the Simulator.

- **A new Apple TV [optional]**: You do not need an new Apple TV since you can work with the Apple TV simulator, but it's deinitely handy to test with a physical remote - plus awesome to see the games on the big screen!

If you don't have the latest version of Xcode installed, be sure to do that before continuing with the book.

Who this book is for

This book is for beginning to advanced iOS developers. Wherever you fall on that spectrum, you will learn a lot from this book!

This book does require some basic knowledge of Swift. If you do not know Swift, you can still follow along with the book because all of the instructions are in step-by-step format. However, there will likely be parts that are confusing due to gaps in your knowledge. Before beginning this book, you might want to go through our Swift Apprentice series, which covers the basics of Swift development:

- www.raywenderlich.com/store

How to use this book

There are two ways to use this book, depending on whether you are a complete beginner to iOS game development or an advanced developer with knowledge of other 2D game frameworks.

If you are a complete beginner

If you're a complete beginner to iOS game development, the best way to read this book is from cover to cover. We have arranged the chapters to introduce the material in the most logical manner to build up your skills one layer at a time.

If you are an advanced developer

If you're an advanced developer with knowledge of other 2D game frameworks, you will have an easier time adapting to Sprite Kit, as the core concepts and syntax will look very familiar.

Our suggestion is to skim through the early chapters and focus more on the later, more advanced chapters, or where you have a particular interest.

Don't worry – you can jump right into any chapter in the book, because we'll always have a starter project waiting for you!

What's ahead: an overview

2D iOS & tvOS Games by Tutorials is split into five sections, moving from beginning to advanced topics. In each section, you will create a complete mini-game, from scratch! The book also includes some bonus chapters at the end that we think you'll enjoy.

Let's take a look at what's ahead!

Section I: Getting started

This section covers the basics of making 2D games with Sprite Kit. These are the most important techniques, the ones you'll use in almost every game you make. By the time you reach the end of this section, you'll be ready to make your own simple game.

Throughout this section you will create an action game called Zombie Conga, where you take the role of a happy-go-lucky zombie who just wants to party!

You will build this game across seven chapters, in stages:

1. **Chapter 1, Sprites**: Get started by adding your first sprites to the game: the background and the zombie.

2. **Chapter 2, Manual Movement**: You'll make the zombie follow your touches around the screen and get a crash-course in basic 2D vector math.

3. **Chapter 3, Actions**: You'll add cats and crazy cat ladies to the game, as well as basic collision detection and gameplay.

4. **Chapter 4, Scenes**: You'll add a main menu to the game, as well as win and lose scenes.

5. **Chapter 5, Camera**: You'll make the game scroll from left to right, and finally, add the conga line itself.

6. **Chapter 6, Labels**: You'll add a label to show the zombie's lives and the number of cats in his conga line.

7. **Chapter 7, Beginning tvOS**: You'll get Zombie Conga working on tvOS, in just a few simple steps!

Section II: Physics and nodes

In this section, you will learn how to use the built-in 2D physics engine included with Sprite Kit to create movement as realistic as that in Angry Birds or Cut the Rope. You will also learn how to use special types of nodes that allow you to play videos or create shapes in your game.

In the process, you will create a physics puzzle game called Cat Nap, where you take the role of a cat who has had a long day and just wants to go to bed.

You will build this game across five chapters, in stages:

8. **Chapter 8, Scene Editor**: You'll begin by creating the first level of the game. By the end, you'll have a better understanding of Xcode's level designer, better known as the scene editor.

9. **Chapter 9, Beginning Physics**: In this chapter, you're going to make a little detour in order to learn the basics of creating physics simulations for your games. As a bonus, you'll learn how to prototype games inside an Xcode playground.

10. **Chapter 10, Intermediate Physics**: You'll learn about physics-based collision detection and create custom classes for your Sprite Kit nodes.

11. **Chapter 11, Advanced Physics:** You'll add two more levels to the game as you learn about interactive bodies, joints between bodies, composed bodies and more.

12. **Chapter 12, Crop, Video and Shape Nodes:** You'll add special new blocks to Cat Nap while learning about additional types of nodes that allow you to do amazing things—like play videos, crop images and create dynamic shapes.

13. **Chapter 13, Intermediate tvOS:** In this last chapter you are going to bring Cat Nap to the silver screen. You are going to take the fully developed game and add support for tvOS so the player can relax on their couch and play the game using only the remote.

Section III: Juice

In this section, you'll also learn how to take a good game and make it great by adding a ton of special effects and excitement – a.k.a. "juice."

In the process, you will create a game called Drop Charge, where you're a space hero with a mission to blow up an alien space ship - and escape with your life before it explodes. To do this, you must jump from platform to platform, collecting special boosts along the way. Just be careful not to fall into the red hot lava!

You will build this game across four chapters, in stages:

14. **Chapter 14, Making Drop Charge**: You'll put together the basic gameplay using the

scene editor and code, flexing the Sprite Kit muscles you've developed working through previous chapters.

15. **Chapter 15, State Machines**: You'll learn what state machines are and how to use them.

16. **Chapter 16, Particle Systems**: You'll learn how to use particle systems to create amazing special effects.

17. **Chapter 17, Juice Up Your Game**: You'll trick out your game with music, sound, animation, more particles and other special effects, experiencing for yourself the benefits of mastering the details.

Section IV: GameplayKit

In this section, you'll learn how to use iOS 9's new GameplayKit to improve your game's architecture and reusability, along with adding pathfinding and basic game AI.

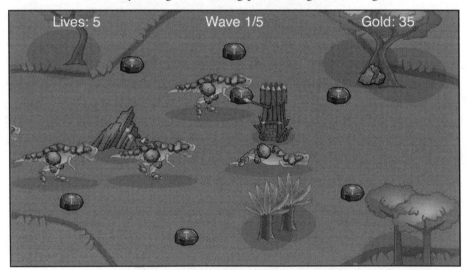

In the proces, you'll create a fun tower defense game called Dino Defense where you construct a perfect defense to save your village from an onslaught of angry dinosaurs!

You will build this game across three chapters, in stages:

18. **Chapter 18, Entity-Component System:** You'll learn all about modeling your game's objects using the new `GKEntity` and `GKComponent` objects provided with GameplayKit, and you'll use what you've learned to implement your first dinosaur and tower.

19. **Chapter 19, Pathfinding:** You'll use GameplayKit's pathfinding features to move

your dinosaurs across the scene, avoiding obstacles and towers.

20. **Chapter 20, Agents, Goals and Behaviors:** Finally, you'll add a second dinosaur to your game that will use a GKAgent with GKGoal and GKBehavior objects to move across the scene as a more organic alternative to pathfinding.

Section V: Advanced Topics

In this section, you'll delve into some more advanced topics like procedural level generation, GameplayKit randomization, and game controllers.

In the process, you'll create a tile-based dungeon crawler called Delve where you try to guide your miner through a rock-elemental infested dungeon.

You will build this game across four chapters, in stages:

21. **Chapter 21, Tile Map Games**: You'll learn techniques for building tile map levels, including how to create a fully functional tile map game.

22. **Chapter 22, Randomization**: Take advantage of the new GameplayKit class GKRandom to generate the game world.

23. **Chapter 23, Procedural Levels**: Remove some of the random aspects of the level generation to make the process more predictable, but still an adventure into the unknown.

24. **Chapter 24, Game Controllers**: This game is perfect for external game controllers; you'll be adding a tvOS target and exploring how to use the Apple TV remote as a game controller.

Section VI: Bonus chapters

And that's not all – on top of the above, we have some bonus chapters for you!

These bonus chapters come as an optional PDF download, which you can download for free here:

- www.raywenderlich.com/store/2d-ios-tvos-games-by-tutorials/bonus-chapters

In these bonus chapters, you'll learn about some APIs other than Sprite Kit that are good to know when making games for iOS. In particular, you will learn how add Game Center leaderboards and achievements into your game, use the new iOS 9 ReplayKit API, and add iAds into your game.

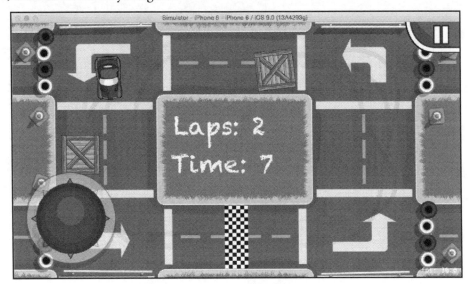

In the process, you will integrate these APIs into a top-down racing game called Circuit Racer, where you take the role of an elite racecar driver out to set a world record. It would be no problem if it weren't for the debris on the track!

You will work with this game across four chapters, in stages:

25. **Chapter 25, Game Center Achievements**: Enable Game Center for your game and award the user achievements for accomplishing certain feats.

26. **Chapter 26, Game Center Leaderboards**: Set up various leaderboards for your game and track and report the player's scores.

27. **Chapter 27, ReplayKit**: You'll learn how to allow players to record and share videos of their games with iOS 9's new ReplayKit.

28. **Chapter 28, iAd**: You'll learn how to integrate iAds into your game so you can have

a nice source of revenue!

We have also included a bonus chapter about making your own game art:

29. **Chapter 29, Making Art for Programmers**: If you liked the art in these mini-games and want to learn how to either hire an artist or make some art of your own, look no further than this chapter! This chapter guides you through drawing a cute cat in the style of this book with Illustrator.

Book source code and forums

You can get the source code for the book here:

- www.raywenderlich.com/store/2d-ios-tvos-games-by-tutorials/source-code

Some of the chapters have starter projects or other required resources that are also included, and you'll definitely want to have these on hand as you go through the book.

We've set up an official forum for the book at raywenderlich.com/forums. This is a great place to ask any questions you have about the book or about making games with Sprite Kit, or to submit any errata you may find.

PDF Version

We also have a PDF version of this book available, which can be handy if you ever want to copy/paste code or search for a specific term through the book as you're developing.

And speaking of the PDF version, we have some good news!

Since you purchased the physical copy of this book, you are eligible to buy the PDF version at a significant discount if you would like (if you don't have it already). For more details, see this page:

- www.raywenderlich.com/store/2d-ios-tvos-games-by-tutorials/upgrade

License

By purchasing 2D iOS & tvOS Games by Tutorials, you acquire the following license:

- You are allowed to use and/or modify the source code provided with 2D iOS & tvOS Games by Tutorials in as many games as you want, with no attribution required.

- You are allowed to use and/or modify all art, music and sound effects that are included

Acknowledgements

We would like to thank many people for their assistance in making this book possible:

- **Our families**: For bearing with us during this hectic time as we worked all hours of the night to get this book ready for publication!

- **Everyone at Apple**: For developing an amazing 2D game framework and other helpful APIs for games, for constantly inspiring us to improve our apps and skills, and for making it possible for many developers to have their dream jobs! Special thanks for the Apple TV dev kits as well. :]

- **Ricardo Quesada**: Ricardo is the lead developer of Cocos2D, which got many of us into making games. Sprite Kit seems to draw quite a bit of inspiration from Cocos2D, so Ricardo deserves "mad props" for that as well.

- And most importantly, **the readers of raywenderlich.com and you**! Thank you so much for reading our site and purchasing this book. Your continued readership and support is what makes this all possible!

Section I: Getting Started

This section covers the basics of making 2D games with Sprite Kit. These are the most important techniques, the ones you'll use in almost every game you make. By the time you reach the end of this section, you'll be ready to make your own simple game.

Throughout this section you will create an action game called Zombie Conga, where you take the role of a happy-go-lucky zombie who just wants to party!

Chapter 1: Sprites

Chapter 2: Manual Movement

Chapter 3: Actions

Chapter 4: Scenes

Chapter 5: Camera

Chapter 6: Labels

Chapter 7: Beginning tvOS

Chapter 1: Sprites

By Ray Wenderlich

Now that you know what Sprite Kit is and why you should use it, it's time to try it out for yourself!

The first minigame you will build in this book is called Zombie Conga. Here's what it will look like when you're finished:

In Zombie Conga, you take the role of a happy-go-lucky zombie who wants to party!

Luckily, the beach town you occupy has an overly abundant cat population. You simply need to bite them and they'll join your zombie conga line.

But watch out for crazy cat ladies! These wizened warriors in red dresses won't take kindly to anyone stealing their beloved cats and will do their best to make the zombie rest in peace—permanently.

You will build this game across the next seven chapters, in stages:

1. **Chapter 1, Sprites**: You are here! Get started by adding your first sprites to the game: the background and the zombie.

2. **Chapter 2, Manual Movement**: You'll make the zombie follow your touches around the screen and get a crash-course in basic 2D vector math.

3. **Chapter 3, Actions**: You'll add cats and crazy cat ladies to the game, as well as basic collision detection and gameplay.

4. **Chapter 4, Scenes**: You'll add a main menu to the game, as well as win and lose scenes.

5. **Chapter 5, Camera**: You'll make the game scroll from left to right, and finally, add the conga line itself.

6. **Chapter 6, Labels**: You'll add a label to show the zombie's lives and the number of cats in his conga line.

7. **Chapter 7, Beginning tvOS**: You'll get Zombie Conga working on tvOS, in just a few simple steps!

Let's get this conga started!

Getting started

Start Xcode and select **File\New\Project...** from the main menu. Select the **iOS \Application\Game** template and click **Next**.

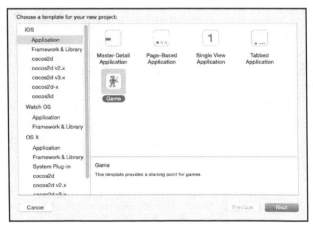

Enter **ZombieConga** for the Product Name, choose **Swift** for Language, **SpriteKit** for Game Technology, **Universal** for Devices and click **Next**.

Select somewhere on your hard drive to save your project and click **Create**. At this point, Xcode will generate a simple Sprite Kit starter project for you.

Take a look at what Sprite Kit made. In Xcode's toolbar, select the iPhone 6 and click **Play**.

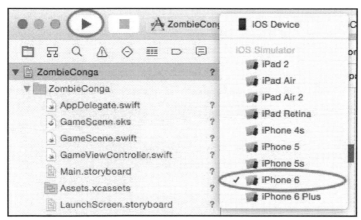

After a brief splash screen, you'll see a single label that says, "Hello, World!" When you click on the screen, a rotating space ship will appear.

In Sprite Kit, a single object called a scene controls each "screen" of your app. A scene is a subclass of Sprite Kit's SKScene class.

Right now this app just has a single scene, GameScene. Open **GameScene.swift** and you'll see the code that displays the label and the rotating space ship. It's not important to understand this code quite yet—you're going to remove it all and build your game one step at a time.

For now, delete everything in **GameScene.swift** and replace it with the following:

```
import SpriteKit

class GameScene: SKScene {
  override func didMoveToView(view: SKView) {
    backgroundColor = SKColor.blackColor()
  }
}
```

didMoveToView() is the method that Sprite Kit calls before it presents your scene in a view; it's a good place to do some initial setup of your scene's contents. Here, you simply set the background color to black.

Zombie Conga is designed to run in landscape mode, so let's configure the app for this. Select the **ZombieConga** project in the project navigator and then select the **ZombieConga** target. Go to the **General** tab and make sure only **Landscape Left** and **Landscape Right** are checked:

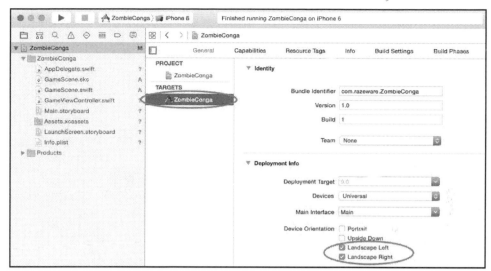

You also need to modify this in one more spot. Open **Info.plist** and find the **Supported interface orientations (iPad)** entry. Delete the entries for **Portrait (bottom home button)** and **Portrait (top home button)** that you see there, so only the landscape options remain.

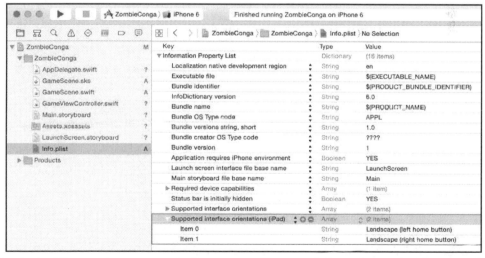

The Sprite Kit template automatically creates a file named **GameScene.sks**. You can edit this file with Xcode's built-in scene editor to lay out your game scene visually. Think of the scene editor as a simple Interface Builder for Sprite Kit.

You'll learn all about the scene editor in Chapter 7, "Scene Editor", but you won't be using it for Zombie Conga, as it will be easier and more instructive to create the sprites programmatically instead.

So, control-click **GameScene.sks**, select **Delete** and then select **Move to Trash**. Since you're no longer using this file, you'll have to modify the template code appropriately.

Open **GameViewController.swift** and replace the contents with the following:

```
import UIKit
import SpriteKit

class GameViewController: UIViewController {
  override func viewDidLoad() {
    super.viewDidLoad()
    let scene =
      GameScene(size:CGSize(width: 2048, height: 1536))
    let skView = self.view as! SKView
    skView.showsFPS = true
    skView.showsNodeCount = true
    skView.ignoresSiblingOrder = true
    scene.scaleMode = .AspectFill
    skView.presentScene(scene)
  }
  override func prefersStatusBarHidden() -> Bool  {
    return true
  }
}
```

Previously, the view controller loaded the scene from **GameScene.sks**, but now it creates the scene by calling an initializer on GameScene instead.

Notice that when you create the scene, you pass in a hardcoded size of **2048x1536** and set the scale mode to AspectFill. This is a good time for a quick discussion about how this game is designed to work as a universal app.

Universal app support

> **Note**: This section is optional and for those who are especially curious. If you're eager to get coding as soon as possible, feel free to skip to the next section, "Adding the art".

We've designed all the games in this book as universal apps, which means they will work on the iPhone and the iPad.

The scenes for the games in this book have been designed with a base size of 2048x1536, or reversed for portrait orientation, with the scale mode set to aspect fill. Aspect fill instructs Sprite Kit to scale the scene's content to fill the entire screen, even if Sprite Kit needs to cut off some of the content to do so.

This results in your scene appearing as-is on the iPad Retina, which has a resolution of

2048x1536, but as scaled/cropped on the iPhone to fit the phone's smaller size and different aspect ratio.

Here are a few examples of how the games in this book will look in landscape orientation on different devices, moving from smallest to largest aspect ratio:

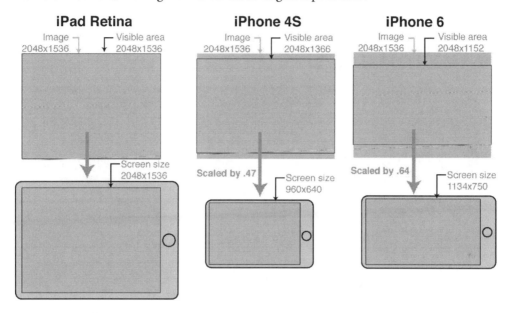

- **iPad Retina [4:3 or 1.33]**: Displayed as-is to fit the 2048x1536 screen size.

- **iPad Non-Retina [4:3 or 1.33]**: Aspect fill will scale a 2048x1536 visible area by 0.5 to fit the 1024x768 screen.

- **iPhone 4S [3:2 or 1.5]**: Aspect fill will scale a 2048x1366 visible area by 0.47 to fit the 960x640 screen.

- **iPhone 5 [16:9 or 1.77]**: Aspect fill will scale a 2048x1152 visible area by 0.56 to fit the 1136x640 screen.

- **iPhone 6 [16:9 or 1.77]**: Aspect fill will scale a 2048x1152 visible area by 0.64 to fit the 1334x750 screen.

- **iPhone 6 Plus [16:9 or 1.77]**: Aspect fill will scale a 2048x1152 visible area by 0.93 to fit the 1920x1080 screen.

Since aspect fill will crop the scene on the top and bottom for iPhones, we've designed the games in this book to have a main "playable area" that is guaranteed to be visible on all devices. Basically, the games will have a 192-pixel margin on the top/bottom in landscape and the left/right in portrait, in which you should avoid putting essential content. We'll show you how to visualize this later in the book.

Note that you need only one set of art for this to work: the art to fit the maximum screen size, 2048x1536. The art will be downscaled on devices other than the iPad Retina.

> **Note**: The con of this approach is that the art will be bigger than necessary for some devices, such as the iPhone 4s, thereby wasting texture memory and space. The pro of this approach is that the game stays nice and simple and works well on all devices.
>
> An alternate approach would be to add different images for each device and scale factor (i.e. iPad @1x, iPad @2x, iPhone@2x, iPhone @3x), leveraging the power of Apple's asset catalogs. However, at the time of writing this chapter, Sprite Kit does not properly load the correct image from the asset catalog based on device and scale factor in all cases, so we will stay with this simple route for now.

Adding the art

Next, you need to add the game art to the project.

In Xcode, open **Assets.xcassets**, select the **Spaceship** entry and press your delete key to remove it— unfortunately, this is not a game about space zombies! ☺ At this point, only **AppIcon** will remain:

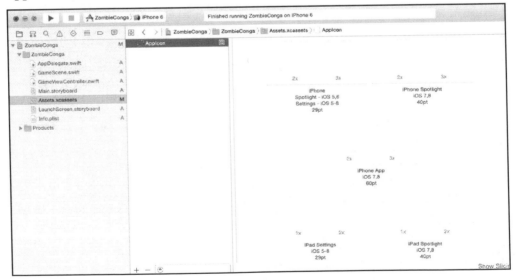

With **AppIcon** selected, drag the appropriate icon from **starter\resources\icons** into each slot:

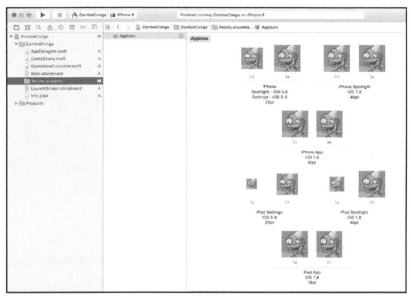

Then drag all of the files from **starter\resources\images** into the left sidebar:

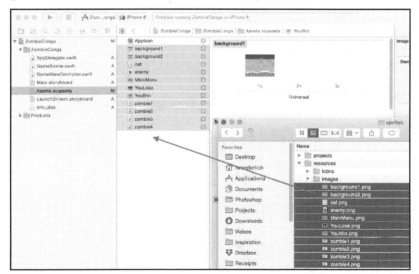

By including your images in the asset catalog, behind the scenes Xcode will build **texture atlases** containing these images and use them in your game, which will automatically increase performance.

Launch screen

> **Note:** This is another optional section, as it won't have any impact on gameplay; you'll simply add a "nice-to-have" feature that you'd typically want in a game. If you'd rather get straight to coding, feel free to skip to the next section, "Displaying a sprite".

There's one last thing you should do to get this game started on the right foot: configure the launch screen.

The launch screen is what iOS displays when your app is first loading, which usually takes a few seconds. A launch image gives the player the impression that your app is starting quickly—the default black screen, needless to say, does not. For Zombie Conga, you'll show a splash screen with the name of the game.

Your app actually has a launch screen already. When you launched your app earlier, you may have noticed a brief, blank white screen. That was it!

In iOS, apps have a special **launch screen** file; this is basically a storyboard, LaunchScreen.storyboard in this project, that you can configure to present something onscreen while your app is loading. The advantage of this over the old method of just displaying an image is that you can use Auto Layout to have much finer control of how this screen looks on different devices.

Let's try this out. Open **LaunchScreen.storyboard**. You'll see the following:

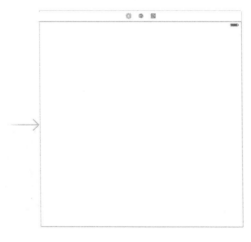

In the Object Library on the right sidebar, drag an image view into the view and resize it to fill the entire area:

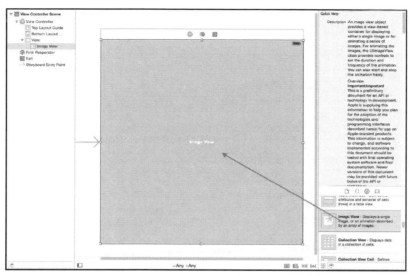

Next, you need to set the image view so that it always has the same width and height as its containing view. To do this, make sure the image view is selected and then click the **Pin** button in the lower right—it looks like a tie fighter. In the Add New Constraints screen, click the four light-red lines so that the image view is pinned to each edge. Make sure that **Constrain to margins** isn't checked and that all values are set to 0, then click **Add 4 Constraints**:

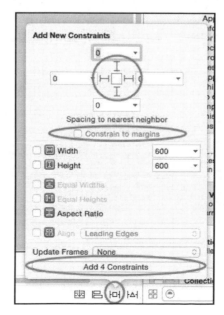

With the image view still selected, make sure the Attributes Inspector is selected—it's the fourth tab on the right. Set the **Image** to **MainMenu** and set the **View Mode** to **Aspect Fill**:

Build and run your app again. This time, you'll see a brief Zombie Conga splash screen:

Which is quickly followed by a (mostly) blank, black screen:

This may not look like much, but you now have a starting point upon which to build your first Sprite Kit game.

Let's move on to the next task, which also happens to be one of the most important and common when making games: displaying an image on the screen.

Displaying a sprite

When making a 2D game, you usually put images on the screen representing your game's various elements: the hero, enemies, bullets and so on. Each of these images is called a **sprite**.

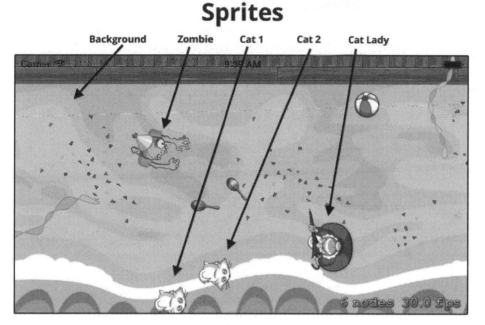

Sprite Kit has a special class called SKSpriteNode that makes it easy to create and work with sprites. This is what you'll use to add all your sprites to the game. Let's give it a try.

Creating a sprite

Open **GameScene.swift** and add this line to didMoveToView(), right after you set the background color:

```
let background = SKSpriteNode(imageNamed: "background1")
```

You don't need to pass the image's extension, as Sprite Kit will automatically determine that for you.

Build and run, ignoring the warning for now. Ah, you thought it was simple, but at this point you still see a blank screen—what gives?

Adding a sprite to the scene

It actually is simple. It's just that a sprite won't show up onscreen until you add it as a child of the scene, or as one of the scene's descendent **nodes**.

To do this, add this line of code right after the previous line:

```
addChild(background)
```

You'll learn about nodes and scenes later. For now, build and run again, and you'll see part of the background appear in the bottom left of the screen:

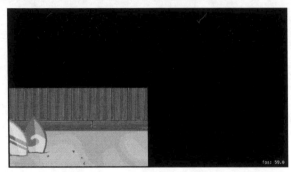

Obviously, that's not quite what you want. To get the background in the correct spot, you have to set its position.

Positioning a sprite

By default, Sprite Kit positions sprites at (0, 0), which in Sprite Kit represents the bottom left. Note that this is different from the UIKit coordinate system in iOS, where (0, 0) represents the top left.

Try positioning the background somewhere else by setting the position property. Add this line of code right before calling addChild(background):

```
background.position = CGPoint(x: size.width/2, y: size.height/2)
```

Here you set the background to the center of the screen. Even though this is a single line of code, there are four important things to understand:

1. The type of the position property is CGPoint, which is a simple structure that has x and y components:

```
struct CGPoint {
  var x: CGFloat
  var y: CGFloat
}
```

2. You can easily create a new `CGPoint` with the initializer shown above.

3. Since you're writing this code in an `SKScene` subclass, you can access the size of the scene at any time with the `size` property. The `size` property's type is `CGSize`, which is a simple structure like `CGPoint` that has width and height components.

```
struct CGSize {
   var width: CGFloat
   var height: CGFloat
}
```

4. A sprite's position is within the coordinate space of its parent node, which in this case is the scene itself. You'll learn more about this in Chapter 5, "Camera".

Build and run, and now your background is fully visible:

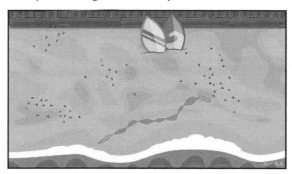

> **Note**: You may notice you can't see the entire background on iPhone devices—parts of it overlap on the top and bottom. This is by design, so the game works on both the iPad and the iPhone, as discussed in the "Universal app support" section earlier in this chapter.

Setting a sprite's anchor point

Setting the position of the background sprite means setting the *center* of the sprite to that position.

This explains why you could only see the upper half of the sprite earlier. Before you set the position, it defaulted to (0, 0), which placed the center of the sprite in the lower-left corner of the screen, so you could only see the top half.

You can change this behavior by setting a sprite's anchor point. Think of the anchor point as "the spot within a sprite that you pin to a particular position". Here's an illustration showing a sprite positioned at the center of the screen, but with different anchor points:

Position: center screen

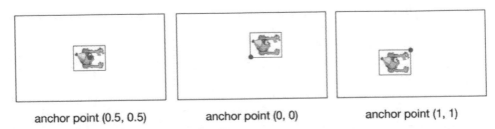

anchor point (0.5, 0.5)   anchor point (0, 0)   anchor point (1, 1)

To see how this works, find the line that sets the background's position to the center of the screen and replace it with the following:

```
background.anchorPoint = CGPoint.zero
background.position = CGPoint.zero
```

CGPoint.zero is a handy shortcut for (0, 0). Here, you set the anchor point of the sprite to (0, 0) to pin the lower-left corner of the sprite to whatever position you set—in this case, also (0, 0).

Build and run, and the image is still in the right spot:

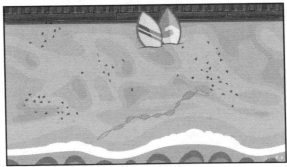

This works because now you're pinning the lower-left corner of the background image to the lower-left corner of the scene.

Here you changed the anchor point of the background for learning purposes. However, usually you can leave the anchor point at its default of (0.5, 0.5), unless you have a specific need to rotate the sprite around a particular point—an example of which is described in the next section.

So, in short: when you set the position of a sprite, by default you are positioning the center of the sprite.

Rotating a sprite

To rotate a sprite, you simply set its zRotation property. Try it out on the background sprite by adding this line right before the call to addChild():

```
background.zRotation = CGFloat(M_PI) / 8
```

Rotation values are in radians, which are units used to measure angles. This example rotates the sprite π / 8 radians, which is equal to 22.5 degrees. Also notice that you convert M_PI, which is a Double, into a CGFloat. You do this because zRotation requires a CGFloat and Swift doesn't automatically convert between types like some other languages do.

> Note: I don't know about you, but I find it easier to think about rotations in degrees rather than in radians. Later in the book, you'll create helper routines to convert between degrees and radians.

Build and run, and check out your rotated background sprite:

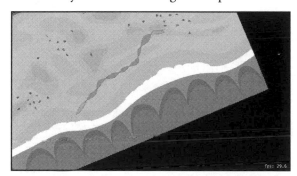

This demonstrates an important point: Sprites are rotated about their anchor points. Since you set this sprite's anchor point to (0, 0), it rotates around its bottom-left corner.

> Note: Remember that on the iPhone, the bottom-left of this image is actually offscreen! If you're not sure why this is, refer back to the "Universal app support" section earlier in this chapter.

Try rotating the sprite around the center instead. Replace the lines that set the position and anchor point with these:

```
background.position = CGPoint(x: size.width/2, y: size.height/2)
background.anchorPoint = CGPoint(x: 0.5, y: 0.5) // default
```

Build and run, and this time the background sprite will have rotated about the center:

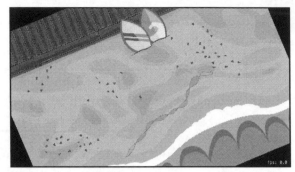

This is all good to know! But for Zombie Conga, you don't want a rotated background, so comment out that line:

```
// background.zRotation = CGFloat(M_PI) / 8
```

If you're wondering when you might want to change the anchor point in a game, imagine you're creating a character's body out of different sprites—one each for the head, torso, left arm, right arm, left leg and right leg:

If you wanted to rotate these body parts at their joints, you'd have to modify the anchor point for each sprite, as shown in the diagram above.

But again, usually you should leave the anchor point at default unless you have a specific need, like the one shown here.

Getting the size of a sprite

Sometimes when you're working with a sprite, you want to know how big it is. A sprite's size defaults to the size of the image. In Sprite Kit, the class representing this image is called a texture.

Add these lines after the call to addChild() to get the size of the background and log it to the console:

```
let mySize = background.size
print("Size: \(mySize)")
```

Build and run, and in your console output, you'll see something like this:

```
Size: (2048.0, 1536.0)
```

Sometimes it's useful to get the size of a sprite programmatically, as you do above, instead of hard-coding numbers. Your code will be much more robust and adaptable for it.

Sprites and nodes

Earlier, you learned that to make a sprite appear onscreen, you need to add it as a child of the scene, or as one of the scene's descendent **nodes**. This section will delve more deeply into the concept of nodes.

Everything that appears on the screen in Sprite Kit derives from a class called SKNode. Both the scene class (SKScene) and the sprite class (SKSpriteNode) derive from SKNode.

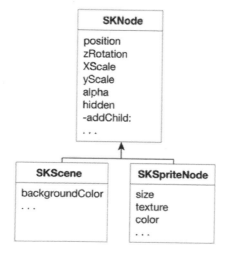

SKSpriteNode inherits a lot of its capabilities from SKNode. It turns out that the position and rotation properties are derived from `SKNode` rather than being particular to `SKSpriteNode`. This means that, just as you can set the position or rotation of a sprite, you can do the same thing with the scene itself or with anything else that derives from `SKNode`.

You can think of everything that appears on the screen together as a graph of nodes, often referred to as a **scene graph**. Here's an example of what such a graph might look like for Zombie Conga if there were one zombie, two cats and one crazy cat lady in the game:

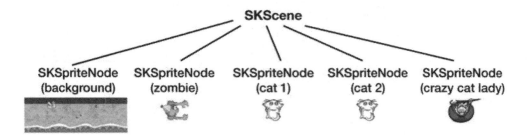

You'll learn more about nodes and the neat things you can do with them in Chapter 5, "Camera". For now, you'll add your sprites as direct children of the scene.

Nodes and z-position

Every node has a property you can set called `zPosition`, which defaults to 0. Each node draws its child nodes in the order of their z-position, from lowest to highest.

Earlier in this chapter, you added this line to **GameViewController.swift**:

```
skView.ignoresSiblingOrder = true
```

- **If ignoresSiblingOrder is true**, Sprite Kit makes no guarantees as to the order in which it draws each node's children with the same `zPosition`.

- **If ignoresSiblingOrder is false**, Sprite Kit will draw each node's children with the same `zPosition` in the order in which they were added to their parent.

In general, it's good to set this property to true, because it allows Sprite Kit to perform optimizations under the hood to make your game run faster.

However, setting this property to `true` can cause problems if you're not careful. For example, if you were to add a zombie to this scene at the same `zPosition` as the background—which would happen if you left them at the default position of 0—Sprite Kit might draw the background on top of the zombie, covering the zombie from the player's view. And if zombies are scary, just imagine invisible ones!

To avoid this, you'll set the background's `zPosition` to -1. This way, Sprite Kit will draw it before anything else you add to the scene, which will default to a `zPosition` of 0.

In **GameScene.swift**, add this line right before the call to `addChild()`:

```
background.zPosition = -1
```

Phew! No invisible zombies.

Finishing touches

That's it for this chapter! As you can see, adding a sprite to a scene takes only three or four lines of code:

1. Create the sprite.

2. Position the sprite.

3. Optionally set its z-position.

4. Add the sprite to the scene graph.

Now it's time for you to test your newfound knowledge by adding the zombie to the scene.

Challenges

It's important for you to practice what you've learned, on your own, so each chapter in this book has one to three challenges, progressing from easy to hard.

I highly recommend giving all the challenges a try, because while following a step-by-step tutorial is educational, you'll learn a lot more by solving a problem by yourself. In addition, each chapter will continue where the previous chapter's challenges left off, so you'll want to stay in the loop!

If you get stuck, you can find solutions in the resources for this chapter—but to get the most from this book, give these your best shot before you look!

Challenge 1: Adding the zombie

Right now, your game has a nice background, but it's missing the star of the show. As your first challenge, you can give your zombie a grand entrance.

Here are a few hints:

• Inside `GameScene`, add a constant property named `zombie` of type `SKSpriteNode`. Initialize it with the image named **zombie1**.

- Inside `didMoveToView()`, position the zombie sprite at (400, 400).

- Also inside `didMoveToView()`, add the zombie to the scene.

If you've got it right, you'll see the zombie appear onscreen like so:

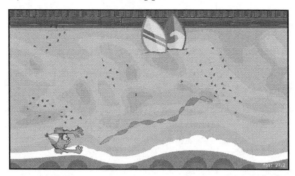

Run your game on the iPad Air 2 simulator to prove it works there, as well—just with a bigger viewable area!

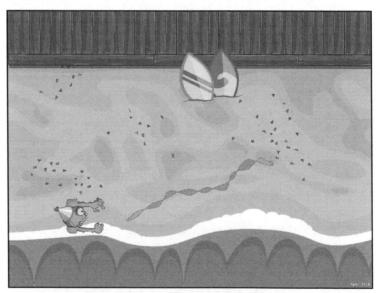

Challenge 2: Further documentation

This chapter covers everything you need to know about sprites and nodes to keep working on the game.

However, it's good to know where to find more information in case you ever have questions or get stuck. I highly recommend you check out Apple's *SKNode Class Reference* and *SKSpriteNode Class Reference*, as these cover the two classes you'll use most often in Sprite Kit, and it's good to have a basic familiarity with the properties and methods they contain.

You can find the references in Xcode by selecting **Help\Documentation and API Reference** from the main menu and searching for SKNode or SKSpriteNode.

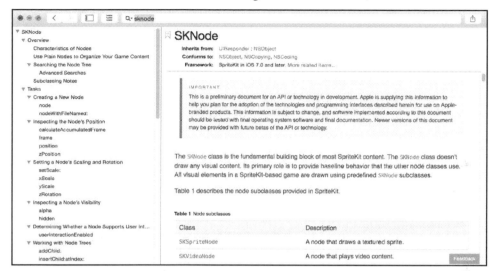

And now for your second challenge: Use the information in these docs to double (scale to 2x) the zombie's size. Answer this question: Did you use a method of SKSpriteNode or SKNode to do this?

Chapter 2: Manual Movement

By Ray Wenderlich

If you completed the challenges from the previous chapter, you now have a rather large zombie on the screen:

> **Note:** If you were unable to complete the challenges or skipped ahead from the previous chapter, don't worry—simply open the starter project from this chapter to pick up where the previous chapter left off.

Of course, you want the sprite to move around, not just stand there—this zombie's got an itch to boogie!

There are two ways to make a sprite move in Sprite Kit:

1. As you might have noticed in the previous chapter—if you looked at the template code provided by Apple—you can make a sprite move using a concept called **actions**. You'll learn more about actions in the next chapter.

2. You can make a sprite move in the more "classic" way—and that's to set the position manually over time. It's important to learn this way first, because it affords the most control and will help you understand what actions do for you.

However, to set a sprite's position over time, you need a method that the game calls periodically as it runs. This introduces a new topic: the Sprite Kit game loop.

The Sprite Kit game loop

A game works like a flipbook animation. You draw a successive sequence of images, and when you flip through them fast enough, it gives the illusion of movement.

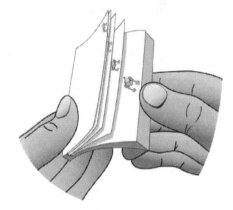

Each individual picture that you draw is called a **frame**. Games typically try to draw frames between 30 to 60 times per second so that the animations feel smooth. This rate of drawing is called the **frame rate**, or specifically **frames per second (FPS)**. By default, Sprite Kit displays this in the bottom-right corner of your game:

> **Note**: It's handy of Sprite Kit to show your frames per second onscreen by default, because you want to keep an eye on the FPS as you develop your game to make sure your game is performing well. Ideally, you want at least 30 FPS.

You should only pay attention to the FPS display on an actual device, though, as you'll get very different performance on the simulator.

In particular, your Mac has a faster CPU and way more memory than an iPhone or iPad, but abysmally slow emulated rendering, so you can't count on any accurate performance measurements from your Mac—again, always test performance on a device!

Besides the FPS, Sprite Kit also displays the count of nodes that it rendered in the last pass.

You can remove the FPS and node count from the screen by going into **GameViewController.swift** and setting both `skView.showsFPS` and `skView.showsNodeCount` to `false`.

Behind the scenes, Sprite Kit runs an endless loop, often referred to as the **game loop**, which looks like this:

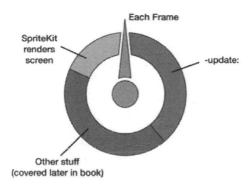

This illustrates that each frame, Sprite Kit does the following:

1. **Calls a method on your scene called `update()`**. This is where you can put code that you want to run every frame—making it the perfect spot for code that updates the position or rotation of your sprites.

2. **Does some other stuff**. You'll revisit the game loop in other chapters, filling in your understanding of the rest of this diagram as you go.

3. **Renders the scene**. Sprite Kit then draws all of the objects that are in your scene graph, issuing OpenGL draw commands for you behind the scenes.

Sprite Kit tries to draw frames as fast as possible, up to 60 FPS. However, if `update()` takes too long, or if Sprite Kit has to draw more sprites than the hardware can handle at one time, the frame rate might decrease.

Here are two tips to keep your game running fast:

1. **Keep update() fast**. For example, you want to avoid slow algorithms in this method since it's called each frame.

2. **Keep your node count as low as possible**. For example, it's good to remove nodes from the scene graph when they're offscreen and you no longer need them.

Now you know that update() is called each frame and is a good spot to update the positions of your sprites—so let's make this zombie move!

Moving the zombie

You're going to implement the zombie movement code in five iterations. This is so you can see some common beginner mistakes and solutions, and in the end, understand how movement works step by step.

To start, you'll implement a simple but not ideal method: moving the zombie a fixed amount per frame.

Before you begin, open **GameScene.swift** and comment out the line in didMoveToView() that sets the zombie to double its size:

```
// zombie.setScale(2) // SKNode method
```

This line was just a test, so you don't need it anymore. Zombies scare me enough in normal size! :]

Iteration 1: Fixed movement per frame

Inside **GameScene.swift**, add the following method:

```
override func update(currentTime: NSTimeInterval) {
  zombie.position = CGPoint(x: zombie.position.x + 8,
                            y: zombie.position.y)
}
```

Here, you update the position of the zombie to be eight more points along the x-axis than last time, and keep the same position along the y-axis. This makes the zombie move from left to right.

Build and run, and you'll see the zombie move across the screen:

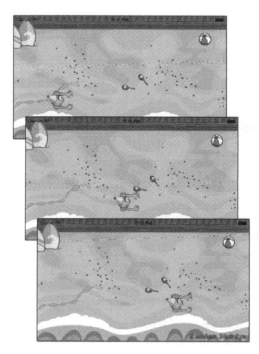

This is great stuff, but the movement feels a bit jagged or irregular. To see why, let's go back to the Sprite Kit game loop.

Remember, Sprite Kit tries to draw frames as quickly as possible. However, there will usually be some variance in the amount of time it takes to draw each frame: sometimes a bit slower, sometimes a bit quicker.

This means the amount of time between calls to your `update()` loop can vary. To see this yourself, add some code to print out the time elapsed since the last update. Add these variables to `GameScene`'s property section, right after the `zombie` property:

```
var lastUpdateTime: NSTimeInterval = 0
var dt: NSTimeInterval = 0
```

Here, you create properties to keep track of the last time Sprite Kit called `update()`, and the delta time since the last update, often abbreviated as `dt`.

Then, add these lines to the beginning of `update()`:

```
if lastUpdateTime > 0 {
  dt = currentTime - lastUpdateTime
} else {
  dt = 0
}
lastUpdateTime = currentTime
print("\(dt*1000) milliseconds since last update")
```

Here, you calculate the time since the last call to update() and store that in dt, then log out the time in milliseconds (1 second = 1000 milliseconds).

Build and run, and you'll see something like this in the console:

```
33.4451289963908 milliseconds since last update
16.3537669868674 milliseconds since last update
34.1878019971773 milliseconds since last update
15.6998310121708 milliseconds since last update
33.9883069973439 milliseconds since last update
33.5779220040422 milliseconds since last update
```

As you can see, the amount of time between calls to update() always varies slightly.

Note: Sprite Kit tries to call your update method 60 times a second (every ~16 milliseconds). However, if it takes too long to update and render a frame of your game, Sprite Kit may call your update method less frequently, and the FPS will drop. You can see that here—some frames are taking over 30 milliseconds.

You're seeing such a low FPS because you're running on the simulator. As mentioned earlier, you can't count on the simulator for accurate performance measurements. If you try running this code on a device, you should see a much higher FPS.

Note that even if your game runs at a smooth 60 FPS, there will always be some small variance in how often Sprite Kit calls your update method. Therefore, you need to take the delta time into account in your calculations—and you'll learn how to do that next!

Since you're updating the position of the zombie a fixed amount per frame rather than taking this time variance into consideration, you're likely to wind up with movement that looks jagged or irregular.

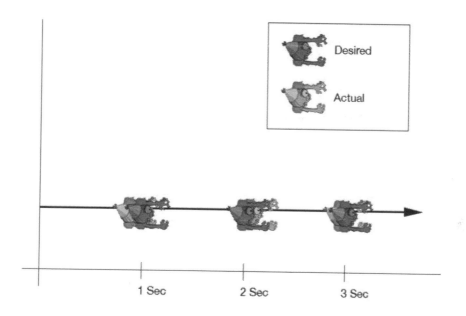

The correct solution is to figure out how far you want the zombie to move per second and then multiply this by the fraction of a second since the last update. Let's give it a shot.

Iteration 2: Velocity multiplied by delta time

Begin by adding this property to the top of GameScene, right after dt:

```
let zombieMovePointsPerSec: CGFloat = 480.0
```

You're saying that in one second, the zombie should move 480 points, about 1/4 of the scene width. You set the type to CGFloat, because you'll be using this value in calculations with other CGFloats inside a CGPoint.

Right after that line, add one more property:

```
var velocity = CGPoint.zero
```

So far, you've used CGPoints to represent positions. However, it's also quite common and handy to use CGPoints to represent **2D vectors**.

A 2D vector represents a **direction** and a **length**:

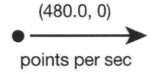

The diagram above shows an example of a 2D vector you might use to represent the zombie's movement. You can see that the orientation of the arrow shows the **direction** in which the zombie should move, while the arrow's **length** indicates how far the zombie should move in a second. The direction and length together represent the zombie's **velocity**–you can think of it as how far and in what direction the zombie should move in 1 second.

However, note that the velocity has no set position. After all, you should be able to make the zombie move in that direction, at that speed, no matter where the zombie starts.

Try this out by adding the following new method:

```
func moveSprite(sprite: SKSpriteNode, velocity: CGPoint) {
  // 1
  let amountToMove = CGPoint(x: velocity.x * CGFloat(dt),
                             y: velocity.y * CGFloat(dt))
  print("Amount to move: \(amountToMove)")
  // 2
  sprite.position = CGPoint(
    x: sprite.position.x + amountToMove.x,
    y: sprite.position.y + amountToMove.y)
}
```

You've refactored the code into a reusable method that takes the sprite to be moved and a velocity vector by which to move it. Let's go over this line by line:

1. Velocity is in points per second, and you need to figure out how many points to move the zombie this frame. To determine that, this section multiplies the points per second by the fraction of seconds since the last update. You now have a point representing the zombie's position—which you can also think of as a vector from the origin to the zombie's position—as well as a vector representing the distance and direction to move the zombie this frame:

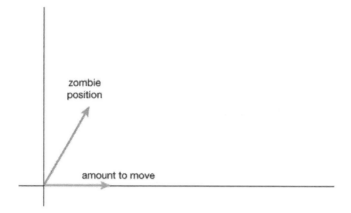

2. To determine the zombie's new position, simply add the vector to the point:

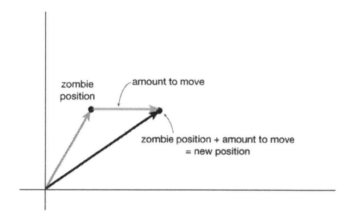

You can visualize this with the diagram above, but in code you simply add the x- and y-components of the point and the vector together.

> **Note**: To learn more about vectors, check out this great guide: http://www.mathsisfun.com/algebra/.

Finally, inside `update()`, replace the line that sets the zombie's position with the following:

```
moveSprite(zombie,
   velocity: CGPoint(x: zombieMovePointsPerSec, y: 0))
```

Build and run, and now the zombie moves much more smoothly across the screen. Look at the console log, and you'll also see that the zombie is now moving a different number of points each frame, based on how much time has elapsed.

```
0.0 milliseconds since last update
Amount to move: (0.0,0.0)
47.8530780237634 milliseconds since last update
Amount to move: (11.4847387257032,0.0)
33.3498929976486 milliseconds since last update
Amount to move: (8.00397431943566,0.0)
34.2196339915972 milliseconds since last update
Amount to move: (8.21271215798333,0.0)
```

If your zombie's movement still looks jittery, be sure to try it on a device instead of on the simulator, which has different performance characteristics.

Iteration 3: Moving toward touches

So far, so good, but now you want to make the zombie move toward whatever spot the player touches. After all, everyone knows zombies are attracted to noise!

Your goal is for the zombie to move toward the point the player taps and keep moving even after passing the tap location, until the player taps another location to draw his attention. There are four steps to make this work—let's cover them one at a time.

Step 1: Find the offset vector

First, you need to figure out the offset between the location of the player's tap and the location of the zombie. You can get this by simply subtracting the zombie's position from the tap position.

Subtracting points and vectors is similar to adding them, but instead of adding the x- and y- components, you—that's right—subtract them! :]

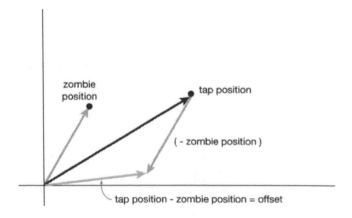

This diagram illustrates that if you subtract the zombie position from the tap position, you get a vector showing the offset amount. You can see this even more clearly if you move the offset vector so it begins from the zombie's position:

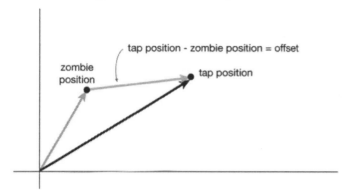

By subtracting these two positions, you get something with a direction and a length. Call this the offset vector.

Try it out by adding the following method:

```
func moveZombieToward(location: CGPoint) {
  let offset = CGPoint(x: location.x - zombie.position.x,
                       y: location.y - zombie.position.y)
}
```

You're not done writing this method; this is only the beginning!

Step 2: Find the length of the offset vector

Now you need to figure out the length of the offset vector, a piece of information you'll need in Step 3.

Think of the offset vector as the hypotenuse of a right triangle, where the lengths of the other two sides of the triangle are defined by the x- and y- components of the vector:

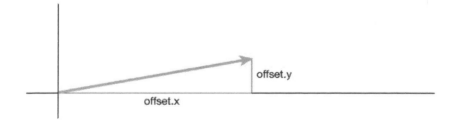

You want to find the length of the hypotenuse. To do this, you can use the Pythagorean theorem. You may remember this simple formula from geometry—it says that the length of the hypotenuse is equal to the square root of the sum of the squares of the two sides.

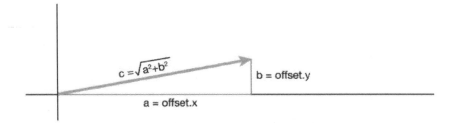

Put this theory into practice. Add the following line to the bottom of `moveZombieToward()`:

```
let length = sqrt(
  Double(offset.x * offset.x + offset.y * offset.y))
```

You're not done yet!

Step 3: Make the offset vector a set length

Currently, you have an offset vector where:

- The **direction** points toward where the zombie should go.
- The **length** is the length of the line between the zombie's current position and the tap location.

What you want is a velocity vector where:

- The **direction** points toward where the zombie should go.
- The **length** is `zombieMovePointsPerSec`, the constant you defined earlier as 480 points per second.

So you're halfway there—your vector points in the right direction, but isn't the right length. How do you make a vector pointing in the same direction as the offset vector, but of a certain length?

The first step is to convert the offset vector into a **unit vector**, which means a vector of length 1. According to geometry, you can do this by simply dividing the offset vector's x- and y- components by the offset vector's length.

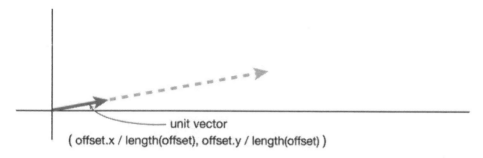

unit vector
(offset.x / length(offset), offset.y / length(offset))

This process of converting a vector into a unit vector is called **normalizing** a vector.

Once you have this unit vector, which you know is of length 1, it's easy to multiply it by `zombieMovePointsPerSec` to make it the exact length you want.

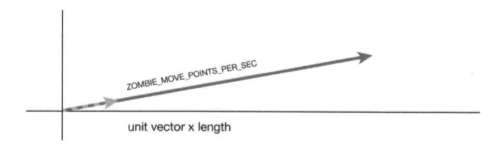

ZOMBIE_MOVE_POINTS_PER_SEC

unit vector x length

Give it a try. Add the following lines to the bottom of `moveZombieToward()`:

```
let direction = CGPoint(x: offset.x / CGFloat(length),
                        y: offset.y / CGFloat(length))
velocity = CGPoint(x: direction.x * zombieMovePointsPerSec,
                   y: direction.y * zombieMovePointsPerSec)
```

Now you've got a velocity vector with the correct direction and length. There's only one step left!

Step 4: Hook up to touch events

In Sprite Kit, to get notifications of touch events on a node, you simply need to set that node's `userInteractionEnabled` property to `true` and then override that node's `touchesBegan(withEvent:)`, `touchesMoved(withEvent:)` and/or `touchesEnded(withEvent:)` methods. Unlike other `SKNode` subclasses, `SKScene`'s `userInteractionEnabled` property is set to `true` by default.

To see this in action, implement these touch handling methods for `GameScene`, as follows:

```
func sceneTouched(touchLocation:CGPoint) {
  moveZombieToward(touchLocation)
}

override func touchesBegan(touches: Set<UITouch>,
  withEvent event: UIEvent?) {
    guard let touch = touches.first else {
      return
    }
    let touchLocation = touch.locationInNode(self)
    sceneTouched(touchLocation)
}

override func touchesMoved(touches: Set<UITouch>,
  withEvent event: UIEvent?) {
    guard let touch = touches.first else {
      return
    }
    let touchLocation = touch.locationInNode(self)
    sceneTouched(touchLocation)
}
```

Finally, inside `update()`, edit the call to `moveSprite()` so it passes in velocity (based on the touch) instead of the preset amount:

```
moveSprite(zombie, velocity: velocity)
```

That's it! Build and run, and now the zombie will chase your taps. Just don't get too close —he's hungry!

> **Note:** You can also use gesture recognizers with Sprite Kit. These can be especially handy if you're trying to implement complicated gestures, such as pinching or rotating.

You can add the gesture recognizer to the scene's view in `didMoveToView()`, and you can use `SKScene`'s `convertPointFromView()` and `SKNode`'s `convertPoint(toNode:)` methods to get the touch in the coordinate space you need.

For a demonstration of this, see the sample code for this chapter, where I've included a commented-out demonstration of gesture recognizers for you. Since it does the same thing as the touch handlers you implemented, comment out your touch handlers when you run with the gesture recognizers if you want to be sure the gestures are working.

Iteration 4: Bounds checking

As you play the latest version of the game, you might notice that the zombie happily runs straight off the screen if you let him. While I admire his enthusiasm, in Zombie Conga you'd like him to stay on the screen at all times, bouncing off an edge if he hits one.

To do this, you need to check if the newly calculated position is beyond any of the screen edges and make the zombie bounce away, if so. Add this new method:

```
func boundsCheckZombie() {
  let bottomLeft = CGPointZero
  let topRight = CGPoint(x: size.width, y: size.height)

  if zombie.position.x <= bottomLeft.x {
    zombie.position.x = bottomLeft.x
    velocity.x = -velocity.x
  }
  if zombie.position.x >= topRight.x {
    zombie.position.x = topRight.x
    velocity.x = -velocity.x
  }
  if zombie.position.y <= bottomLeft.y {
    zombie.position.y = bottomLeft.y
    velocity.y = -velocity.y
  }
  if zombie.position.y >= topRight.y {
    zombie.position.y = topRight.y
    velocity.y = -velocity.y
  }
}
```

First, you make constants for the bottom-left and top-right coordinates of the scene.

Then, you check the zombie's position to see if it's beyond or on any of the screen edges. If it is, you clamp the position and reverse the appropriate velocity component to make the zombie bounce in the opposite direction.

Now call your new method at the end of update():

```
boundsCheckZombie()
```

Build and run, and you have a zombie bouncing around the screen. I told you he was ready to party!

Iteration 5: Playable area

Run the game on your iPhone 6 simulator and move your zombie toward the top of the screen. Notice that your zombie moves offscreen before he bounces back!

Run the game on the iPad simulator, and you'll see the game works as expected. Does this give you a clue as to what's going on?

Recall from the "Universal app support" section in Chapter 1 that Zombie Conga has been designed with a 4:3 aspect ratio (2048x1536). However, you want to support up to a 16:9 aspect ratio (1136x640), which is what the iPhone 5, 6, and 6 Plus use.

Let's take a look at what happens with a 16:9 device. Since you've configured the scene to use aspect fill, Sprite Kit first calculates the largest 16:9 rectangle that fits within the 2048x1536 space: that's 2048x1152. It then centers that rectangle and scales it to fit the actual screen size; for example, the iPhone 6's 1134x750 screen requires scaling by 0.64.

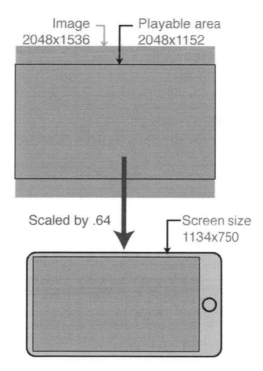

This means that on 16:9 devices, there are 192-point gaps at the top and bottom of the scene that won't be visible (1536 - 1152 = 384. 384 / 2 = 192). Hence, you should avoid critical gameplay in those areas—such as letting the zombie move in those gaps.

Let's solve this problem. First, add a new property to GameScene to store the playable rectangle:

```
let playableRect: CGRect
```

Then, add this initializer to set the value appropriately:

```
override init(size: CGSize) {
  let maxAspectRatio:CGFloat = 16.0/9.0 // 1
  let playableHeight = size.width / maxAspectRatio // 2
  let playableMargin = (size.height-playableHeight)/2.0 // 3
  playableRect = CGRect(x: 0, y: playableMargin,
                        width: size.width,
                        height: playableHeight) // 4
  super.init(size: size) // 5
}

required init(coder aDecoder: NSCoder) {
  fatalError("init(coder:) has not been implemented") // 6
}
```

Line by line, here's what this code does:

1. Zombie Conga supports aspect ratios from 3:2 (1.33) to 16:9 (1.77). Here you make a constant for the max aspect ratio supported: 16:9 (1.77).

2. With aspect fit, regardless of aspect ratio, the playable width will always be equal to the scene width. To calculate the playable height, you divide the scene width by the max aspect ratio.

3. You want to center the playable rectangle on the screen, so you determine the margin on the top and bottom by subtracting the playable height from the scene height and dividing the result by 2.

4. You put it all together to make a centered rectangle on the screen, with the max aspect ratio.

5. You call the initializer of the superclass.

6. Whenever you override the default initializer of a Sprite Kit node, you must also override the required `NSCoder` initializer, which is used when you're loading a scene from the scene editor. Since you're not using the scene editor in this game, you simply add a placeholder implementation that logs an error.

To visualize this, add a helper method to draw this playable rectangle to the screen:

```
func debugDrawPlayableArea() {
    let shape = SKShapeNode()
    let path = CGPathCreateMutable()
    CGPathAddRect(path, nil, playableRect)
    shape.path = path
    shape.strokeColor = SKColor.redColor()
    shape.lineWidth = 4.0
    addChild(shape)
}
```

For the moment, don't worry about how this works; you'll learn all about `SKShapeNodes` in Chapter 11, "Crop, Video and Shape Nodes". For now, consider this a black box that draws the debug rectangle to the screen.

Next, call this method at the end of `didMoveToView()`:

```
debugDrawPlayableArea()
```

And finally, modify the first two lines in `boundsCheckZombie()` to take into consideration the y-values in `playableRect`:

```
let bottomLeft = CGPoint(x: 0,
                         y: CGRectGetMinY(playableRect))
let topRight = CGPoint(x: size.width,
                       y: CGRectGetMaxY(playableRect))
```

Build and run, and you'll see the zombie now bounces correctly, according to the playable rectangle, drawn in red and matched to the corners of the screen:

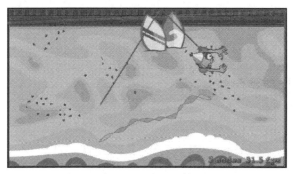

Then build and run on an iPad simulator, and you'll see the zombie bounces correctly there, as well, according to the playable rectangle:

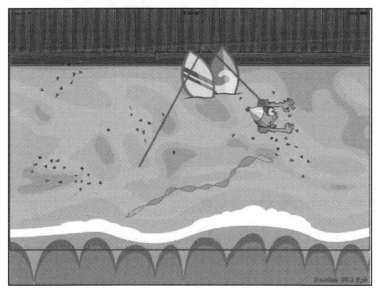

The playable area outlined in red is exactly what you see on the iPhone device, which has the largest supported aspect ratio, 16:9.

Now that you have a playable rectangle, you simply need to make sure the rest of the gameplay takes place in this box—and your zombie can party everywhere!

Note: An alternate method would be to restrict the zombie's movement based on the visible area of the current device. In other words, you could let the zombie move all the way to the edges of the iPad, rather than restricting him to the minimum playable area.

However, this would make the game easier on the iPad, as there'd be more space to avoid enemies. For Zombie Conga, we think it's more important to have the same difficulty across all devices, so we're keeping the core gameplay in the guaranteed playable area.

Rotating the zombie

The zombie is moving nicely, but he always faces the same direction. Granted, he's undead, but this zombie is on the curious side and would like to turn to see where he's going!

You already have a vector that includes the direction the zombie is facing: velocity. You just need to find the rotation angle to get the zombie facing in that direction.

Once again, think of the direction vector as the hypotenuse of a right triangle. You want to find the angle:

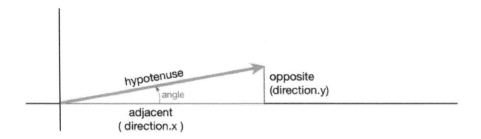

You may remember from trigonometry the mnemonic *SOH CAH TOA*, where the last part stands for:

```
tan(angle) = opposite / adjacent
```

Since you have the lengths of the opposite and adjacent sides, you can rewrite the above formula as follows to get the angle of rotation:

```
angle = arctan(opposite / adjacent)
```

If none of this trigonometry rings any bells, don't worry. Just think of it as a formula that you type in to get the angle—that's all you need to know.

Give this formula a try by adding the following new method:

```
func rotateSprite(sprite: SKSpriteNode, direction: CGPoint) {
  sprite.zRotation = CGFloat(
    atan2(Double(direction.y), Double(direction.x)))
}
```

This uses the equation from above. It includes a bunch of casting because `CGFloat` is defined as a `Double` on 64-bit machines and as a `Float` on 32-bit machines.

This works because the zombie image faces to the right. If the zombie image were instead facing the top of the screen, you'd have to add an additional rotation to compensate, because an angle of 0 points to the right.

Now call this new method at the end of `update`:

```
rotateSprite(zombie, direction: velocity)
```

Build and run, and the zombie rotates to face the direction in which he's moving:

Congratulations, you've given your zombie life! The sprite moves smoothly, bounces off the edges of the screen and rotates on both the iPhone and the iPad—a great start to a game.

But you're not done yet. It's time for you to try some of this stuff on your own to make sure you've got it down.

Challenges

This chapter has three challenges, and they're particularly important ones. Performing these challenges will give you useful practice with vector math and introduce new math utilities you'll use throughout the rest of the book.

As always, if you get stuck, you can find solutions in the resources for this chapter—but give it your best shot first!

Challenge 1: Math utilities

As you've no doubt noticed while working on this game, you frequently have to perform calculations on points and vectors: adding and subtracting points, finding lengths and so on. You've also been doing a lot of casting between `CGFloat` and `Double`.

So far in this chapter, you've done all of this yourself inline. That's a fine way of doing things, but it can get tedious and repetitive in practice. It's also error-prone.

Create a new file with the **iOS\Source\Swift File** template and name it **MyUtils**. Then replace the contents of **MyUtils.swift** with the following:

```
import Foundation
import CoreGraphics

func + (left: CGPoint, right: CGPoint) -> CGPoint {
  return CGPoint(x: left.x + right.x, y: left.y + right.y)
}

func += (inout left: CGPoint, right: CGPoint) {
  left = left + right
}
```

In Swift, you can make operators like +, −, * and / work on any type you want. Here, you make them work on `CGPoint` (sometimes in combination with `CGFloat`). [TODO: I want to get rid of the parentheses here, but I'm confused because I don't see `CGFloat` anywhere in the above code.]

Now you can add points like the ones below—but don't add this anywhere; it's just an example:

```
let testPoint1 = CGPoint(x: 100, y: 100)
let testPoint2 = CGPoint(x: 50, y: 50)
let testPoint3 = testPoint1 + testPoint2
```

Let's override operators for subtraction, multiplication and division on `CGPoint`s as well. Add this code to the end of **MyUtils.swift**:

```
func − (left: CGPoint, right: CGPoint) -> CGPoint {
  return CGPoint(x: left.x − right.x, y: left.y − right.y)
}

func −= (inout left: CGPoint, right: CGPoint) {
  left = left − right
}

func * (left: CGPoint, right: CGPoint) -> CGPoint {
  return CGPoint(x: left.x * right.x, y: left.y * right.y)
}
```

```
func *= (inout left: CGPoint, right: CGPoint) {
  left = left * right
}

func * (point: CGPoint, scalar: CGFloat) -> CGPoint {
  return CGPoint(x: point.x * scalar, y: point.y * scalar)
}

func *= (inout point: CGPoint, scalar: CGFloat) {
  point = point * scalar
}

func / (left: CGPoint, right: CGPoint) -> CGPoint {
  return CGPoint(x: left.x / right.x, y: left.y / right.y)
}

func /= (inout left: CGPoint, right: CGPoint) {
  left = left / right
}

func / (point: CGPoint, scalar: CGFloat) -> CGPoint {
  return CGPoint(x: point.x / scalar, y: point.y / scalar)
}

func /= (inout point: CGPoint, scalar: CGFloat) {
  point = point / scalar
}
```

Now you can subtract, multiply or divide a CGPoint by another CGPoint. You can also multiply and divide points by scalar CGFloat values, as below—again, don't add this anywhere; it's just an example:

```
let testPoint5 = testPoint1 * 2
let testPoint6 = testPoint1 / 10
```

Finally, add a class extension on CGPoint with a few helper methods:

```
#if !(arch(x86_64) || arch(arm64))
func atan2(y: CGFloat, x: CGFloat) -> CGFloat {
  return CGFloat(atan2f(Float(y), Float(x)))
}

func sqrt(a: CGFloat) -> CGFloat {
  return CGFloat(sqrtf(Float(a)))
}
#endif

extension CGPoint {

  func length() -> CGFloat {
    return sqrt(x*x + y*y)
```

```
  }

  func normalized() -> CGPoint {
    return self / length()
  }

  var angle: CGFloat {
    return atan2(y, x)
  }
}
```

The #if/#endif block is true when the app is running on 32-bit architecture. In this case, CGFloat is the same size as Float, so this code makes versions of atan2 and sqrt that accept CGFloat/Float values rather than the default of Double, allowing you to use atan2 and sqrt with CGFloats, regardless of the device's architecture.

Next, the class extension adds some handy methods to get the length of the point, return a normalized version of the point (i.e., length 1) and get the angle of the point.

Using these helper functions will make your code a lot more concise and clean. For example, look at moveSprite(velocity:):

```
func moveSprite(sprite: SKSpriteNode, velocity: CGPoint) {
  let amountToMove = CGPoint(x: velocity.x * CGFloat(dt),
                             y: velocity.y * CGFloat(dt))
  print("Amount to move: \(amountToMove)")
  sprite.position = CGPoint(
    x: sprite.position.x + amountToMove.x,
    y: sprite.position.y + amountToMove.y)
}
```

Simplify the first line by multiplying velocity and dt using the * operator, and avoid the cast. Also, simplify the final line by adding the sprite's position and amount to move using the += operator.

Your end result should look like this:

```
func moveSprite(sprite: SKSpriteNode, velocity: CGPoint) {
  let amountToMove = velocity * CGFloat(dt)
  print("Amount to move: \(amountToMove)")
  sprite.position += amountToMove
}
```

Your challenge is to modify the rest of Zombie Conga to use this new helper code, and verify that the game still works as expected. When you're done, you should have the following calls, including the two mentioned already:

- += operator: 1 call

- – operator: 1 call

- ∗ operator: 2 calls
- `normalized`: 1 call
- `angle`: 1 call

You'll also notice when you're done that your code is a lot cleaner and easier to understand. In future chapters, you'll use a math library we made that's very similar to the one you created here.

Challenge 2: Stop that zombie!

In Zombie Conga, when you tap the screen, the zombie moves toward the tap point—but then continues beyond it.

That's the behavior you want for Zombie Conga, but in another game, you might want the zombie to stop where you tap. Your challenge is to modify the game to do this.

Here are a few hints for one possible implementation:

- Create an optional property called `lastTouchLocation` and update it whenever the player touches the scene.

- Inside `update()`, check the distance between the last touch location and the zombie's position. If that remaining distance is less than or equal to the amount the zombie will move this frame (`zombieMovePointsPerSec * dt`), then set the zombie's position to the last touch location and the velocity to zero. Otherwise, call `moveSprite(velocity:)` and `rotateSprite(direction:)` like normal. `boundsCheckZombie()` should always occur.

- To do this, use the – operator once and call `length()` once using the helper code from the previous challenge.

Challenge 3: Smooth moves

Currently, the zombie immediately rotates to face the tap location. This can be a bit jarring—it would be nicer if the zombie rotated smoothly over time to face the new direction.

To do this, you need two new helper routines. Add these to the bottom of **MyUtils.swift** (to type π, use Option-p):

```
let π = CGFloat(M_PI)

func shortestAngleBetween(angle1: CGFloat,
                          angle2: CGFloat) -> CGFloat {
  let twoπ = π * 2.0
```

```
  var angle = (angle2 - angle1) % twoπ
  if (angle >= π) {
    angle = angle - twoπ
  }
  if (angle <= -π) {
    angle = angle + twoπ
  }
  return angle
}

extension CGFloat {
  func sign() -> CGFloat {
    return (self >= 0.0) ? 1.0 : -1.0
  }
}
```

`sign()` returns 1 if the `CGFloat` is greater than or equal to 0; otherwise it returns -1.

`shortestAngleBetween()` returns the shortest angle between two angles. It's not as simple as subtracting the two angles, for two reasons:

1. Angles "wrap around" after 360 degrees (2 * `M_PI`). In other words, 30 degrees and 390 degrees represent the same angle.

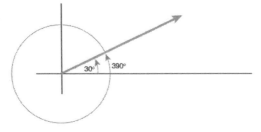

2. Sometimes the shortest way to rotate between two angles is to go left, and other times to go right. For example, if you start at 0 degrees and want to turn to 270 degrees, it's shorter to turn -90 degrees than to turn 270 degrees. You don't want your zombie turning the long way around—he may be undead, but he's not stupid!

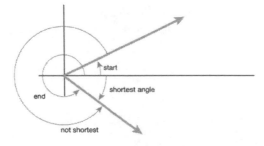

So this routine finds the difference between the two angles, chops off any amount greater than 360 degrees and then decides if it's faster to go right or left.

Your challenge is to modify rotateSprite(direction:) to take and use a new parameter: the number of radians the zombie should rotate per second.

Define the constant as follows:

```
let zombieRotateRadiansPerSec:CGFloat = 4.0 * π
```

And modify the method signature as follows:

```
func rotateSprite(sprite: SKSpriteNode, direction: CGPoint,
                  rotateRadiansPerSec: CGFloat) {
  // Your code here!
}
```

Here are a few hints for implementing this method:

- Use shortestAngleBetween() to find the distance between the current angle and the target angle. Call this shortest.

- Figure out the amount to rotate this frame based on rotateRadiansPerSec and dt. Call this amtToRotate.

- If the absolute value of shortest is less than the amtToRotate, use that instead.

- Add amountToRotate to the sprite's zRotation—but multiply it by sign() first, so that you rotate in the correct direction.

- Don't forget to update the call to rotate the sprite in update() so that it uses the new parameter.

If you've completed all three of these challenges, great work! You really understand moving and rotating sprites, using the "classic" approach of updating the values yourself over time.

Ah, but the classic, while essential to understand, always gives way to the modern. In the next chapter, you'll learn how Sprite Kit can make some of these common tasks much easier, through the magic of actions!

Chapter 3: Actions

By Ray Wenderlich

So far, you've learned how to move and rotate Sprite Kit nodes—a node being anything that appears onscreen—by manually setting their positions and rotations over time.

This do-it-yourself approach works and is quite powerful, but Sprite Kit provides an easier way to move sprites incrementally: **actions**.

Actions allow you to do things like rotate, scale or change a sprite's position over time—with only one line of code! You can also chain actions together to create movement combinations quite easily.

In this chapter, you'll learn all about Sprite Kit actions as you add enemies, collectibles and basic gameplay logic to your game.

You'll see how actions can simplify your game-coding life, and by the time you've finished this chapter, Zombie Conga will be action-packed!

> **Note:** This chapter begins where the previous chapter's Challenge 3 left off. If you were unable to complete the challenges or skipped ahead from an earlier chapter, don't worry—simply open the starter project from this chapter to pick up where the previous chapter left off.

Move action

Right now, your zombie's "life" is a bit too carefree. Let's add action to this game by introducing enemies to dodge: crazy cat ladies!

Open **GameScene.swift** and create the start of a new method to spawn an enemy:

```
func spawnEnemy() {
  let enemy = SKSpriteNode(imageNamed: "enemy")
  enemy.position = CGPoint(x: size.width + enemy.size.width/2,
                           y: size.height/2)
  addChild(enemy)
}
```

This code is a review from the previous two chapters: You create a sprite and position it at the vertical center of the screen, just out of view to the right.

Now you'd like to move the enemy from the right of the screen to the left. If you were to do this manually, you might update the enemy's position each frame according to a velocity.

No need to trouble yourself with that this time! Simply add these two lines of code to the bottom of spawnEnemy():

```
let actionMove = SKAction.moveTo(
  CGPoint(x: -enemy.size.width/2, y: enemy.position.y),
  duration: 2.0)
enemy.runAction(actionMove)
```

To create an action in Sprite Kit, you call one of several static constructors on the SKAction class, such as the one you see here, moveTo(duration:). This particular constructor returns an action that moves a sprite to a specified position over a specified duration (in seconds).

Here, you set up the action to move the enemy along the x-axis at whatever speed is necessary to take it from its current position to just off the left side of the screen in two seconds.

Once you've created an action, you need to run it. You can run an action on any SKNode by calling runAction(), as you did in the above code.

Give it a try! For now, call this method inside `didMoveToView()`, right after calling `addChild(zombie)`:

```
spawnEnemy()
```

Build and run, and you'll see the crazy cat lady race across the screen:

Not bad for only two lines of code, eh? You could have even done it with a single line of code if you didn't need to use the `actionMove` constant for anything else.

Here you saw an example of `moveTo(duration:)`, but there are a few other move action variants:

- **moveToX(duration:)** and **moveToY(duration:)**. These allow you to specify a change in only the x- or y-position; the other is assumed to remain the same. You could have used `moveToX(duration:)` in the example above to save a bit of typing.

- **moveByX(y:duration:)**. The "move to" actions move the sprite to a particular point, but sometimes it's convenient to move a sprite as an offset from its current position, wherever that may be. You could've used `moveByX(y:duration:)` in the example above, passing `-(size.width + enemy.size.width)` for x and 0 for y.

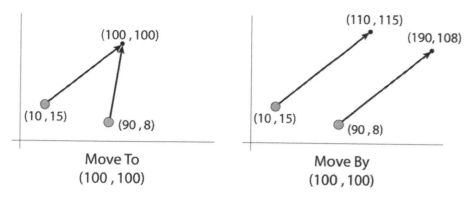

You'll see this pattern of "[action] to" and "[action] by" variants for other action types, as well. In general, you can use whichever of these is more convenient for you—but keep in mind that if either works, the "[action] by" actions are preferable because they're reversible. For more on this topic, keep reading.

Sequence action

The real power of actions lies in how easily you can chain them together. For example, say you want the cat lady to move in a V—down toward the bottom of the screen, then up to the goal position.

To do this, replace the lines that create and run the move action in `spawnEnemy()` with the following:

```
// 1
let actionMidMove = SKAction.moveTo(
  CGPoint(x: size.width/2,
          y: CGRectGetMinY(playableRect) + enemy.size.height/2),
  duration: 1.0)
// 2
let actionMove = SKAction.moveTo(
  CGPoint(x: -enemy.size.width/2, y: enemy.position.y),
  duration:1.0)
// 3
let sequence = SKAction.sequence([actionMidMove, actionMove])
// 4
enemy.runAction(sequence)
```

Let's go over this line by line:

1. Here you create a new move action, just like you did before, except this time it represents the "mid-point" of the action—the bottom middle of the playable rectangle.

2. This is the same move action as before, except you've decreased the duration to 1.0, since it will now represent moving only half the distance: from the bottom of the V, offscreen to the left.

3. Here's the new sequence action! As you can see, it's incredibly simple—you use the `sequence:` constructor and pass in an `Array` of actions. The sequence action will run one action after another.

4. You call `runAction()` in the same way as before, but pass in the sequence action this time.

That's it! Build and run, and you'll see the crazy cat lady "bounce" off the bottom of the playable rectangle:

The sequence action is one of the most useful and commonly used actions—chaining actions together is just so powerful! You'll use the sequence action many times in this chapter and throughout the rest of this book.

Wait-for-duration action

The wait-for-duration action does exactly what you'd expect: It makes the sprite wait for a period of time, during which the sprite does nothing.

"What's the point of that?" you may be wondering. Well, wait-for-duration actions only truly become interesting when combined with a sequence action.

For example, let's make the cat lady briefly pause when she reaches the bottom of the V-shape. To do this, replace the line in `spawnEnemy()` that creates a sequence with the following lines:

```
let wait = SKAction.waitForDuration(0.25)
let sequence = SKAction.sequence(
  [actionMidMove, wait, actionMove])
```

To create a wait-for-duration action, call `waitForDuration()` with the amount of time to wait in seconds. Then, simply insert it into the sequence of actions where you want the delay to occur.

Build and run, and now the cat lady will briefly pause at the bottom of the V:

Run-block action

At times, you'll want to run your own block of code in a sequence of actions. For example, let's say you want to log a message when the cat lady reaches the bottom of the V.

To do this, replace the line in `spawnEnemy()` that creates a sequence with the following lines:

```
let logMessage = SKAction.runBlock() {
  print("Reached bottom!")
}
let sequence = SKAction.sequence(
  [actionMidMove, logMessage, wait, actionMove])
```

To create a run-block action, simply call `runBlock()` and pass in a block of code to execute.

Build and run, and when the cat lady reaches the bottom of the V, you'll see the following in the console:

```
Reached bottom!
```

> **Note**: If your project still includes the `print` statements from earlier chapters, now would be a great time to remove them. Otherwise, you'll have to search your console for the above log statement—it's doubtful you'll notice it within the sea of messages scrolling by.
>
> While you're at it, you should remove any comments as well, to keep your project nice and clean.

Of course, you can do far more than log a message here—since it's an arbitrary code block, you can do anything you want!

You should be aware of one more action related to running blocks of code:

- **runBlock(queue:)** allows you to run the block of code on an arbitrary dispatch queue instead of in the main Sprite Kit event loop. You'll learn more about this in Chapter 28, "Performance: Tips and Tricks".

Reversing actions

Let's say you want to make the cat lady go back the way she came: After she moves in a V to the left, she should move in a V back to the right.

One way to do this would be, after she goes offscreen to the left, to have her run the existing `actionMidMove` action to go back to the middle, and creating a new `moveTo(duration:)` action to send her back to the start position.

But Sprite Kit gives you a better option. You can reverse certain actions in Sprite Kit simply by calling `reversedAction()` on them, resulting in a new action that is the opposite of the original action.

For example, if you run a `moveByX(y:duration:)` action, you can run the reverse of that action to go back the other way:

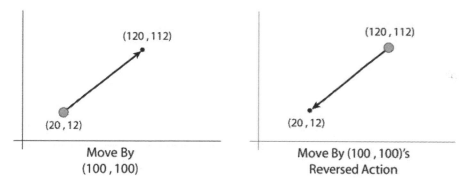

Not all actions are reversible—for example, `moveTo(duration:)` is not. To find out if an action is reversible, look it up in the `SKAction` class reference, which indicates it plainly.

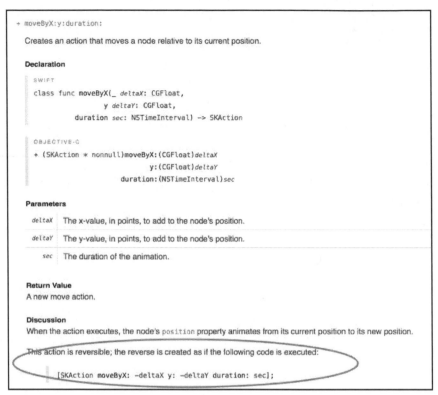

Let's try this out. First, replace the declarations of `actionMidMove` and `actionMove` in `spawnEnemy()` with the following code:

```
let actionMidMove = SKAction.moveByX(
  -size.width/2-enemy.size.width/2,
  y: -CGRectGetHeight(playableRect)/2 + enemy.size.height/2,
  duration: 1.0)
let actionMove = SKAction.moveByX(
  -size.width/2-enemy.size.width/2,
  y: CGRectGetHeight(playableRect)/2 - enemy.size.height/2,
  duration: 1.0)
```

Here, you switch the `moveTo(duration:)` actions to the related `moveByX(y:duration:)` variant, since that is reversible.

Now replace the line in `spawnEnemy()` that creates `sequence` with the following lines:

```
let reverseMid = actionMidMove.reversedAction()
let reverseMove = actionMove.reversedAction()
let sequence = SKAction.sequence([
  actionMidMove, logMessage, wait, actionMove,
  reverseMove, logMessage, wait, reverseMid
])
```

First, you switch the `moveTo(duration:)` actions to the related `moveByX(y:duration:)` variant, since that is reversible.

Then, you create the reverse of those actions by calling `reversedAction()` on each, and insert them into the sequence.

Build and run, and now the cat lady will go one way, then back the other way:

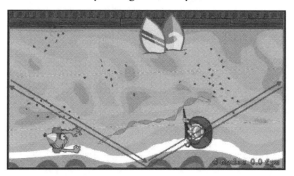

> **Note**: If you try to reverse an action that isn't reversible, then `reversedAction()` will return the same action.

Because sequence actions are also reversible, you can simplify the above code as follows. **Remove** the lines where you create the reversed actions and replace the sequence creation with the following lines:

```
let halfSequence = SKAction.sequence(
  [actionMidMove, logMessage, wait, actionMove])
let sequencc = SKAction.sequence(
  [halfSequence, halfSequence.reversedAction()])
```

This simply creates a sequence of actions that moves the sprite one way, and then reverses the sequence to go back the other way.

Astute observers may have noticed that the first half of the sequence logs a message as soon as the sprite reaches the bottom of the screen, but on the way back, the message isn't logged until after the sprite has waited at the bottom for one second.

This is because the reversed sequence is the exact opposite of the original, unlike your first implementation of the reversal. Later in this chapter, you'll read about the group action, which you could use to fix this behavior.

Repeating actions

So far, so good, but what if you want the cat lady to repeat this sequence multiple times? Of course, there's an action for that!

You can repeat an action a certain number of times using `repeatAction(count:)`, or an endless number of times using `repeatActionForever()`.

Let's go with the endless variant. Replace the line that runs your action in `spawnEnemy()` with the following two lines:

```
let repeatAction = SKAction.repeatActionForever(sequence)
enemy.runAction(repeatAction)
```

Here, you create an action that repeats the sequence of other actions endlessly, and run that repeat action on the enemy.

Build and run, and now your cat lady will continuously bounce back and forth. I told you she's crazy!

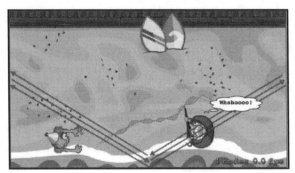

Congratulations! You now understand many useful types of actions:

- Move actions
- Sequence actions
- Wait-for-duration actions
- Run-block actions
- Reversing actions
- Repeating actions

Next, you're going to put all of these together in a new and interesting way to make cat ladies spawn periodically, so your zombie can never get too comfortable.

Periodic spawning

Right now, the game spawns a single cat lady at launch. To prepare for periodic spawning, you'll revert the `spawnEnemy()` code to the original version that simply moves the cat lady from right to left. You'll also introduce random variance so the cat lady doesn't always spawn at the same y-position.

First things first: You need a helper method to generate a random number within a range of values. Add this new method to **MyUtils.swift**, alongside the other math utilities you added in the challenges section of the previous chapter:

```swift
extension CGFloat {
  static func random() -> CGFloat {
    return CGFloat(Float(arc4random()) / Float(UInt32.max))
  }

  static func random(min min: CGFloat, max: CGFloat) -> CGFloat
  {
    assert(min < max)
    return CGFloat.random() * (max - min) + min
  }
}
```

This extends `CGFloat` to add two new methods: The first gives a random number between 0 and 1, and the second gives a random number between specified minimum and maximum values.

It's not important for you to understand these methods beyond that. But if you're really curious, you can read the following note:

> **Note:** `random()` calls `arc4random()`, which gives you a random integer between 0 and the largest value possible to store with an unsigned 32-bit integer, represented by `UInt32.max`. If you divide that number by `UInt32.max`, you get a float between 0 and 1.
>
> Here's how `random(min:max:)` works. If you multiply the result of `random()` — remember, that's a float between 0 and 1 — by the range of values (`max - min`), you'll get a float between 0 and the range. If you add to that the `min` value, you'll get a float between `min` and `max`.

This is a very simple way of generating a random number. If you need more advanced control, check out Chapter 20, "Randomization".

Voilà, job done!

Next, head back to **GameScene.swift** and replace the current version of spawnEnemy() with the following:

```
func spawnEnemy() {
  let enemy = SKSpriteNode(imageNamed: "enemy")
  enemy.position = CGPoint(
    x: size.width + enemy.size.width/2,
    y: CGFloat.random(
      min: CGRectGetMinY(playableRect) + enemy.size.height/2,
      max: CGRectGetMaxY(playableRect) - enemy.size.height/2))
  addChild(enemy)

  let actionMove =
    SKAction.moveToX(-enemy.size.width/2, duration: 2.0)
  enemy.runAction(actionMove)
}
```

You've modified the fixed y-position to be a random value between the bottom and top of the playable rectangle, and you've reverted the movement back to the original implementation—well, the moveToX(duration:) variant of the original implementation, anyway.

Now it's time for some action. Inside didMoveToView(), replace the call to spawnEnemy() with the following:

```
runAction(SKAction.repeatActionForever(
  SKAction.sequence([SKAction.runBlock(spawnEnemy),
                     SKAction.waitForDuration(2.0)])))
```

This is an example of chaining actions together inline instead of creating separate variables for each. You create a sequence of calling spawnEnemy() and waiting two seconds, and repeat this sequence forever.

Note that you're running the action on the scene itself. This works because the scene is a node, and any node can run actions.

Note: You can pass spawnEnemy directly as an argument to runBlock(), because a function with no arguments and no return value has the same type as the argument to runBlock(). Handy, eh?

Build and run, and the crazy cat ladies will spawn endlessly, at varying positions:

Remove-from-parent action

If you keep the game running for a while, there's a problem.

You can't see it, but there are a big army of cat ladies offscreen to the left. This is because you never remove the cat ladies from the scene after they've finished moving.

A never-ending list of nodes in a game is not a good thing. This node army will eventually consume all of the memory on the device, and at that point, the OS will automatically terminate your app, which from a user's perspective will look like your app crashed.

To keep your game running smoothly, a good rule of thumb is "If you don't need it anymore, remove it." And as you may have guessed, there's an action for that, too! When you no longer need a node and want to remove it from the scene, you can either call `removeFromParent()` directly or use the remove-from-parent action.

Give this a try. Replace the call to `runAction()` inside `spawnEnemy()` with the following:

```
let actionRemove = SKAction.removeFromParent()
enemy.runAction(SKAction.sequence([actionMove, actionRemove]))
```

Build and run, and now your nodes will clean up properly. Ah—much better!

> Note: removeFromParent() removes the node that's running that action from its parent. This raises a question: What happens to actions after you run them? Calling runAction() stores a strong reference to the action you give it, so won't that slowly eat up your memory?
>
> The answer is no. Sprite Kit nodes do you the favor of automatically removing their references to actions when the actions finish running. So you can tell a node to run an action and then forget about it, feeling confident that you haven't leaked any memory.

Animation action

This one is super useful, because animations add a lot of polish and fun to your game.

To run an animation action, you first need to gather a list of images called **textures** that make up the frames of the animation. A sprite has a texture assigned to it, but you can always swap out the texture with a different one at runtime by setting the texture property on the sprite.

In fact, this is what animations do for you: automatically swap out your sprite's textures over time, with a slight delay between each.

Zombie Conga already includes some animation frames for the zombie. As you can see below, you have four textures to use as frames to show the zombie walking:

zombie1.png   zombie2.png   zombie3.png   zombie4.png

You want to play the frames in this order:

1   2   3   4   3   2

You can then repeat this endlessly for a continuous walk animation.

Give it a shot. First, create a property for the zombie animation action:

```
let zombieAnimation: SKAction
```

Then, add the following code to `init(size:)`, right before the call to
`super.init(size:)`:

```
// 1
var textures:[SKTexture] = []
// 2
for i in 1...4 {
   textures.append(SKTexture(imageNamed: "zombie\(i)"))
}
// 3
textures.append(textures[2])
textures.append(textures[1])

// 4
zombieAnimation = SKAction.animateWithTextures(textures,
   timePerFrame: 0.1)
```

Let's go over this one section at a time:

1. You create an array that will store all of the textures to run in the animation.

2. The animation frames are named **zombie1.png**, **zombie2.png**, **zombie3.png** and
    zombie4.png. This makes it easy to fashion a loop that creates a string for each
    image name and then makes a texture object from each name using the
    `SKTexture(imageNamed:)` initializer.

    The first `for` loop adds frames 1 to 4, which is most of the "forward walk."

3. This adds frames 3 and 2 to the list—remember, the textures array is 0-based. In
    total, the textures array now contains the frames in this order: 1, 2, 3, 4, 3, 2. The
    idea is to loop this for a continuous animation.

4. Once you have the array of textures, running the animation is easy—you simply
    create and run an action with `animateWithTextures(timePerFrame:)`.

Finally, add this line to `didMoveToView()`, just after calling `addChild(zombie)`:

```
zombie.runAction(SKAction.repeatActionForever(zombieAnimation))
```

This runs the action wrapped in a repeat-forever action, which will seamlessly cycle
through the frames 1,2,3,4,3,2,1,2,3,4,3,2,1,2....

Build and run, and now your zombie will strut in style!

Stopping action

Your zombie's off to a good start, but there's one annoying thing: When the zombie stops moving, his animation keeps running. Ideally, you'd like to stop the animation when the zombie stops moving.

In Sprite Kit, whenever you run an action, you can give the action a key by using a variant of `runAction()` called `runAction(withKey:)`. This is handy because it allows you to stop the action by calling `removeActionForKey()`.

Give it a shot by adding these two new methods:

```
func startZombieAnimation() {
  if zombie.actionForKey("animation") == nil {
    zombie.runAction(
      SKAction.repeatActionForever(zombieAnimation),
      withKey: "animation")
  }
}

func stopZombieAnimation() {
  zombie.removeActionForKey("animation")
}
```

The first method starts the zombie animation. It runs the animation as before, but tags it with a key called "animation".

Also note that the method first uses `actionForKey()` to make sure there isn't already an action running with the key "animation"; if there is, the method doesn't bother running another one.

The second method stops the zombie animation by removing the action with the key "animation".

Now go to `didMoveToView()` and comment out the line that runs the action there:

```
// zombie.runAction(
//   SKAction.repeatActionForever(zombieAnimation))
```

Call `startZombieAnimation()` at the beginning of `moveZombieToward()`:

```
startZombieAnimation()
```

And call `stopZombieAnimation()` inside `update()`, right after the line of code that sets `velocity = CGPointZero`:

```
stopZombieAnimation()
```

Build and run, and now your zombie will only move when he should!

Scale action

You have an animated zombie and some crazy cat ladies, but the game is missing one very important element: cats! Remember, the player's goal is to gather as many cats as she can into the zombie's conga line.

In Zombie Conga, the cats won't move from right to left like the cat ladies do—instead, they'll appear at random locations on the screen and remain stationary. Rather than have the cats appear instantly, which would be jarring, you'll start them at a scale of 0 and grow them to a scale of 1 over time. This will make the cats appear to "pop in" to the game.

To implement this, add the following new method:

```
func spawnCat() {
  // 1
  let cat = SKSpriteNode(imageNamed: "cat")
  cat.position = CGPoint(
    x: CGFloat.random(min: CGRectGetMinX(playableRect),
                      max: CGRectGetMaxX(playableRect)),
    y: CGFloat.random(min: CGRectGetMinY(playableRect),
                      max: CGRectGetMaxY(playableRect)))
  cat.setScale(0)
  addChild(cat)
  // 2
  let appear = SKAction.scaleTo(1.0, duration: 0.5)
  let wait = SKAction.waitForDuration(10.0)
  let disappear = SKAction.scaleTo(0, duration: 0.5)
  let removeFromParent = SKAction.removeFromParent()
  let actions = [appear, wait, disappear, removeFromParent]
  cat.runAction(SKAction.sequence(actions))
}
```

Let's go over each section:

1. You create a cat at a random spot inside the playable rectangle. You set the cat's scale to 0, which makes the cat effectively invisible.

2. You create an action to scale the cat up to normal size by calling scaleTo(duration:). This action isn't reversible, so you also create a similar action to scale the cat back down to 0. In sequence, the cat appears, waits for a bit, disappears and is then removed from the parent.

You want the cats to spawn continuously from the start of the game, so add the following inside didMoveToView(), just after the line that spawns the enemies:

```
runAction(SKAction.repeatActionForever(
  SKAction.sequence([SKAction.runBlock(spawnCat),
                     SKAction.waitForDuration(1.0)])))
```

This is very similar to the way you spawned the enemies. You run a sequence that calls spawnCat(), waits for one second and then repeats.

Build and run, and you'll see cats pop in and out of the game:

You should be aware of a few variants of the scale action:

- **scaleXTo(duration:)**, **scaleYTo(duration:)** and **scaleXTo(y:duration:)**: These allow you to scale the x-axis or the y-axis of a node independently, which you can use to stretch or squash a node.

- **scaleBy(duration:)**: The "by" variant of scaling, which multiples the passed-in scale by the current node's scale. For example, if the current scale of a node is 1.0 and you scale it by 2.0, it is now at 2x. If you scale it by 2.0 again, it is now at 4x. Note that you couldn't use scaleBy(duration:) in the previous example, because anything multiplied by 0 is still 0!

- **scaleXBy(y:duration:)**: Another "by" variant, but this one allows you to scale x and y independently.

Rotate action

The cats in this game should be appealing enough that the player wants to pick them up, but right now they're just sitting motionless.

Let's give them some charm by making them wiggle back and forth while they sit.

To do this, you need the rotate action. To use it, you call the `rotateByAngle(duration:)` constructor, passing in the angle (in radians) by which to rotate.

Replace the declaration of the `wait` action in `spawnCat()` with the following:

```
cat.zRotation = -π / 16.0
let leftWiggle = SKAction.rotateByAngle(π/8.0, duration: 0.5)
let rightWiggle = leftWiggle.reversedAction()
let fullWiggle = SKAction.sequence([leftWiggle, rightWiggle])
let wiggleWait = SKAction.repeatAction(fullWiggle, count: 10)
```

Then, inside the declaration of the `actions` array, replace the `wait` action with `wiggleWait`, as shown below:

```
let actions = [appear, wiggleWait, disappear, removeFromParent]
```

Rotations go counterclockwise in Sprite Kit, so negative rotations go clockwise. First, you rotate the cat clockwise by 1/16 of π (11.25 degrees) by setting its `zRotation` to −π/16. The user won't see this because at this point, the cat's scale is still 0.

Then you create `leftWiggle`, which rotates counterclockwise by 22.5 degrees over a period of 0.5 seconds. Since the cat starts out rotated clockwise by 11.25 degrees, this results in the cat being rotated counterclockwise by 11.25 degrees.

Because this is a "by" variant, it's reversible, so you use `reversedAction()` to create `rightWiggle`, which simply rotates back the other way to where the cat started.

You create a `fullWiggle` by rotating left and then right. Now the cat has completed its wiggle and is back to its start position. This "full wiggle" takes a total of one second, so in `wiggleWait`, you repeat this 10 times to have a 10-second wiggle duration.

Build and run, and now your cats look like they've had some catnip!

Group action

So far, you know how to run actions one after another in sequence, but what if you want to run two actions at exactly the same time? For example, in Zombie Conga, you want to make the cats scale up and down slightly as they're wiggling.

For this sort of multitasking, you can use what's called the group action. It works in a similar way as the sequence action, where you pass in a list of actions. However, instead of running them one at a time, a group action runs them all at once.

Let's try this out. Replace the declaration of the `wiggleWait` action in `spawnCat()` with the following:

```
let scaleUp = SKAction.scaleBy(1.2, duration: 0.25)
let scaleDown = scaleUp.reversedAction()
let fullScale = SKAction.sequence(
  [scaleUp, scaleDown, scaleUp, scaleDown])
let group = SKAction.group([fullScale, fullWiggle])
let groupWait = SKAction.repeatAction(group, count: 10)
```

This code creates a sequence similar to that of the wiggle sequence, except it scales up and down instead of wiggling left and right.

The code then sets up a group action to run the wiggling and scaling at the same time. To use a group action, you simply provide it with the list of actions that should run simultaneously.

Now replace `wiggleWait` with `groupWait` inside the declaration of the actions array, as shown below:

```
let actions = [appear, groupWait, disappear, removeFromParent]
```

Build and run, and your cats will bounce with excitement:

> **Note:** The duration of a group action is equal to the longest duration of any of the actions it contains. So if you include an action that takes one second and another that takes 10 seconds, both actions will begin to run at the same time, and after one second, the first action will be complete. The group action will continue to execute for nine more seconds until the other action is complete.

Collision detection

You've got a zombie, you've got cats, you've even got crazy cat ladies—but you don't have a way to detect when they collide.

There are multiple ways to detect collisions in Sprite Kit, including by using the built-in physics engine, as you'll learn in Chapter 9, "Intermediate Physics". In this chapter, you'll take the simplest and easiest approach: bounding-box collision detection.

There are three basic ideas you'll use to implement this:

1. You need a way of getting all of the cats and cat ladies in a scene into lists, so that you can check for collisions one by one. An easy solution is to give nodes a name when you create them, allowing you to use `enumerateChildNodesWithName(usingBlock:)` on the scene to find all the nodes with a certain name.

2. Once you have the lists of cats and cat ladies, you can loop through them to check for collisions. Each node has a `frame` property that gives you a rectangle representing the node's location onscreen.

3. If you have the frame for either a cat or a cat lady, and the frame for the zombie, you can use the built-in method `CGRectIntersectsRect()` to see if they collide.

Let's give this a shot. First, set the name for each node. Inside `spawnEnemy()`, right after creating the enemy sprite, add this line:

```
enemy.name = "enemy"
```

Similarly, inside `spawnCat()`, right after creating the cat sprite, add this line:

```
cat.name = "cat"
```

Then add these new methods to the file:

```
func zombieHitCat(cat: SKSpriteNode) {
  cat.removeFromParent()
}

func zombieHitEnemy(enemy: SKSpriteNode) {
  enemy.removeFromParent()
}

func checkCollisions() {
  var hitCats: [SKSpriteNode] = []
  enumerateChildNodesWithName("cat") { node, _ in
    let cat = node as! SKSpriteNode
    if CGRectIntersectsRect(cat.frame, self.zombie.frame) {
      hitCats.append(cat)
    }
  }
  for cat in hitCats {
    zombieHitCat(cat)
  }

  var hitEnemies: [SKSpriteNode] = []
  enumerateChildNodesWithName("enemy") { node, _ in
    let enemy = node as! SKSpriteNode
    if CGRectIntersectsRect(
      CGRectInset(node.frame, 20, 20), self.zombie.frame) {
      hitEnemies.append(enemy)
    }
  }
  for enemy in hitEnemies {
    zombieHitEnemy(enemy)
  }
}
```

Here, you enumerate through any child of the scene that has the name "cat" or "enemy" and cast it to an `SKSpriteNode`, since you know it's a sprite node if it has that name.

You then check if the frame of the cat or enemy intersects with the frame of the zombie. If there is an intersection, you simply add the cat or enemy to an array to keep track of it. After you finish enumerating the nodes, you loop through the `hitCats` and `hitEnemies` arrays and call a method that removes the cat or enemy from the scene.

Note that you don't remove the nodes from within the enumeration. It's unsafe to remove a node while enumerating over a list of them, and doing so can crash your app.

Also, notice that you do a little trick for the cat lady. Remember that the frame of a sprite is the sprite's entire image, including transparent space:

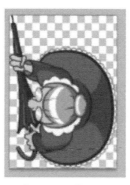

That means if the zombie went into the area of transparent space at the top of the cat lady image, it would "count" as a hit. Totally unfair!

To resolve this, you shrink the bounding box a little by using `CGRectInset()`. It's not a perfect solution, but it's a start. You'll learn a better way to do this in Chapter 10, "Advanced Physics".

Add the following call to your collision detection method at the end of `update()`:

```
checkCollisions()
```

Build and run, and now when you collide with a cat or enemy, it disappears from the scene. It's your first small step toward the zombie apocalypse!

The Sprite Kit game loop, round 2

There's a slight problem with the way you're detecting collisions, and it's related to Sprite Kit's game loop.

Earlier, you learned that during Sprite Kit's game loop, first `update()` gets called, then some "other stuff" occurs, and finally Sprite Kit renders the screen:

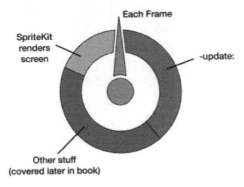

One of the things in the "other stuff" section is the evaluation of the actions you've been learning about in this chapter:

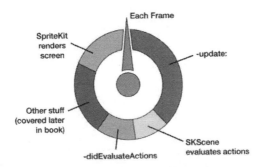

Herein lies the problem with your current collision detection method. You check for collisions at the end of the `update()` loop, but Sprite Kit doesn't evaluate the actions until *after* this `update()` loop. Therefore, your collision detection code is always one frame behind!

As you can see in your new event loop diagram, it would be much better to perform collision detection after Sprite Kit evaluates the actions and all the sprites are in their new spots. So comment out the call at the end of `update()`:

```
// checkCollisions()
```

And implement `didEvaluateActions()` as follows:

```
override func didEvaluateActions() {
   checkCollisions()
}
```

You probably won't notice much of a difference in this case, because the frame rate is so fast, it's hard to tell it was behind. But it could be quite noticeable in other games, so it's best to do things properly.

Sound action

The last type of action you'll learn about in this chapter also happens to be one of the most fun—it's the action that plays sound effects!

Using the `playSoundFileNamed(waitForCompletion:)` action, it takes just one line of code to play a sound effect with Sprite Kit. The node on which you run this action doesn't matter, so typically you'll run it as an action on the scene itself.

First, you need to add sounds to your project. In the resources for this chapter, find the folder named **Sounds** and drag it into your project. Make sure that **Copy items if needed**, **Create Groups** and the **ZombieConga** target are selected, and click **Finish**.

Now for the code. Add this line to the end of `zombieHitCat()`:

```
runAction(SKAction.playSoundFileNamed("hitCat.wav",
   waitForCompletion: false))
```

Then add this line to the end of `zombieHitEnemy()`:

```
runAction(SKAction.playSoundFileNamed("hitCatLady.wav",
   waitForCompletion: false))
```

Here, you play the appropriate sound action for each type of collision. Build and run, move the zombie around and enjoy the sounds of the smash-up!

Sharing actions

In the previous section, perhaps you noticed a slight pause the first time the sound plays. This can occur whenever the sound system loads a sound file for the first time. The solution to this problem also demonstrates one of the most powerful features of Sprite

Kit's actions: sharing.

The `SKAction` object doesn't itself maintain any state, and that allows you to do something cool: reuse actions on any number of nodes simultaneously! For example, the action you create to move the cat ladies across the screen looks something like this:

```
let actionMove =
  SKAction.moveToX(-enemy.size.width/2, duration: 2.0)
```

But you're creating this action for every cat lady. Instead, you could create an `SKAction` property, store this action in it and then use that property wherever you're currently using `actionMove`.

> Note: In fact, you could modify Zombie Conga so it reuses most of the actions you've created so far. This would reduce the amount of memory your system uses, but that's a performance improvement you probably don't need to make in such a simple game.

But how does this relate to the sound delay?

The application is loading the sound the first time you create an action that uses it. So to prevent the sound delay, you can create the actions in advance and then use them when necessary.

Create the following properties:

```
let catCollisionSound: SKAction = SKAction.playSoundFileNamed(
  "hitCat.wav", waitForCompletion: false)
let enemyCollisionSound: SKAction = SKAction.playSoundFileNamed(
  "hitCatLady.wav", waitForCompletion: false)
```

These properties hold shared instances of the sound actions you want to run.

Finally, replace the line that plays the sound in `zombieHitCat()` with the following:

```
runAction(catCollisionSound)
```

And replace the line that plays the sound in `zombieHitEnemy()` with the following:

```
runAction(enemyCollisionSound)
```

Now you're reusing the same sound actions for all collisions rather than creating a new one for each collision.

Build and run again. You'll no longer experience any pauses before the sound effects play.

As for music, stay tuned (no pun intended!)—you'll learn about that in the next chapter, where you'll wrap up the core gameplay by adding a win/lose scene to the game.

But before you move on, be sure to get some practice with actions by working through the challenges for this chapter!

Challenges

This chapter has three challenges, and as usual, they progress from easiest to hardest.

Be sure to do these challenges. As a Sprite Kit developer, you'll be using actions all the time, so it's important to practice with them before moving further.

As always, if you get stuck, you can find solutions in the resources for this chapter—but give it your best shot first!

Challenge 1: The ActionsCatalog demo

This chapter covers the most important actions in Sprite Kit, but it doesn't cover all of them. To help you get a solid understanding of all the actions available to you, I've created a little demo called ActionsCatalog, which you can find in the resources for this challenge.

Open the project in Xcode and build and run. You'll see something like the following:

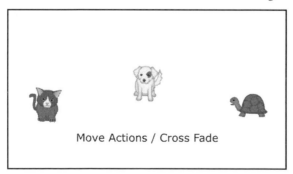

Each scene in the app demonstrates a particular set of actions, shown as the part of the label before the backslash. This first example demonstrates the various move actions.

Each time you tap the screen, you'll see a new set of actions. As the scenes transition, you'll also see different transition effects, shown as the part of the label after the backslash.

Your challenge is to flip through each of these demos, then take a look at the code to answer the following questions:

1. What action constructor would you use to make a sprite follow a certain pre-defined path?

2. What action constructor would you use to make a sprite 50% transparent, regardless of what its current transparency settings are?

3. What are "custom actions" and how do they work at a high level?

You can check your answers in a comment at the top of GameScene.swift in the solution project for this chapter.

Challenge 2: An invincible zombie

Currently, when an enemy hits the zombie, it destroys the enemy. This is a sneaky way of avoiding the problematic scenario of the enemy colliding with the zombie multiple times in a row as it moves through the zombie, which would result in the squish sound effect playing just as many times in rapid succession.

Usually in a video game, you'd resolve this problem by making the player sprite invincible for a few seconds after it gets hit, so the player has time to get his or her bearings.

Your challenge is to modify the game to do just this. When the zombie collides with a cat lady, he should become temporarily invincible instead of destroying the cat lady.

While the zombie is invincible, he should blink. To do this, you can use the custom blink action that's included in ActionsCatalog. Here's the code for your convenience:

```
let blinkTimes = 10.0
let duration = 3.0
let blinkAction = SKAction.customActionWithDuration(duration) {
  node, elapsedTime in
  let slice = duration / blinkTimes
  let remainder = Double(elapsedTime) % slice
  node.hidden = remainder > slice / 2
}
```

If you'd like a detailed explanation of this method, see the comment in the solution for the previous challenge. Here are some hints for solving this challenge:

* You should create a variable property to track whether or not the zombie is invincible.

* If the zombie is invincible, you shouldn't bother enumerating the scene's cat ladies.

* If the zombie collides with a cat lady, don't remove the cat lady from the scene. Instead, set the zombie as invincible. Next, run a sequence of actions that first makes the zombie blink 10 times over three seconds, then runs the block of code described below.

* The block of code should set hidden to false on the zombie, making sure he's visible at the end no matter what, and set the zombie as no longer invincible.

Challenge 3: The conga train

This game is called Zombie Conga, but there's no conga line to be seen just yet!

Your challenge is to fix that. You'll modify the game so that when the zombie collides with a cat, instead of disappearing, the cat joins your conga line!

In the process of doing this, you'll get more practice with actions, and you'll also review the vector math material you learned in the last chapter. Yes, that stuff still comes in handy when working with actions!

First, when the zombie collides with a cat, don't remove the cat from the scene. Instead, do the following:

1. Set the cat's name to "train" instead of "cat".

2. Stop all actions currently running on the cat by calling `removeAllActions()`.

3. Set the scale of the cat to 1 and its rotation to 0.

4. Run an action to make the cat turn green over 0.2 seconds. If you're not sure what action to use for this, check out `ActionsCatalog`.

After this, there are three more things you have to do:

1. Create a constant `CGFloat` property to keep track of the cat's move points per second. Set it to 480.0.

2. Set the zombie's `zPosition` to 100, which will make the zombie appear on top of the other sprites. Larger `z` values are "out of the screen" and smaller values are "into the screen", and the default value is 0.

3. Make a new method called `moveTrain`. The basic idea for this method is that every so often, you make each cat move toward the current position of the previous cat. This creates a conga line effect!

Use the following template:

```
func moveTrain() {
  var targetPosition = zombie.position

  enumerateChildNodesWithName("train") {
    node, _ in
    if !node.hasActions() {
      let actionDuration = 0.3
      let offset = // a
      let direction = // b
      let amountToMovePerSec = // c
      let amountToMove = // d
      let moveAction = // e
      node.runAction(moveAction)
    }
    targetPosition = node.position
  }
}
```

You need to fill in **a** through **d** by using the `CGPoint` operator overloads and utility functions you created last chapter, and **e** by creating the appropriate action. Here are some hints:

1. You need to figure out the offset between the cat's current position and the target position.

2. You need to figure out a unit vector pointing in the direction of the offset.

3. You need to get a vector pointing in the direction of the offset, but with a length of the cat's move points per second. This represents the amount and direction the cat should move in a second.

4. You need to get a fraction of the `amountToMovePerSec` vector, based on the `actionDuration`. This represents the offset the cat should move over the next `actionDuration` seconds. Note that you'll need to cast `actionDuration` to a `CGFloat`.

5. You should move the cat a relative amount based on the `amountToMove`.

Finally, don't forget to call `moveTrain` at the end of `update()`.

And that's it—who said you couldn't herd cats? If you got this working, you've truly made this game live up to its name: Zombie Conga!

Chapter 4: Scenes

By Ray Wenderlich

Zombie Conga is beginning to look like a real game. It has character movement, enemies, sounds, animation, collision detection—and if you finished the challenges from the last chapter, even its namesake: a conga line!

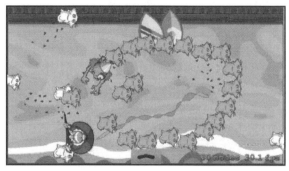

However, right now all the action takes place in a single **scene** of the game: the default GameScene created for you by the Sprite Kit project template.

In Sprite Kit, you don't have to place everything within the same scene. Instead, you can create multiple unique scenes, one for each "screen" of the app, much like how view controllers work in iOS development.

In this short chapter, you'll add two new scenes: one for when the player wins or loses the game and another for the main menu. You'll also learn a bit about using the cool transitions you saw in the ActionsCatalog demo from last chapter's Challenge 1.

But first, you need to wrap up some gameplay logic so you can detect when the player should win or lose the game. Let's get started!

Note: This chapter begins where the previous chapter's Challenge 3 left off. If you were unable to complete the challenges or skipped ahead from an earlier chapter, don't worry—simply open the starter project from this chapter to pick up where the previous chapter left off.

Win and lose conditions

Here's how the player will win or lose Zombie Conga:

- **Win Condition**: If the player creates a conga line of 15 or more cats, the player wins!

- **Lose Condition**: The player will start with five lives. If the player spends all of his or her lives, the player loses.

Right now, when a crazy cat lady collides with the zombie, nothing bad happens—there's only a sound. To make this game challenging, you'll change this so collisions with a cat lady result in the following effects:

1. The zombie loses a life.

2. The zombie loses two cats from his conga line.

Let's make it so. Inside **GameScene.swift**, add a new property to keep track of the zombie's lives and another to keep track of whether the game is over:

```
var lives = 5
var gameOver = false
```

Next, add this new helper method to make the zombie lose two cats from his conga line:

```
func loseCats() {
  // 1
  var loseCount = 0
  enumerateChildNodesWithName("train") { node, stop in
    // 2
    var randomSpot = node.position
    randomSpot.x += CGFloat.random(min: -100, max: 100)
    randomSpot.y += CGFloat.random(min: -100, max: 100)
    // 3
    node.name = ""
    node.runAction(
      SKAction.sequence([
        SKAction.group([
          SKAction.rotateByAngle(π*4, duration: 1.0),
          SKAction.moveTo(randomSpot, duration: 1.0),
          SKAction.scaleTo(0, duration: 1.0)
        ]),
```

```
        SKAction.removeFromParent()
    ]))
  // 4
  loseCount++
  if loseCount >= 2 {
    stop.memory = true
  }
 }
}
```

Let's go over this section by section:

1. Here, you set up a variable to track the number of cats you've removed from the conga line so far, then you enumerate through the conga line.

2. You find a random offset from the cat's current position.

3. You run a little animation to make the cat move toward the random spot, spinning around and scaling to 0 along the way. Finally, the animation removes the cat from the scene. You also set the cat's name to an empty string so it's no longer considered a normal cat or a cat in the conga line.

4. You update the variable that's tracking the number of cats you've removed from the conga line. Once you've removed two or more, you set the `stop` Boolean to `true`, which causes Sprite Kit to stop enumerating the conga line.

Now that you have this helper method, call it in `zombieHitEnemy()`, right after playing the enemy collision sound, and add a line to subtract 1 from the `lives` counter:

```
loseCats()
lives--
```

You're ready to add the code that checks if the player should win or lose. Begin with the lose condition. Add this to the end of `update()`:

```
if lives <= 0 && !gameOver {
  gameOver = true
  print("You lose!")
}
```

Here, you check if the number of remaining lives is 0 or less, and you make sure the game isn't already over. If both of these conditions are met, you set the game to be over and log out a message.

To check for the win condition, you'll make a few modifications to `moveTrain()`. First, add this variable at the beginning of the method:

```
var trainCount = 0
```

You'll use `trainCount` to keep track of the number of cats in the train. Increment this counter with the following line inside the enumerateChildNodesWithName() block, before the call to hasActions():

```
trainCount++
```

Finally, add this code at the end of moveTrain():

```
if trainCount >= 15 && !gameOver {
  gameOver = true
  print("You win!")
}
```

Here, you check if there are more than 15 cats in the train, and you make sure the game isn't over already. If both of these conditions are met, you set the game to be over and log out a message.

Build and run, and see if you can collect 15 cats.

When you do, you'll see the following message in the console:

```
You win!
```

That's great, but when the player wins the game, you want something a bit more dramatic to happen. Let's create a proper game over scene.

Creating a new scene

To create a new scene, you simply create a new class that derives from SKScene. You can then implement init(size:), update(), touchesBegan(withEvent:) or any of the other methods you overrode in GameScene to implement the behavior you want.

For now, you're going to keep things simple with a bare-bones new scene. In Xcode's main menu, select **File\New\File...**, select the **iOS\Source\Swift File** template and click **Next**.

Enter **GameOverScene.swift** for **Save As**, make sure the **ZombieConga** target is checked and click **Create**.

Open **GameOverScene.swift** and replace its contents with some bare-bones code for the new class:

```
import Foundation
import SpriteKit

class GameOverScene: SKScene {
}
```

With this, you've created an empty class, derived from SKScene, which defaults to a blank screen when presented. Later in this chapter, you'll return to this scene to add artwork and logic.

Now, how do you get to this new scene from your original scene?

Transitioning to a scene

There are three steps to transition from one scene to another:

1. **Create the new scene**. First, you create an instance of the new scene itself. Typically, you'd use the default init(size:) initializer, although you can always choose to create your own custom initializer if you want to be able to pass in extra parameters. Later in this chapter, you'll do just that.

2. **Create a transition object**. Next, you create a transition object to specify the type of

animation you'd like to use to display the new scene. For example, there are crossfade transitions, flip transitions, door-opening transitions and many more.

3. **Call the SKView's presentScene(transition:) method**. In iOS, SKView is the UIView that displays Sprite Kit content on the screen. You can get access to this via a property on the scene: view. You can then call presentScene(transition:) to animate to the passed-in scene (created in step 1) with the passed-in transition (created in step 2).

It's time to give this a try.

Open **GameScene.swift** and add the following lines in moveTrain(), right after the code that logs "You Win!" to the console (within the if statement):

```
// 1
let gameOverScene = GameOverScene(size: size)
gameOverScene.scaleMode = scaleMode
// 2
let reveal = SKTransition.flipHorizontalWithDuration(0.5)
// 3
view?.presentScene(gameOverScene, transition: reveal)
```

These three lines correspond exactly to the three steps above.

Notice that after creating the game over scene, you set its scale mode to the same as the current scene's scale mode to make sure the new scene behaves the same way across different devices.

Also notice that to create a transition, there are various constructors on SKTransition, just as there are various constructors for actions on SKAction. Here, you choose a flip horizontal animation, which flips up the scene into view from the bottom of the screen. For a demo of all the transitions, refer to ActionsCatalog, as discussed in the previous chapter's challenges.

Now add the exact same lines as above to update(), right after the code that logs "You lose!" to the console (again, within the if statement):

```
// 1
let gameOverScene = GameOverScene(size: size)
gameOverScene.scaleMode = scaleMode
// 2
let reveal = SKTransition.flipHorizontalWithDuration(0.5)
// 3
view?.presentScene(gameOverScene, transition: reveal)
```

Build and run, and either win or lose the game. Feel free to cheat and change the number of cats to win to less than 15—after all, you're the developer!

Whether you win or lose, when you do, you'll see the scene transition to a new blank scene:

That's really all there is to scene transitions! Now that you have a new scene, you can do whatever you like in it, just as you did in GameScene.

For Zombie Conga, you'll modify this new scene to show either a "You Win" or a "You Lose" background. To make this possible, you need to create a custom scene initializer to pass in either the win or lose condition.

Creating a custom scene initializer

Open **GameOverScene.swift** and modify GameOverScene as follows:

```
class GameOverScene: SKScene {
  let won:Bool

  init(size: CGSize, won: Bool) {
    self.won = won
    super.init(size: size)
  }

  required init(coder aDecoder: NSCoder) {
    fatalError("init(coder:) has not been implemented")
  }
}
```

Here, you add a custom initializer that takes just one extra parameter: a Boolean that should be true if the player won and false if the player lost. You store this value in a property named won.

Next, implement didMoveToView() to configure the scene when it's added to the view hierarchy:

```
override func didMoveToView(view: SKView) {

  var background: SKSpriteNode
  if (won) {
    background = SKSpriteNode(imageNamed: "YouWin")
```

```
    runAction(SKAction.sequence([
      SKAction.waitForDuration(0.1),
      SKAction.playSoundFileNamed("win.wav",
        waitForCompletion: false)
    ]))
  } else {
    background = SKSpriteNode(imageNamed: "YouLose")
    runAction(SKAction.sequence([
      SKAction.waitForDuration(0.1),
      SKAction.playSoundFileNamed("lose.wav",
        waitForCompletion: false)
    ]))
  }

  background.position =
    CGPoint(x: self.size.width/2, y: self.size.height/2)
  self.addChild(background)

  // More here...
}
```

This looks at the won Boolean and chooses the proper background image to set and sound effect to play.

In Zombie Conga, you want to display the game over scene for a few seconds and then automatically transition back to the main scene. To do this, add these lines of code right after the "More here..." comment:

```
let wait = SKAction.waitForDuration(3.0)
let block = SKAction.runBlock {
  let myScene = GameScene(size: self.size)
  myScene.scaleMode = self.scaleMode
  let reveal = SKTransition.flipHorizontalWithDuration(0.5)
  self.view?.presentScene(myScene, transition: reveal)
}
self.runAction(SKAction.sequence([wait, block]))
```

By now, this is all review for you. The code runs a sequence of actions on the scene, first waiting for three seconds and then calling a block of code. The block of code creates a new instance of GameScene and transitions to that with a flip animation.

One last step: You need to modify your code in GameScene to use this new custom initializer. Open **GameScene.swift** and inside update(), change the line that creates the GameOverScene to indicate that this is the lose condition:

```
let gameOverScene = GameOverScene(size: size, won: false)
```

Inside moveTrain(), change the same line, but indicate that this is the win condition:

```
let gameOverScene = GameOverScene(size: size, won: true)
```

Build and run, and play until you win the game. When you do, you'll see the win scene, which will then flip back to a new game after a few seconds:

Now that your game is close to done, it's a good time to turn off the debug drawing for the playable rectangle. Comment out this line in didMoveToView():

```
// debugDrawPlayableArea()
```

Background music

You almost have a complete game, but you're missing one thing: awesome background music!

Luckily, we've got you covered. Open **MyUtils.swift** and add the following to the bottom of the file:

```
import AVFoundation

var backgroundMusicPlayer: AVAudioPlayer!

func playBackgroundMusic(filename: String) {
  let resourceUrl = NSBundle.mainBundle().URLForResource(
    filename, withExtension: nil)
  guard let url = resourceUrl else {
    print("Could not find file: \(filename)")
    return
  }

  do {
    try backgroundMusicPlayer = AVAudioPlayer(contentsOfURL:
url)
    backgroundMusicPlayer.numberOfLoops = -1
    backgroundMusicPlayer.prepareToPlay()
    backgroundMusicPlayer.play()
  } catch {
    print("Could not create audio player!")
```

```
        return
    }
  }
```

Sprite Kit has no built-in way to play background music, so you'll have to fall back on other iOS APIs to do it. One easy way to play music in iOS is to use the `AVAudioPlayer` class inside the AVFoundation framework. The above helper code uses an `AVAudioPlayer` to play some background music in an endless loop.

Back in **GameScene.swift**, try it out by adding this line to the top of `didMoveToView()`:

```
playBackgroundMusic("backgroundMusic.mp3")
```

Here, you make the game play the background music when the scene first loads.

Finally, you need to stop the background music when the player switches scenes, so they can hear the "you win" or "you lose" sound effects. To do this, add this line right after the "You Win!" log line in `moveTrain()`:

```
backgroundMusicPlayer.stop()
```

Also add that same line right after the "You Lose!" log line in `update()`:

```
backgroundMusicPlayer.stop()
```

Build and run, and enjoy your groovy tunes!

Challenges

This was a short and sweet chapter, and the challenges will be equally so. With only one challenge for this chapter, it's time to add a main menu scene to the game.

As always, if you get stuck, you can find the solution in the resources for this chapter—but give it your best shot first!

Challenge 1: Main menu scene

Usually, it's best to start a game with an opening or main menu scene, rather than throw the player right into the middle of the action. The main menu often includes options to start a new game, continue a game, access game options and so on.

Zombie Conga's main menu scene will be very simple: It will show an image and allow the player to tap to continue straight to a new game. This will effectively be the same as the splash screen, except it will allow the player more time to get his or her bearings.

Your challenge is to implement a main menu scene that shows the **MainMenu.png** image as a background and upon a screen tap, uses a "doorway" transition over 1.5 seconds to transition to the main action scene.

Here are a few hints for how to accomplish this:

1. Create a new class that derives from `SKScene` named `MainMenuScene`.

2. Implement `didMoveToView()` on `MainMenuScene` to display **MainMenu.png** in the center of the scene.

3. Inside **GameViewController.swift**, edit `viewDidLoad()` to make it start with `MainMenuScene` instcad of `GameScene`.

4. Build and run, and make sure the main menu image appears. So far, so good!

5. Finally, implement `touchesBegan(_:withEvent:)` in `MainMenuScene` to call a helper method, `sceneTapped()`. `sceneTapped()` should transition to `GameScene` using a "doorway" transition over 1.5 seconds.

If you've gotten this working, congratulations! You now have a firm understanding of how to create and transition between multiple scenes in Sprite Kit.

Chapter 5: Camera

By Ray Wenderlich

So far, Zombie Conga's background is stationary. In contrast, many games have large scrolling worlds, like the original *Super Mario Bros.*:

The red box shows what you can see on the screen, but the level continues beyond to the right. As the player moves Mario to the right, you can think of the background as moving to the left:

There are two ways to accomplish this kind of scrolling in Sprite Kit:

1. **Move the background**. Make the player, enemies and power-ups children of the "background layer." Then, to scroll the game, you can simply move the background layer from right to left, and its children will move with it.

2. **Move the camera**. New in iOS 9, Sprite Kit includes SKCameraNode, which makes creating scrolling games even easier. You simply add a camera node to the scene, and the camera node's position represents the center of the current view.

In this chapter, you're going to use SKCameraNode to scroll the game, since this is the easiest method and likely what developers will use the most, now that it's available. It's time to get scrolling!

> **Note**: This chapter begins where the previous chapter's Challenge 1 left off. If you were unable to complete the challenges or skipped ahead from an earlier chapter, don't worry—simply open the starter project from this chapter to pick up where the previous chapter left off.

Lights, camera, action!

Working with SKCameraNode is a cinch. You simply:

1. Create an SKCameraNode;

2. Add it to the scene and set the scene's camera property to the camera node;

3. Set the camera node's position, which will represent the center of the screen.

Give this a try. Open **GameScene.swift** and add the following new property for the camera node:

```
let cameraNode = SKCameraNode()
```

This completes step 1. Next, add these lines to the end of didMoveToView():

```
addChild(cameraNode)
camera = cameraNode
cameraNode.position = CGPoint(x: size.width/2, y: size.height/2)
```

This completes steps 2 and 3, centering the view in the middle of the scene.

Build and run on your **iPad Air 2** simulator (I'll explain why the iPad Air and not the iPhone later), and you'll see the following:

The game works as before, except now you're using a camera node. To see the benefit of this, make the camera follow the zombie by adding this line of code to the end of update():

```
cameraNode.position = zombie.position
```

Build and run on your **iPad Air 2** simulator, and you'll see that the camera now follows the zombie:

That was easy! But right now, the background is only sized to match the visible area. You don't want your zombie walking through the void, so comment out that line for now.

```
// cameraNode.position = zombie.position
```

Now try running this on your **iPhone 6** simulator. At the time of writing, there appears to be a bug that makes the background a little off-center:

Luckily, there's a workaround. Add these methods to the bottom of GameScene:

```
func overlapAmount() -> CGFloat {
  guard let view = self.view else {
    return 0
  }
  let scale = view.bounds.size.width / self.size.width
  let scaledHeight = self.size.height * scale
  let scaledOverlap = scaledHeight - view.bounds.size.height
  return scaledOverlap / scale
}

func getCameraPosition() -> CGPoint {
  return CGPoint(x: cameraNode.position.x, y:
cameraNode.position.y + overlapAmount()/2)
}

func setCameraPosition(position: CGPoint) {
  cameraNode.position = CGPoint(x: position.x, y: position.y -
overlapAmount()/2)
}
```

Don't worry too much about how these work; just remember that you should use getCameraPosition() and setCameraPosition() instead of getting or setting the camera's position directly.

Try this out in didMoveToView() by replacing the line that sets the camera's position with the following:

```
setCameraPosition(CGPoint(x: size.width/2, y: size.height/2))
```

Build and run on your **iPhone 6** simulator, and you'll see the scene is now centered correctly!

A scrolling background

As you may remember from Chapter 2, you're using a background named **background1** that's the same size as the scene itself. Your project contains a second background named **background2** that's designed to be placed to the right of background1, like so:

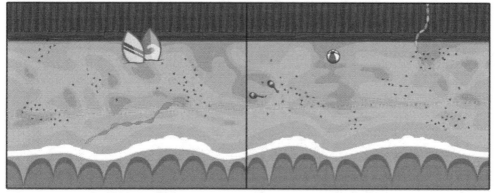

background1   **background2**

Your first task is simple: combine these two background images into a single node so you can easily scroll them both at the same time.

Add this new method to GameScene:

```
func backgroundNode() -> SKSpriteNode {
  // 1
  let backgroundNode = SKSpriteNode()
  backgroundNode.anchorPoint = CGPoint.zero
  backgroundNode.name = "background"
```

```
// 2
let background1 = SKSpriteNode(imageNamed: "background1")
background1.anchorPoint = CGPoint.zero
background1.position = CGPoint(x: 0, y: 0)
backgroundNode.addChild(background1)
// 3
let background2 = SKSpriteNode(imageNamed: "background2")
background2.anchorPoint = CGPoint.zero
background2.position =
  CGPoint(x: background1.size.width, y: 0)
backgroundNode.addChild(background2)
// 4
backgroundNode.size = CGSize(
  width: background1.size.width + background2.size.width,
  height: background1.size.height)
return backgroundNode
}
```

Let's go over this section by section:

1. You create a new **SKNode** to contain both background sprites as children. In this case, instead of using **SKNode** directly, you use an **SKSpriteNode** with no texture. This is so you can conveniently set the size property on the **SKSpriteNode** to the combined size of the background images.

2. You create an **SKSpriteNode** for the first background image and pin the bottom-left of the sprite to the bottom-left of **backgroundNode**.

3. You create an **SKSpriteNode** for the second background image and pin the bottom-left of the sprite to the bottom-right of **background1** inside **backgroundNode**.

4. You set the size of the **backgroundNode** based on the size of the two background images.

Next, replace the code that creates the background sprite in **didMoveToView()** with the following:

```
let background = backgroundNode()
background.anchorPoint = CGPoint.zero
background.position = CGPoint.zero
background.name = "background"
addChild(background)
```

This simply creates the background using your new helper method rather than basing it on a single background image.

Also note that before, you had the background centered onscreen. Here, you pin the lower-left corner to the lower-left of the scene, instead.

Changing the anchor point to the lower-left like this will make it easier to calculate positions when the time comes. You also name the background, "background", so you can readily find it.

Your goal is to make this camera scroll from left to right. To do this, add a property for the camera's scrolling speed:

```
let cameraMovePointsPerSec: CGFloat = 200.0
```

Next, add this helper method to move the camera:

```
func moveCamera() {
  let backgroundVelocity =
    CGPoint(x: cameraMovePointsPerSec, y: 0)
  let amountToMove = backgroundVelocity * CGFloat(dt)
  cameraNode.position += amountToMove
}
```

This calculates the amount the camera should move this frame, and updates the camera's position accordingly.

Finally, call this new method inside `update()`, right after the call to `moveTrain()`:

```
moveCamera()
```

Build and run, and now you have a scrolling background:

But as the screen scrolls, the zombie disappears offscreen, the cats stop spawning—and eventually, you see the void:

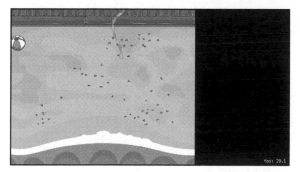

Don't worry. It's not the end of the world yet; it's only a minor zombie apocalypse! Nonetheless, it's time to fix these problems—starting by endlessly scrolling the background.

An endlessly scrolling background

The most efficient way to continuously scroll your background is to make two background nodes instead of one and lay them side by side:

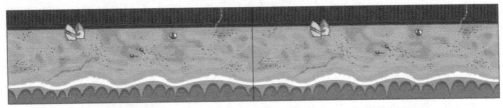

Then, as you scroll both images from right to left, as soon as one of the images goes offscreen, you simply reposition it to the right:

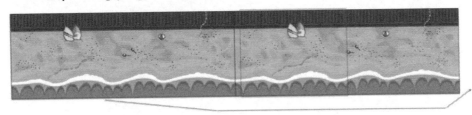

To do this, replace the code that creates the background node in `didMoveToView()`: with the following:

```
for i in 0...1 {
  let background = backgroundNode()
  background.anchorPoint = CGPointZero
  background.position =
    CGPoint(x: CGFloat(i)*background.size.width, y: 0)
  background.name = "background"
  addChild(background)
}
```

Also, if you still have the lines that get and log the background's size, comment them out.

The above wraps the code in a `for`-loop that creates two copies of the background and then sets their positions, so the second copy begins after the first ends.

Next, add this new method:

```
var cameraRect : CGRect {
  return CGRect(
    x: getCameraPosition().x - size.width/2
      + (size.width - playableRect.width)/2,
    y: getCameraPosition().y - size.height/2
      + (size.height - playableRect.height)/2,
    width: playableRect.width,
    height: playableRect.height)
}
```

This is a helper method that calculates the current "visible playable area". You'll be using this for calculations throughout the rest of the chapter.

Next, add the following code to the bottom of `moveCamera()`:

```
enumerateChildNodesWithName("background") { node, _ in
  let background = node as! SKSpriteNode
  if background.position.x + background.size.width <
self.cameraRect.origin.x {
    background.position = CGPoint(
        x: background.position.x + background.size.width*2,
        y: background.position.y)
  }
}
```

You check to see if the right-hand side of the background is less than the left hand side of the current visible playable area—in other words, if it's offscreen. Remember, you set the anchor point of the background to the bottom-left.

If part of the background is offscreen, you simply move the background node to the right by double the width of the background. Since there are two background nodes, this places the first node immediately to the right of the second.

Build and run, and now you have an continuously scrolling background! You saved the world from ending—even if it still has zombies.

Fixing the gameplay

You've fixed the background, but the gameplay is still wonky. Nothing appears to stay on the screen!

WHAT IZ   HAPPEN...?

Start by reining in the zombie. In **GameScene.swift**, review boundsCheckZombie() and see if you can spot the problem:

```
let bottomLeft = CGPoint(x: 0,
  y: CGRectGetMinY(playableRect))
let topRight = CGPoint(x: size.width,
  y: CGRectGetMaxY(playableRect))
```

This code assumes that the visible portion of the scene never changes from its original position. To correct that assumption, change the lines above so they look like this:

```
let bottomLeft = CGPoint(x: CGRectGetMinX(cameraRect),
  y: CGRectGetMinY(cameraRect))
let topRight = CGPoint(x: CGRectGetMaxX(cameraRect),
  y: CGRectGetMaxY(cameraRect))
```

Here you grab the coordinates from the visible playable area, rather than hardcoding a fixed position.

The cats have a similar problem. Inside spawnCat(), change the lines that set the cat's position to the following:

```
cat.position = CGPoint(
  x: CGFloat.random(min: CGRectGetMinX(cameraRect),
    max: CGRectGetMaxX(cameraRect)),
  y: CGFloat.random(min: CGRectGetMinY(cameraRect),
    max: CGRectGetMaxY(cameraRect)))
cat.zPosition = 50
```

This updates the cat so it spawns within the visible playable area rather than at a hardcoded position. You also update the cat's zPosition to make sure it stays on top of the background, but below the zombie.

There's one last thing: Since the background is continuously scrolling, your gameplay will be a lot more dynamic if you disable the code that stops the zombie once he reaches the target point - this way the zombie will always keep running. Remember, this was the zombie's original behavior before your second challenge in Chapter 2.

To let your zombie loose, comment out the relevant code in update(), as shown below:

```
/*
if let lastTouchLocation = lastTouchLocation {
  let diff = lastTouchLocation - zombie.position
  if (diff.length() <= zombieMovePointsPerSec * CGFloat(dt)) {
    zombie.position = lastTouchLocation
    velocity = CGPointZero
    stopZombieAnimation()
  } else {
  */
    moveSprite(zombie, velocity: velocity)
    rotateSprite(zombie, direction: velocity,
rotateRadiansPerSec: zombieRotateRadiansPerSec)
  /*}
}*/
```

Build and run, and now most of the gameplay works smoothly:

w00t, you're almost done—the only thing left to fix are the enemies! And that challenge is left to you. :]

Challenges

There's only one challenge this time: fixing the gameplay for the enemies.

As always, if you get stuck, you can find the solutions in the resources for this chapter—but give it your best shot first!

Challenge 1: Fixing the enemies

After awhile, the crazy cat ladies stop spawning and in some cases appear behind the background.

Look at `spawnEnemy()` and you'll see this is because you're still selecting the spawn point assuming the camera never moves, rather than using the currently visible playable area.

Your challenge is to modify this method to instead spawn enemies right outside of the currently visible playable area. Also, be sure to set the enemies' `zPosition` to match that of the cat so they don't appear below the background.

After you do this, you'll notice that as the level goes on, the enemies spawn faster and faster. Find out why this is and fix it.

> **Hint**: It has something to do with `actionMove`—is there an alternative action type you can use instead?

If you got this working, congratulations - you now have a complete scrolling game! There's just one bit of polish to wrap things up before we move on to another game: adding some labels to the game.

Chapter 6: Labels

By Ray Wenderlich

It's often useful in games to display text to keep your player informed. For example, currently in Zombie Conga, there's no indication of how many lives you have remaining —which can be quite frustrating if you die unexpectedly!

In this chapter, you'll learn how to display fonts and text within your game. Specifically, you'll add two labels to Zombie Conga: one to display your current lives and one to display your count of cats.

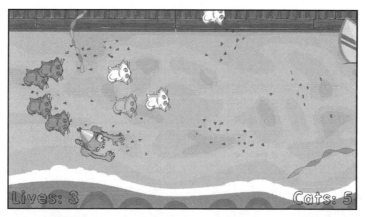

Note: This chapter begins where the previous chapter's Challenge 1 left off. If you were unable to complete the challenge or skipped ahead from an earlier chapter, don't worry—simply open the starter project from this chapter to pick up where the previous chapter left off.

Built-in fonts and font families

In iOS, fonts are broken into sets named "families". A font "family" consists of variants of the same font—such as lighter or heavier versions of the font—which may be useful in different situations.

For example, the "Thonburi" font family contains of three fonts:

1. **Thonburi-Light**: A thin/light version of the font.

2. **Thonburi**: A standard version of the font.

3. **Thonburi-Bold**: A bold version of the font.

Some font families have even more variants; the "Avenir" family has 12!

iOS ships with a number of built-in font families and fonts, so before you start using labels, you need to know what's available to you. To find out, you'll create a simple Sprite Kit project that lets you see these different fonts at a glance.

Create a new project in Xcode by selecting **File\New\Project...** from the main menu. Select the **iOS\Application\Game** template and click **Next**.

Enter **AvailableFonts** for the Product Name, select **Swift** as the language, **SpriteKit** as the Game Technology, **Universal** for Devices and then click **Next**.

Select a location on your hard drive to store the project and click **Create**. You now have a simple Sprite Kit project open in Xcode that you'll use to list the font families and fonts available in iOS.

You want this app to run in portrait mode, so select the **AvailableFonts** project in the project navigator and then select the **AvailableFonts** target. Go to the General tab, check **Portrait** and uncheck all other orientations.

Just like in Zombie Conga, you'll be creating this scene programmatically rather than using the scene editor. To do this, select **GameScene.sks** and delete it from your project. Then, open **GameViewController.swift** and replace the contents with the following:

```swift
import UIKit
import SpriteKit

class GameViewController: UIViewController {
  override func viewDidLoad() {
    super.viewDidLoad()
    let scene =
      GameScene(size:CGSize(width: 2048, height: 1536))
    let skView = self.view as! SKView
    skView.showsFPS = false
    skView.showsNodeCount = false
    skView.ignoresSiblingOrder = true
```

```
    scene.scaleMode = .AspectFill
    skView.presentScene(scene)
}

override func prefersStatusBarHidden() -> Bool {
    return true
}
}
```

This is the same code you used in Zombie Conga; it simply creates and presents
GameScene to the screen.

It's time to add that code. Open **GameScene.swift** and replace its contents with the
following:

```
import SpriteKit

class GameScene: SKScene {

  var familyIdx: Int = 0

  required init?(coder aDecoder: NSCoder) {
    super.init(coder: aDecoder)
  }

  override init(size: CGSize) {
    super.init(size: size)
    showCurrentFamily()
  }

  func showCurrentFamily() {
    // TODO: Coming soon...
  }

  override func touchesBegan(touches: Set<UITouch>,
    withEvent event: UIEvent?) {
      familyIdx++
      if familyIdx >= UIFont.familyNames().count {
        familyIdx = 0
      }
      showCurrentFamily()
  }
}
```

You begin by displaying the font family with index 0. Every time the user taps, you
advance to display the next font family name. In iOS, you can get a list of the built-in
font family names by calling UIFont.familyNames().

The code to display the fonts in the current font family will be in `showCurrentFamily()`, so implement that now by placing the following code inside that method:

```
// 1
removeAllChildren()

// 2
let familyName = UIFont.familyNames()[familyIdx]
print("Family: \(familyName)")

// 3
let fontNames =
  UIFont.fontNamesForFamilyName(familyName)

// 4
for (idx, fontName) in fontNames.enumerate() {
  let label = SKLabelNode(fontNamed: fontName)
  label.text = fontName
  label.position = CGPoint(
    x: size.width / 2,
    y: (size.height * (CGFloat(idx+1))) /
      (CGFloat(fontNames.count)+1))
  label.fontSize = 50
  label.verticalAlignmentMode = .Center
  addChild(label)
}
```

OK! Let's review this code section by section:

1. You remove all of the children from the scene so that you start with a blank slate.

2. You get the current family name based on the index that you increment with each tap. You also log out the family name, in case you're curious about it.

3. `UIFont` has another helper method to get the names of the fonts within a family, named `fontNamesForFamilyName()`. You call this here and store the results.

4. You then loop through the block and create a label using each font; the text of each label displays the name of the corresponding font. Since labels are the subject of this chapter, you'll review them in more detail next.

Creating a label

Creating a label is easy: You simply call `SKLabelNode(fontNamed:)` and pass in the name of the font:

```
let label = SKLabelNode(fontNamed: fontName)
```

The most important property to set is the text, because this is what you want the font to display.

```
label.text = fontName
```

You also usually want to set the font size (unless you want the default of 32 points).

```
label.fontSize = 50
```

Finally, just as with any other node, you position it and add it as a child of another node —in this case, the scene itself:

```
label.position = yourPosition
addChild(label)
```

For now, don't worry too much about the math you're using to position the labels. Also, don't worry about your use of `verticalAlignmentMode`—that's simply a little code magic to space the labels evenly up and down the screen. You'll learn more about alignment later in this chapter.

Build and run. Now, every time you tap the screen, you'll see a different built-in font family:

Tap through to get an idea of what's available. Try to find the font named "Chalkduster"—you'll be using that shortly in Zombie Conga.

This app will also be a handy reference in the future, when you're wondering what font would be the perfect match for your game.

Adding a label to Zombie Conga

Now that you know a little more about the available fonts, it's time to use what you've learned to add a label to Zombie Conga. You'll start with a simple label to show the player's remaining lives.

Open your Zombie Conga project, using either your post-challenge project file from the previous chapter or the starter project for this chapter.

With the appropriate project loaded in Xcode, open **GameScene.swift** and add this line to the bottom of the list of properties:

```
let livesLabel = SKLabelNode(fontNamed: "Chalkduster")
```

Here, you create an SKLabelNode, passing in the "Chalkduster" font you discovered in AvailableFonts earlier.

Next, add these lines to the bottom of `didMoveToView(_:)`:

```
livesLabel.text = "Lives: X"
livesLabel.fontColor = SKColor.blackColor()
livesLabel.fontSize = 100
livesLabel.zPosition = 100
livesLabel.position = CGPoint(x: size.width/2, y: size.height/2)
addChild(livesLabel)
```

Here, you do the same sorts of things you've already learned about: set the text to a placeholder, set the position to the center of the screen, set the font size and then add the node as a child of the scene. You also set a new property, `fontColor`, to set the color of the text.

Build and run, and you'll see the label. But wait! It scrolls off the screen as the camera moves!

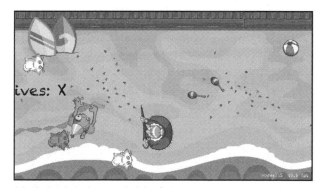

It's because you added the label as a child of the scene; as you move the camera, it "looks at" different parts of the scene.

What you really want is for the label to stay in the same position, regardless of how the camera moves. To do this, you need to add the label as a child of the camera node instead.

To do this, change the last two lines to the following:

```
livesLabel.position = CGPoint.zero
cameraNode.addChild(livesLabel)
```

Remember, a node's position is relative to the center of its parent, so `CGPoint.zero` means the center of the camera. This is aside from the bug with the camera that was mentioned in the previous chapter, which you'll address with a workaround a little later.

Build and run, and you'll see the label is now in a fixed position near the center of the screen:

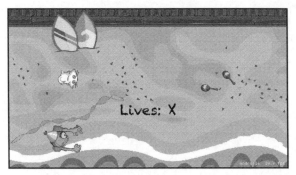

This looks good, except for Zombie Conga, it would look better if this label were aligned to the bottom-left of the playable area. For you to understand how to do this, I'd like to introduce you to the concept of **alignment modes**.

Alignment modes

So far, you know you can place a label by setting its position, but how can you control the placement of the text in relation to the position?

Unlike `SKSpriteNode`, `SKLabelNode` doesn't have an `anchorPoint` property. In its place, you can use the `verticalAlignmentMode` and `horizontalAlignmentMode` properties.

The `verticalAlignmentMode` controls the text's vertical placement in relation to the label's position, and the `horizontalAlignmentMode` controls the text's horizontal placement. You can see this visually in the following diagram:

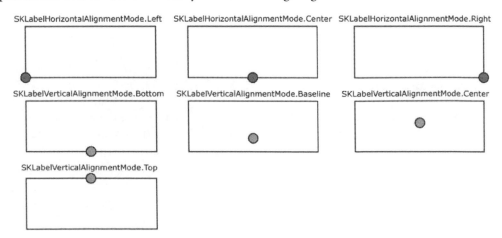

The red and blue points in the diagram show, for the different alignment modes, where each label's bounding box will be rendered in relation to the label's position. There are two things worth noting here:

- The default alignment modes of SKLabelNode are Center for horizontal and Baseline for vertical.

- Baseline uses the actual font's baseline, which you can think of as the "line" on which you would draw a font, if you were writing on ruled paper. For example, the tails of letters such as **g** and **y** will hang below the defined position.

To align the lives label to the bottom-left of the screen, you want to set the alignment modes to Left for horizontal and Bottom for vertical. This way, you can simply set the position to the bottom-left of the playable area.

It's time to try this out. Delete the line that sets the label's position and replace it with the following:

```
livesLabel.horizontalAlignmentMode = .Left
livesLabel.verticalAlignmentMode = .Bottom
livesLabel.position = CGPoint(x: -playableRect.size.width/2 +
CGFloat(20),
   y: -playableRect.size.height/2 + CGFloat(20) +
overlapAmount()/2)
```

Here you set the alignment modes as discussed, and then set the position to the bottom-left of the playable area. Here's a diagram to help you visualize this:

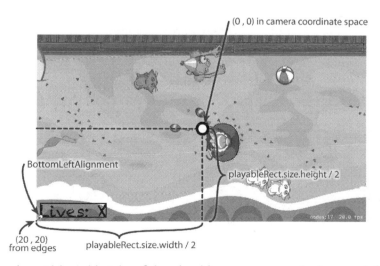

You subtract the width and height of the playable area to get to the bottom-left corner, and then you add a 20-point margin to provide a little space between the label and the edges.

Note: As a workaround to resolve the camera behavior bug mentioned in the previous chapter, you also add `overlapAmount()/2` to the y-axis; the diagram does not show this.

Build and run, and now you'll see the label correctly positioned in the bottom-left of the playable area.

Loading custom fonts

While the list of built-in fonts is large, there will be times you want to use fonts that aren't included by default.

For example, in Zombie Conga, it would be nice to switch to a font that's less intrusive in the game, but none of the fonts included by default are going to meet your needs. Luckily, Apple has made it super simple to use a **True Type Font** (TTF) in your project.

First, you need to find the font you want to use. One excellent source of fonts is http://www.dafont.com. Open your browser of choice and enter the URL. You'll see there's a large selection of categories from which to choose, including one named **Fancy/Cartoon**.

Click on that category, and you'll see a huge list of fonts with example text. Some people could spend hours looking through these fonts just for fun, so take as much time as you like to see what's available.

Now that you're back, the font you're going to use is named **Glimstick** by Uddi Uddi. Type that name into the search bar on the dafont.com website. A font preview will appear:

Glimstick by Uddi Uddi

In Fancy > Cartoon

72,848 downloads (18 yesterday) 100% Free

Download

Glimstick

This fun cartoony font is a perfect fit for the minigame you're creating. Click the **Download** button. Once the download is complete, unzip the package and find the file named **GLIMSTIC.TTF**. The resources for this chapter also include a copy of this font, in case you have trouble downloading it.

> **Note**: It's important to check the license for any fonts you want to use in your project. Some fonts require permission or a license before you can use them, so checking now could save a lot of headache and cost later.

> You can see just above the download button that the Glimstick font you're using is marked as **Free**, but to be sure, always check the license information included in the downloaded zip file.

Now that you have your font, drag **GLIMSTIC.TTF** into your Zombie Conga project. Make sure that **Copy items if needed** and the **ZombieConga** target are checked, and click **Finish**.

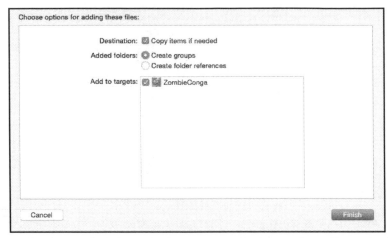

Next, open **Info.plist** and click on the last entry in the list, and you'll see plus (+) and minus (-) buttons appear next to that title.

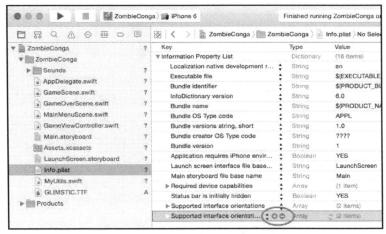

Click the plus button and a new entry will appear in the table, along with a drop-down list of options:

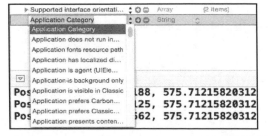

In the drop-down box, type **Fonts**, making sure to use a capital **F**. The first option that comes up will be **Fonts provided by application**. Press **Return** to select that option.

Click the triangle to the left of the new entry to expand it, and double-click inside the value field.

Inside the textbox that appears, type **GLIMSTIC.TTF**. This is the name of the font file you downloaded and the one you're going to use in the game. Be sure to spell it correctly or your app won't be able to load it.

▼ Fonts provided by application	Array	(1 item)
Item 0	String	GLIMSTIC.TTF

Now, to try out this font! Open **GameScene.swift** and replace your line that declares the livesLabel property with the following:

```
let livesLabel = SKLabelNode(fontNamed: "Glimstick")
```

> **Note**: Notice how the font filename (i.e. "GLIMSTIC.TTF") does not necessarily have to match the actual name of the font (i.e. "Glimstick"). You can find the actual name of the font by double clicking the .TTF file.

Build and run, and you'll see your new font appear:

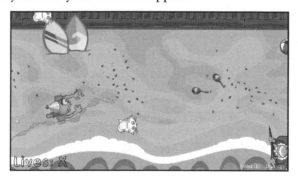

Updating the label text

One last thing: The label is still showing the placeholder text. To update the text, simply add this line to the bottom of moveTrain():

```
livesLabel.text = "Lives: \(lives)"
```

Build and run, and now your lives will properly update!

Challenges

This is your final challenge for Zombie Conga. Your game is 99% complete, so don't leave it hanging!

As always, if you get stuck, you can find the solutions in the resources for this chapter—but give it your best shot first!

Challenge 1: A cat count

Your challenge is to add a second label to the game to keep track of the count of cats in your conga train. This label should be in the bottom-right of the playable area.

Here are a few hints:

- Create a property named `catsLabel` like you did for the `livesLabel`.
- In `didMoveToView()`, configure the `catsLabel` similarly to the `livesLabel`. However, you'll have to change the `text`, `horizontalAlignmentMode` and `position`.
- For the `position`, refer to the diagram earlier in the chapter if you get stuck.
- Finally, in `moveTrain`, update the `catsLabel.text` based on `trainCount`.

If you've made it this far, a huge congratulations—you've completed your first Sprite Kit minigame, from scratch! Think of all you've learned to do:

• Add sprites to a game;

• Move them around manually;

• Move them around with actions;

• Create multiple scenes in a game;

• Make it a scrolling game with a camera;

• Add labels to the game.

Believe it or not, this knowledge is sufficient to make 90% of Sprite Kit games. The rest is just icing on the cake! :]

Chapter 7: Beginning tvOS

By Ray Wenderlich

At this point, Zombie Conga is complete as a Universal app for iPhone and iPad.

"But wait a minute", you may be thinking. "This book is called *2D iOS & tvOS Games by Tutorials*—where in the heck is the tvOS part?!"

```
I was
promised
full-screen
zombies!
```

Never fear, that's what this chapter is all about.

In this chapter, you'll port Zombie Conga to the Apple TV. By the time you're done, your game will be running on the big screen!

Believe it or not, porting your game is easier than it seems. Sprite Kit works the same on tvOS as it does on iOS, so getting the game to work on tvOS requires only a few simple steps.

So prepare to bring zombies into your living room—just have your shotgun ready.

> **Note**: This chapter begins where the previous chapter's Challenge 1 left off. If you were unable to complete the challenge or skipped ahead from an earlier chapter, don't worry—simply open the starter project from this chapter to pick up in the right place.

tvOS user input

Before you begin to port Zombie Conga to tvOS, it's important to understand one way developing for tvOS is different from developing for iOS: **user input**.

- **On iOS devices**, you touch the screen directly.

- **On tvOS devices**, you don't touch the screen directly—after all, we're too busy lazing on the couch! :] Instead, you move your finger on the remote's touchpad.

Since you aren't touching the screen itself on tvOS devices, your touch handlers can't receive exact coordinates of the touch location like they do on iOS.

Instead, this is what happens on tvOS:

1. When you start touching the remote's touchpad, tvOS calls touchesBegan() with coordinates of the center of the scene, regardless of where you began to touch on the touchpad.

2. As you move your finger along the remote's touchpad, tvOS calls touchesMoved() with coordinates relative to the previous coordinates, based on how you move your finger.

If this isn't clear yet, don't worry—the best way to understand how this works is with an example.

Getting started

Open Xcode and go to **File\New\Project....** Select the **tvOS\Application\Game** template and click **Next**.

Enter **tvOSTouchTest** for **Product Name**, choose **Swift** for **Language** and choose
SpriteKit for **Game Technology**. Then, click **Next**.

Choose a directory to save your project and click **Create**.

You won't be using the Sprite Kit scene editor for this chapter, so delete **GameScene.sks** from your project and choose **Move to Trash**.

Next, open **GameViewController.swift** and replace its contents with the following:

```
import UIKit
import SpriteKit

class GameViewController: UIViewController {
  let gameScene = GameScene(size:CGSize(width: 2048, height:
1536))

  override func viewDidLoad() {
    super.viewDidLoad()
    let skView = self.view as! SKView
    skView.showsFPS = true
    skView.showsNodeCount = true
    skView.ignoresSiblingOrder = true
    gameScene.scaleMode = .AspectFill
    skView.presentScene(gameScene)
  }
}
```

This simply creates the GameScene of size 2048x1536 and adds it to the SKView, just as you did earlier for Zombie Conga.

Next, open GameScene.swift and replace its contents with the following:

```
import SpriteKit

class GameScene: SKScene {

  // 1
  let pressLabel = SKLabelNode(fontNamed: "Chalkduster")
  // 2
  let touchBox = SKSpriteNode(color: UIColor.redColor(), size:
CGSize(width: 100, height: 100))

  override func didMoveToView(view: SKView) {

    // 3
    pressLabel.text = "Move your finger!"
    pressLabel.fontSize = 200
    pressLabel.verticalAlignmentMode = .Center
    pressLabel.horizontalAlignmentMode = .Center
    pressLabel.position = CGPoint(x: size.width/2, y:
size.height/2)
    addChild(pressLabel)

    // 4
    addChild(touchBox)
```

```
  }

  // 5
  override func touchesBegan(touches: Set<UITouch>, withEvent
event: UIEvent?) {
    for touch in touches {
      let location = touch.locationInNode(self)
      touchBox.position = location
    }
  }

  override func touchesMoved(touches: Set<UITouch>, withEvent
event: UIEvent?) {
    for touch in touches {
      let location = touch.locationInNode(self)
      touchBox.position = location
    }
  }
}
```

Take a look at what you're doing with this code, section by section:

1. Here you initialize a label node, just as you learned to do in the previous chapter.

2. In addition to creating sprite nodes from images, you can create a sprite node that's a simple color of a specified size. This is often handy for quick tests, like the one you're doing here. In this case, you initialize a sprite that's a 100x100 red box.

3. You set the text of the label to "Move your finger!" and center it on the screen. This is a review from the previous chapter.

4. In your touch handler methods, you simply move the red box to the location the touch handlers report. This will help you visualize what you're receiving for these methods.

Build and run on the Apple TV simulator, and you'll see the following:

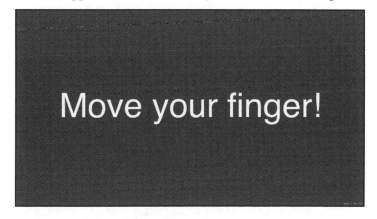

Next, bring up the Apple TV remote by clicking **Hardware\Show Apple TV Remote** from the simulator's main menu. Click the remote to focus it, then move your mouse over the touchpad area, hold down **Option** and **drag**. You'll start to see a red box moving around the screen, representing the coordinates you're receiving in your touch handler:

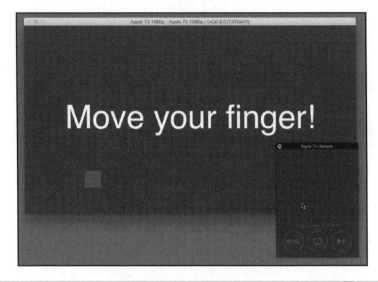

> **Note**: If you don't see the red box appear and move around, be sure to hold down Option as you drag your mouse inside the Apple TV remote.

Play around for a bit to see with your own eyes how touches work. As a reminder, here's what's going on:

1. When you start touching the remote's touchpad, tvOS calls `touchesBegan()` with the coordinates of the center of the scene, regardless of where you begin to touch on the touchpad.

2. As you move your finger along the remote's touchpad, tvOS calls `touchesMoved()` with coordinates relative to the previous coordinates, based on how you move your finger.

Once you're satisfied, keep reading to learn about one more difference in user input on tvOS.

> **Note:** You may have noticed that the input to your touch methods can go outside of the scene's coordinates. This is because the coordinates you receive aren't related to your view or scene, and instead only represent relative movement.

Button presses

A second difference in user input on tvOS is that the remote has a lot more buttons you might want to use.

Again, the best way to understand this is through a little demo.

Still in your **tvOSTouchTest** project, open **GameScene.swift** and implement these new methods at the bottom of the file:

```
// 1
override func pressesBegan(presses: Set<UIPress>, withEvent
event: UIPressesEvent?) {
  for press in presses {
    // 2
    switch press.type {
      case .UpArrow:
        pressLabel.text = "Up arrow"
      case .DownArrow:
        pressLabel.text = "Down arrow"
      case .LeftArrow:
        pressLabel.text = "Left arrow"
      case .RightArrow:
        pressLabel.text = "Right arrow"
      case .Select:
        pressLabel.text = "Select"
      case .Menu:
        pressLabel.text = "Menu"
      case .PlayPause:
        pressLabel.text = "Play/Pause"
    }
  }
}

override func pressesEnded(presses: Set<UIPress>, withEvent
event: UIPressesEvent?) {
  // 3
  self.removeAllActions()
  runAction(SKAction.sequence([
    SKAction.waitForDuration(1.0),
    SKAction.runBlock() {
      self.pressLabel.text = ""
    }
  ]))
}
```

Here's what you're doing, section by section:

1. To receive information about button presses in tvOS, you implement the pressesBegan() and pressesEnded() methods, which are called when you begin and stop pressing a button on the remote, respectively.

2. Each press has a `type` field that indicates which button the user is pressing. Based on the button, you update the label appropriately.

3. You want to clear the label after the user stops pressing a button, but you do so after a delay, giving the player time to see the button they pressed before you remove the label.

At the time of writing, these methods aren't called on an `SKScene` automatically, so you have to route the calls to your scene through your view controller. To do this, open **GameViewController.swift** and implement these two new methods:

```
override func pressesBegan(presses: Set<UIPress>, withEvent
event: UIPressesEvent?) {
  gameScene.pressesBegan(presses, withEvent: event)
}

override func pressesEnded(presses: Set<UIPress>, withEvent
event: UIPressesEvent?) {
  gameScene.pressesEnded(presses, withEvent: event)
}
```

These simply forward both calls to your `GameScene`.

Build and run, and tap the play/pause button on the remote to see the label update:

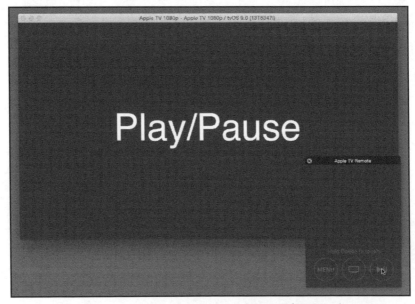

If you have an Apple TV, try running this app on the actual TV and try to get each type of touch to show up on the label. Here's what to do for each:

1. **Up/down/left/right**: Tap on the appropriate edge of the touchpad.

2. **Select**: Press down on the touchpad.

3. **Menu/PlayPause**: Press the appropriate button on the remote.

> **Note**: At the time of writing, pressing the menu button while debugging can confuse the Apple TV and create a state where you can't move around the main menu. If you have any trouble, just reset your Apple TV.

All right, now that you understand how user input works in tvOS, it's time to apply this to Zombie Conga.

Adding a tvOS target

Open your ZombieConga project from after you completed the previous chapter's challenge.

Click on your **ZombieConga** project in the project navigator and make sure the **General** tab is selected:

So far, there's only one target listed for your project: **ZombieConga**, which builds the project for iOS. To build this project for tvOS, you need to add a tvOS.

> **Note**: If you don't see the list of targets in the left sidebar, click the button just to the left of the General tab to reveal them.

To add a new target, click the plus (+) button at the bottom-left of the list of targets:

Just as you did before, select the **tvOS\Application\Game** template and click **Next**:

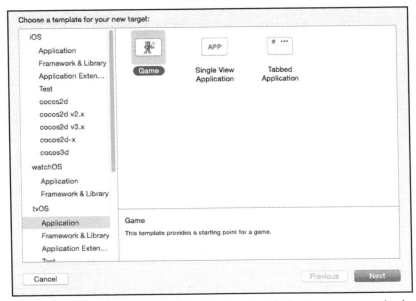

Enter **ZombieCongaTV** for **Product Name**, select **Swift** for **Language** and select **Sprite Kit** for **Game Technology**. Then, click **Finish**:

You'll see a new target appear in the list, along with a set of files that belong to that target in the project navigator:

Your goal is to reuse the files from your ZombieConga target in your ZombieCongaTV target. To do this, right-click your ZombieConga project located in the project navigator —it's the blue one at the very top, not the yellow folder—and select **New Group**. Name the group **Shared** and drag the following files from your yellow **ZombieConga** group to Shared:

1. **GLIMSTIC.TTF**

2. The entire **Sounds** group

3. **MainMenuScene.swift**

4. **GameSene.swift**

5. **GameOverScene.swift**

6. **Assets.xcassets**

7. **MyUtils.swift**

Next, rename **Shared\Assets.xcassets** to **Shared\Game.xcassets**. You need to do this so there's not a name conflict when you share this file with the ZombieCongaTV project.

Now, select all of the files you just added to Shared, including the files in the Sounds group, but not the group itself. Then, in the File Inspector on the right sidebar, click the checkbox for the **ZombieCongaTV** target:

This effectively includes all of these files in both targets.

There's just a little cleanup left to do. In your **ZombieCongaTV** group, delete **GameScene.sks**, **GameScene.swift** and **Game.xcassets**, since you either don't need them, or they're already included in the shared files. You can move them to the trash.

Then, open **ZombieCongaTV\Info.plist** and add the same **Fonts provided by application** entry for **GLIMSTIC.TTF** as you did in the previous chapter:

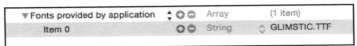

Finally, open **ZombieCongaTV\GameViewController.swift** and replace the contents with the following:

```swift
import UIKit
import SpriteKit

class GameViewController: UIViewController {
  override func viewDidLoad() {
    super.viewDidLoad()
    let scene =
      MainMenuScene(size:CGSize(width: 2048, height: 1536))
    let skView = self.view as! SKView
    skView.showsFPS = true
    skView.showsNodeCount = true
    skView.ignoresSiblingOrder = true
    scene.scaleMode = .AspectFill
    skView.presentScene(scene)
  }
}
```

This is the same initialization code you're using in the iOS version of Zombie Conga.

In the upper left of Xcode, switch to the **ZombieCongaTV\tvOS Simulator**:

That's it—build and run, and enjoy Zombie Conga on the big screen!

Are you wondering how the game works seamlessly with the tvOS resolution? Recall from Chapter 1 that your strategy was to make the art at the biggest possible size and aspect ratio, and downscale it for other devices using Aspect Fill. The Apple TV renders at 1920x1080, so Aspect Fill will scale a 2048x1152 viewable scene size by 0.93 to fit the 1920x1080 screen size. This is the same as the iPhone 6 Plus. :]

> **Note:** At the time of writing this chapter, if you leave Zombie Conga by hitting the home menu on your game then return to the game, sometimes the background sprites will disappear. This appears to be a bug in Sprite Kit on tvOS.

Fixing the touch handling

At first glance, the controls for Zombie Conga seem to work out-of-the-box. But after playing for awhile, you might notice strange problems with the controls.

To see what I mean, add your old friend, the red touch box, from tvOSTouchTest into

Zombie Conga.

Open **GameScene.swift** and add this new property:

```
let touchBox = SKSpriteNode(color: UIColor.redColor(), size:
CGSize(width: 100, height: 100))
```

Then, add these lines to the bottom of `didMoveToView()` to add it to the scene:

```
touchBox.zPosition = 1000
addChild(touchBox)
```

Finally, add this line to the end of `touchesBegan()`:

```
touchBox.position = touchLocation
```

Also, add that same line to the end of `touchesMoved()`:

```
touchBox.position = touchLocation
```

Build and run, and try moving around.

You'll notice that every time you start a new touch, the touch location always reverts back to the center of the screen, which can sometimes make the zombie backtrack or move in unexpected directions.

Since tvOS touches don't map directly to scene coordinates, the best way to fix this is to set the zombie's velocity based on the recent direction of movement of the user's touches.

First, add a new property to `GameScene`:

```
var priorTouch: CGPoint = CGPoint.zero
```

Then, update `touchesBegan()` as follows:

```
override func touchesBegan(touches: Set<UITouch>,
  withEvent event: UIEvent?) {
    guard let touch = touches.first else {
      return
    }
    let touchLocation = touch.locationInNode(self)
    touchBox.position = touchLocation
    #if os(tvOS)
      priorTouch = touchLocation
    #else
      sceneTouched(touchLocation)
    #endif
}
```

This makes it so that on tvOS, rather than calling the old `sceneTouched()` method, you simply store the touch location—that is, the center of the scene, where it begins—in `priorTouch`.

Next, update `touchesMoved()` as follows:

```
override func touchesMoved(touches: Set<UITouch>,
  withEvent event: UIEvent?) {
  guard let touch = touches.first else {
    return
  }
  let touchLocation = touch.locationInNode(self)
  #if os (tvOS)
    // 1
    let offset = touchLocation - priorTouch
    let direction = offset.normalized()
    velocity = direction * zombieMovePointsPerSec

    // 2
    priorTouch = (priorTouch * 0.75) + (touchLocation * 0.25)

    // 3
    touchBox.position = zombie.position + (direction*200)
  #else
    touchBox.position = touchLocation
    sceneTouched(touchLocation)
  #endif
}
```

Once again, let's review this section by section:

1. This sets the velocity based on the direction between the current touch and `priorTouch`, rather than trying to move toward a particular point on the screen.

2. You don't want to set `priorTouch` to `touchLocation` directly, because you'd get a lot of noise from minute finger movements. Instead, use a blend: 75% of the previous `priorTouch` and 25% of the new `touchLocation`.

3. Update the touchBox to help visualize the current direction of movement.

Build and run, and you'll see the zombie's movement is much improved!

Mwahaha! This zombie is under my command!

Now that this is working, turn off the red box by adding this to the end of `didMoveToView()`:

```
touchBox.hidden = true
```

Top-shelf image and 3D icons

The gameplay for Zombie Conga is complete, so it's time to polish it up by adding a tvOS top-shelf image, launch image and 3D icon.

Open **ZombieCongaTV\Assets.xcassets** and expand the **Launch Image**.

In the resources for this chapter, you'll find a folder named **LaunchImage**; copy the image from this folder into this slot.

Still in **Assets.xcassets**, expand the **Top Shelf Image** and drag the file from the **resources \Top Shelf Image** into this slot.

Next, open **App Icon - Large** in **Assets.xcassets** and make sure the Attributes Inspector is open. In the Layers box, click the **+** button two more times so there are five layers in total:

The layers are ordered from frontmost to backmost. Drag the files from **resources\App Icon - Large** into each slot from top to bottom:

You can drag your mouse around and see a preview of the 3D image—cool!

Repeat this same process to set up the **App Icon - Small**.

Finally, open **ZombieCongaTV\Info.plist** and set the **Bundle name** to **Zombie Conga** so that it looks nice on the home screen of the Apple TV.

Build and run, and press the menu button to see the Apple TV home screen. Now Zombie Conga's got style!

Congratulations, you've made your first complete iOS and tvOS game! There's no challenge this time, so you can take a well-deserved break.

When you come back, there are new iOS and tvOS games waiting for you to make! :]

Section II: Physics and Nodes

In this section, you will learn how to use the built-in 2D physics engine included with Sprite Kit to create movement as realistic as that in Angry Birds or Cut the Rope. You will also learn how to use special types of nodes that allow you to play videos or create shapes in your game.

In the process, you will create a physics puzzle game called Cat Nap, where you take the role of a cat who has had a long day and just wants to go to bed.

Chapter 8: Scene Editor

Chapter 9: Beginning Physics

Chapter 10: Intermediate Physics

Chapter 11: Advanced Physics

Chapter 12: Crop, Video and Shape Nodes

Chapter 13: Intermediate tvOS

Chapter 8: Scene Editor

By Marin Todorov

In this chapter, you'll begin to build the second minigame in this book: a puzzle game called Cat Nap. Here's what it will look like when you're finished:

In Cat Nap, you take the role of a cat who's had a long day and just wants to go to bed.

However, a thoughtless human has cluttered the cat's bed with scrap materials from his recent home renovation. This silly human's bad choices are preventing the cat from falling asleep! Of course, since cats don't care much about—well, anything—he sits on top of the scrap anyway.

Your job is to destroy the blocks by tapping them so the cat can comfortably fall into place. Be careful, though: If you cause the cat to fall on the floor or tip onto his side, he'll wake up and get really cranky.

The puzzle is to destroy the blocks in the correct order, so the cat falls straight down. One wrong choice and—queue evil music—you face the Wrath of Kitteh!

You'll build this game across the next six chapters, in stages:

1. **Chapter 8, Scene Editor**: You are here! You'll begin by creating the first level of the game, pictured above. By the end, you'll have a better understanding of Xcode's level designer, better known as the scene editor.

2. **Chapter 9, Beginning Physics**: In this chapter, you're going to make a little detour in order to learn the basics of creating physics simulations for your games. As a bonus, you'll learn how to prototype games inside an Xcode playground.

3. **Chapter 10, Intermediate Physics**: You'll learn about physics-based collision detection and create custom classes for your Sprite Kit nodes.

4. **Chapter 11, Advanced Physics:** You'll add two more levels to the game as you learn about interactive bodies, joints between bodies, composed bodies and more.

5. **Chapter 12, Crop, Video and Shape Nodes:** You'll add special new blocks to Cat Nap while learning about additional types of nodes that allow you to do amazing things—like play videos, crop images and create dynamic shapes.

6. **Chapter 13, Intermediate tvOS:** In this last chapter you are going to bring Cat Nap to the silver screen. You are going to take the fully developed game and add support for tvOS so the player can relax on their couch and play the game using only the remote.

It's time to get started—there's nothing worse (or perhaps funnier) than an impatient cat!

Getting started

Start Xcode and select **File\New\Project…** from the main menu. Select the **iOS \Application\Game** template and click **Next**.

Enter **CatNap** for the Product Name, **Swift** for the Language, **Sprite Kit** for the Game Technology and **Universal** for the Devices. Click **Next**, then choose a place on your hard drive to save your project and click **Create**.

You want this app to run in landscape rather than portrait mode. Just like you did in

Chapter 1, "Sprites", select the **CatNap** project in the project navigator and then select the **CatNap** target. Go to the **General** tab and verify that only the device orientations for **Landscape Left** and **Landscape Right** are checked.

You also need to modify this in one more spot. Open **Info.plist** and find the **Supported interface orientations (iPad)** entry. Delete the entries for **Portrait (bottom home button)** and **Portrait (top home button)** so that only the landscape options remain.

To get this game started on the right foot, or should we say paw, you need to set up an app icon. To do this, select **Assets.xassets** in the project navigator on the left and then select the **AppIcon** entry. Then, in the resources for this chapter, drag all of the files from the **Icons\iOS** subfolder into the area on the right. You might need to drag a few individual files until Xcode matches all required icons. You'll see the following when you're done:

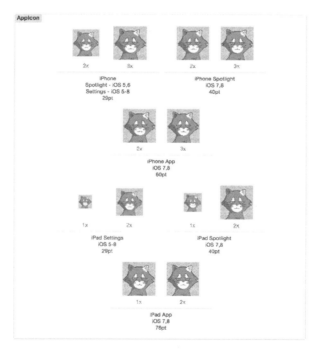

There's one final step. Open **GameViewController.swift** and modify the line that sets skView.ignoresSiblingOrder from true to false:

```
skView.ignoresSiblingOrder = false
```

This makes it so nodes with the same zPosition are drawn in the order in which they are added to the scene, which will make developing Cat Nap a bit simpler. Keep in mind, though, that there's a performance cost incurred by changing this setting to false. Luckily, for a simple game like this, it's not a problem.

Build and run the project on the **iPhone simulator**. You'll see the "Hello, World!" message nicely positioned in the center of the screen, in landscape mode.

Introducing texture atlases

Before you can add sprites to the scene, you need images for them, right? In the resources for this chapter, locate the **Resources** folder; this includes all the images, sounds and other files you'll need for Cat Nap. (It's the folder where the project icons were located.)

In Xcode, open **Assets.xcassets** and drag in all of the images from the **Resources\Images** folder. Also delete **Spaceship** from the asset catalog; this cat prefers both paws on the ground! At this point, your asset catalog should look like this:

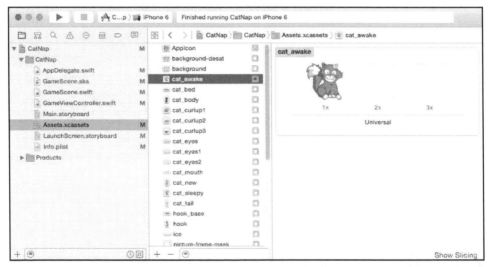

Next, drag the **Resources\Sounds** into your project and make sure that **Copy items if needed**, **Create groups** and the **CatNap** target are all checked. At this point, your project navigator should look like this:

Woo-hoo! You've finished setting up your project. Now it's time to fire up the scene editor.

Getting started with the scene editor

As mentioned previously, Cat Nap is a puzzle game in which players need to solve one level after another. This is the perfect reason to learn how to use the scene editor, a built-in Xcode tool designed to help you build levels without having to write everything in code.

The default Sprite Kit project template contains a scene file already. Look in the project navigator and you'll see a file called **GameScene.sks**. Select that file and you'll see a new editor panel that shows a gray background:

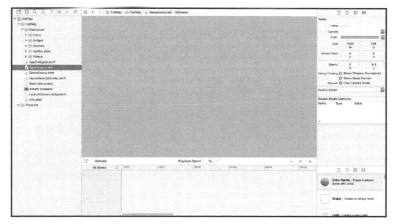

Click the minus (–) button in the mid-right corner several times until you see a yellow rectangle appear—you might need to click it five or six times if you're on a laptop. This is the boundary of your scene. The default size for a new scene is 1024x768 points.

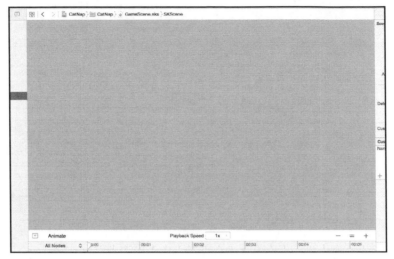

Remember from Chapter 1, "Sprites", that the strategy we're taking for games in this book is to use a single set of images sized for a 2048x1536 scene, and let Sprite Kit downscale the images for all devices with smaller screen resolutions. Resizing the scene is straightforward.

So let's resize the scene to our preferred 2048x1536 size. To do this, make sure the utilities editor on the right-hand side is open; if it's not, click **View\Utilities\Show Attributes Inspector**.

Within the **Attributes Inspector** for the scene, enter the new dimensions:

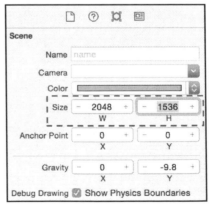

Now the scene has established a suitable size for supporting all devices.

The Object Library

At the bottom of the utilities editor, if it's not already selected, select the **Object Library**:

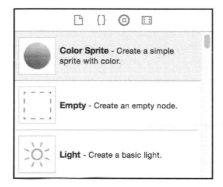

> **Note:** If the utilities editor on the right-hand side isn't open, click **View\Utilities \Show Object Library**.

The Object Library displays a list of objects that you can drop onto your scene and configure. When you load the scene file, those objects will appear in their correct positions based on the properties you set for them in the scene editor. That's much better than writing code to position and adjust every game object one by one, isn't it?

Here are some of the objects you can use:

- **Color sprite:** This is the object you use to put sprites onscreen and the one you'll use most often throughout this chapter and the next.

- **Shape node:** These are special types of nodes in Sprite Kit that allow you to easily draw squares, circles and other shapes. You'll learn more about these in Chapter 12, "Crop, Video and Shape Nodes".

- **Label:** You already know how to create labels programmatically, but with the scene editor, you can create them simply by dragging and dropping them onto the scene.

- **Emitter:** These are special types of nodes in Sprite Kit that allow you to create particle systems, which you can use for special effects like explosions, fire, or rain. You'll learn more about these in Chapter 16, "Particle Systems".

- **Light:** You can place a light node in your scene for a spotlight effect and have your scene objects cast shadows. You'll learn more about these in chapter 23, "2D Lighting".

The best thing about the scene editor is that it's not just an editor—it also serves as a simulator, allowing you to easily preview scenes without running the app. You'll see this later.

Adding and positioning sprites

Make sure the yellow frame of your scene is visible and that it fits into the editor window. Drag and drop a **color sprite** object into the editor area.

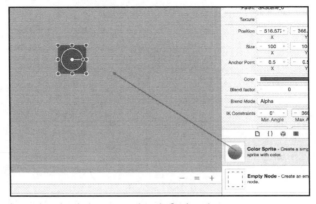

With the sprite selected, which happens by default when you create it, you'll see the available properties listed in the Attributes Inspector.

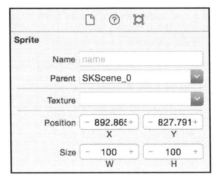

You may recognize a lot of these properties from before—you used many of them programmatically in your Zombie Conga project (such as `position` and `name`).

In the Attributes Inspector, you can set the sprite's name, parent node and the image file you want to use as the texture. You can also set the sprite's position, size and anchor point, either by hand or by dragging with the mouse.

Further down in the same panel, you'll see the controls to adjust the sprite's scale, z-axis position and z-axis rotation:

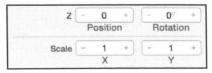

But wait! There's more! Even further down, listed in a section called **Physics Definition**, you'll find more properties you can set:

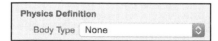

Notice that your sprite doesn't have a physics body, which means it is not taking part in a physics simulation. You'll be returning to this setting in future chapters, where you'll learn more about Sprite Kit physics.

In the meantime, let's begin by designing Cat Nap's first level!

Laying out your first scene

Select the sprite you just added to your scene and on the right-hand side, in the Attributes Inspector, set its properties to the following values:

- **Texture: background**
- **Position X: 1024**
- **Position Y: 768**

This should start you off nicely with the level's background image:

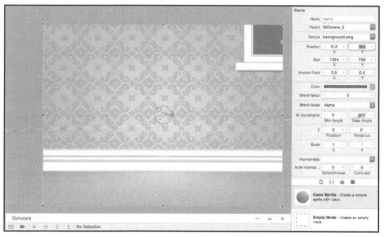

That was easy!

Next, you're going to add the cat bed to the scene. Drag another **color sprite** onto the scene and set its properties as follows:

- **Name: bed**
- **Texture: cat_bed**
- **Position: (1024, 272)** (enter X and Y into the respective boxes)

This will position the cat bed a bit off the bottom of the scene.

Now let's move on to those wooden blocks that get in the cat's way. There will be four blocks in total, but you'll add them two by two.

Drop two **color sprite** objects onto the scene. Edit their properties like so:

- **First block**: Texture **wood_vert1**, Position X **1024**, Position Y **330**
- **Second block**: Texture **wood_vert1**, Position X **1264**, Position Y **330**

Now you'll see this:

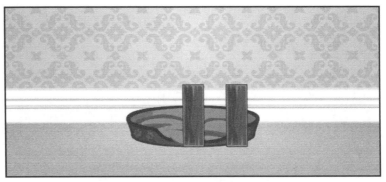

Take a moment to appreciate how much easier it is to set objects onscreen via the scene editor instead of through code. Of course, that doesn't mean you shouldn't understand what goes on behind the scenes. In fact, knowing how to do both is a huge plus.

OK! It's time to add the horizontal blocks. Drop two more **color sprite** objects onto the scene and adjust their properties as follows:

- **First block**: Texture **wood_horiz1**, Position X **1050**, Position Y **580**
- **Second block**: Texture **wood_horiz1**, Position X **1050**, Position Y **740**

Your scene continues to develop, and all of the obstacles are present now. At this point, you're only missing your main character:

Drop one last **color sprite** object onto the scene. This will be the cat. Edit as follows:

- **Cat**: Texture **cat_sleepy**, Position X **1024**, Position Y **1036**

Finally, you've completed the basic setup of the first Cat Nap level:

Build and run. Notice that your scene appears on the screen. Also notice the "Hello, World" label from the template code in **GameScene.swift**—don't worry about that now:

These are the basic skills you need to design levels using the scene editor. Luckily, it's capable of much more than laying down sprites on a scene. In the next section, you'll build more complex stuff!

File references

A cool feature (introduced in iOS 9) is that the scene editor allows you to reference content from other scene (.sks) files.

This means you can put together a bunch of sprites, add some effects like animations and then save those in a reusable .sks file. Then, you can reference the same content from multiple scenes, and they'll all dynamically load the same content from the reusable .sks file.

Now comes the best part: If you need to change the referenced content in *all* scenes, you only need to edit the original content and you're good to go.

As you may have guessed, this is perfect for level-based games where you often have characters or other parts of the scene recurring throughout the game. In Cat Nap, such a recurring character is everybody's favorite kitten:

In this section, you're going to extract the sleepy cat into its own .sks file and add more nodes and animations. Then you'll reference all of these as a bundle from within **GameScene.sks**.

First and foremost, since you're going to have more than one .sks file, it's time to organize them neatly. Control-click the yellow **CatNap** group and select **New Group**. Rename the group **Scenes**, and move **GameScene.sks** inside the newly created folder.

Once you're done, it should look like this:

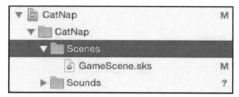

Next, control-click **Scenes** and from the pop-up menu, click **New File...**. Choose the **iOS/Resource/SpriteKit Scene** file template and then click **Next**. Call the new file **Cat.sks** and save it in the project folder.

Xcode automatically opens the newly created **Cat.sks** file and presents you with an empty, gray editor window. In exactly the same way as before, your task is to resize the scene to your needs and add some sprites.

Set the scene size to **380x440** points (the size of the cat) and since you have that particular pane open, set the Anchor Point to **(0.5, 0.5)**. Doing so lets you position the nodes inside the scene relative to the scene center; this is slightly easier placing them relative to the lower left, as most nodes will be centered either horizontally or vertically:

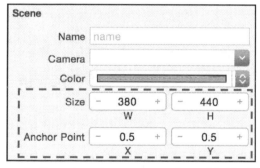

Now that the scene is ready for prime time, you need to add all of the cat's elements. First you'll add the torso. Drag in two **color sprite** nodes from the Object Library and set their properties like so:

- **Cat Body**: Name **cat_body**, Texture **cat_body**, Position X **22**, Position Y **-112**

- **Cat Head**: Name **cat_head**, Parent **cat_body**, Texture **cat_head**, Position X **18**, Position Y **192**

Note you set the cat body as the parent of the cat head. Since each Sprite Kit node can have as many sub-nodes as needed, sometimes it's handy to have one of your nodes act as the root node—that is, as a parent to other nodes. This way, if you need to copy or move all nodes, you only need to work with the root node, and the rest will move along with it.

Now your cat's body and head are nicely positioned within the scene while leaving space on the left for the big, fluffy tail that you're adding next.

Speaking of big, fluffy tails, drag in a **color sprite** from the Object Library and set its properties like so:

- **Tail**: Name **tail**, Texture **cat_tail**, Parent **cat_body**, Anchor Point **(0, 0)**, Position **(-206, -70)**, Z Position **-1**

Later in this chapter, you'll animate the tail so it rotates gently along its (0, 0) position. This will make it appear as if the cat is swinging its tail slowly in the air, giving him that cat swagger.

So far the cat scene looks like this:

Now it's time to add the rest of the cat parts. Add two **color sprite** objects to the scene and adjust their properties like so:

- **Cat mouth**: Name **mouth**, Parent **cat_head**, Texture **cat_mouth**, Position X **6**, Position Y **-67**

- **Cat eyes**: Name **eyes**, Parent **cat_head**, Texture **cat_eyes**, Position X **6**, Position Y **2**

This completes the cat, and your scene will look like this:

Now you will remove the static cat image from **GameScene.sks** and use your newly designed cat scene.

To do this, open **GameScene.sks** and delete the static cat sprite. In its place, drop a **reference node** from the Object Library:

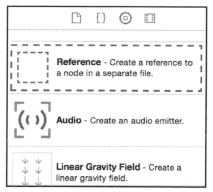

The empty reference node appears like a hollow, dashed rectangle:

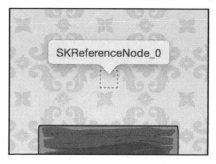

Set the following property values for the selected reference node:

- **Name: cat_shared**
- **Reference:** select **Cat.sks** from the drop-down menu
- **Position: (1030, 1045)**
- **Z-Position: 10**

Here, you're loading the content of the file **Cat.sks** and positioning it where the static cat image used to be. Additionally, you're setting a higher z-position to make sure the contents of **Cat.sks** appear above the level's background image.

With this done, you've successfully created a reusable piece of content that you can use throughout your game. Nice job!

Note: Due to a bug in Xcode 7 you might not see the cat appear on the scene when you add the reference. To solve this just close Xcode and start it again - this time around your reference will show the cat just like on the screenshot above.

There's one problem with your cat—it doesn't do anything interesting. It's just a bunch of nodes stuck together!

It's time to correct that by creating what's called an "idle animation". This will help to make the scene come alive.

Animations and action references

So far, you've been creating node actions using code. As you saw in the previous chapters, with only a few lines of code, you can create an SKAction to move a sprite along the screen, rotate it and scale it. But sometimes it's nice to do that visually, especially when prototyping animations or level design.

In this section, you're going to learn how to add actions to the nodes in your scene. Later, you'll learn how to extract those actions into their own .sks files and reuse them to animate different sprites.

Adding actions to nodes

Open **Cat.sks** and find this arrow button towards the bottom of Xcode's window:

If the arrow on the button points upward, like in the screenshot above, click it to open the **action editor**:

The action editor displays all the nodes in the scene and a timeline with rows corresponding to each node. If you've ever worked with animation or video software, you might be familiar with this type of user interface.

You're going to use the action editor to animate the cat's tail.

Grab a **RotateToAngle action** object from the Object Library and drop it onto the timeline track for the **tail** node. While dragging the action over the tail track, a new strip will open and show you a live preview where the new action will appear when dropped.

Drop the action and position it at the beginning of the timeline—that is, at the 0:00 time mark:

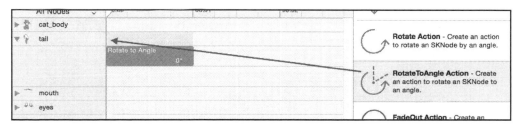

Cool! You've just added a rotate action to the tail sprite. You only need to polish the action a bit before giving it a try. In the **Attributes Inspector**, set the following two values:

- **Duration: 2**
- **Degrees: 5**

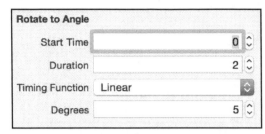

While you're at it, add one more action just after the first one.

Drag another **RotateToAngle action** object to the **tail** node and snap it to the end of the first one; set its properties as follows:

• **Start Time: 2**

• **Duration: 1.5**

• **Degrees: 0**

This action will swing the cat's tail back to its initial position. The timeline will now look like so:

The best thing about the scene editor is that you don't need to run your game in the simulator or on a device in order to test your scenes.

Find the **Animate** button at the top of the action editor and click it; the scene editor will play the actions you just added. This allows you to quickly find any issues you may have with your animations.

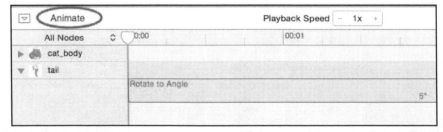

If you want more control over the playback, you can simply grab the timeline scrubber and move it back and forth:

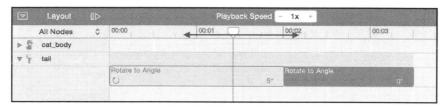

Notice how the **Animate** button turns into a **Layout** button. This indicates that you're currently animating the scene. If you'd like to work again on the layout, click on **Layout** to switch back to that mode.

When you click **Layout**, the timeline position resets, and you can again move sprites around and edit their properties.

More about the timeline

Timeline is very powerful when it comes to designing complex scenes and animations. Before moving on you will go on a quick tour.

To the right of the Animate button you will see a Playback Speed control. While you are playing back your actions you can choose the speed of replay. This makes sense since when you are loading those animations from code you can tell Sprite Kit the speed you want to use for the animations.

Change the playback speed to **2x**.

Click **Animate** and notice how the tail moves two times faster than before. This feature is very useful when you are prototyping animations in scene editor - if you are not really sure about the duration of some of your actions you can easily experiment by just changing the playback speed until you are satisfied.

Reset the playback speed to **1x** before moving on.

The timeline lists all views in your scene in the order you added them to the scene. You started with the cat body and added the eyes last and you see the nodes in that exact order too:

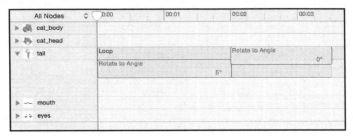

As you can imagine the more complex a scene is the more fields you will have in this list. Once you have so many nodes that you have to scroll continuously up and down to find the one you're looking for you will feel the need to navigate the list in a more convenient way.

You have two ways to filter the timeline node list. First in the top left corner just under Animate you will see a drop list menu:

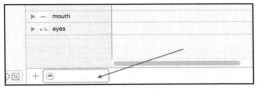

The item selected by default is All Nodes but you can choose from two more:

- **Nodes with Actions**: Filters the node list to show you only the nodes that already have actions attached. Using this option is useful when you want to modify an existing action and you want to see only the nodes that possibly the action runs on.

- **Selected Nodes**: This option will dynamically show you only the nodes you have currently selected in scene editor. This is a powerful mode as it shows you only the timeline for the selected scene items.

The second control allowing you to filter the node list is the search field at the bottom left corner:

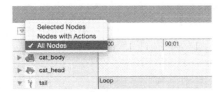

This field allows you to quickly filter the node list to only those nodes whose names contain the given search term. This comes very handy in the cases when you want to work with a given node and you have its name off the top of your head.

Last but not least in the bottom right corner there is a slider that allows you to scale up or down the timeline so you can see more or less actions without having to scroll through:

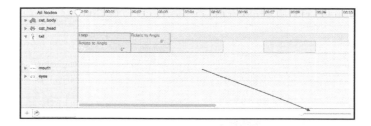

Repeating actions

You're almost done, but there's one more thing you need to do - make the cat's tail wave continuously. This cat refuses to sit still!

Making an action repeat a set number of times, or indefinitely, is easy to do using the action editor. For your tail animation, you'll first need to group the two actions you just created, and then repeat that action group so the tail can continuously swing back and forth.

First, select both actions in the action editor's timeline while pressing the **Command** key; if you do this properly, you'll see both actions appear highlighted:

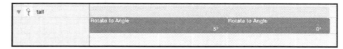

While both actions are selected, right-click on one of them and select **Create Loop** from the pop-up menu.

In the popover menu, select the infinity symbol ∞ to indicate that you want this action to repeat continuously (the button will remain selected to show you your current looping preference):

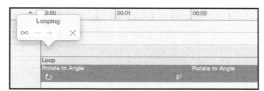

The timeline shows you the currently selected loop in blue and all of the repeats in an orange tint so you can easily see, which one is the "original" and its repetitions.

Besides an indefinitely repeating loop you can choose from three more options.

When you clicked **Create Loop** in first place Xcode created a loop that plays once and repeats one more time. So if you wanted an action that plays a total of two times - you would not have had to do anything more.

The popup menu gives you few more options to control the repeat count of the loop:

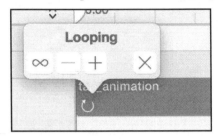

- ∞ loops the action forever;

- **+** adds one more repeat;

- **-** removes one repeat;

- **X** removes all repeats from the action.

For your tail-rotation action, you chose ∞ to make the cat gently swing its tail throughout the whole game.

> **Note:** It's natural to think that the X button closes the popup. In this case however it removes the looping from your animation instead. To close the popup window simply click somewhere outside of it and it will automatically go away.

That's pretty cool! And even cooler is that you've got a little content hierarchy going on in your game to maximize resource reuse:

1. **Cat.sks** contains sprites and actions, and configures the looping and duration of the actions.

2. **GameScene.sks** contains a complete level setup, and it also references the cat character from **Cat.sks**.

This setup allows you to load the cat with all its body parts and attached to them actions from any level in your game. In fact - you are going to load the cat in **each** level in your game!

Further you are going to create more .sks files containing different cat animations, which you are going to load and use in different stages of the game.

> **Note:** The original Sprite Kit feature list introduced with iOS 9 includes the ability to also create actions in their own .sks file and re-use those actions for different nodes in different scenes. This is pretty cool because it alows you to use one more level of resource abstraction.

However this feature does not work on 32bit systems - i.e. if your game load actions from .sks files that runs on iPhone6, iPhone 6s, and newer but crashes on iPhone5, iPhone 4s and earlier. This bug is present in Xcode 7 and is not fixed in Xcode 7.1 so this chapter does not cover it.

Now build and run your project to see how far you've come:

Look at that cat swinging its tail like a boss.

This is a pretty long chapter, and you're probably a bit tired. If so, take a five minute break to fool around. Better yet, why not drag more reference nodes from the Object Library and load up the scene with more cats?

Good fun! Just make sure you remove all of the extra cats before going further. :]

In this chapter you have learned how to find your way around scene editor, how to plan and design game scenes, add and edit nodes and run basic actions on them. The interface of scene editor is fairly simple but it allows you to achieve quite a lot.

So far you have designed the very first Cat Nap level, which is not that complex but you will keep applying your new skills throughout the two chapters that follow and create a number of additional levels, which will get progressively more complex.

The next chapters, in which you get to work on Cat Nap, focus more on creating sprites and actions from code. It's important for you to know how to design and fine tune your game's levels both from within Scene Editor and your code so you can always use the best approach for your current project.

With that being said make sure that you really got a good command of the Scene Editor interface before moving on. The two challenges that follow are a perfect opportunity to exercise your newly acquired Scene Editor skills.

Once you are finished working through the challenges and you have your cat fully animated you will be ready to move on to getting to know the ropes of physics simulation in SpriteKit.

Challenges

There are two challenges this time, to get you some additional practice with the scene editor; creating actions and laying out levels.

As always, if you get stuck, you can find the solution sin the resources for this chapter—but give it your best shot first!

Challenge 1: Creating further cat actions

You've constructed the cat using a few nodes, like its body, head, tail, eyes and, of course, its gorgeous smile. So far, you've animated the tail by using a repeating sequence of two rotate actions.

In this challenge, you'll use additional types of actions to complete the cat's idle animation.

Follow the general steps below to create a new action inside **Cat.sks**. Add the actions listed below to the cat's mouth node, setting their properties like so:

- **Move Action**: Start Time **5**, Duration **0.75**, Timing **Ease Out**, Offset **(0, 5)**
- **Move Action**: Start Time **5.75**, Duration **0.75**, Timing **Ease In**, Offset **(0, -5)**
- **PlaySoundFileNamed Action**: Start Time **5.25**, Duration **1**

For the filename of the sound action, select **mrreow.mp3** from the drop-down menu.

If you're wondering how you can make the actions overlap on the timeline, here's a hint for you. The final result looks like this:

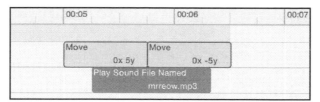

Since you would like the actions to repeat including the 5 seconds of waiting time you need to do a little trick.

Add one more action at the beginning of the timeline for the mouth node:

- **Move Action**: Start Time **0**, Duration **1**, Offset **(0, 0)**

Then select all four actions and create a loop of them like you did earlier in this chapter. You should see the four actions grouped in a loop like so:

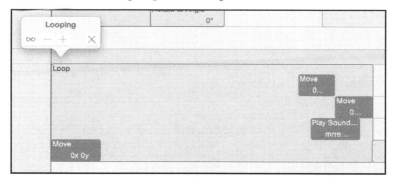

> **Note:** Once more - this loop could have been easier to create without a *cheat* node had Sprite Kit not been crashing on 32bit systems.

While you're at it, create one more action and drop it on the eyes node in the scene timeline. Drag in an **AnimateWithTextures Action** and set the Start Time to **6.5** and the Duration to **0.75**.

Then, in the fourth tab in the bottom right (the Media Library), drag **cat_eyes**, **cat_eyes1**, and **cat_eyes2** onto the Textures list of your newly created action.

Finally, click the loop button on your action to add one more repetition. Keep in mind that sometimes, depending on the timeline zooming, your actions are too small to accommodate the button - if you don't see it when hovering with your mouse over an action, try zooming in on that action by using the slider in the bottom-right corner of the timeline pane.

Also, tick the **Restore** checkbox; this way when the animation completes, it will go back to its initial frame.

The final setup should look like this:

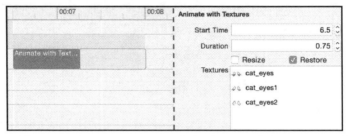

Once more, in order to trick Sprite Kit to include the initial 6.5 seconds of waiting time in your loop, add a *cheat* action:

- **Move Action**: Start Time **0**, Duration **1**, Offset **(0, 0)**

Select both actions you added to the cat eyes and create a loop that repeats forever.

Well done so far! Your complete timeline should now look like this:

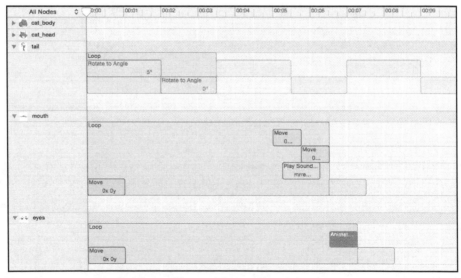

Build and run to enjoy the fruits of your labour. Watch as the cat sits quietly waving its tail, and every now and again, sleepily blinks and purrs. Neat, huh?

Challenge 2: Creating further cat scenes

In this challenge, you'll create two more .sks files, which you'll use later to load the cat's "win" and "lose" animations.

Create a new **CatCurl.sks** file and set the scene size to (380, 440). Add one **color sprite** object with the following properties:

- **Cat Curl**: Name **cat_curl**, Texture **cat_curlup1**, Position **(190, 220)**, Size **(380, 440)**

In the actions editor, add one action to the **cat_curl** sprite node as follows:

- **AnimateWithTextures Action**: Start Time **0**, Duration **1**

Make sure Restore is **not** checked. For Textures, drag in the following files from the Media Library:

- **cat_curlup1.png**
- **cat_curlup2.png**
- **cat_curlup3.png**

You can scrub the timeline view to preview this animation; later you will load and run this when the player successfully solves a level in Cat Nap:

There's one more scene left to create: the animation to play when your player fails to solve a level. The process is similar to creating the winning sequence.

Create a new **CatWakeUp.sks** file and set the scene size to (380, 440). Add one **color sprite** object with the following properties:

- **Cat Awake**: Name **cat_awake**, Texture **cat_awake**, Position **(190, 220)**, Size **(380, 440)**

In the actions editor, add one action to the **cat_awake** sprite node with the following properties:

- **AnimateWithTextures Action**: Start Time **0**, Duration **0.5**

Make sure Restore is **not** checked. For Textures, drag in the following files from the Media library:

- **cat_awake.png**
- **cat_sleepy.png**

Make the action repeat indefinitely.

You can scrub the timeline view to preview this animation; later you will load and run this scene when the cat falls off a wooden block and onto the ground, causing the player to fail the level:

Who ever said cats always land on their feet?

Phew! That was a long chapter with lots of instructions. If you need to take another break, no one will blame you. However, the next chapter introduces you to the world of actions, collisions and crazy physics experiments, so don't wait too long to turn the page.

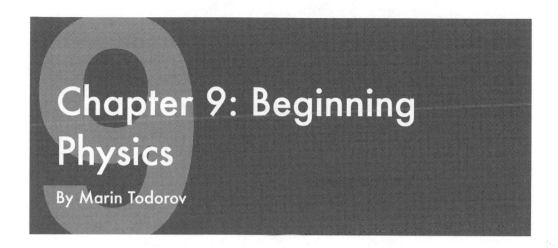

Chapter 9: Beginning Physics

By Marin Todorov

So far, you've learned to move sprites by manually positioning them and by running actions. But what if you want to simulate more complex behavior, like a ball bouncing against a wobbly pillar, a chain of dominos falling down or a house of cards collapsing?

You could accomplish the above with plenty of math, but there's an easier way. Sprite Kit contains a powerful and user-friendly physics engine that will help you move your objects realistically—in ways both simple and complex—without breaking a sweat.

With a physics engine, you can accomplish effects like those you see in many popular iOS games:

- **Angry Birds** uses a physics engine to simulate what happens when the bird collides with the tower of bricks.

- **Tiny Wings** uses a physics engine to simulate the bird riding the hills and flying into the air.

- **Cut the Rope** uses a physics engine to simulate the movement of the ropes and the effect of gravity on the candy.

Combing a physics engines with touch controls can give your games a wonderfully realistic dynamism—and as you can see in Angry Birds, sometimes in the name of destruction!

If you like this kind of lifelike behavior and you want to know how to build your own physics-based game, you're in the right chapter.

Since you'll be playing around with physics—while learning, of course—a playground is the best place to get started. And I don't mean an actual playground; I mean an Xcode playground, which is perfect for experimenting with code.

In this chapter, you'll take a break to learn Sprite Kit physics basics in a playground. But don't worry - in the next two chapters you'll return to your old friend Cat Nap and integrate the physics engine there.

Physics in Sprite Kit

Under the hood, Sprite Kit uses a library called Box2D to perform all the physics calculations. Box2D is open-source, full-featured, fast and powerful. A lot of popular games already use Box2D—on the iPhone, Android, BlackBerry, Nintendo DS, Wii, OS X and Windows—so it's nice to see the library as a part of Sprite Kit.

However, Box2D has two main drawbacks for iOS developers: It's written in C++, and it could stand to be more user-friendly, especially for beginners.

Apple doesn't expose Box2D directly, instead it abstracts it behind its own API in Sprite

Kit. In fact, Box2D is walled so well that Apple could choose to change the physics engine in a later version of iOS, and you wouldn't even know it.

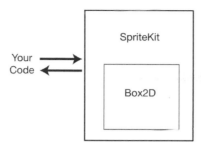

To make a long story short, in Sprite Kit, you get access to all the power of a super-popular engine, but through a friendly, polished, Apple-style API.

Physics bodies

For the physics engine to control the movement of one of your sprites, you have to create a **physics body** for the sprite. You can think of a physics body as a rough boundary for your sprite that the engine will use for collision detection.

The illustration below depicts a typical physics body for a sprite. Note that the shape of the physics body doesn't need to match the boundaries of the sprite exactly. Usually, you'll choose a simpler shape to help the collision detection algorithms run faster.

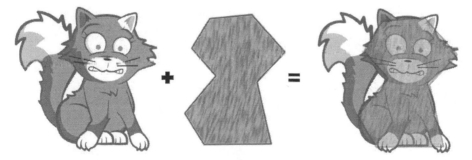

If you need a more precise shape, you can tell Sprite Kit's physics engine to detect the shape of your sprite by ignoring all transparent parts of the image. This is a good strategy if you want a more lifelike collision between the objects in your game. For the cat, the automatically-detected, transparency-based physics body would look something like this:

You may be thinking, "Excellent! I'll just use that all the time."

Think twice. Before you rush into anything, understand that it takes *much* more processing power to calculate the physics for a complex shape like this one, as compared to a simpler polygonal shape.

Once you set a physics body for your sprite, it will move similarly to how it would in real life: It will fall with gravity, be affected by impulses and forces and move in response to collisions with other objects.

You can adjust the properties of your physics bodies, such as how heavy or bouncy they are. You can also alter the laws of the entire simulated world—for example, you can decrease gravity so that a ball, upon falling to the ground, will bounce higher and travel farther.

Imagine you throw two balls and each bounces for a while—the red one under normal Earth gravity and the blue one under low gravity, such as on the Moon. It would look something like this:

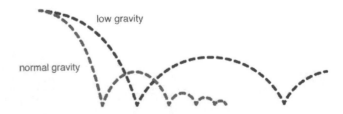

There are few things you should know about physics bodies:

- **Physics bodies are rigid**. In other words, physics bodies can't be squished or deformed under pressure and won't change shape as a consequence of the physics simulation. For example, you can't use a physics body to simulate a squishy ball that deforms as it rolls along the floor.

- **Complex physics bodies have a performance cost**. While it may be convenient to use the alpha mask of your images as the physics body, you should only use this feature when absolutely necessary. If you have many shapes onscreen colliding with each other, try using an alpha mask only for your main character or for two to three main characters, and set the rest to rectangles or circles.

- **Physics bodies are moved by forces or impulses**. Impulses, such as the transfer of energy when two physics bodies collide, adjust the object's momentum immediately. Forces, such as gravity, affect the object gradually over time. You can apply your own forces or impulses to physics bodies, as well—for example, you may use an impulse to simulate firing a bullet from a gun, but use a force to simulate launching a rocket. You'll learn more about forces and impulses later in this chapter.

Sprite Kit makes all of these features, and many more, incredibly easy to manage. In Apple's typical manner, most of the configuration is fully pre-defined, meaning a blank Sprite Kit project will already include lifelike physics with absolutely no set up required.

Getting started

Let's learn about physics in Sprite Kit in the best way possible: by experimenting in real time inside an Xcode playground.

Launch Xcode and from its initial dialogue, select **Get started with a playground**.

> **Note**: If you previously disabled the startup dialogue, select **File\New \Playground...** from the main menu.

In the next dialogue, enter **SpriteKitPhysicsTest** for the **Name** and select **iOS** for the **Platform**.

Click **Next** and select a location to save the playground.

Xcode will create a new, empty playground, importing only the UIKit framework, so you can use all of the data types, classes and structures you're used to working with in your iOS projects.

The empty playground window will look like this:

This view may seem a little strange if you haven't used playgrounds before. Don't worry —this next section covers the interface and how to experiment (play!) in a playground.

> **Note:** If you're already comfortable working in playgrounds, you can skip the next section and move on to "Creating a Sprite Kit playgound".

Your first playground

In previous chapters, you've worked with Xcode projects, which usually include many source files, resources, storyboards, game scenes and so forth. A playground, on the other hand, is just a single file with a **.playground** extension.

Playgrounds allow you to experiment with code in real time. But before you do that, it's a good idea to get familiar with the interface.

Take a look at your empty playground window:

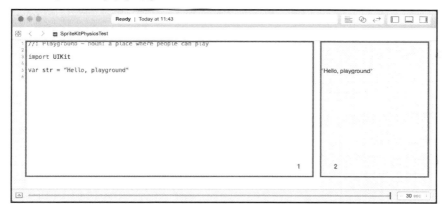

On the left-hand side is the source editor *(1)* and on the right-hand side is the results sidebar *(2)*. As you type code, Xcode evaluates and executes every line and produces the results in the results sidebar, as you'd expect.

For example, if you change "Hello, playground" to "Sprite Kit rules!", you'll immediately see the results sidebar update to reflect this change. You can experiment with anything you like, but right now give the code below a try:

```
let number = 0.4
let string = "Sprite Kit is #\(5-4)"
let numbers = Array(1...5)

var j = 0
for i in 1..<10 {
  j += i*2
}
```

As soon as you paste or type in the code, you'll see the results sidebar update and neatly align the output of every line against the corresponding code in the editor.

The first line of code produces the result you'd expect:

```
let number = 0.4
0.4
```

> **Note**: For clarity, we'll display the code line followed by the corresponding result.

This is a static value, so to see the output of an expression, as well as prove the code really gets executed in real time, look at the result of the second line:

```
let string = "Sprite Kit is #\(5-4)"
"Sprite Kit is #1"
```

Xcode wraps the result in quotes to show you that the data type of that result is a `String`. The next example shows you the result of an even more elaborate piece of code:

```
let numbers = Array(1...5)
[1, 2, 3, 4, 5]
```

The code creates a new array containing `Int` elements with values from 1 to 5.

When you enter an expression like that, on a line by itself, Xcode will evaluate it and send the result to the results sidebar. This is incredibly useful for debugging purposes—rather than use a separate log function as you would in a project, simply write a variable name or an expression, and you'll immediately see its value to the right.

The final example produces a somewhat surprising result—the text **(9 times)**:

```
var j = 0
for i in 1..<10 {
    j += i*2
}

(9 times)
```

If you consider everything you've learned so far, you might expect this. The result is aligned to the code, so even though the line `j += i*2` is executed nine times in the loop, it can still produce only a single line of text. The line tells you how many times the loop ran, but that's far from what would actually be useful to you: to see the values of the variables while the loop runs.

No fear—a playground is smarter than that! Hover with your mouse cursor over the text **(9 times)**. You'll see an extra button appear along with a little tip:

Click the + button to show the history of the value over the nine loop iterations. This history is displayed directly under the line of code that calculates the value of `j`. Click on the points representing the loop iterations to see the value of your tracked expression in a little pop-up.

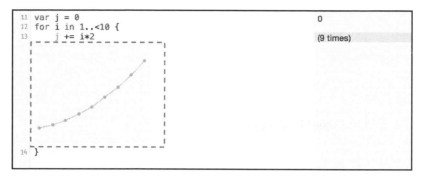

Good work. This is the basic knowledge you need to use an Xcode playground. Now comes the interesting part: conducting physics experiments in a playground.

Creating a Sprite Kit playground

Delete any code you have in your playground and add these imports at the top:

```
import UIKit
import SpriteKit
import XCPlayground
```

These import the basic `UIKit` classes, the Sprite Kit framework and the handy `XCPlayground` module, which will help you visualize your Sprite Kit scene right inside the playground window.

Since you already know how to create a new game scene, you'll do that first.

Make sure Xcode's assistant editor is open; it usually stays in the right-hand side of the window. To show the assistant editor, select **View/Assistant Editor/Show Assistant Editor** from Xcode's main menu.

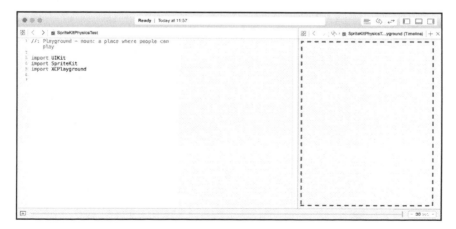

Now, add the following to your playground's source code:

```
let sceneView = SKView(frame: CGRect(x: 0, y: 0, width: 480,
height: 320))

let scene = SKScene(size: CGSize(width: 480, height: 320))
sceneView.showsFPS = true
sceneView.presentScene(scene)

XCPShowView("My Scene", view: sceneView)
```

Most of this code is surely familiar, though you've never seen it in this context. Let's have a look at what you achieve above.

First, you create a new `SKView` instance and give it a frame size of 480 by 320 pixels. Then, you create an empty default `SKScene` instance and give it the same size. This is what the code in your view controllers has been doing for you in the previous chapters of this book.

Next, you tell the `SKView` to present the scene.

Finally, you call `XCPShowView` from the **XCPlayground** module and pass in a string title and the view. As you can see, `XCPShowView` is quite handy and helps with a few things:

1. First and foremost, it tells Xcode *not* to abort executing your playground as soon as it runs through the source code. In a game prototype, you'd like things to keep running, right? In this case, the playground will continue to run for the default duration of 30 seconds every time you change the source code.

2. It renders the current state of the view in the assistant editor.

3. Finally, it records the view over time so you can rewind, fast forward and skim through the recorded session. You'll see this momentarily.

In the assistant editor, you'll see your game scene:

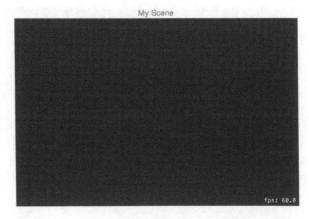

Do you see the frame rate label flickering as it renders different rates? This tells you that the scene is rendering live. Wait until the 30 seconds of execution time are up, and then drag the little slider below the scene left and right. You're dragging through the recorded session—how cool is that?

Playing with an empty game scene is not so much fun. Fortunately, that's easy to change! You have a nice, blank slate; your next step is to add sprites to the scene.

Add this code to the playground to create a new sprite with the image **square.png**:

```
let square = SKSpriteNode(imageNamed: "square")
```

Hover the mouse over the results sidebar where it reads **SKSpriteNode** and click on the eye icon to see the sprite you just created:

Oh no! The preview shows a broken image. That's because you didn't add any assets to your playground, and Sprite Kit is letting you know that it couldn't find an image named **square.png**.

From Xcode's main menu, select **View/Navigators/Show Project Navigator**. Have a look at the file structure of your playground:

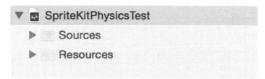

The playground contains two empty folders. The first, **Sources**, contains code you want to pre-compile and make available to your playground, while the second, **Resources**, contains assets you want to use, like images, sounds and so forth.

In the **Resources** folder for this chapter, you'll find a **Shapes** folder that includes all of the artwork you need for your playground. Grab all the files inside **Shapes** and drop them into the **Resources** folder in your playground.

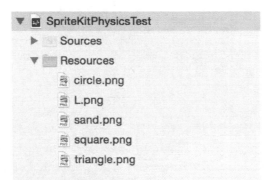

Excellent! Now, switch back to Xcode and click the eye icon next to your sprite node in the results sidebar. This time, you'll see a blue patterned image. With your assets in place, you're ready to proceed.

Add this code to the end of the file:

```
square.name = "shape"
square.position = CGPoint(x: scene.size.width * 0.25, y:
scene.size.height *
0.50)

let circle = SKSpriteNode(imageNamed: "circle")
circle.name = "shape"
circle.position = CGPoint(x: scene.size.width * 0.50, y:
scene.size.height *
0.50)

let triangle = SKSpriteNode(imageNamed: "triangle")
triangle.name = "shape"
triangle.position = CGPoint(x: scene.size.width * 0.75, y:
scene.size.height *
0.50)
```

This code creates three constants: square, circle and triangle. All of them are sprite nodes, and you initialize them with the textures **square.png**, **circle.png** and **triangle.png**, respectively.

At this point, you can see in the results sidebar that the three sprites have been created successfully, but you still can't see them onscreen. You need to add them to your scene, so do that with the following code:

```
scene.addChild(square)
scene.addChild(circle)
scene.addChild(triangle)
```

This creates three sprites in the center of the screen: a square, a circle and a triangle. Check them out:

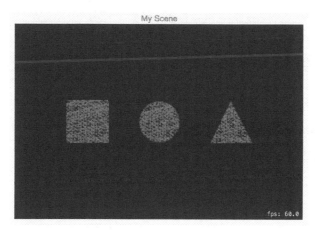

For the most part, this has been a review of creating sprites and positioning them manually onscreen, although this time, you've done it using a playground. But now it's time to introduce something new—controlling these objects with physics!

Circular bodies

Remember two things from earlier in this chapter:

1. For the physics engine to control the movement of a sprite, you must create a **physics body** for the sprite.

2. You can think of a physics body as a rough boundary for your sprite that the physics engine uses for collision detection.

Let's attach a physics body to the circle. Add this at the bottom of the file:

```
circle.physicsBody = SKPhysicsBody(circleOfRadius:
circle.size.width/2)
```

Since the `circle` sprite uses an image shaped like a circle, it's best to create a physics body of roughly the same shape. `SKPhysicsBody` has a convenience initializer method, `SKPhysicsBody(circleRadius:)`, that creates a circular body. Because you need to supply the radius of the circle, you'll be dividing the width of the circle sprite by 2.

> **Note:** The radius of a circle is the distance from the center of the circle to its edge.

Believe it or not, thanks to Sprite Kit's pre-configured physics simulation, you're all done!

Once you save your file, the playground will automatically re-execute your code and you'll see the circle drop with gravity:

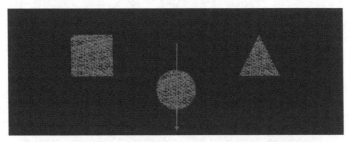

But wait a minute—the circle keeps falling offscreen and disappears! Not to mention that by the time the scene is rendered, the circle is almost out of sight—you don't see much of the fall happen.

The easiest way to fix this is to turn off gravity at the start of your scene and then turn it back on a few seconds later. Yes—you heard me right—turn off gravity!

Skim through your Swift code and find the line where you call `presentScene()` on your `SKView`. Just before this line, add the code to turn off gravity:

```
scene.physicsWorld.gravity = CGVector(dx: 0, dy: 0)
```

Your scene has a property named `physicsWorld` that represents the basic physics setup of your game. When you alter the `gravity` vector of your physics world, you change the constant acceleration that is applied to every physics body in your scene each frame.

As soon as you enter the code to reset gravity to a zero vector, you'll see that now the circle stays at its initial position without falling down. So far, so good.

Now you're going to create a little helper function named `delay`. Since you'll write it once, and not need to re-compile it each time the playground executes, you may put it aside in the **Sources** folder.

The easiest way to add a source file is to right-click on **Sources** and choose **New File** from the pop-up menu.

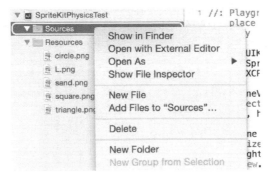

Name the newly added file **SupportCode.swift** and then open it in the source editor. Once it's opened, add the following code to it:

```
import UIKit

public func delay(seconds seconds: Double, completion:()->()) {

    let popTime = dispatch_time(DISPATCH_TIME_NOW,
        Int64( Double(NSEC_PER_SEC) * seconds ))

    dispatch_after(popTime,
        dispatch_get_global_queue(DISPATCH_QUEUE_PRIORITY_LOW, 0)) {
            completion()
    }
}
```

Don't worry too much about this code. All you need to know is that you're using it to delay code execution, something you'll be doing throughout this chapter.

With that done, open the playground again by clicking on **SpriteKitPhysicsTest** in the project navigator, at the top.

Now scroll back down to the end of the code and add the following to re-establish gravity two seconds after the scene is created:

```
delay(seconds: 2.0, completion: {
    scene.physicsWorld.gravity = CGVector(dx: 0, dy: -9.8)
})
```

> **Note:** Keep this piece of code at the bottom of the file—all the code you add from here on out, you'll add *just above* it.

Now that you've paused gravity, you'll be able to see the circle shape appear in the assistant editor and then fall under the pull of gravity, two seconds later.

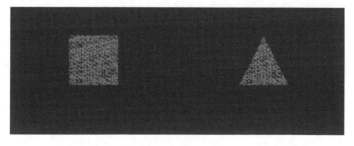

> **Note**: While you were editing **SupportCode.swift**, Xcode might have switched
> the contents of the assistant editor so you won't see the rendered scene. In that
> case, click on the quick jump bar at the top of the assistant editor and choose
> **Timeline/SpriteKitPhysicsTest.playground**.

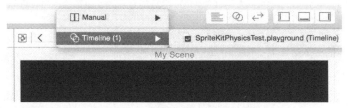

But that's still not exactly what you want! For this demo, you want the circle to stop
when it hits the bottom of the screen and stay there.

Luckily, Sprite Kit makes this easy to do using something called an **edge loop body**.

Edge loop bodies

To put bounds around the scene, which is something you'll need to do in many physics-
based games, add this line of code just before you present the scene:

```
scene.physicsBody = SKPhysicsBody(edgeLoopFromRect: scene.frame)
```

First you set the physics body for the scene itself. Any Sprite Kit node can have a physics
body, and remember, a scene is a node, too!

Next, you create a different type of body—an edge loop rather than a circle. There is a
major difference between these two types of bodies:

- The circle body is a **dynamic** physics body—that is, it moves. It's solid, has mass and
  can collide with any other type of physics body. The physics simulation can apply
  various forces to move volume-based bodies.

- The edge loop body is a **static** physics body—that is, it does not move. As the name
  implies, an edge loop only defines the edges of a shape. It doesn't have mass, cannot
  collide with other edge loop bodies and is never moved by the physics simulation.
  Other objects can be inside or outside its edges.

The most common use for an edge loop body is to define collision areas to describe your
game's boundaries, ground, walls, trigger areas or any other type of unmoving collision
space.

Since you want to restrict bodies to movement within the screen's edges, you create the scene's physics body to be an edge loop with the scene's `frame` CGRect:

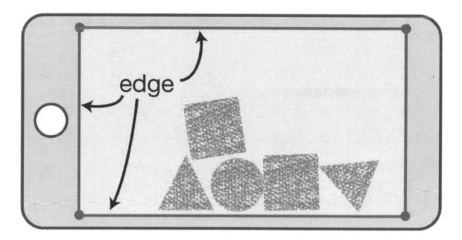

As you saw when Xcode ran your playground, the circle now stops when it hits the bottom of the screen and even bounces a little:

Rectangular bodies

Next, you'll add the physics body for the square sprite. Add the following line to the end of your code:

```
square.physicsBody = SKPhysicsBody(rectangleOfSize:
square.frame.size)
```

You can see that creating a rectangular physics body is very similar to creating a circular body. The only difference is that instead of passing in the radius of the circle, you pass in a `CGSize` representing the width and height of the rectangle.

Now that it has a physics body attached to it, the square will fall down to the bottom of the scene, too... well, in two seconds, thanks to you having paused gravity—like a boss!

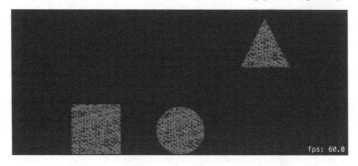

Custom-shaped bodies

Right now, you have two very simple shapes—a circle and a square. What if your shape is more complicated? For example, there's no built-in triangle shape.

You can create arbitrarily-shaped bodies by giving Sprite Kit a **Core Graphics path** that defines the boundary of the body. The easiest way to understand how this works is by looking at an example—so let's try it out with the triangle shape.

Add the following code:

```
var trianglePath = CGPathCreateMutable()

CGPathMoveToPoint(trianglePath, nil, -triangle.size.width/2,
-triangle.size.height/2)

CGPathAddLineToPoint(trianglePath, nil, triangle.size.width/2,
-triangle.size.height/2)

CGPathAddLineToPoint(trianglePath, nil, 0, triangle.size.height/
2)

CGPathAddLineToPoint(trianglePath, nil, -triangle.size.width/2,
-triangle.size.height/2)

triangle.physicsBody = SKPhysicsBody(polygonFromPath:
trianglePath)
```

Let's go through this step by step:

1. First, you create a new `CGMutablePathRef`, which you'll use to plot out the triangle's points.

2. Next, you move your virtual "pen" to the triangle's first point, which in this case is the bottom left, by using `CGPathMoveToPoint()`. Note that the coordinates are relative to the sprite's anchor point, which by default is its center.

3. You then draw three lines, one to each of the three corners of the triangle, by calling CGPathAddLineToPoint(). Note the terms "draw" and "line" do not refer to things you'll see onscreen—rather, they represent the notion of virtually defining the points and line segments that make up a triangle.

4. Finally, you create the body by passing the trianglePath to SKPhysicsBody(polygonFromPath:).

As expected, all three objects fall down when gravity is restored:

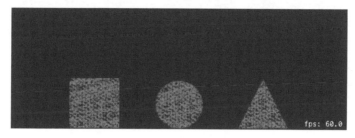

Visualizing the bodies

Each of the three objects now has a physics body that matches its shape, but at the moment, you can't prove that the physics bodies are indeed different for each sprite.

Before beginning the code for this section, add one more utility function to make your code shorter and easier to read. You'll need a random function that returns a CGFloat value in a given range, so open **Sources/SupportCode.swift** and add the following:

```
public func random(min min: CGFloat, max: CGFloat) -> CGFloat {
    return CGFloat(Float(arc4random()) / Float(0xFFFFFFFF)) * (max
    - min) + min
}
```

> **Note:** You can force the use of an external parameter name by including the external and internal parameter names, separated by a space, as shown here with the min parameter. These names don't need to be the same, though they are in this case. Sometimes forcing the parameter name for the first parameter helps to provide a better understanding of the values being passed into the function.

With that done, let's pour particles over the objects to observe their true physical shapes.

Return to your playground and add this function *before* your call to
`delay(seconds:completion:)`:

```
func spawnSand() {

  let sand = SKSpriteNode(imageNamed: "sand")

  sand.position = CGPoint(
    x: random(min: 0.0, max: scene.size.width),
    y: scene.size.height - sand.size.height)

  sand.physicsBody = SKPhysicsBody(circleOfRadius:
sand.size.width/2)

  sand.name = "sand"
  scene.addChild(sand)
}
```

In this function, you make a small circular body, just like you did before, out of the
texture named **sand.png** and position the sprite in a random location at the top of the
scene. You also give the sprite the name **sand** for easy access to it later.

Let's add 100 of these sand particles and see what happens! Modify your call to
`delay(seconds:completion:)` by replacing what's there now with this:

```
delay(seconds: 2.0) {
  scene.physicsWorld.gravity = CGVector(dx: 0, dy: -9.8)
  scene.runAction(
    SKAction.repeatAction(
      SKAction.sequence([
        SKAction.runBlock(spawnSand),
        SKAction.waitForDuration(0.1)
        ]),
      count: 100)
  )
}
```

Finally, some (SK-)action! :]

The new `delay(seconds:completion:)` creates a sequence of actions that calls
`spawnSand` and then waits for `0.1` seconds before executing the sequence 100 times on
the scene.

When the scene starts rendering in the assistant editor, you'll see a "sand storm" as the
100 sand particles rain down and fill the spaces between the three bodies on the ground:

Observe how the sand bounces off of the shapes, proving that your shapes indeed have unique bodies.

After 30 seconds of execution, move the recording slider left and right to see the comical action of the sand going up and down and bouncing off the shapes.

Have some fun with that—you've earned it!

Bodies with complex shapes

The code to create `CGPath` instances is not easy to read, especially if it's been awhile since you wrote it. In addition, if you have a complex body shape to create, it's going to be a long and cumbersome process to create the path for it by code.

While it's useful to know how to create bodies out of custom paths, there's a much easier way to handle complex shapes.

Before you begin, there's one more shape you need to add to your scene, and it looks a bit like a rotated capital letter L:

Considering the code you wrote to define a triangular path, you probably already realize that the shape above will be painful to put together in code.

Let's use the alpha mask of the image to create the physics body for the sprite. Add this to your code:

```
let l = SKSpriteNode(imageNamed:"L")
l.name = "shape"
l.position = CGPoint(x: scene.size.width * 0.5, y:
scene.size.height * 0.75)
l.physicsBody = SKPhysicsBody(texture: l.texture!, size: l.size)
scene.addChild(l)
```

The initializer `SKPhysicsBody(texture:size:)` is the one that lifts the burden from your shoulders and automatically detects the shape of your sprite. It takes two parameters, an `SKTexture` and a `CGSize`.

In the example above, you use the texture of the sprite to generate the physics body for that sprite—but you aren't restricted to using the sprite's texture. If your sprite's texture has a very complex shape, you can also use a different image with a rough outline of your sprite to improve the performance of your game.

You can also control the size of the created body by adjusting the `size` parameter of `SKPhysicsBody(texture:size:)`.

Look at the scene now, and you'll see that the L shape automatically got a physics body that follows its outline. It conveniently falls onto the circle shape for a strong visual effect:

I'm sure you're already wondering how would you debug a real game scene with many complex shapes—you can't always have particles raining over your game objects!

Apple to the rescue!

The Sprite Kit physics engine provides a very convenient feature: an API that enables physics debug output to your live scene. You can see the outlines of your objects, the joints between them, the physics constraints you create and more.

Find the line in your code that enables the frame counter label, `sceneView.showsFPS = true`, and add this line below it:

```
sceneView.showsPhysics = true
```

As soon as the scene starts rendering anew, you'll see the shapes of all your bodies drawn in bright green (it may be hard to see in this screenshot but it's there):

Thanks to this feature, you can do some serious debugging of your physics setup.

Properties of physics bodies

There's more to physics bodies than collision detection. A physics body also has several properties you can set, such as, colloquially speaking, slipperiness, bounciness and heaviness.

To see how a body's properties affect the game physics, you'll adjust the properties for the sand. Right now, the sand falls as though it's very heavy, much like granular rock. What if the pieces were made of soft, elastic rubber?

Add the following line to the end of `spawnSand()`:

```
sand.physicsBody!.restitution = 1.0
```

The `restitution` property describes how much energy the body loses when it bounces off of another body—a fancy way of saying "bounciness".

Values can range from `0.0`, where the body does not bounce at all, to `1.0`, where the body bounces with the same force with which it started the collision. The default value is `0.2`.

Oh my! The "sand" goes crazy:

> **Note:** Sprite Kit sets all properties of physics bodies to *reasonable* values by default. An object's default weight is based on how big it looks onscreen; `restitution` and `friction` ("slipperiness") default to values matching the material of most everyday objects, and so forth.

One more thing: While valid `restitution` values must be from `0` to `1`, the compiler won't complain if you supply values outside of that range. However, think about what it would mean for a body to have a `restitution` value greater than 1, for example. The body would end a collision with *more* energy than it had initially. That's not realistic behavior and it would quickly break your physics simulation, as the values would grow too large for the physics engine to calculate accurately. It's not something I'd recommend in a real app, but give it a try if you want to have some fun.

Next, let's make the particles much more dense, so that they're effectively heavier than the other shapes. Given how bouncy they are now, it should be an interesting sight!

Add this line to the end of `spawnSand()`:

```
sand.physicsBody!.density = 20.0
```

Density is defined as mass per unit volume—in other words, the higher the density of an object, the heavier it will be for its size. Density defaults to 1.0, so here you set the sand to be 20x as dense as usual.

This results in the sand being heavier than any of the other shapes—in comparison, the other shapes behave as if they're made of styrofoam. After the simulation settles down, you'll end up with something like this onscreen:

The red particles literally throw their considerable weight around and push the bigger, but lighter, blue shapes aside. When you control the physics, size doesn't necessarily matter!

Here's a quick tour of the rest of the properties on a physics body:

- **friction**: This sets an object's "slipperiness". Values can range from `0.0`, where the body slides smoothly along surfaces like an ice cube, to `1.0`, where the body quickly slows and stops when sliding along surfaces. The default value is `0.2`.

- **dynamic**: Sometimes you want to use physics bodies for collision detection, but move the node yourself with manual movement or actions. If this is what you want, simply set `dynamic` to `false`, and the physics engine will ignore all forces and impulses on the physics body and let you move the node yourself.

- **usesPreciseCollisionDetection**: By default, Sprite Kit doesn't perform precise collision detection, because it's often best to sacrifice some precision to achieve faster performance. However, this has a side effect: If an object is moving very quickly, like a bullet, it might pass through another object. If this ever happens, try turning this flag on to enable more accurate collision detection.

- **allowsRotation**: You might have a sprite you want the physics engine to simulate, but never rotate. If this is the case, simply set this flag to `false`.

- **linearDamping** and **angularDamping**: These values affect how much the linear velocity (translation) or angular velocity (rotation) decrease over time. Values can range from `0.0`, where the speed never decreases, to `1.0`, where the speed decreases immediately. The default value is `0.1`.

- **affectedByGravity**: All objects are affected by gravity by default, but you can turn this off for a body simply by setting this to `false`.

- **resting**: The physics engine has an optimization where objects that haven't moved in a while are flagged as "resting" so the physics engine doesn't have to perform calculations on them any more. If you ever need to "wake up" a resting object manually, simply set this flag to `false`.

- **mass and area**: These are automatically calculated for you based on the shape and density of the physics body. However, if you ever need to manually override the `mass`, you can. The `area` is read-only.

- **node**: The physics body has a handy pointer back to the `SKNode` to which it belongs. This is a read-only property.

- **categoryBitMask**, **collisionBitMask**, **contactBitMask** and **joints**: You'll learn all about these in Chapter 9, "Intermediate Physics" and Chapter 10, "Advanced Physics".

Applying an impulse

To wrap up this introduction to physics in Sprite Kit, you're going to add a special effect to your test scene. Every now and then, you'll apply an impulse to the particles, making them jump.

The effect will look like a seismic shock that throws everything into the air. Remember, impulses adjust an object's momentum immediately, like a bullet firing from a gun.

To try it out, add this new method to your playground *before* your call to `delay(seconds:completion:)`:

```
func shake() {
  scene.enumerateChildNodesWithName("sand") { node, _ in
    node.physicsBody!.applyImpulse(
      CGVector(dx: 0, dy: random(min: 20, max: 40))
    )
  }
}
```

This function loops over all of the nodes in your scene with the name **sand** and applies an impulse to each of them. You apply an upward impulse by having the x-component always equal zero and having a random positive y-component between 20 and 40.

You create the impulse as a CGVector, which is just like a CGPoint but named so that it's clear it's used as a vector. You then apply the impulse to the anchor point of each particle. Since the strengths of the impulses are random, the shake effect will look pretty realistic.

Of course, you need to call the function before you'll see the particles jump. Locate the call to delay(seconds:completion:) and replace it with this one:

```
delay(seconds: 2.0) {
  scene.physicsWorld.gravity = CGVector(dx: 0, dy: -9.8)
  scene.runAction(
    SKAction.repeatAction(
      SKAction.sequence([
        SKAction.runBlock(spawnSand),
        SKAction.waitForDuration(0.1 )
        ]),
      count: 100)
  )
  delay(seconds: 12, completion: shake)
}
```

You call shake() after 12 seconds have passed, giving the scene time to settle down so you can observe the seismic shock.

It's a bit odd that the shapes don't jump by themselves but are rather "lifted" by the sand particles. Add this code to your shake() function to make the shapes jump, too:

```
scene.enumerateChildNodesWithName("shape") { node, _ in
  node.physicsBody!.applyImpulse(
    CGVector(dx: random(min:20, max:60),
      dy: random(min:20, max:60))
  )
}

delay(seconds: 3, completion: shake)
```

First, you loop through all the shapes and apply a random vector impulse to each of them. Then, you call delay(seconds:completion:) and tell it to call shake() again in three seconds.

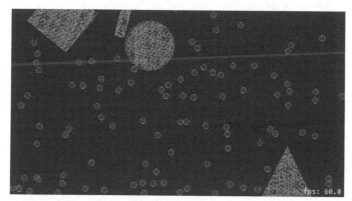

Don't forget to replay those shakes using the scrubber—it's pretty funny!

Well done. You've covered the basics of Sprite Kit's physics engine, and you're almost ready to put these concepts to use in a real game. But first, it's time to push yourself to prove all that you've learned so far!

Challenges

This chapter has two challenges that will get you ready to create your first physics game. You'll learn about forces and create a dynamic sprite with collision detection.

As always, if you get stuck, you can find the solutions in the resources for this chapter—but do give it your best shot before peeking!

Challenge 1: Forces

So far, you've learned how to make the sand move immediately by applying an impulse. But what if you wanted to make objects move more gradually, over time?

Your first challenge is to simulate a very windy day that will blow your objects back and forth across the screen. Below are some guidelines for how to accomplish this.

First, add these variables:

```
var blowingRight = true
var windForce = CGVector(dx: 50, dy: 0)
```

Then, add this stub implementation of update():

```
// 1
NSTimer.scheduledTimerWithTimeInterval(0.05, target: scene,
selector: "windWithTimer:", userInfo: nil, repeats: true)

NSTimer.scheduledTimerWithTimeInterval(3.0, target: scene,
selector: "switchWindDirection:", userInfo: nil, repeats: true)

extension SKScene {

  // 2
  func windWithTimer(timer: NSTimer) {
    // TODO: apply force to all bodies
  }

  // 3
  func switchWindDirection(timer: NSTimer) {
    blowingRight = !blowingRight
    windForce = CGVector(dx: blowingRight ? 50 : -50, dy: 0)
  }
}
```

Let's go over this section by section:

1. You declare two timers. The first fires 20 times per second and calls windWithTimer(_:) on your scene—this is where you'll apply force to all the bodies. The second timer fires once every three seconds and calls switchWindDirection(_:), where you'll toggle blowingRight and adjust the windForce vector accordingly.

2. Inside windWithTimer(_:), enumerate over all sand particles and shape bodies and apply the current windForce to each. Look up the method named applyForce(_:), which works in a similar way to applyImpulse(_:), which you already know.

3. Inside switchWindDirections(_:), you simply toggle blowingRight and update windForce.

Remember the difference between forces and impulses: You apply a force every frame while the force is active, but you fire an impulse once and only once.

If you get this working, you'll see the objects slide back and forth across the screen as the wind changes direction:

Challenge 2: Kinematic bodies

In your games, you might have some sprites you want to move with manual movement or custom actions, and others you want the physics engine to move. But you'll still want collision detection to work on all of these sprites, including the ones you move yourself.

As you learned earlier in this chapter, you can accomplish this by setting the `dynamic` flag on a physics body to `false`. Bodies that you move yourself, but that still have collision detection, are sometimes called **kinematic bodies**.

Your second challenge in this chapter is to try this out for yourself by making the circle sprite move not by the physics engine, but by an `SKAction`. Here are a few hints:

- Set the `dynamic` property of the circle's physics body to `false` after creating it.

- Create an `SKAction` to move the circle horizontally back and forth across the screen, and make that action repeat forever.

If you get this working, you'll see that everything is affected by the gravity, wind and impulses, except for the circle. However, the objects still collide with the circle as usual:

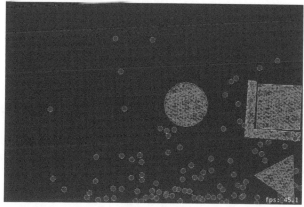

If you made it through both of these challenges, congratulations! You now have a firm grasp of the most important concepts of Sprite Kit's physics engine, and you're 100% ready to put these concepts to use in Cat Nap. Meow!

Chapter 10: Intermediate Physics

By Marin Todorov

In Chapter 8, "Scene Editor", you got acquainted with Sprite Kit's level designer by building the first level of a game called Cat Nap.

Then in Chapter 9, "Beginning Physics", you took up physics in Sprite Kit by experimenting in real time inside a playground. You learned how to add bodies to sprites, create shapes, customize physics properties and even apply forces and impulses.

In this chapter, you're going to use your newly acquired scene editor and physics skills to add physics into Cat Nap, creating your first fully playable level! By the end of this chapter, you'll finally be able to help the sleepy cat settle into his bed:

Purr-fect!

> **Note**: This chapter begins where the Chapter 8's Challenge 2 left off. If you were unable to complete the challenges or skipped ahead from an earlier chapter, don't worry—simply open the starter project from this chapter to pick up where Chapter 8's Challenge 2 left off.

Getting started

Open your CatNap project, and make sure **GameScene.swift** is open.

First, you're going to do some more scene initialization by overriding the scene's didMoveToView(_:). Just as you did for Zombie Conga, you need to set the scene's playable area so that when you're finished developing Cat Nap, it will fully support both iPhone and iPad screen resolutions.

To get rid of the default code added by Xcode, replace the contents of **GameScene.swift** with the following:

```
import SpriteKit

class GameScene: SKScene {

  override func didMoveToView(view: SKView) {
    // Calculate playable margin

    let maxAspectRatio: CGFloat = 16.0/9.0 // iPhone 5
    let maxAspectRatioHeight = size.width / maxAspectRatio
    let playableMargin: CGFloat = (size.height -
maxAspectRatioHeight)/2

    let playableRect = CGRect(x: 0, y: playableMargin,
      width: size.width, height: size.height-playableMargin*2)

    physicsBody = SKPhysicsBody(edgeLoopFromRect: playableRect)
  }
}
```

Just as you did for Zombie Conga, you begin with the aspect ratio of the iPhone 5 screen and then define the frame of the playable area based on the current scene size.

Since Cat Nap is a physics-based game, you set the detected playable frame as the edge loop for the scene. That's all there is to it—Sprite Kit will now automatically confine your game objects within the area you designate for the gameplay.

Now you're ready to put to work those sprites you placed in the scene editor!

Custom node classes

When you place objects in the scene editor, you choose from the list provided in the Object Library. As you already know, you can drag-and-drop a generic node, a sprite node showing an image, or a label. At run-time, Sprite Kit creates the nodes from the respective built-in type and sets them up the way you want.

This, however, leaves you with limited room for customization—you can't add new methods or simply override one of the built-in functionalities with your own implementation.

In this section, you'll learn how to create and employ your own custom node classes, which will give you exactly the behavior you need for your game from every node in your level.

You'll start by adding a simple class for the cat bed node. From Xcode's main menu, select **File/New/File...** and for the file template, choose **iOS/Source/Swift file**. Name the new file **BedNode.swift** and save it.

Replace the default contents with an empty SKSpriteNode subclass:

```
import SpriteKit

class BedNode: SKSpriteNode {
}
```

You've created an empty class that derives from SKSpriteNode; now you need to link this class to the bed sprite in the scene editor. To do this, open **GameScene.sks** in the scene editor and select the cat bed. In the utilities area, switch to the **Custom Class Inspector**, which is the last tab on the right.

For **Custom Class**, enter **BedNode**.

Custom Class	
Custom Class	BedNode
Module	

This way, when you launch your game, instead of creating a plain SKSpriteNode for the cat bed, Sprite Kit will make a new instance of BedNode. Now you can customize your BedNode class to behave in the way you'd like.

Next, to understand how much you can do with custom node classes, you're going to add an event method that will get called when the node is added to the scene. If you're familiar with building UIKit apps for iOS, it will be similar to UIView.didMoveToWindow().

First, you need a new protocol for all the nodes that implement your custom event. Open **GameScene.swift** and add the following after the import statement:

```
protocol CustomNodeEvents {
  func didMoveToScene()
}
```

Now, switch back to **BedNode.swift** and make the class conform to the new protocol by adding a `didMoveToScene()` method stub that prints out a message. The class will now look like this:

```
import SpriteKit

class BedNode: SKSpriteNode, CustomNodeEvents {
  func didMoveToScene() {
    print("bed added to scene")
  }
}
```

As the final step, you need to call the new method. A good place to do that is at the bottom of the `didMoveToView(_:)` of your scene class.

Back in **GameScene.swift**, add the following code at the end of `didMoveToView(_:)`:

```
enumerateChildNodesWithName("//*", usingBlock: {node, _ in
  if let customNode = node as? CustomNodeEvents {
    customNode.didMoveToScene()
  }
})
```

Here you use `enumerateChildNodesWithName(_:usingBlock:)`, an `SKNode` method that loops over all the nodes that exist in the scene. While `childNodeWithName(_:)` finds the first node matching the given name or search pattern, `enumerateChildNodesWithName(_:usingBlock:)` returns an array containing all the nodes that match the name or pattern you're looking for.

As the first parameter, you can specify either a node name or a search pattern. If you've worked extensively with XML, you'll notice the similarities:

- **/name**: Search for nodes named "name" in the root of the hierarchy

- **//name**: Search for nodes named "name" starting at the root and moving recursively down the hierarchy

- *****: Matches zero or more characters; e.g. "name*" will match name1, name2, nameABC and name

> **Note**: For additional examples, review the section "Advanced Searches" in Apple's `SKNode` docs: http://apple.co/1I9QfBz

Now you can decipher the search pattern from the last code block: "**//*** ". When your search pattern starts with **//**, the search starts at the top of the node hierarchy, and when you search for *****, which means *any name*, you loop over all existing nodes, regardless of their names or their locations in the node hierarchy.

As a second parameter, enumerateChildNodesWithName(_:usingBlock:) gets a closure; the code inside is executed once per each matching node. The first closure parameter is the node result, and the second gives you an opportunity to stop the search at that point.

Build and run the game. You'll see your test message show up—your code looped over all nodes, matched the ones implementing CustomNodeEvents and called didMoveToScene() on each one:

This proves that your game is using your custom BedNode SKSpriteNode subclass for the cat bed. w00t!

Now you can put all your node setup code in didMoveToScene() for each respective node class. That way, you won't clog your scene class with code that's relevant only to specific nodes. In your scene class, you'll add the code that has to do with the entire scene or interaction between nodes.

To give custom classes another try, add a custom class for the cat. From Xcode's main menu, select **File/New/File...** and for the file template, choose **iOS/Source/Swift file**. Name the new file **CatNode.swift** and save it.

Replace the default contents with the following SKSpriteNode subclass:

```
import SpriteKit

class CatNode: SKSpriteNode, CustomNodeEvents {
  func didMoveToScene() {
    print("cat added to scene")
  }
}
```

Just like before, you make sure that when the method gets called, it prints a statement.

One last thing before moving on: You don't want to change the class in **GameScene.sks**; you want to change the class in **Cat.sks**. Remember, **GameScene.sks** only holds a reference to **Cat.sks**, so you need to go to **Cat.sks** to set the appropriate class for your cat node.

Open **Cat.sks** and select the cat_body sprite node. In the Custom Class Inspector, set the **Custom Class** to **CatNode**.

Build and run the game again. The output in the console is now:

The cat is one step closer to taking a nap!

Next you need to connect the nodes you created in the scene editor to variables, so you can access the sprites in code.

Connecting sprites to variables

For those familiar with UIKit development, connecting nodes to variables is somewhat like connecting views in your storyboard to outlets.

Open **GameScene.swift** and add two instance variables to the GameScene class:

```
var bedNode: BedNode!
var catNode: CatNode!
```

catNode and bedNode are—or will be in a moment—the cat and cat bed sprite nodes, respectively. Notice that you use their custom classes, because the scene editor takes care to use the correct type when creating the scene nodes.

Open **GameScene.sks** and select the cat bed. In the Attributes Inspector, notice that the sprite has the name **bed**. This is how you'll find that sprite in the scene from code—by its name. In UIKit development, the name of the sprite is much like a view's tag property.

Switch back to **GameScene.swift** and add the following code to didMoveToView(_:):

```
bedNode = childNodeWithName("bed") as! BedNode
```

childNodeWithName(_:) loops through a node's children and returns the *first node* with the required name. In this case, you loop through the scene's children, looking for the bed sprite, which is based on the name you set in the scene editor.

For the cat sprite, you need a different approach. You don't want to work with the cat reference; instead, you want to work with the cat body. After all, only the cat's body will have its own physics body—you don't need to apply physics simulation to the eyes or the whiskers!

Since the cat_body sprite is not a direct child of the scene, you can't simply provide the name cat_body to childNodeWithName(_:) and expect to get it back. Instead, you need to recursively search through all the children of the children of the scene!

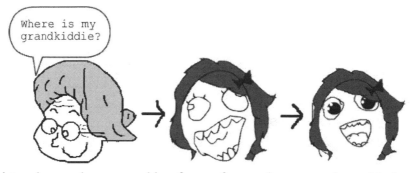

Consulting the search pattern table reference from earlier, you end up with the simple pattern **//cat_body**. That being the case, add this line to `didMoveToView(_:)`:

```
catNode = childNodeWithName("//cat_body") as! CatNode
```

Now you have a reference to each sprite, so you can modify them in code. To test this, add the following two lines to the end of `didMoveToView(_:)`:

```
bedNode.setScale(1.5)
catNode.setScale(1.5)
```

Build and run, and you'll see Giganto-Cat!

Now that you've proved you can modify the sprites in code, comment out those two lines to revert the cat and bed back to normal:

```
// bedNode.setScale(1.5)
// catNode.setScale(1.5)
```

Sorry about that, Giganto-cat, but cats already have a big enough ego! :]

Congratulations - now you know how to connect objects in the scene editor to code. Now it's time to move onto physics!

Adding physics

Recall from the previous chapter that for the physics engine to kick in, you need to create physics bodies for your sprites. In this section, you're going to learn three different ways to do that:

1. Creating simple bodies in the scene editor

2. Creating simple bodies from code

3. Creating custom bodies

Let's try each of these methods, one at a time.

Creating simple bodies in the scene editor

Looking at your scene as it is now, you can't help but notice that those wooden blocks would make perfect use of rectangular physics bodies.

From your experiments in the previous chapter, you already know how to create rectangular bodies in code, so let's look at how to do it in the scene editor.

Open **GameScene.sks** and select the four block sprites in your scene. Press and hold the **Command** key on your keyboard and click on each block until you've selected them all:

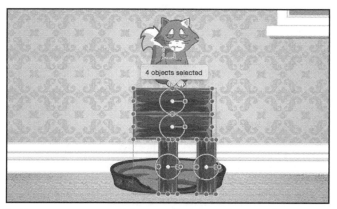

In the **Physics Definition** section of the Attributes Inspector, change the selection for **Body Type** to **Bounding Rectangle**. This will open a section with additional properties, allowing you to control most aspects of a physics body. You read about each of these properties in the previous chapter.

The default property values look about right for your wooden blocks: The bodies will be **dynamic**, can **rotate** when falling and are **affected by gravity**. The **Mass** field reads **Multiple Values**, because Sprite Kit assigned a different mass to each wooden block based on its size.

That's all you need to do to set up the blocks' physics bodies. Notice now that when you deselect the blocks, they're faintly outlined in blue-green, indicating they have physics bodies:

There's one last thing to do: Select all four wooden blocks again, scroll to the top of the Attributes Inspector and enter **block** in the **Name** field. Now you can easily enumerate all the blocks in the scene and also easily see which ones are blocks when you debug the scene.

> **Note:** This kind of node setup is something you could implement in a custom node class. Don't worry—you'll learn how to set up your bodies both from the scene editor and from code. But you can only do one at a time. :]
>
> In fact, you'll add a custom class for the block nodes later, when you add user interaction to them.

Simulating the scene

Let's quickly explore another feature of the scene editor.

You know that clicking the **Animate** button will run any sprite actions you add to sprites. But what about physics? Will the same button also fire up the good old physics engine? Click **Animate** and watch what happens:

You'll see the blocks fall down off the screen. They won't stop at the edges, because the animate button does not run the code that creates the edge loop that you added to `GameScene`, but this is still a handy way to do some basic testing.

Creating simple bodies from code

What if you want a physics body to be smaller than a node's bounding rectangle or circle? For example, you might want to be "forgiving" in the collision detection between two objects to make the gameplay easier or more fun, similar to how you reduced the collision box for the crazy cat lady in Zombie Conga.

Making the physics body a different shape than the sprite itself is easy to do, and also gives you an opportunity to apply your skills from the previous chapter to Cat Nap.

The cat bed itself won't participate in the physics simulation; instead, it will remain static on the ground and exempt from collisions with other bodies in the scene. It will still have a physics body, though, because you need to detect when the cat falls onto the bed. So you're going to give the bed small, non-interactive body for the purpose of detecting contacts.

Since you've already connected your `bedNode` instance variable to the bed sprite, you can create the body in code.

Switch to **BedNode.swift** and add the following to `didMoveToScene()`:

```
let bedBodySize = CGSize(width: 40.0, height: 30.0)
physicsBody = SKPhysicsBody(rectangleOfSize: bedBodySize)
physicsBody!.dynamic = false
```

As you learned in the previous chapter, a sprite's physics body doesn't necessarily have to match the sprite's size or shape. For the cat bed, you want the physics body to be much smaller than the sprite, because you only want the cat to fall happily asleep when he hits the exact center of the bed. Cats are known to be picky, after all!

Since you never want the cat bed to move, you set its dynamic property to `false`. This makes the body static, which allows the physics engine to optimize its calculations, because it can ignore any forces applied to this object.

> **Note**: You need to force-unwrap the `physicsBody` property—it's an *optional* property, so you need to use `!` if you're sure there's a body attached to the sprite, or `?` if you're not.

Open **GameViewController.swift** and add the following line inside `viewDidLoad()`, just after the code that declares `skView`:

```
skView.showsPhysics = true
```

Build and run the project, and you'll see your scene come alive:

Look at the little rectangle toward the bottom of the screen—that's the physics body of the cat bed! It's green so that you remember it's not a dynamic physics body.

But your carefully built obstacle tower appears a little off-center. That happened because the bed body pushed aside your central wooden block. To fix this, you'll need to set the block bodies and the bed body so they don't collide with each other, something you'll learn how to do a bit later.

Creating custom bodies

Looking at the cat sprite, you can instantly guess that a rectangular or a circular body won't do—you'll have to use a different approach and create a custom-shaped physics body.

To do this, you'll load a separate image that describes the shape of the cat's physics body and use it to create the body object itself. Open **CatNode.swift** and add this code to `didMoveToScene()`:

```
let catBodyTexture = SKTexture(imageNamed: "cat_body_outline")
parent!.physicsBody = SKPhysicsBody(texture: catBodyTexture,
size: catBodyTexture.size())
```

You create a new texture object out of an image named **cat_body_outline.png.** From the project navigator, open **cat_body_outline** from your assets catalog and you'll see it contains this blue shape:

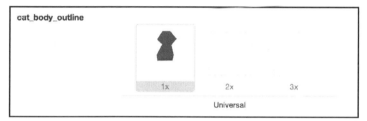

This shape doesn't include the cat's head or tail, and it doesn't follow the outline of the paws. Instead, it uses a flat bottom edge, so the cat will remain stable on those wooden blocks.

Next, you create a body for the cat sprite using an `SKPhysicsBody` instance and the appropriate texture, scaling it to the node's own `size`. You're already familiar with how to do this from the previous chapter.

Build and run the project again, and check out the debug drawing of the cat's body. Excellent work!

Now that you've set up the first level, why don't you take a break from all this physics and get the player in the mood for puzzles by turning on some soothing and delightful music?

Introducing SKTUtils

In the first few chapters of this book, while you were working on Zombie Conga, you created some handy extensions to allow you to do things like add and subtract two CGPoints by using the + or − operators.

Rather than make you continuously re-add these extensions in each mini-game, we've combined them and created a library named SKTUtils.

Besides handy geometry and math functions, this library also includes a useful class that helps you easily play an audio file as your game's background music.

Now you're going to add SKTUtils to your project so you can make use of these methods throughout the rest of the chapter. Happy birthday!

Locate SKTUtils in the root folder for this book and drag the entire **SKTUtils** folder into the project navigator in Xcode. Make sure **Copy items if needed**, **Create Groups** and the **CatNap** target are all checked, and click **Finish**.

Take a minute to review the contents of the library. It should look quite familiar, with a few additions and tweaks:

Now every class in your project has access to these timesaving functions.

Background music

Now that you've added `SKTUtils`, it will be a cinch to add background music. Open **GameScene.swift** and add this code to `didMoveToView(_:)` to start the music:

```
SKTAudio.sharedInstance().playBackgroundMusic("backgroundMusic.m
p3")
```

Build and run the project, and enjoy the merry tune!

> **Note**: You still have many more build and runs ahead of you in this chapter. If at any time you feel like muting the background music, just comment out this last line.

Controlling your bodies

So far, you know how to create physics bodies for sprites and let the physics engine do its thing.

But in Cat Nap, you want a bit more control than that. For example:

- **Categorizing bodies**. You want to keep the cat bed from colliding with the blocks, and vice versa. To do this, you need a way to categorize bodies and set up collision flags.

- **Finding bodies**. You want to enable the player to destroy a block by tapping it. To do this, you need a way to find a body at a given point.

- **Detecting collisions between bodies**. You want to detect when the cat hits the cat bed, so he can get his beauty sleep. To do this, you need a way to detect collisions.

You'll investigate these areas over the next three sections. By the time you're done, you'll have implemented the most important parts of this mini-game!

Categorizing bodies

Sprite Kit's default behavior is for all physics bodies to collide with all other physics bodies. If two objects are occupying the same point, like the brick and the cat bed, the physics engine will automatically move one of them aside.

The good news is, you can override this default behavior and specify whether or not two physics bodies should collide. There are three steps to do this:

1. **Define the categories**. The first step is to define categories for your physics bodies, such as block bodies, cat bodies and cat bed bodies.

2. **Set the category bit mask**. Once you have a set of categories, you need to specify the categories to which each physics body belongs—a physics body can belong to more than one category—by setting its category bit mask.

3. **Set the collision bit mask**. You also need to specify the collision bit mask for each physics body. This controls which categories of bodies the body will collide with.

As with most things, the best place to start is at the beginning—in this case, by defining the categories for Cat Nap. In **GameScene.swift**, add the category constants **outside** the GameScene class, preferably at the top:

```swift
struct PhysicsCategory {
  static let None:  UInt32 = 0
  static let Cat:   UInt32 = 0b1 // 1
  static let Block: UInt32 = 0b10 // 2
  static let Bed:   UInt32 = 0b100 // 4
}
```

Now you can comfortably access body categories like `PhysicsCategory.Cat` and `PhysicsCategory.Bed`.

You've probably already spotted that each of the categories turns on another bit:

- **PhysicsCategory.None**: Decimal **0**, Binary **00000000**

- **PhysicsCategory.Cat**: Decimal **1**, Binary **00000001**

- **PhysicsCategory.Block**: Decimal **2**, Binary **00000010**

- **PhysicsCategory.Bed**: Decimal **4**, Binary **00000100**

This is very handy, and very fast for the physics engine to calculate, when you want to specify that the cat should collide with all block bodies and the bed. You can then say the collision bitmask for the cat is `PhysicsCategory.Block | PhysicsCategory.Bed`— read this as "block OR bed"—which produces the logical OR of the two values:

- **PhysicsCategory.Block | PhysicsCategory.Bed**: Decimal **6**, Binary **00000110**

> **Note**: If you aren't quite at ease with binary arithmetic, you can read more about bitwise operations here: http://en.wikipedia.org/wiki/Bitwise_operation

Now you can move on to steps two and three: setting the category and collision bit masks for each object, starting with the blocks.

Go back to **GameScene.sks** and select the **four wooden blocks**, as you did earlier. Look at the current **Category Mask** and **Collision Mask**:

Category Mask	4294967295
Collision Mask	4294967295
Field Mask	4294967295
Contact Mask	0

Both are set to the biggest integer value possible, thus making all bodies collide with all other bodies. If you convert the default value of 4294967295 to binary, you'll see that it has all bits turned *on*, and therefore, it collides with all other objects:

```
4294967295 = 11111111111111111111111111111111
```

It's time to implement custom collisions. Edit the blocks' properties like so:

For **Category Mask**, enter the raw value of `PhysicsCategory.Block`, which is **2**;

For **Collision Mask**, enter the bitwise `OR` value of `PhysicsCategory.Cat | PhysicsCategory.Block`, which is **3**.

> **Note**: Just put the decimal values in the boxes—that is, for the Collision Mask, enter **3**.

Category Mask	2
Collision Mask	3

This means you've set each block's body to be of the `PhysicsCategory.Block` category, and you've set all of the blocks to collide with both the cat and other blocks.

Next, set up the bed. You created this body from code, so go back to **BedNode.swift** and add the following to the end of `didMoveToScene()`:

```
physicsBody!.categoryBitMask = PhysicsCategory.Bed
physicsBody!.collisionBitMask = PhysicsCategory.None
```

With the code above, you set the category of the bed body and then set its collision mask to `PhysicsCategory.None`—you don't want the bed to collide with any other game objects.

> **Note**: As promised earlier, you're learning how to do things both from the scene editor and from code—when you're on your own, just pick whichever suits you. I personally like the code approach a little better, because you can use the defined enumeration members; in the scene editor, you have to use hard-coded integer values.

At this point, you've set up both the wooden blocks and the cat bed with the proper categories and collision masks. Build and run the project one more time:

As expected, you see a block right in front of the bed's body without either body pushing the other away. Nice!

Finally, set the bitmasks for the cat. Since you created the physics body for your cat sprite in code, you also have to set the category and collision masks in code, specifically in **CatNode.swift**. Open that file and add this to the end of `didMoveToScene()`:

```
parent!.physicsBody!.categoryBitMask = PhysicsCategory.Cat
parent!.physicsBody!.collisionBitMask = PhysicsCategory.Block
```

You put the cat into its own category, `PhysicsCategory.Cat`, and set it to collide only with blocks. Note how you add the physics body to the parent node (i.e. the compound node that holds all cat parts).

> **Note:** A physics body's `collisionBitMask` value specifies which categories of objects will affect the movement of *that* body when those two bodies collide. But remember, you set the bed's `dynamic` property to `false`, which already ensures that no forces will ever affect the bed—so there's no need to set the bed's `collisionBitMask`.
>
> Generally, there's never a reason to set the `collisionBitMask` for an object with its `dynamic` property set to `false`. Likewise, edge loop bodies are always treated as if their `dynamic` property is `false`, even if it isn't—so there's never a reason to set the `collisionBitMask` for an edge loop, either.

Now you know how to make a group of bodies pass through some bodies and collide with others. You'll find this technique useful for many types of games. For example, in some games you want players on the same team to pass through each other, but collide with enemies from the other team. Often, you don't want game physics to imitate real life!

Handling touches

In this section, you'll implement the first part of the gameplay. When the player taps a block, you'll destroy it with a *pop*.

To distinguish nodes you can tap on and those node that are just static decoration you will add a new protocol. Open **GameScene.swift** and add under the existing protocol declaration for `CustomNodeEvents`:

```
protocol InteractiveNode {
  func interact()
}
```

When you create a custom node for the level's block nodes you will make that class adhere to `Interactive` and will add the method `interact()` where you will place all code to react to the player's touches.

Since `SKNode` inherits from `UIResponder`, you can handle touches on each node from the node's own custom class by overriding `touchesBegan(_:withEvent:)`, `touchesEnded(_:withEvent:)` or other `UIResponder` methods.

Since right now you're interested in simple taps on the block nodes, a `BlockNode` class with just `touchesEnded(_:withEvent:)` will suffice.

You're already quite familiar with creating custom node classes, so this should be a breeze. From Xcode's main menu, select **File/New/File...** and for the file template, choose **iOS/Source/Swift file**. Name the new file **BlockNode.swift** and save it.

Replace the default contents with the following:

```
import SpriteKit

class BlockNode: SKSpriteNode, CustomNodeEvents, InteractiveNode
{
  func didMoveToScene() {
    userInteractionEnabled = true
  }

  func interact() {
    userInteractionEnabled = false
  }

  override func touchesEnded(touches: Set<UITouch>, withEvent
event: UIEvent?) {
    super.touchesEnded(touches, withEvent: event)
    print("destroy block")
    interact()
  }
}
```

For this type of node, you did all the physics body setup from the scene editor, so you only need to enable user interactions inside didMoveToScene(). By default, userInteractionEnabled is off to keep the responder chain as light as possible—but for your blocks, you definitely want to handle touches, so you set it to true.

Further, you override touchesEnded(_:withEvent:), so you can handle simple taps on the block node - in the code above you simply call interact() and leave it do all the work.

Since you will allow the players to destroy a block by simply tapping it once, as soon as interact() is being called you turn off userInteractionEnabled to ignore further touches on the same block.

The final step before you test that code is to set this custom class to all block nodes, in the scene editor. Open **GameScene.sks** and select the four wooden blocks just as you did before. In the Custom Class Inspector, enter **BlockNode** for the **Custom Class**:

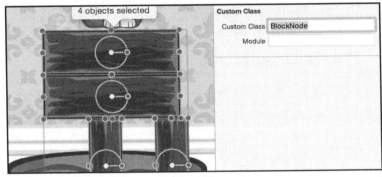

Build and run the project, and start tapping some blocks. You should see one line in the console for each of your taps on a block:

Now for the fun part! You want to destroy those blocks and remove them from the scene. Add this to interact() in **BlockNode.swift**:

```
runAction(SKAction.sequence([
  SKAction.playSoundFileNamed("pop.mp3", waitForCompletion:
false),
  SKAction.scaleTo(0.8, duration: 0.1),
  SKAction.removeFromParent()
  ]))
```

Here you're running a sequence of three actions: The first action plays an amusing *pop* sound, the next scales down the sprite and the last removes it from the scene. This should be enough to make the level's basic physics work.

Build and run the project again. This time, when you tap the blocks, you've got your game on:

Detecting collisions between bodies

Very often in games, you'd like to know if certain bodies are in contact. Two or more bodies can "touch" or "pass through" each other, depending on whether or not they're set to collide. In both cases, they're in contact:

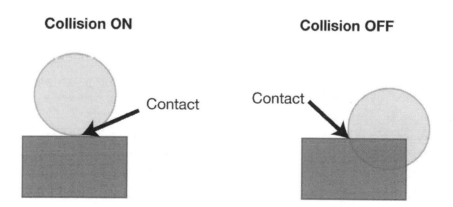

In Cat Nap, you want to know whether certain pairs of bodies touch:

1. If **the cat touches the floor**, it means he's on the ground, but out of his bed, so the player fails the level.

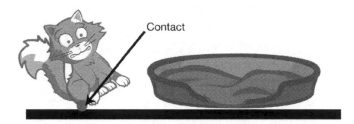

2. If **the cat touches the bed**, it means he landed successfully on the bed, so the player wins the level.

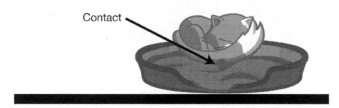

Sprite Kit makes it easy for you to receive a callback when two physics bodies make contact. The first step is to implement the SKPhysicsContactDelegate methods.

In Cat Nap, you'll implement these methods in GameScene. Open **GameScene.swift** and add the SKPhysicsContactDelegate protocol to the class declaration line, so it looks like this:

```
class GameScene: SKScene, SKPhysicsContactDelegate {
```

The SKPhysicsContactDelegate protocol defines two methods you'll implement in GameScene:

• didBeginContact(_:) tells you when two bodies first make contact.

• didEndContact(_:) tells you when two bodies end their contact.

The diagram below shows how you'd call these methods in the case of two bodies passing through each other:

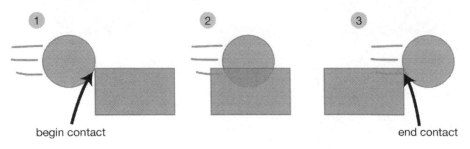

You'll most often be interested in didBeginContact(_:), because much of your game logic will occur when two objects touch.

However, there are times you'll want to know when objects stop touching. For example, you may want to use the physics engine to test when a player is within a trigger area. Perhaps entering the area sounds an alarm, while leaving the area silences it. In a case such as this, you'll need to implement didEndContact(_:), as well.

To try this out, you first need to add a new category constant for the edges of the screen, since you want to be able to detect when the cat collides with the floor. Scroll to the top of **GameScene.swift** and add this new PhysicsCategory value:

```
static let Edge:  UInt32 = 0b1000 // 8
```

Then, find this line inside didMoveToView(_:):

```
physicsBody = SKPhysicsBody(edgeLoopFromRect: playableRect)
```

And just below it, add the following:

```
physicsWorld.contactDelegate = self
physicsBody!.categoryBitMask = PhysicsCategory.Edge
```

First, you set GameScene as the contact delegate of the scene's physics world. Then, you assign PhysicsCategory.Edge as the body's category.

Build and run the project to see the results of your actions so far.

Hmm... that's not right. All the blocks fall through the edge—but just seconds ago, the project worked fine!

The issue here is that the world edge now has a category, PhysicsCategory.Edge, but the blocks aren't set to collide with it. Therefore, they fall through the floor. Meanwhile, the cat bed's dynamic property is set to false, so it can't move at all.

With no blocks on the screen, you have no game! Open **GameScene.sks** in the scene editor and select the four wooden blocks, just as you did before. Then, change the

Collision Mask for their bodies from 3 to **11**.

- **PhysicsCategory.Block | PhysicsCategory.Cat | PhysicsCategory.Edge**: Decimal **11**,
  Binary **00001110**

Build and run the project now, and you'll see the familiar scene setup. But try popping
all the blocks out of the cat's way, and you'll see the cat fall through the bottom of the
screen and disappear. Goodbye, Kitty!

By now, you probably know what's wrong: The cat doesn't collide with the scene's edge
loop, of course!

Go to **CatNode.swift** and change the line where you set the cat's collision mask so that
the cat also collides with the scene's boundaries:

```
parent!.physicsBody!.collisionBitMask = PhysicsCategory.Block |
PhysicsCategory.Edge
```

This should keep that pesky feline from falling off the screen!

Build and run the project again, and everything will appear (and behave!) as it should.

Detecting contact between bodies

You've learned to use the `categoryBitMask` to set a physics body's categories, and the
`collisionBitMask` to set the colliding categories for a physics bodies. Well, there's
another bit mask: `contactTestBitMask`.

You use `contactTestBitMask` to detect contact between a physics body and designated
categories of objects. Once you've set this up, Sprite Kit will call your physics contact
delegate methods at the appropriate time.

In Cat Nap, you want to receive callbacks when the cat makes contact with either the edge loop body or the bed body, so switch to **CatNode.swift** and add this line to the end of `didMoveToScene()`:

```
parent!.physicsBody!.contactTestBitMask = PhysicsCategory.Bed |
PhysicsCategory.Edge
```

That's all the configuration you need to do. Every time the cat body makes contact with either the bed body or the edge loop body, you'll get a message.

Now to handle those contact messages. Back in **GameScene.swift**, add this contact delegate protocol method to your class:

```
func didBeginContact(contact: SKPhysicsContact) {

  let collision = contact.bodyA.categoryBitMask |
contact.bodyB.categoryBitMask

  if collision == PhysicsCategory.Cat | PhysicsCategory.Bed {
    print("SUCCESS")
  } else if collision == PhysicsCategory.Cat |
PhysicsCategory.Edge {
    print("FAIL")
  }
}
```

Look at the parameter this method receives—it's of class `SKPhysicsContact` and tells you a lot about the contacting bodies:

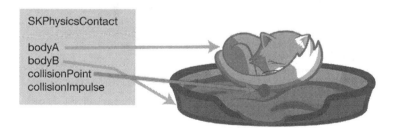

There's no way to guarantee a particular object will be in **bodyA** or **bodyB**. But there are various ways you can find out, such as by checking the body's category or looking for some property of the body's node.

This simple game contains only four categories so far, which correspond to the integer values 1, 2, 4 and 8. That makes it simple to check for contact combinations—simply use bitwise `OR` as you did to define the collision and contact bitmasks.

Categories	2-Category Combinations
Cat: 1	Cat (1) | Block (2) = 3
Block: 2	Block (2) | Block (2) = 2
Bed: 4	Cat (1) | Bed (4) = 5
Edge: 8	... other combinations

> **Note**: If you feel the ground loosening under your feet when you think about comparing bitmasks, consider reading this short but informative article: http://en.wikipedia.org/wiki/Mask_(computing).

Inside your implementation of `didBeginContact(_:)`, you first add the categories of the two bodies that collided and store the result in `collision`. The two `if` statements check `collision` for the combinations of bodies in which you're interested:

- If the two contacting bodies are the **cat** and the **bed**, you print out "SUCCESS".

- If the two contacting bodies are the **cat** and the **edge**, you print out "FAIL".

Build and run the project to verify you've got this working thus far. You'll see a message in the console when the cat makes contact with either the bed or the floor.

> **Note**: When the cat falls on the ground, you'll see several FAIL messages. That's because the cat bounces off the ground just a little by default, so it ends up making contact with the ground more than once. You'll fix this soon.

Finishing touches

You're almost there—you already know when the player should win or lose, so you just need to do something about it.

There are three steps remaining in this chapter:

- **Add an in-game message**
- **Handle losing**
- **Handle winning**

Adding an in-game message

First, add this new category value to the `PhysicsCategory` structure in **GameScene.swift**:

```
static let Label: UInt32 = 0b10000 // 16
```

Next, you need a new custom class; it will inherit from `SKLabelNode`, the built-in Sprite Kit label class, but it will implement some custom behavior.

From Xcode's main menu, select **File/New/File…** and for the file template, choose **iOS/ Source/Swift file**. Name the new file **MessageNode.swift** and save it.

Replace the default code with the following:

```swift
import SpriteKit

class MessageNode: SKLabelNode {

  convenience init(message: String) {

    self.init(fontNamed: "AvenirNext-Regular")

    text = message
    fontSize = 256.0
    fontColor = SKColor.grayColor()
    zPosition = 100

    let front = SKLabelNode(fontNamed: "AvenirNext-Regular")
    front.text = message
    front.fontSize = 256.0
    front.fontColor = SKColor.whiteColor()
    front.position = CGPoint(x: -2, y: -2)
    addChild(front)

  }
}
```

You add a new `convenience init` that expects a parameter for the text to show onscreen. To initialize the label node, you call another built-in `convenience init` that sets the label with the AvenirNext font.

Next, you set the label's text, font size, color and z-position; you want the text to display over all other scene nodes and 100 is an acceptable value.

To make things a bit more interesting, you add another label as a child to the current one, the second one having a different color and offset by a few points. Essentially, you're creating a poor man's drop-shadow for the text by combining dark and light copies of the message.

Now, to make the message more amusing, add some physics to it by appending the following to the `convenience init` of `MessageNode`:

```
physicsBody = SKPhysicsBody(circleOfRadius: 10)
physicsBody!.collisionBitMask = PhysicsCategory.Edge
physicsBody!.categoryBitMask = PhysicsCategory.Label
physicsBody!.restitution = 0.7
```

You create a circular physics body for the label and set it to bounce off of the scene's edge. You also assign it to its own physics category, `PhysicsCategory.Label`.

When you add the label to the scene, it will bounce around until it rests on the "ground", like so:

To make showing an in-game message even easier, add a short utility method to **GameScene.swift**:

```
func inGameMessage(text: String) {
   let message = MessageNode(message: text)
   message.position = CGPoint(x: CGRectGetMidX(frame), y:
CGRectGetMidY(frame))
   addChild(message)
}
```

In this method, you create a new message node and add it at the center of the scene. Once that's done, the physics engine will take care of the rest.

Now you'll add the methods that run the winning and losing sequences, and you'll use inGameMessage(_:) from there.

Losing scenario

First of all, you're going to add a method to restart the current level. To do that, you'll simply call presentScene(_:) again on the SKView of your game, and it will reload the whole scene.

Still in **GameScene.swift**, add this new method:

```
func newGame() {
    let scene = GameScene(fileNamed:"GameScene")
    scene!.scaleMode = scaleMode
    view!.presentScene(scene)
}
```

In just a few lines of code, you:

- Create a new instance of GameScene out of **GameScene.sks** by using the init(fileNamed:) initializer;

- Set the scale mode of the scene to match the scene's current sacale mode;

- Pass the new GameScene instance to presentScene(_:), which removes the current scene and replaces it with the shiny new scene.

With all preparations complete, it's time to add the initial version of the lose method to **GameScene.swift**:

```
func lose() {
  //1
  SKTAudio.sharedInstance().pauseBackgroundMusic()
  runAction(SKAction.playSoundFileNamed("lose.mp3",
waitForCompletion: false))

  //2
  inGameMessage("Try again...")

  //3
  performSelector("newGame", withObject: nil, afterDelay: 5)
}
```

With this snippet of code, you do a few things:

1. You play a fun sound effect when the player loses. To make the effect more prominent, you pause the in-game music by calling pauseBackgroundMusic() on SKTAudio. Then, you run an action to play the effect on the scene.

2. You also spawn a new in-game message that reads, "Try again...", to keep your players motivated. :]

3. Finally, you wait for five seconds and then restart the level by calling newGame().

That's it for now—locate didBeginContact(_:) and add the following line after print("FAIL"):

```
lose()
```

You now have a working fail sequence. Build and run the project, and give it a try:

Oops! Something isn't quite right, and it's a problem you've noticed before.

As the cat bounces off the floor, it produces numerous contact messages, and since the contact is always between the cat and the scene's edge, you get many calls to your shiny, new lose() method.

To prevent this from happening, you need a mechanism to stop in-game interactions once the player has failed or completed the level. This calls for a state machine!

For Cat Nap, you're going to build a very simple state machine, but don't let that sink your motivation level—you're going to learn much more about building solid game state machines in Chapter 15, "State Machines".

A basic state machine

Your Cat Nap state machine will handle two distinct states: when the level is playable, and when the level is inactive. In the latter state, contacts produced by bodies won't have any effect.

Add a new instance variable to your GameScene class to hold the state of your level:

```
var playable = true
```

The level is playable as soon as it loads and appears onscreen. However, you want the level to become inactive as soon as you call lose(), because the player should never be able to lose multiple times without trying again. :]

Insert the following line at the top of lose():

```
playable = false
```

Finally, to prevent more successful contacts, insert the following at the top of `didBeginContact(_:)`:

```
if !playable {
  return
}
```

This should suffice for now—your level is playable at launch. Then, as soon as the player fails, it becomes inactive. When the level restarts, it's playable again.

Build and run the program, and test it once more. You've solved the multi-message problem and the game restarts after a few seconds:

Good work—it was an easy fix that introduced you to the importance of handling your game state!

Playing an animation

There's something that feels incomplete about this losing sequence—the cat seems emotionless about his grand failure to comfortably sneak in a nap.

It's finally time to put the wake-up animation you designed in Chapter 8, "Scene Editor", to work.

Remember, you created the a wake up action in **CatWakeUp.sks**? To wrap up this section, you're going to show the wake animation when the player fails to solve the level.

Open **CatNode.swift** and add a new method:

```swift
func wakeUp() {
  // 1
  for child in children {
    child.removeFromParent()
  }
  texture = nil
  color = SKColor.clearColor()


  // 2
  let catAwake = SKSpriteNode(fileNamed:
"CatWakeUp")!.childNodeWithName("cat_awake")!

  // 3
  catAwake.moveToParent(self)
  catAwake.position = CGPoint(x: -30, y: 100)
}
```

You call this method on the cat node to "wake up" the cat. The method consist of two sections:

1. In the first section, you loop over all of the cat's child nodes—the cat "parts"—and remove them from the cat body. Then you set the current texture to `nil`. Finally, you set the cat's background to a transparent color, which effectively resets the cat to an empty node.

2. In the second section, you load **CatWakeUp.sks** and fetch the scene child named **cat_awake**. Review the contents of that .sks file, and you'll see that **cat_awake** is the name of the only sprite found there. This is also the sprite on which the **cat_wake** action runs.

3. Finally, you change the sprite's parent from the **CatWakeUp.sks** scene to the `CatNode`. You set the node's position to make sure that it will appear exactly over the existing texture.

> **Note**: I hope you noticed the use of `moveToParent:`. If a sprite already has a parent, you can't use `addChild(_:)` directly to add it elsewhere; `moveToParent(_:)` removes it from its current hierarchy and adds it at the new location you specify.

That's it! Switch back to **GameScene.swift** and add the following at the bottom of `lose()`:

```swift
catNode.wakeUp()
```

Build and run the project and enjoy your complete sequence:

Winning scenario

Now that you have a losing sequence, it's only fair to give the player a winning sequence. Add this new method to your GameScene class:

```
func win() {
  playable = false

  SKTAudio.sharedInstance().pauseBackgroundMusic()
  runAction(SKAction.playSoundFileNamed("win.mp3",
waitForCompletion: false))

  inGameMessage("Nice job!")

  performSelector("newGame", withObject: nil, afterDelay: 3)
}
```

This code looks almost identical to what you did in lose(), with few differences, of course. When you pause the music, you play an uplifting win song and show the rewarding **Nice job!** message.

Just like before, you'll add an extra method in your cat node class to load the winning animation. Open **CatNode.swift** and add the following:

```
func curlAt(scenePoint: CGPoint) {
  parent!.physicsBody = nil
  for child in children {
    child.removeFromParent()
  }
  texture = nil
  color = SKColor.clearColor()

  let catCurl = SKSpriteNode(fileNamed:
"CatCurl")!.childNodeWithName("cat_curl")!
  catCurl.moveToParent(self)
  catCurl.position = CGPoint(x: -30, y: 100)
}
```

This is exactly the same as `wakeUp()`, with a couple of differences:

1. You remove the cat's physics body, because you'll animate the cat manually into the bed;

2. You load the happy curl animation from **CatCurl.sks**.

`curlAt(_:)` expects a single `CGPoint` parameter, which is the bed location in the scene's coordinate system. To find the curl point in the cat coordinate system, you need to first convert the location. That's easy thanks to the `convertPoint(_:fromNode:)` API, which converts positions from one node's coordinate system to another node's coordinate system.

Append to the bottom of `curlAt(_:)`:

```
var localPoint = parent!.convertPoint(scenePoint, fromNode:
scene!)
localPoint.y += frame.size.height/3
```

In the first line, you call `convertPoint(_:fromNode:)` on the cat body's parent—that is, the cat reference you load from the .sks file. You need to work with the body's parent coordinates while the body itself is positioned at those coordinates. Thus, you need the target curl point within a coordinate system in which you can animate the body.

In the second line, you add one third of the cat's height to the curl point, which makes the curl happen toward the bottom of the bed, not in its center.

Finally, add the animation to the cat in `curlAt(:_)` in **CatNode.swift**:

```
runAction(SKAction.group([
  SKAction.moveTo(localPoint, duration: 0.66),
  SKAction.rotateToAngle(0, duration: 0.5)
]))
```

This action group animates the cat to the center of the bed, and it also straightens up the cat in case he was falling over.

You've reached the final steps to put everything together. Open **GameScene.swift** and in `win()`, append this line at the bottom:

```
catNode.curlAt(bedNode.position)
```

Then, inside `didBeginContact(_:)`, find the `print("SUCCESS")` line and add this line after it:

```
win()
```

Build and run the project. You now have a winning sequence in place (pun intended):

Believe it or not, you've completed another mini-game! And this time, your game also has a complete physics simulation. Give yourself a pat on the back.

Don't be sad that your game has only one level. You'll continue to work on Cat Nap in the next two chapters, adding two more levels as well as some crazy features before you're done.

Challenges

Make sure you aren't rushing through these chapters. You're learning a lot of new concepts and APIs, so iterating over what you've learned is the key to retaining it.

That's one reason why the challenges at the end of each chapter are so important. If you feel confident about everything you've covered so far in Cat Nap, move on to the challenge.

This chapter introduced a lot of new APIs, so in case you get stuck, the solutions are in the resources folder for this chapter. But have faith in yourself—you can do it!

Challenge 1: Count the bounces

Think about the in-game message you show when the player wins or loses the level. Your challenge is to fine-tune when it disappears from the scene.

More specifically, your challenge is to count the number of times the label bounces off the bottom margin of the screen and remove the message on exactly the fourth bounce. Working through this will teach you more about custom node behaviors, and it will be a nice iteration over what you've already learned.

Try implementing the solution on your own, but if you need a little help, follow the directions below.

1. Add a variable in MessageNode to keep track of the number of bounces. Also, add a didBounce() method that increases the counter and removes the node from its parent on the fourth bounce.

2. Enable contact detection between the label's physics body and the edge of the screen. To do that you will need to set the contactTestBitMask of MessageNode.

3. In didBeginContact(_:) of your GameScene class, add a check for contact between two physics bodies with the categories PhysicsCategory.Label and PhysicsCategory.Edge. Keep in mind, you need to add this check *before* the line if !playable {, because otherwise, your bounce contact messages will fire in vain.

Locate the node body by accessing its node property or by looking for the message node; for example:

```
let labelNode = (contact.bodyA.categoryBitMask ==
PhysicsCategory.Label) ? contact.bodyA.node : contact.bodyB.node
```

3. Once you grab the node, you can cast it to a MessageNode and call your custom method that increases its bounce counter. Finally, don't forget to add a contact mask to your custom label node, so that it produces contact notifications when it bounces off the scene's edge.

This exercise will get you on the right path to implementing more complicated contact handlers. Imagine the possibilities—all the custom actions you could make happen in a game depending on how many times two bodies touch, or how many bodies of one category touch the edge, and so forth.

Chapter 11: Advanced Physics

By Marin Todorov

In the last chapter, you saw how easy it is to create responsive game worlds with Sprite Kit, especially when using the scene editor. By now, you're a champion of creating sprites and physics bodies and configuring them to interact under simulated physics.

But perhaps you're already thinking in bigger terms. So far, you can move shapes by letting gravity, forces and impulses affect them. But what if you want to constrain the movement of shapes with respect to other shapes—for example, maybe you want to pin a hat to the top of the cat's head, and have it rotate back and forth based on physics? Dr. Seuss would be proud!

In this chapter, you'll learn how to do things like this by adding two new levels to Cat Nap—three, if you successfully complete the chapter's challenge! By the time you're done, you'll have brought your knowledge of Sprite Kit physics to an advanced level and will be able to apply this newfound force in your own apps.

> **Note**: This chapter begins where the previous chapter's Challenge 1 left off. If you were unable to complete the challenge or skipped ahead from an earlier chapter, don't worry—simply open the starter project from this chapter to pick up in the right place.

The Sprite Kit game loop, round 3

To get you back on track with Cat Nap, you're going to add one last touch to Level 1: a smarter failure detection system.

Specifically, you want to detect whether the cat is leaning to either side by more than 25 degrees. If he is, you want to wake up the cat, at which point the player should fail the level.

To achieve this, you'll check the position of the cat every frame, but only after the physics engine does its job. That means you have to understand a bit more about the Sprite Kit game loop.

Back in the third chapter of this book, you learned that the Sprite Kit game loop looks something like this:

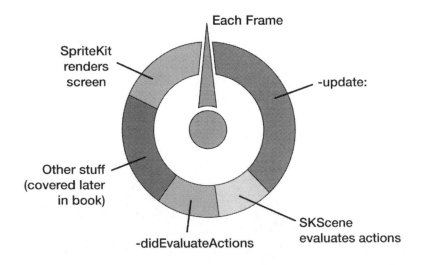

Now it's time to introduce the next piece of the game loop: simulating physics. Here's your new version of the loop:

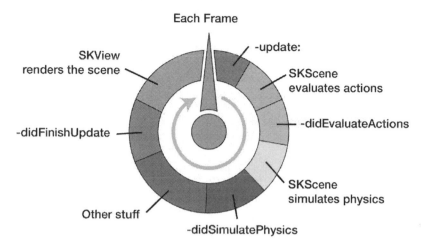

After evaluating the sprite actions, but just before rendering the sprites onscreen, Sprite Kit performs the physics simulation and moves the sprites and bodies accordingly, represented by the yellow chunk in your new diagram. At that point, you have a chance to perform any code you might like by implementing `didSimulatePhysics()`, represented by the red chunk.

This is the perfect spot to check if the cat is tilting too much!

> **Note**: The new loop also includes `didFinishUpdate()`. This is a method you can override if you want do something after all the other processing has beeen completed.

To write your code to check for the cat's tilt, you'll use a function from `SKTUtils`, the library of helper methods you added to the project in the previous chapter. In particular, you'll use a handy method that converts degrees into radians.

Make sure you have CatNap open where you left it off in the previous chapter's challenge. Then inside **GameScene.swift**, implement `didSimulatePhysics()` as follows:

```
override func didSimulatePhysics() {
  if playable {
    if fabs(catNode.parent!.zRotation) >
CGFloat(25).degreesToRadians() {
      lose()
    }
  }
}
```

Here you perform two tests:

- **Is the game currently playable?** You check if `playable` is `true` to see if the player is still solving the level.

- **Is the cat tilted too much?** Specifically, is the absolute value of the cat's `zRotation` property more than the radian equivalent of 25 degrees?

When both of these conditions are `true`, then you call `lose()` right away, because obviously the cat is falling over and should wake up immediately!

One more thing to note is that `catNode` never rotates; this node is contained by the cat reference and is therefore pinned to its parent node. That's why you need to keep an eye on the rotation of the cat as a whole by referencing `catNode.parent!`.

Build and run, and then fail the level on purpose. The cat wakes up while he's still in the air, before he even touches the ground.

This is more realistic behavior, as it's hard to sleep when falling to the ground!

Introducing Level 2

So far, you've been working on a game with a single game scene. Cat Nap, however, is a level-based puzzle game.

In this section of the chapter, you're going to give the game the ability to present different levels onscreen, and you'll add a second level right away. Level 2 will feature new interactive physics objects, like springs, ropes and hooks.

Except for this game, you'll call the springs *catapults*. See what I did there? =]

Fortunately for the cat, this level will have just one catapult. Here's how the level will look when you're finished:

I know, I know. That catapult underneath the cat and the hook on the ceiling look rather nefarious, but I promise no animals will be harmed in the making of this game.

To win the level, the player first needs to tap the catapult. This will launch the cat upward, where the hook will catch and hold him suspended. With the cat safely out of the way, the player can destroy the blocks. Once the blocks are destroyed, the player can tap the hook to release the cat, who will then descend safely to his bed below.

On the other hand, if the player destroys the blocks first and then taps the catapult, the cat won't rise high enough to reach the hook, causing the player to lose the level.

Loading levels

Lucky for you, you're already loading levels in your game.

You have a single level so far, and the level file is named **GameScene.sks**. You load it, show it onscreen, and then you implement the game logic in your GameScene class.

You need to create another **.sks** file for each of Cat Nap's levels. Then, you need to load and display these new levels, one after the next, as the player solves them.

First of all, to avoid confusion, rename **GameScene.sks** to **Level1.sks**.

Next, you need to add a factory method on your `GameScene` class that takes a level number and creates a scene by loading the corresponding **.sks** file from the game bundle.

To do this, add the following property and class function to `GameScene`:

```
//1
var currentLevel: Int = 0

//2
class func level(levelNum: Int) -> GameScene? {
  let scene = GameScene(fileNamed: "Level\(levelNum)")!
  scene.currentLevel = levelNum
  scene.scaleMode = .AspectFill
  return scene
}
```

You'll use the `currentLevel` property to hold the current level's number. The class method `level(_:)` takes in a number and calls `GameScene(fileNamed:)`. If the level file loads successfully, you set the current level number on the scene and scale correctly.

Now you need to make a few changes to your view controller. Open **GameViewController.swift** and find the following line in `viewDidLoad()`:

```
if let scene = GameScene(fileNamed: "GameScene") {
```

Replace it with this:

```
if let scene = GameScene.level(1) {
```

That's much nicer on the eye, isn't it?

Next, open **GameScene.swift** and locate `newGame()`. To improve it with the new factory method, replace the complete method body with this:

```
view!.presentScene(GameScene.level(currentLevel))
```

Build and run to verify the game works as usual.

Good work. Now you can focus on building Level 2.

Scene Editor, round 2

After doing so much in code, it'll be nice to use the scene editor again.

From Xcode's menu, select **File\New\File...**. Then choose **iOS\Resource\SpriteKit**

Scene and click **Next**.

Name the new file **Level2.sks** and click **Create**.

As soon as you save the file, Xcode opens it in the scene editor. Zoom out until you see the yellow border:

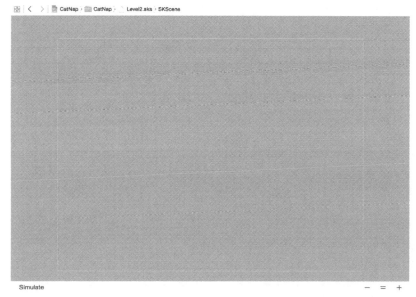

With the scene editor skills you already possess from previous chapters, setting up this scene will be simple—as well as a great way to review what you've learned.

First, resize the scene to 2048x1536:

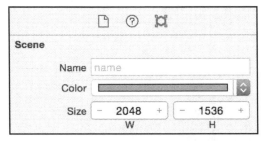

Next, add five color sprite objects to the scene and set their properties as follows:

- **Background**: Texture **background.png**, Position **(1024, 768)**
- **Bed**: Texture **cat_bed.png**, Name **bed**, Position **(1024, 272)**, Custom Class **BedNode**
- **Block1**: Texture **wood_horiz1.png**, Name **block**, Position **(1024, 260)**, Body Type **Bounding Rectangle**, Category Mask **2**, Collision Mask **43**, Custom Class **BlockNode**
- **Block2**: Texture **wood_horiz1.png**, Name **block**, Position **(1024, 424)**, Body Type **Bounding Rectangle**, Category Mask **2**, Collision Mask **43**, Custom Class **BlockNode**
- **Spring**: Texture **spring.png**, Name **spring**, Position **(1024, 588)**, Body Type **Bounding Rectangle**, Category Mask **32**, Collision Mask **11**, Custom Class **SpringNode**

Whoa, that's a lot of objects! Much of what you're doing is recreating the elements from Level 1: a background image, a cat bed, and some blocks.

For this level, you added a sprite for the spring; it uses a new physics category, 32, and a new custom class, SpringNode. You don't have those yet, but you can quickly add them right now.

Open **GameScene.swift** and find the PhysicsCategory struct at the top of the file. Add a new constant to use for your springs:

```
static let Spring:UInt32 = 0b100000 // 32
```

> **Note**: For practice, see if you can figure out why you set the category mask to 43 for the two blocks in the level. If you get stuck, open Calculator on your Mac, switch to Programmer mode and enter in 43 to see the number in binary.

Next, create a new file by choosing **File/New/File...** and select **iOS/Source/Cocoa Touch Class** for the template. Name the new class **SpringNode**, make it a subclass of

SKSpriteNode and click **Next**, then **Create**.

Xcode will automatically open the file. When it does, replace the contents of the file with this:

```
import SpriteKit

class SpringNode: SKSpriteNode, CustomNodeEvents,
InteractiveNode {

  func didMoveToScene() {

  }

  func interact() {

  }
}
```

Look familiar? Your custom node class implements the `CustomNodeEvents` protocol and has an empty `didMoveToScene()` method, where you'll add some code momentarily. In addition, this class conforms to `InteractiveNode`, because you want to let the player tap on the spring node and interact with it.

There's only one key component missing from your new level—the cat!

Open **Level2.sks** and drag in a **reference** from the Object Library:

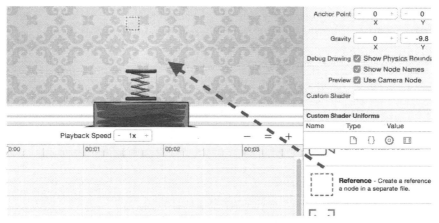

Give the reference object the following properties, matching the cat's configuration in Level 1:

• Name **cat_shared**, Reference **Cat.sks**, Position **(983, 894)**, Z Position **10**.

Next, it's time to test the level.

Head over to **GameViewController.swift** and replace `if let scene = GameScene.level(1) {` with this:

```
if let scene = GameScene.level(2) {
```

Now the game begins with Level 2, rather than Level 1. That's right: Not only does this make it quicker to test Level 2—now you can cheat in your own game! =]

Build and run the project, and you'll see the initial setup for your new level:

You'll see the cat pass straight through the spring. That happens because your existing code doesn't know about your new spring objects. You're about to change that.

Catapults

Since catapults are a new category of objects for your game, you need to tell your scene how other objects should interact with them. The code for this will be quite familiar to you, so I won't spell out all of the details; feel free to move through this part quickly.

Note: In this chapter, I use the words **catapults** and **springs** interchangeably.

To make the cat sit on top of the catapult, you need to enable collisions between the cat and the catapult.

Open **CatNode.swift**, and in `didMoveToScene()`, change the line responsible for setting the cat's `collisionBitMask` to include `PhysicsCategory.Spring`:

```
parent!.physicsBody!.collisionBitMask = PhysicsCategory.Block |
    PhysicsCategory.Edge | PhysicsCategory.Spring
```

Now your catapult and cat should behave as expected.

Build and run the game, and check it out.

One small change in code; one big step for sleepy cats!

Next, it's time to make the catapult hurl that kitty when the player taps on the spring sprite. It's actually quite easy; if the player taps on the catapult, you need to apply an impulse to the spring, which will then bounce the cat—if, of course, the cat is on top of the spring.

The first step is to enable user interaction on the spring node so it will react to taps.

Switch to **SpringNode.swift** and add the following line inside `didMoveToScene()`:

```
userInteractionEnabled = true
```

And just like you did for the block nodes, add the respective `UIResponder` method to detect taps:

```
override func touchesEnded(touches: Set<UITouch>, withEvent
event: UIEvent?) {
  super.touchesEnded(touches, withEvent: event)
  interact()
}
```

Now, add the code for the interaction in `interact()`:

```
userInteractionEnabled = false

physicsBody!.applyImpulse(CGVector(dx: 0, dy: 250),
  atPoint: CGPoint(x: size.width/2, y: size.height))

runAction(SKAction.sequence([
  SKAction.waitForDuration(1),
  SKAction.removeFromParent()
]))
```

When the player taps a spring node, you apply an impulse to its body using applyImpulse(_:atPoint:); this is similar to what you did in Chapter 9, "Beginning Physics", with the sand particles. Because a spring can "jump" only once, you disable the user input on that node as soon as it receives a tap. Finally, you remove the catapult after a delay of one second.

Build and run the game again, and this time, tap on the catapult:

Houston, we have lift off... and a slight problem.

Right now, when catapulted, the kitty flips through the air and lands on its head. That's why you need to add the ceiling hook to grab him!

The idea is that the catapult will bounce the kitty right onto the hook, which will hold him while the player clears the blocks. Once the blocks are gone, you'll release the kitty so he falls straight into his bed. Mrrow!

Joints: An overview

To implement the ceiling hook, you need **joints**. In Sprite Kit, there are five types of joints available, each of which lets you constrain the positions of two bodies relative to each other. This section describes them in turn.

> **Note**: Because joints are a heavily-used concept in physics-based games, it's a good idea to familiarize yourself with them.

Fixed joint

A fixed joint gives you the ability to attach two physics bodies together.

Imagine you have two objects and you nail them together with a few rusty nails. If you take one of them and throw it, the other one will fly right along with it.

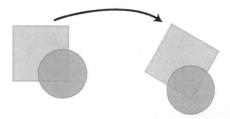

Sometimes, you want to make an object immoveable. The quickest way to do that is to fix it to the scene's edge loop, and you're ready to go.

Other times, you want a complex object a player can destroy—and perhaps break into many pieces. If that's the case, simply fix the pieces together, and when the player hits the object, remove the joints so the pieces fall apart.

Limit joint

You can use a limit joint to set the maximum distance between two physics bodies. Although the two bodies can move closer to each other, they can never be farther apart than the distance you specify.

Think of a limit joint as a soft but strong rope that connects two objects. In the diagram below, the ball is connected to the square via a limit joint; it can bounce around, but it can never move farther away than the length of the limit joint:

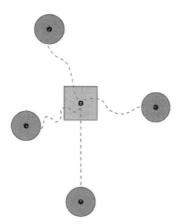

These types of joints are useful when you want to connect two objects, but let one move independently of the other within a certain radius—like a dog on a leash!

Spring joint

A spring joint is much like a limit joint, but the connection behaves more like a rubber band: it's elastic and springy.

Like a limit joint, a spring joint is useful for simulating rope connections, especially ropes made of elastic. If you have a bungee-jumping hero, the spring joint will be of great help!

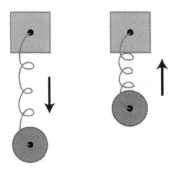

Pin joint

A pin joint fixes two physics bodies around a certain point, the anchor of the joint. Both bodies can rotate freely around the anchor point—if they don't collide, of course.

Think of the pin joint as a big screw that keeps two objects tightly together, but still allows them to rotate:

If you were to build a clock, you'd use a pin joint to fix the hands to the dial; if you were to build a physics body for an airplane, you'd use a pin joint to attach the propeller to the plane's nose.

Sliding joint

A sliding joint fixes two physics bodies on an axis along which they can freely slide; you can further define the minimum and maximum distances the two bodies can be from each other while sliding along the axis.

The two connected bodies behave as though they're moving on a rail with limits on the distance between them:

A sliding joint might come in handy if you're building a roller coaster game and you needed the two car objects to stay on the track, but to keep some distance from one another.

> **Note:** It's possible to apply more than one joint to a physics body. For example, you could use one pin joint to attach an hour hand to a clock face, and add a second pin joint to connect the minute hand to the clock face.

Joints in use

The easiest way to learn how to use joints is to try them out for yourself. And what better way to do that than by creating the hook object and attaching it to the ceiling.

Consider this blueprint for the hook object:

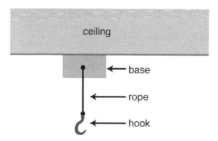

There's one body fixed to the ceiling (the base), another body for the hook, and a third body that connects them together (the rope).

To make this structure work, you'll be using two types of joints:

- **A fixed joint** to fix the base to the ceiling.
- **A spring joint** to connect the hook to the base. The spring joint will be your rope.

Using a fixed joint

First, you need to add the relevant sprites in the scene editor. Open **Level2.sks** and add two color sprites, configured as follows:

- **Hook mount**: Texture **wood_horiz1.png**, Position **(1024, 1466)**
- **Hook base**: Texture **hook_base.png**, Name **hookBase**, Position **(1024, 1350)**, Body Type **Bounding Rectangle**, Custom Class **HookNode**

hookBase is the node to which the hook and its rope will be attached. The base itself is going to be fixed on the ceiling by a joint to the scene edge body.

You might wonder what purpose the wood block serves. It doesn't even have a physics body! Take a look at the playable area on an iPhone and an iPad:

On a 4" iPhone, the scene cuts out somewhere just before the top edge of the hook base —it looks like the hook base is built into the ceiling. But remember that an iPad's screen aspect ratio is different, which is why on the iPad, you can see more of the scene. If it weren't for the wood piece on top, it would look like the hook base were just floating in midair.

So the wood block's only role is to make things look nice. On an iPhone, it's outside of the screen bounds, so the player won't even see it.

Perhaps you've noticed that the hook has a custom node class; you're going to add that to the project now.

Create a new file by choosing **File/New/File...**, and select the file template **iOS/Source/ Cocoa Touch Class**. Name the new class **HookNode**, make it a subclass of **SKSpriteNode** and click **Next** and then **Create**. Xcode will automatically open the file once it's created.

To clear the error you see in Xcode by default, replace `import UIKit` with:

```
import SpriteKit
```

HookNode is a little different than the other custom nodes you've created so far. Since the hook is a compound object made of a base, a swinging rope and the hook itself, you'll use only one custom class for the whole structure.

You're also going to create the rope and the hook in code rather than in the scene editor.

First, you need a way to access the parts of the hook, so add the following properties in **HookNode.swift**:

```
private var hookNode = SKSpriteNode(imageNamed: "hook")
private var ropeNode = SKSpriteNode(imageNamed: "rope")
private var hookJoint: SKPhysicsJointFixed!

var isHooked: Bool {
  return hookJoint != nil
}
```

The first two properties are the nodes you need in order to finish building the hook object, and hookJoint is something you'll use later when the kitty bounces and is "hooked" by the rope. Finally, there's a dynamic property named isHooked; this checks if there's already a stored physics joint in hookJoint.

Next, make your new class conform to the CustomNodeEvents protocol by adding the declaration to the class line:

```
class HookNode: SKSpriteNode, CustomNodeEvents {
```

Also, add the initial stub for didMoveToScene():

```
func didMoveToScene() {
  guard let scene = scene else {
    return
  }
}
```

You check to see if the node has already been added to the scene; if so, you bail out.

Now in didMoveToScene(), you're going to configure and add hookNode and ropeNode. Then, you're going to finish constructing the hook. You'll do this in a few steps.

First, add the following, after the guard statement but not within it:

```
let ceilingFix =
SKPhysicsJointFixed.jointWithBodyA(scene.physicsBody!, bodyB:
physicsBody!, anchor: CGPoint.zero)
scene.physicsWorld.addJoint(ceilingFix)
```

Here, you use a factory method of SKPhysicsJointFixed to create a joint instance between the current node's body and the scene's own body, which is the edge loop.

You're also giving the joint an anchor point, which tells the scene at what location to create the connection between the two bodies.

You always specify the anchor point in scene coordinates. When you attach a body to the scene's body, you can safely pass any value as the anchor point, so you use (0, 0). Also note that you must have already added the sprites as children of the scene before you can create the joint.

Finally, you add the joint to the scene's physics world. Now, these two bodies are connected until the end of time—or until you remove the joint.

> **Note:** When you create a fixed joint, the two bodies don't need to be touching—each body simply maintains its relative position from the anchor point.
>
> In addition, you could get this same behavior without using a joint at all. Instead, you could make the physics body static, either by unchecking the **Dynamic** field in the scene editor or by setting the dynamic property of the physicsBody to false. This would be more efficient for the physics engine, but you're using a fixed joint here for learning purposes.

Build and run the game, and you'll see the hook base fixed securely to the top of the screen:

> **Note**: If you don't see it, try running the game on an iPad or iPad Simulator.

Look at that line going from the bottom-left corner to the top of the scene—this is the debug physics drawing representing the joint you just created. It indicates there's a joint connecting the scene itself—with a position of (0, 0)—to the hook.

Since you're on a roll, add the sprite for the rope, too.

Back in **HookNode.swift**, and in didMoveToScene(), add the following at the end:

```
ropeNode.anchorPoint = CGPoint(x: 0, y: 0.5)
ropeNode.zRotation = CGFloat(270).degreesToRadians()
ropeNode.position = position
scene.addChild(ropeNode)
```

This positions the rope just under the hook base, sets its anchor point to be its top—since it's going to swing like a pendulum—and aligns it so it points down.

Now it's time to add the hook itself, which will use a different type of joint.

Using a spring joint

First, you need one more body category for the hook, so switch back to **GameScene.swift** and add this new value to the PhysicsCategory:

```
static let Hook:  UInt32 = 0b1000000 // 64
```

Now, go back to **HookNode.swift** and add the following to the end of didMoveToScene():

```
hookNode.position = CGPoint(
  x: position.x,
  y: position.y - ropeNode.size.width )

hookNode.physicsBody =
  SKPhysicsBody(circleOfRadius: hookNode.size.width/2)
hookNode.physicsBody!.categoryBitMask = PhysicsCategory.Hook
hookNode.physicsBody!.contactTestBitMask = PhysicsCategory.Cat
hookNode.physicsBody!.collisionBitMask = PhysicsCategory.None

scene.addChild(hookNode)
```

This creates a sprite, sets its position and creates a physics body for it. It also sets the category bitmask to PhysicsCategory.Hook, and sets the contactTestBitMask such that it detects contacts between the hook and the cat.

The hook doesn't need to collide with any other objects. Later, you'll implement some custom behavior for it that default Sprite Kit physics doesn't provide.

> **Note**: You position the hook sprite just under the ceiling base, because the distance between the base and the hook is precisely the length of the rope that will hold them together.

Now, create a spring joint to connect the hook and its ceiling holder by adding the following to didMoveToScene():

```
let hookPosition = CGPoint(x: hookNode.position.x,
  y: hookNode.position.y+hookNode.size.height/2)

let ropeJoint =
SKPhysicsJointSpring.jointWithBodyA(physicsBody!,
  bodyB: hookNode.physicsBody!,
  anchorA: position,
  anchorB: hookPosition)
scene.physicsWorld.addJoint(ropeJoint)
```

First, you calculate the position of the hookNode where the joint should attach itself and store that position in hookPosition.

Then, using a factory method similar to the one you used for the ceiling joint, you connect the hookNode body and the hook's base body with a spring joint. You also specify the precise points in the scene's coordinate system where the rope connects to the two bodies.

Build and run the game now. If all's well, you'll see your hook hanging in the air just under the ceiling:

The rope joint works fine, but that rope doesn't move.

The Sprite Kit game loop, round 4

At long last, it's time to introduce the final missing piece of the Sprite Kit game loop.

As you can see below, after Sprite Kit finishes simulating physics, it performs one last step: applying something named **constraints** to the scene and notifying your scene that this has happened.

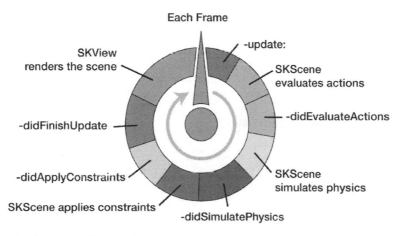

Let's take a look at how this works.

Constraints: An overview

Constraints are a handy Sprite Kit feature that let you easily ensure certain relationships are true regarding the position and rotation of sprites within your game.

The best way to understand constraints is to see them in action.

Open **GameScene.swift** and add the following code to the end of didMoveToView(_:):

```
let rotationConstraint =  SKConstraint.zRotation(
  SKRange(lowerLimit: -π/4, upperLimit: π/4))
catNode.parent!.constraints = [rotationConstraint]
```

There are two steps to using a constraint:

- **Create the constraint**. This example creates a constraint that limits z rotation from -45° to 45°, and applies it to the cat node.

- **Add the constraint to a node**. To add the constraint to a node, simply add it to the constraints array on the node.

> **Note**: To type π in your source code, press and hold the **Alt** key on your keyboard and press **P**. π is a constant defined in SKTUtils; you can press Command and click on it in Xcode to jump to its definition. If you prefer, you can use CGFloat(M_PI) instead.

After Sprite Kit finishes simulating the physics, it runs through each node's constraints and updates the position and rotation of the node so that the constraint is met.

Build and run to see this in action:

As you can see, even though the physics simulation sometimes determines that the cat should fall over beyond 45°, during the constraint phase of the game loop, Sprite Kit updates the cat's rotation to 45° so the constraint remains true.

This was just a test, so comment out the previous code:

```
//let rotationConstraint =
//  SKConstraint.zRotation(
// SKRange(lowerLimit: −π/4, upperLimit: π/4))
//catNode.parent!.constraints = [rotationConstraint]
```

You could also add constraints to do such things as:

- Limit a sprite so it stays within a certain rectangle;
- Make a turret in your game point in the direction in which it's shooting;
- Constrain a sprite's movement along the x-axis;
- Limit the rotation of a sprite to a certain range.

After this crash course in constraints, you're ready to use a real constraint in your Cat Nap game. Specifically, you'll finish the hook object by adding the final piece: the rope constraint.

Implementing a rope with a constraint

Now you're going to use a constraint to make sure the rope is always oriented toward the hook sprite, making it appear as if the rope is connected to the hook.

In **HookNode.swift**, add the following code at the end of didMoveToScene():

```
let range = SKRange(lowerLimit: 0.0, upperLimit: 0.0)
let orientConstraint = SKConstraint.orientToNode(hookNode,
offset: range)
ropeNode.constraints = [orientConstraint]
```

SKConstraint.orientToNode(_:offset:) produces a constraint object that automatically changes the zRotation of the node to which its being applied, so that the node always points toward another "target" node.

You can also provide an offset range to the constraint if you don't want to orient the node with perfect precision. Since you want the end of the rope and the hook to be tightly connected, you provide a zero range for the constraint.

Finally, you set the orientConstraint as the sole constraint for the ropeNode.

One last step. There's nothing that moves the hook—which makes it look kind of odd. Add this line to the end of didMoveToScene():

```
hookNode.physicsBody!.applyImpulse(CGVector(dx: 50, dy: 0))
```

This applies an impulse to the hook node so that it swings from its base.

Build and run the game again. Check out your moving, customized level object:

Remember, there are two things going on here that make this behavior work:

• You set up a **joint** connecting the hook to the base. This makes it so the hook is always a certain distance from the base, so it appears to "swing" from the base.

• You set up a **constraint** that makes the rope always orient itself toward the hook so that it appears to follow the hook.

Together, this makes for a pretty sweet effect!

> **Note**: A previous version of this chapter instructed readers to manually orient the rope inside the scene's `update()` method. On every invocation of `update()`, the code calculated the angle between the base and hook sprites and set this angle for the `zRotation` of the rope.
>
> This is still a perfectly valid strategy, but since Sprite Kit now has built-in constraints that can handle this for you, this edition uses the new approach. In your games, choose whichever is easiest for you.

There's one thing I should mention to keep my conscience clear: Right now, the rope is represented by just one sprite. That means your rope is more like a rod.

If you'd like to create an object that better resembles a rope, you could create several shorter sprite segments and connect them to each other, like so:

In this case, you might want to create physics bodies for each rope segment and connect them to each other with pin joints.

More constraints

So far, you've seen examples of the `zRotation()` and `orientToNode(_:offset:)` constraints.

There are a number of other types of constraints you can create in Sprite Kit beyond these. Here's a reference of what's available:

- `positionX()`, `positionY()` and `positionX(y:)`: These let you restrict the position of a sprite to within a certain range on the x-axis, y-axis or both. For example, you could use these to restrict the movement of a sprite to be within a certain rectangle on the screen.

- `orientToPoint(_:offset:)` and `orientToPoint(_:inNode:offset:)`: Just like you can make a sprite orient itself toward another sprite, as you made the rope orient itself toward the hook, you can make a sprite always orient itself toward a certain point. For example, you could use these to make a turret point toward where the user taps.

- `distance(_:toNode:)`, `distance(_:toPoint:)` and `distance(_:toPoint:inNode)`: These let you ensure that two nodes, or a node and a point, are always within a certain distance of each other. The function is similar to a limit joint, except these work on any node, whether or not it has a physics body.

Creating and removing joints dynamically

You need to add a few final touches to get the whole cat-hooking process to work: You need to check for hook-to-cat contact, and you need to create and remove a joint to fix the cat to the rope dynamically.

Open **GameScene.swift** and scroll to `didBeginContact()`. This is the place where you detect when object bodies in your game touch. You need to check if the two contacting bodies are the hook and the cat. You also need to do an additional check to see if they're already hooked together.

To do these checks, you need an outlet to the hook node. Add a new property to **GameScene.swift**:

```
var hookNode: HookNode?
```

Next, you need to look through the scene hierarchy to find out if there's a hook node. Don't forget, the other levels don't have a hook, and that's why you need an Optional value for that property.

OK! Next, at the bottom of `didMoveToView(_:)`, add the following:

```
hookNode = childNodeWithName("hookBase") as? HookNode
```

That line should be familiar; you simply locate the node by name and assign it to the property you created earlier.

Now scroll back to `didBeginContact()` and add the check for a hook-to-cat contact:

```
if collision == PhysicsCategory.Cat | PhysicsCategory.Hook &&
   hookNode?.isHooked == false {
   hookNode!.hookCat(catNode)
}
```

You check if the collision bitmask matches the cat and hook categories, and that the two aren't hooked together already. If both are true, you call hookCat(_:) on the hook node. Of course, this method doesn't exist yet, so you'll get an error, but that's an easy problem to fix.

Go back to **HookNode.swift** and add a new method to hook the cat:

```
func hookCat(catNode: SKNode) {
  catNode.parent!.physicsBody!.velocity = CGVector(dx: 0, dy: 0)
  catNode.parent!.physicsBody!.angularVelocity = 0
}
```

First, you manually alter the physics simulation by forcing a velocity and angular velocity of zero on the cat's body. You do this to calm things down when the cat's about to get hooked; you don't want to make players wait too long before their next moves while they wait for the hook to stop swinging.

The important point here is that you can manually alter the physics simulation. How great is that? Don't be afraid to do this—making the game fun is your top priority.

Now, add the following to that same method:

```
let pinPoint = CGPoint(
  x: hookNode.position.x,
  y: hookNode.position.y + hookNode.size.height/2)

hookJoint =
SKPhysicsJointFixed.jointWithBodyA(hookNode.physicsBody!,
  bodyB: catNode.parent!.physicsBody!, anchor: pinPoint)
scene!.physicsWorld.addJoint(hookJoint)

hookNode.physicsBody!.contactTestBitMask = PhysicsCategory.None
```

With that block of code, you calculate the position where the two bodies will be fixed together. Using this position, you create a new SKPhysicsJointFixed to connect the hook and cat, and then you add it to the world.

You also need to make didSimulatePhysics() respect the fact that the kitty is "hooked", so that the game is OK with rotating to angles more than the margin of 45 degrees.

Open **GameScene.swift** and inside didSimulatePhysics(), change the if condition from if playable { to this:

```
if playable && hookNode?.isHooked != true {
```

Now when the cat swings on the hook, he won't wake up.

Build and run the game, and play around.

When the cat hangs from the ceiling, you can safely destroy the blocks over the cat bed. But you're still missing one thing—the cat needs to fall off the hook and into the bed. To make that happen, you need to remove the joint you just added.

This time, add the method to destroy the joint before you call it. Open **HookNode.swift** and add the following:

```
func releaseCat() {
  hookNode.physicsBody!.categoryBitMask = PhysicsCategory.None
  hookNode.physicsBody!.contactTestBitMask =
PhysicsCategory.None
  hookJoint.bodyA.node!.zRotation = 0
  hookJoint.bodyB.node!.zRotation = 0
  scene!.physicsWorld.removeJoint(hookJoint)
  hookJoint = nil
}
```

In this method, you simply undo what you did in hookCat(_:). You remove the joint connecting the hook and the cat. Then, you straighten up the cat and the hook.

Next, you'll add the code to let the cat fall off the hook. In the game, the player will need to tap the cat while it swings in midair.

Here you encounter a new problem: The player needs to tap on the cat node, but the hook node needs to react to this action. You don't want to couple the hook and the cat by making them know about each other in some way. You want to keep nodes de-coupled, since different levels feature different node combinations.

To keep the nodes independent from each other, you'll use notifications.

Each time the player taps on the cat, it will send a notification, and nodes that are interested in this event will have the chance to catch the broadcast and react in whatever way is necessary.

First, you're going to handle taps on the cat node. Open **CatNode.swift** and add the following to didMoveToScene():

```
userInteractionEnabled = true
```

Just like before, you need to make this class adhere to InteractiveNode.

Add the protocol to the class declaration:

```
class CatNode: SKSpriteNode, CustomNodeEvents, InteractiveNode {
```

As soon as you do that, Xcode will complain about missing the required protocol method, so add a stub for now:

```
func interact() {
}
```

Then, outside of the class body and just under import SpriteKit, define a new notification name:

```
let kCatTappedNotification = "kCatTappedNotification"
```

Now add the method to handle touches:

```
override func touchesEnded(touches: Set<UITouch>, withEvent
event: UIEvent?) {
  super.touchesEnded(touches, withEvent: event)
  interact()
}
```

Each time the player taps on the cat, a notification needs to be sent via NSNotificationCenter. To make that happen, add the following line of code inside interact():

```
NSNotificationCenter.defaultCenter().postNotificationName(
  kCatTappedNotification, object: nil)
```

You'll do more in interact(), but for now, you simply broadcast a kCatTappedNotification.

> **Note:** This time around, you don't disable user interactions inside interact(). Since other nodes might implement custom logic based on taps on the cat, you can't speculate whether or not further touches on that node would be of interest. To be safe, you keep accepting touches and broadcasting the same notification over and over again.

Next, you're going to observe for the kCatTappedNotification. If one is received, you're going to release the cat from the hook, but—needless to say—only if the cat is already hooked.

Open **HookNode.swift** and in didMoveToScene(), add the following:

```
NSNotificationCenter.defaultCenter().addObserver(self,
  selector: "catTapped", name: kCatTappedNotification, object:
  nil)
```

This code "listens" for a notification named kCatTappedNotification. If it "hears" a notification, it will invoke the catTapped() method on the CatNode class. Of course, you still need to add that method, so do that now:

```
func catTapped() {
  if isHooked {
    releaseCat()
  }
}
```

In catTapped(), you simply check if the cat is currently hanging from the hook, and in that case, you call releaseCat to let it go. That's all!

Build and run the game again, and try to land the cat on the bed. You probably don't need this advice, but: tap on the catapult, tap on all the blocks, and then tap the cat to solve the level.

Creating joints dynamically is a fun and powerful technique. I hope to see you use it a lot in your own games!

Compound shapes

It's time to move on to the third level of Cat Nap.

In this level, you'll tackle another game physics concept, one related to body complexity. With this in mind, have a look at the completed Level 3 and try to guess what's new compared to the previous levels:

You guessed right if you said that in Level 3, one of the blocks has a more complicated shape than your average wooden block.

Perhaps you also noticed that the shape is broken into two sub-shapes. Maybe you even wondered why it was done that way instead of being constructed as a polygon shape, like the shape in the challenge in Chapter 9, "Beginning Physics".

Sometimes in games, for reasons related to game logic, you need an object that's more complex than a single image with a physics body. To better understand the problem, let's go back in time, I mean - back in chapters.

Do you remember your old friend the zombie from the Zombie Conga minigame?

In a physics based game a zombie would have quite a complex shape and you might be temped to use a single texture for it. But if you make the zombie body-parts separate nodes with separate physics bodies you could make him wave his hands, move his legs, etc.

Also - everyone knows that when zombies don't keep a strict diet of fresh brains they start loosing limbs. You have surely seen your green friends drop an arm or a jaw on the way while they chase the hero in the latest Hollywood horror movie.

For example if you use separate nodes for the zombie arms you could simply "detach" them during any point in your game for an added comical effect.

Having said that, in this section you'll build a simple compound body for the next level of Cat Nap.

Designing the third level

Just as before, replace the starting level in **GameViewController.swift**:

```
if let scene = GameScene.level(3) {
```

Creating the third level of Cat Nap in the scene editor will follow much the same process as for Level 2.

Select the **Scenes** group in the project navigator. From Xcode's menu, select **File/New/ File...** and then **iOS/Resource/SpriteKit Scene**. Click **Next**, save the file as **Level3.sks**, and click **Create**.

You'll be rewarded, as usual, with the sight of an empty game scene. Sorry, no flashing lights, screaming fans or bells and whistles. But hey, maybe they'll add that in a future release. =]

OK, first, resize the scene to 2048x1536 points. Then, add the following color sprite objects to the empty scene:

- **Background**: Texture **background.png**, Position **(1024, 768)**
- **Bed**: Texture **cat_bed.png**, Name **bed**, Position **(1024, 272)**, Custom Class **BedNode**
- **Block1**: Texture **wood_square.png**, Name **block**, Position **(946, 276)**, Body Type **Bounding Rectangle**, Category Mask **2**, Collision Mask **11**, Custom Class **BlockNode**, Z Position **2**
- **Block2**: Texture **wood_square.png**, Name **block**, Position **(946, 464)**, Body Type **Bounding Rectangle**, Category Mask **2**, Collision Mask **11**, Custom Class **BlockNode**, Z Position **2**
- **Block3**: Texture **wood_vert2.png**, Name **block**, Position **(754, 310)**, Body Type **Bounding Rectangle**, Category Mask **2**, Collision Mask **11**, Custom Class **BlockNode**, Z Position **2**
- **Block4**: Texture **wood_vert2.png**, Name **block**, Position **(754, 552)**, Body Type **Bounding Rectangle**, Category Mask **2**, Collision Mask **11**, Custom Class **BlockNode**, Z Position **2**

- **Stone1**: Texture **rock_L_vert.png**, Name **stone**, Position **(1282, 434)**, Custom Class **StoneNode**

- **Stone2**: Texture **rock_L_horizontal.png**, Name **stone**, Position **(1042, 714)**, Custom Class **StoneNode**

Finally, drag in a **reference** from the Object Library. Give the reference object the following properties:

- Name **cat_shared**, Reference **Cat.sks**, Position **(998, 976)**.

This is the complete setup for Level 3.

Build and run the game to see what you have so far:

The level in its current state doesn't look very good. The cat falls through the stone L-shaped block as if the block weren't in the scene at all. And no wonder—you didn't create any bodies for the two blocks used to build the L-shape. In the next section, you'll learn how to create a complex body that matches the shape of the new stone block.

Making compound objects

For your stone nodes, you'll have an even more elaborate initialization than for the hook.

You'll develop a custom class called StoneNode. When you add it to the scene, it will search for all stone pieces, remove them from the scene and create a new compound node to hold them all together. As you can see, when it comes to creating custom node behavior, the sky's the limit!

First, create a new file by choosing **File/New/File...** and selecting **iOS/Source/Cocoa Touch Class** for the template. Name the new class **StoneNode**, make it a subclass of **SKSpriteNode** and click **Create**. Xcode will automatically open the new file.

To clear the error you see in Xcode, replace the default contents with the following:

```
import SpriteKit

class StoneNode: SKSpriteNode, CustomNodeEvents, InteractiveNode
{

  func didMoveToScene() {

  }

  func interact() {

  }
}
```

This code looks familiar by now: You create a custom `SKSpriteNode` subclass and adapt your `CustomNodeEvents` protocol.

Next, add the method that will look through the scene nodes and bind together all the stone pieces. Make it a static method:

```
static func makeCompoundNode(inScene scene: SKScene) -> SKNode {
  let compound = StoneNode()
  compound.zPosition = -1

}
```

You initialize an empty `StoneNode` object to hold your stone pieces, and give it a `zPosition` of –1 to make sure the empty node doesn't "stay" in front of some other nodes.

> **Note**: Don't worry about the error. That will disappear after you finishing adding the rest of the code.

Next, find all the stone pieces and remove them from the scene. Then, add each one to `compound`, instead:

```
for stone in scene.children.filter({node in node is StoneNode})
{
  stone.removeFromParent()
  compound.addChild(stone)
}
```

You filter the scene child nodes, taking only the ones of type `StoneNode`. Then, you simply move them from their current places into the hierarchy of the `compound` node.

Next, you need to create physics bodies for each of these pieces. You'll just loop over all the stone nodes now contained in compound node and create a physics body for each one:

```
let bodies = compound.children.map({node in
  SKPhysicsBody(rectangleOfSize: node.frame.size, center:
node.position)
})
```

With this code, you store all the bodies in the bodies array, because in the next bit of code, you'll be supplying them to the initializer of SKPhysicsBody(bodies:) and creating a compound physics body out of all the pieces.

Do that now by adding the following:

```
compound.physicsBody = SKPhysicsBody(bodies: bodies)
compound.physicsBody!.collisionBitMask = PhysicsCategory.Edge |
PhysicsCategory.Cat | PhysicsCategory.Block
compound.physicsBody!.categoryBitMask = PhysicsCategory.Block
compound.userInteractionEnabled = true
compound.zPosition = 1

return compound
```

SKPhysicsBody(bodies:) takes all of the bodies you provide and binds them together; you set the result as the body of the compound node. Finally, you set the collision bitmask of the stone node so that it collides with the cat, the other blocks and the edge of the screen.

Before returning the ready-for-use compound node, you enable user interactions on it. That way, the player can't tap on the separate pieces; only the compound node will accept taps.

> **Note**: Now that you're returning a valid object, the error should be resolved.

All that's left to do is call the new method from didMoveToScene(), so do that now:

```
let levelScene = scene

if parent == levelScene {
  levelScene!.addChild(StoneNode.makeCompoundNode(inScene:
levelScene!))
}
```

For each node, you check if its parent is levelScene. If it is, that means the node hasn't been moved to the compound node, in which case you call makeCompoundNode(inScene:).

Since you're removing the stone nodes from their parents before adding them to `compound` within `makeCompoundNode(inScene:)`, they lose their link to the game scene. That's why, before you start modifying the nodes, you store a pointer to the current scene object in `levelScene` and use that variable until the end of the method.

Build and run the game, and behold the coveted L-shaped stone in all its compound glory!

Destroy one of the **wooden** blocks on the left to see the two stone pieces now behave as one solid body:

Victory! You have a compound body in your scene.

If you try to solve the level, it won't work; that's because you haven't added interactivity to the stone blocks yet.

Switch back to **StoneNode.swift** and override the `UIResponder` method to react to touches:

```
override func touchesEnded(touches: Set<UITouch>, withEvent
event: UIEvent?) {
  super.touchesEnded(touches, withEvent: event)
  interact()
}
```

Then add the relevant code in `interact()`:

```
userInteractionEnabled = false

runAction( SKAction.sequence([
  SKAction.playSoundFileNamed("pop.mp3", waitForCompletion:
false),
  SKAction.removeFromParent()
]))
```

Note that `interact()` will be called on your compound node, so calling `removeFromParent()` will remove the compound node and both of the pieces it contains. Two for the price of one!

No matter which of the pieces the player taps, you remove *all* of the pieces by removing the node that holds them.

Build and run the game again. This time, you'll be able to solve the level.

Level progression

Until this point, you've worked on one level at a time, so you've manually specified which level to load. However, that won't work for players—they expect to proceed to the next level after winning!

This is quite easy to implement. Begin by setting the game to load Level 1. Change the line that loads the scene in **GameViewController.swift** so it looks like this:

```
if let scene = GameScene.level(1) {
```

Then, in **GameScene.swift**, add the following code at the beginning of `win()`. Make sure you add it before all of the other code:

```
if (currentLevel < 3) {
  currentLevel++
}
```

Now, every time the player completes a level, the game will move on to the next one.

Finally, to raise the stakes, add this to the beginning of `lose()`:

```
if (currentLevel > 1) {
  currentLevel--
}
```

That'll certainly make the player think twice before tapping a block!

Congratulations - you now have three unique levels for Cat Nap. You've learned how to use the scene editor and how to create custom classes for your nodes. You've even learned how to implement custom behavior. From here on out, you're ready to start working on your own level-based game. The principles you learned in the last four chapters remain the same in any physics game.

There's one more chapter with Cat Nap to go, where you'll be learning about some more advanced types of nodes you can use in your game. But before you move on - try your hand at the challenge below!

Challenges

By now, you've come a long way toward mastering physics in Sprite Kit.

And because I'm so confident in your skills, I've prepared a challenge for you that will require a solid understanding of everything you've done in the last three chapters—and will ask even more of you.

Challenge 1: Add one more level to Cat Nap

Your challenge is to develop an entirely new level by yourself. If you do everything just right, the finished level will look like this:

As you can see, this time, besides blocks, there's a seesaw between the poor cat and its bed. This cat sure has a hard life.

And yes, it's a real seesaw; it rotates about its center and is fully interactive. And you developed it all by yourself! Er, sorry—you *will* develop it all by yourself. See, I have confidence in you. :]

I'll lay down the main points and you can take it from there.

Here are the objects to place in **Level4.sks**:

- **Background**: Texture **background.png**, Position **(1024, 768)**

- **Bed**: Texture **cat_bed.png**, Name **bed**, Position **(1024, 272)**, Custom Class **BedNode**

- **Block1**: Texture **wood_square.png**, Name **block**, Position **(1024, 626)**, Body type **Bounding Rectangle**, Category Mask **2**, Collision Mask **11**, Custom Class **BlockNode**

- **Block2**: Texture **wood_square.png**, Name **block**, Position **(1024, 266)**, Body type **Bounding Rectangle**, Category Mask **2**, Collision Mask **11**, Custom Class **BlockNode**

- **Seesaw base**: Texture **wood_square.png**, Name **seesawBase**, Position **(514, 448)**, Body type **Bounding Rectangle**, Uncheck **Dynamic** checkbox under Body Type, Category Mask **0**

- **Seesaw**: Texture **ice.png**, Name **seesaw**, Position **(518, 440)**, Body type **Bounding Rectangle**, Category Mask **2**, Collision Mask **11**

And, of course, the cat reference:

- Name **cat_shared**, Position **(996, 943)**, Z position **10**

Once you've placed these objects, the scene should look something like this:

There's not much left to do from here—I'll assume you've done everything perfectly so far!

You'll need to fix the seesaw board to its base on the wall. Do that by creating a pin joint that will anchor the center of the board to the center of the base and let the board rotate around that anchor, like so:

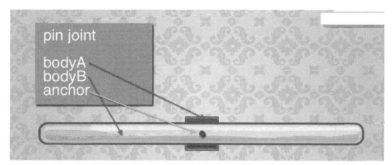

You can create a pin joint in two ways. First, create it in code using `SKPhysicsJointPin.jointWithBodyA(bodyB:anchor:)` to make sure you understand how that works. You'll need to find the node by name and use it to create the joint.

After that, you can remove that code and do the much simpler thing: Check the **Pinned** checkbox in the scene editor, in the seesaw's **Physics Definition** section. This will create a pin joint that connects the node to the scene at the node's anchor point.

That's it. Try solving the level yourself. I'm not going to give you any other tips besides the fact that the order in which you destroy the blocks matters.

Chapter 12: Crop, Video, and Shape Nodes

By Marin Todorov

In the very first chapter of this book, you learned that all of the visual elements in your game scene are nodes. You used a number of different nodes by creating instances of classes that inherit from SKNode.

Whether you created a node from code, or added them using the scene editor, they all inherited from the SKNode base class.

Here's a quick review of the nodes you've used so far:

- **SKNode**: An empty node that doesn't draw anything on the screen; use it to group other nodes by adding them as children to this node.

- **SKScene**: This node represents a single *screen* or a level in your game; add all your level nodes directly or indirectly to this node.

- **SKLabelNode**: From the game score to the player's remaining lives to any in-game message—it's all done with this node.

- **SKSpriteNode**: You've been using this node quite often; it displays an image or a sequence of images onscreen via an action. This is generally the node you use the most when designing a scene.

In this chapter, you'll continue working on Cat Nap, and in the process, you'll learn about three advanced types of nodes:

- **SKCropNode**: This node lets you mask the contents of a node, including its child nodes. This comes in handy when you want to *crop out* part of a texture.

- **SKVideoNode**: This node lets you include videos in your games. As you've probably experienced, developers often use videos to create richer gameplay.

- **SKShapeNode**: This node lets you draw shapes onscreen. You can draw shapes of different complexities, from rectangles and circles to any arbitrary shape.

If these three nodes have anything in common, it's that they all let you add unique effects to your games. These nodes might not seem like much at first, but by the end of this chapter, you'll be able to create amazing and advanced things using them.

Make no mistake—advanced does not necessarily mean difficult. You'll probably find this chapter easier than you expect, and when you're done, you just might have the urge to celebrate with some disco moves.

Without further ado, it's time to add two more levels to Cat Nap.

> **Note:** This chapter begins where the previous chapter's Challenge 1 left off. If you were unable to complete the challenge or skipped ahead from an earlier chapter, don't worry—you can simply open the starter project from this chapter to pick up in the right place.

Getting started

Open the project in Xcode. Then, open the **Assets.xcassets** catalogue.

To work through this chapter, you'll need some extra resources. Look in the **starter \resources** folder for this chapter and drag the **textures** folder into your project's **Assets.xcassets** catalogue. Included in this folder are additional textures you'll need to build this chapter's levels.

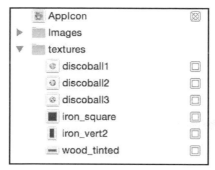

Then, drag the **media** folder into your project—*not* into the assets catalogue, but into the **project navigator**. This folder contains a video that you'll use in this section to spice up one of the new levels and the audio track to go along with it.

Since you're already a pro with the scene editor, I won't ask you to create the last two levels of Cat Nap from scratch. Instead, open the **levels** folder inside **Resources** and drag **Level5.sks** and **Level6.sks** into your project.

To let the player progress to these new levels, open **GameScene.swift** and inside win(), change if (currentLevel < 4) { to this:

```
if (currentLevel < 6) {
```

Also, to save yourself some time while developing, open **GameViewController.swift** and inside viewDidLoad(), change if let scene = GameScene.level(1) { to this:

```
if let scene = GameScene.level(5) {
```

With that, you've completed the project setup and you can lay your hands on SKCropNode to do some cutouts. Snip snip!

Crop nodes

In previous chapters, you used SKSpriteNode to show textures onscreen. For example, if you wanted to display a picture of the main character from this book's first mini-game, Zombie Conga, you could easily do that by creating a new SKSpriteNode and adding it to your scene like so (don't add this code; this is just an example):

```
let picture = SKSpriteNode(imageNamed: "picture")
picture.position = CGPoint(x: 200.0, y: 150.0)
addChild(picture)
```

You would see the picture show up at full size:

But what if you wanted to create a node that's not rectangular in shape? So far, you've used only rectangular textures; when you needed a different shape, you simply used images with transparent backgrounds.

Using transparency works most of the time, but if you're creating a more advanced game, you'll eventually need to take a normal rectangular texture and cut out an arbitrary piece of it to use in your scene.

To crop the contents of a texture, you can apply a mask and cut out only the content you want to keep:

Imagine using a cookie cutter: You press the cutter onto the dough, and it cuts out a piece of the dough in the shape of the cutter. And that's your cookie!

To use `SKCropNode` to achieve a similar effect, you follow four easy steps:

1. **Create a new SKCropNode**. This node doesn't display anything by default; it's only a container node.

2. **Add one or more child nodes** of any type you like to the crop node: labels, sprite nodes and so forth.

3. **Set the crop mask**. The mask is also a node and can be any type, such as a sprite node or a label. The mask node's contents should have transparent and opaque areas; opaque areas will preserve their content, while transparent areas will be masked— that is, hidden or cut out.

4. **Add the crop node to the scene**. Like any other node, you need to add the crop node to the scene to see its contents.

The process looks much like this:

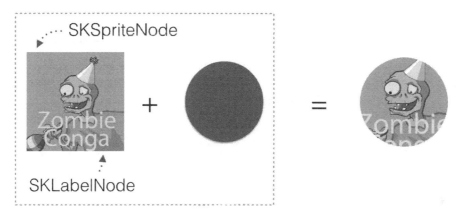

SKCropNode

In this example, a crop node has two child nodes: a sprite node and a label. When you apply a circular mask to the crop, you cut out all of the children nodes' content, as well.

With that in mind, you're good to start working on a very special part of Level 5: a dusty old picture of a zombie who likes the conga!

With a little help from my frames

Run Cat Nap and take a look at Level 5:

You can play around a bit, but here's the bad news: You can't solve the level as-is. You need to add some extra cool crop nodes to help the kitty get to his bed.

> **Note**: The black blocks are just like normal blocks, except they're indestructible; no matter how many times you tap them, they'll remain unharmed.

The new element in this level is obviously the picture frame on the wall. Open **Level5.sks** and select the picture frame node. Switch to the Custom Class Inspector, and you'll see the node is already configured to be an instance of `PictureNode`.

Create a new file by choosing **File/New/File…** and selecting **iOS/Source/Cocoa Touch Class** for the file template. Name the new class **PictureNode**, make it a subclass of **SKSpriteNode** and click **Create**. Xcode will automatically open the new file.

Replace the contents of **PictureNode.swift** with the following:

```
import SpriteKit

class PictureNode: SKSpriteNode, CustomNodeEvents,
InteractiveNode {

  func didMoveToScene() {
    userInteractionEnabled = true

  }

  func interact() {

  }
}
```

This code enables touches on the picture node and gets you ready to add more custom content. At the moment, `PictureNode` only displays a hollow picture frame. Next, you're going to load the zombie picture and crop it to a circle so it will fit in the frame.

As a first step, add the following code to `didMoveToScene()`:

```
let pictureNode = SKSpriteNode(imageNamed: "picture")
let maskNode = SKSpriteNode(imageNamed: "picture-frame-mask")
```

These two lines load images into two sprite nodes:

• In `pictureNode`, you load the zombie picture;

• In `maskNode`, you load an image holding a circle on a transparent background; this will be your mask.

Next, you need to add the crop node. Add these lines:

```
let cropNode = SKCropNode()
cropNode.addChild(pictureNode)
cropNode.maskNode = maskNode
addChild(cropNode)
```

You create an empty crop node and add `pictureNode` as a child. Then, you set your prepared `maskNode` to be the mask of the crop node. Finally, you add the configured crop node to the picture frame node—the one that came from the .sks file and contains all the content.

Build and run the game. You'll see the zombie picture cropped neatly inside the picture frame:

To see exactly what the crop node does, comment out the line `cropNode.maskNode = maskNode`.

This removes the mask so you can see the whole, uncropped content:

Now **uncomment** the line where you set the mask, and you'll have the zombie picture cropped once again and neatly tucked inside the picture frame.

Look more carefully at the picture: It features a green outline denoting a physics body. Switch back to the scene editor and look up the physics body settings of the picture, and you'll notice two things:

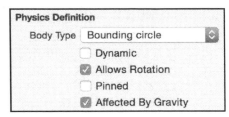

- The picture has a **circular body** that matches the shape of the picture frame. Specifically, the body is a bounding circle.

- The body isn't **dynamic**, because the Dynamic option is unchecked. This means the body isn't affected by the physics world—gravity doesn't pull it down, and when other bodies hit it, it doesn't move.

To finish up the level, you'll add just a bit of interactivity to this node. When the player taps on the picture frame, you'll set its physics body to be dynamic. Since the picture isn't pinned to the wall, it will fall down under the pull of gravity and help the player solve the level.

Open **PictureNode.swift** and add a new method to the `PictureNode` class:

```
override func touchesEnded(touches: Set<UITouch>, withEvent
event: UIEvent?) {
  super.touchesEnded(touches, withEvent: event)
  interact()
}
```

Then, add the interaction code in `interact()`:

```
userInteractionEnabled = false
physicsBody!.dynamic = true
```

Whenever the player taps the picture, you simply set the `dynamic` property on its body to `true`.

Build and run the game. See if you can get kitty to his bed. Also, check out what happens when you tap the picture.

Note: If you have difficulty solving the level, here's a hint: destroy all of the wooden blocks, then tap the picture; when the picture pushes kitty over the center of his bed, tap the long white block.

Crop nodes are straightforward: They let you cut out any shape you want from any texture or node. But you don't have to limit yourself to using images for the mask node. For example, you can use an SKLabelNode as a mask to produce some neat looking text. Here's what happens when you crop the level's background image, specifically the room's wallpaper, using a label node for a mask:

But enough about cutting and cropping—it's time to move on to the next stop on your advanced nodes tour: SKVideoNode.

Video nodes

Videos are everywhere in games—from a lively scene background to cut-off scenes. A video can give your game a number of advantages. For example:

- You can include **3D content** in your 2D game. Produce a scene in 3D modeling software, animate it in some way and finally, export it as video file. Alternatively, buy a cheap 3D royalty free video online! Play the video in your 2D game and boom!—you have 3D content. :]

- You can **save GPU power**. Imagine you have a game taking place at the bottom of the ocean; in the background, you have 200 different fishes swimming happily about. You can create 200 sprite nodes and run 200 repeating actions on them to create the scene, but that would take a toll on the device's GPU and your game's frame rate. If you pre-record the scene and play the video as a background in your game, you can increase your game's performance.

- Finally, you can include content that is simply **a movie**. :] Is your player in command of hundreds of tiny 2D space ships? Then put on a hat and a fake mustache, become Space Admiral Zblorg and use your iPhone to record a video of the player's pep talk for the next level.

I'm sure you don't need any more convincing to get started with SKVideoNode or the next level of Cat Nap.

Creating a video node

Open **GameViewController.swift** and change the starting level to 6 to save yourself the trouble of having to solve Level 5 each time you want to test something:

```
if let scene = GameScene.level(6) {
```

Build and run the game to see this level's starting point:

Since you're familiar with Cat Nap's game mechanics, you'll quickly notice that you don't have a way to solve this level as it is right now.

There are a bunch of wooden pieces lying around, but the kitty is way off the center of the screen; no matter the order in which you destroy the wooden blocks, kitty is just too far from his bed to make it in.

I bet you've also noticed a new element on the screen: a big, shiny disco ball! In this level, you're going to turn the quiet bedroom into a disco each time the player taps the ball.

While the music and lights are on, some special gameplay will take effect. When the player taps the kitty, he'll start to "dance". Each time the kitty dances, he'll end up a bit to the right of his original position.

If the player repeats this routine of tapping the disco ball, the kitty will eventually find himself in the center of the screen. From there, getting into his bed will be as easy as tapping a couple of blocks.

If you look around the level file in the scene editor, you'll see that the custom class for the ball sprite is already set to DiscoBallNode.

So, what are you waiting for? You know the drill—create that class. :]

Create a new file by choosing **File/New/File...** and selecting **iOS/Source/Cocoa Touch Class** for the file template. Name the new class **DiscoBallNode**, make it a subclass of

SKSpriteNode and click **Create**.

Xcode will automatically open the file. Once it does, replace the contents of the file with the following:

```
import SpriteKit
import AVFoundation

class DiscoBallNode: SKSpriteNode, CustomNodeEvents,
InteractiveNode {

  private var player: AVPlayer!
  private var video: SKVideoNode!

  func didMoveToScene() {
    userInteractionEnabled = true

  }

  func interact() {

  }
}
```

You lay down the class basics by inheriting from `SKSpriteNode` and implementing the `CustomNodeEvents` protocol, just as before. This time, though, you have two class variables, as well:

- **player**: This is the `AVPlayer` class from the `AVFoundation` framework. It helps you load local or remote video files for playback. `AVPlayer` doesn't render the video itself; it only loads and manages the video file.

- **video**: This is the node responsible for displaying onscreen the video file you load via `AVPlayer`.

Incidentally, `AVPlayer` creates an instance of `AVPlayerItem`, which represents a single video file in the `AVPlayer` playlist:

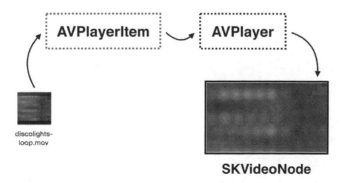

SKVideoNode can automatically load the video file without the help of a separate AVPlayer object, but in that case, you can only start and stop the video, and you lose fine-grained control of playback, such as seeking through and looping the video.

To instantaneously display the video, you'll load the file and have the video node ready when the game loads the level. Initially, you'll have the video node hidden, but when the player taps on the ball, you'll unhide the node and have the video play instantly.

It's time to get this show on the road, so to speak. Add the following to didMoveToScene():

```
let fileUrl = NSBundle.mainBundle().URLForResource("discolights-
loop", withExtension: "mov")!
player = AVPlayer(URL: fileUrl)
video = SKVideoNode(AVPlayer: player)
```

The first line gets the URL to the discolights-loop.mov video file included in your project. You use that URL to create a new AVPlayer instance. Then, SKVideoNode(AVPLayer:) creates a video node that uses the aforementioned AVPlayer object.

And that's it! Your node is ready for prime time.

> **Note**: Did you notice that you didn't have to specify the video format codec the player needs in order to reproduce your file? AVPlayer is really magical in the way it deals with videos. It looks up the video file meta information and decides on its own how to load and decode the video content. Besides being magical, AVPlayer loads and plays any MPEG4 (.mp4), Apple MPEG4 (.m4v) or QuickTime (.mov) file.

Video playback

Since you've loaded the video and initialized your video node, all that's left to do is position and size the node, and, of course, add it to the scene.

Still in didMoveToScene(), add the following lines:

```
video.size = scene!.size
video.position = CGPoint(
  x: CGRectGetMidX(scene!.frame),
  y: CGRectGetMidY(scene!.frame))
video.zPosition = -1
scene!.addChild(video)
```

With this code, you make the video as big as the scene and then center it so it fills the whole screen. Further, you set its zPosition so that the video appears behind the cat, the bed and the blocks, but *in front* of the original background.

Finally, you add the video node to the scene.

Build and run now to see the result:

> **Note:** Due to a bug with the simulator, you have to **test on your device** until the end of this chapter. If you use the simulator, you won't see any of the video content, though you might hear the audio, if your video has audio. From here on out, build and run on your device.

Wow! I told you this would be amazing!

However, there's a slight problem with the video right now—it plays for few seconds, then stops as it reaches the end of the file.

You need to make the video loop, which happens to be a rather simple task.

When `AVPlayer` reaches the end of the video file, it posts a certain notification. You'll listen for that notification and simply rewind the video tape to its start position, and continue the playback from there. And by video tape, I mean the video file. :]

Add the following to `didMoveToScene()`:

```
NSNotificationCenter.defaultCenter().addObserver(self,
  selector: "didReachEndOfVideo",
    name: AVPlayerItemDidPlayToEndTimeNotification, object: nil)
```

You observe for a notification named `AVPlayerItemDidPlayToEndTimeNotification`. As the name suggests, this is the notification that's posted whenever `AVPlayer` reaches the end of the current video file.

Now, you need to add a `didReachEndOfVideo` method to react to the playback having reached the end of the video.

Therefore, add a new method to **DiscoBallNode.swift**:

```
func didReachEndOfVideo() {
  print("rewind!")
  player.currentItem!.seekToTime(kCMTimeZero)
}
```

The `currentItem` property on your player object is an instance of `AVPlayerItem`. This class gives you access to a lot of the aspects of the video player, like positioning through the video, audio mixing, video composition, loaded video buffers and much more.

Using `seekToTime(_:)`, it's possible to move the current position in the video to a given time offset. The handy `kCMTimeZero` constant tells the player item to seek to the beginning of the file.

Additionally, just to make the looping more obvious for this demo, you print a message in the console whenever you jump from the end of the video to the beginning of the video.

Build and run the game on your device. Enjoy the glorious disco lights video on loop.

> **Note:** Isn't that video cool? I made it especially for this chapter's project. I built a small app using Core Animation and my favorite layer, `CAReplicatorLayer`, and then captured the video of the animation from my screen.
>
> If you want to learn how to create cool animations with Core Animation, check out my book about animations, *iOS Animation by Tutorials*:
>
> http://www.raywenderlich.com/store/ios-animations-by-tutorials

The previous screenshot doesn't do much justice to the video, but the output in the console clearly shows that the video loops and plays continuously:

```
☑  ▶  ❚❚  ⌂  ↧  ↥  ▥  ◁  ▣  CatNap
bed added to scene
cat added to scene
rewind!
rewind!
rewind!
rewind!
rewind!
rewind!
rewind!
rewind!
```

Now, to make the video blend a little better, set its opacity to 75% by adding the following line to `didMoveToScene()`:

```
video.alpha = 0.75
```

The change in opacity makes for a more subtle effect that fits the scene perfectly.

Starting and stopping

As per your initial plan, you need to hide the video until the player taps the disco ball. Still in `didMoveToScene()`, add the following two lines:

```
video.hidden = true
video.pause()
```

This will hide the video node as well as pause it, since there's no reason to keep `AVPlayer` busy while the video isn't visible.

Next, you need to add the code to react to touches on the disco ball.

Since the disco ball will work for just a few seconds at a time, you'll need to implement a time-out to turn it off again. The easiest way is to add a new instance property—call it `isDiscoTime`—and show or hide the video whenever the value of that property changes.

Add the following to `DiscoBallNode`:

```
private var isDiscoTime: Bool = false {
  didSet {
    video.hidden = !isDiscoTime

  }
}
```

Any time you change the value of `isDiscoTime`, the `didSet` handler will show or hide the video node accordingly.

Now you can override touchesEnded(_:withEvent:) in your disco ball class, and simply toggle the value of isDiscoTime. Add this to DiscoBallNode:

```
override func touchesEnded(touches: Set<UITouch>, withEvent
event: UIEvent?) {
  super.touchesEnded(touches, withEvent: event)
  interact()
}
```

And, as usual, add the code to handle user taps in interact():

```
if !isDiscoTime {
  isDiscoTime = true
}
```

Build and run the game, and tap the disco ball to make sure everything works as planned:

When you tap the disco ball, the video appears and it's ready to play. Now, you just need to play the video and add a little extra "something" to the disco ball.

First, add a new property to keep a frame animation for your disco ball:

```
private let spinAction = SKAction.repeatActionForever(
  SKAction.animateWithTextures([
    SKTexture(imageNamed: "discoball1"),
    SKTexture(imageNamed: "discoball2"),
    SKTexture(imageNamed: "discoball3")
  ], timePerFrame: 0.2))
```

spinAction is a frame animation action that continuously loops over the discoball1, discoball2, and discoball3 images. That should get you a nice and shiny rotating disco ball animation.

Back in didSet for isDiscoTime, add the following:

```
if isDiscoTime {
  video.play()
  runAction(spinAction)
} else {
  video.pause()
```

```
    removeAllActions()
}
```

This bit of code plays or pauses the video depending upon whether the player turns the disco music on or off. Notice the use of the `play()` and `pause()` methods from `SKVideoNode`; these handy methods control the underlaying `AVPlayer` and are, in fact, the only playback methods the node offers.

Now you have the scene and mood all set - you show the disco lights video, the cat gets dancing but the player keeps listening to the mellow Cat Nap tune. You are about to fix that pretty quickly :]

In the beginning of this chapter you added two new files to your project - the video of the disco lights and an audio file called *disco-sound.m4a*. Why not just have the audio track contained in the video you might ask? Well - the video is just couple of seconds long and it loops a number of times when you play it in the game. The audio track is longer so to keep both files smaller in size you will play it manually alongside the video.

You will just replace the background music with the disco tune whenever you start the video and then bring back the default music whenever disco time is over.

Add just after the last chunk of code you inserted:

```
SKTAudio.sharedInstance().playBackgroundMusic(
    isDiscoTime ? "disco-sound.m4a" : "backgroundMusic.mp3"
)
```

This simple one-liner switches between the Cat Nap tune and disco depending on the current level state.

The final code to add to `didSet` will automatically turn off the disco mode after a few seconds. At the end of that method, append the following:

```
if isDiscoTime {
    video.runAction(SKAction.waitForDuration(5.0), completion: {
        self.isDiscoTime = false
    })
}
```

First, you check if the player is turning on the disco mode; if so, you run a wait action on the video node for 5 seconds. When this action completes, you simply set `isDiscoTime` to `false`, which triggers the `didSet` handler again and pauses and hides the video.

Build and run to see how it's coming together. With that, your video node crash course is complete!

> **Note:** If you'd like to know more about fine-grained playback control, streaming video from the Internet, or just about playing video on iOS, consult the `AVPlayer` class documentation: http://apple.co/1JZPhds.
>
> Also, if you want to learn more about recording and playing video, you can follow this fun tutorial online that will take you on an `AVFoundation` tour: http://bit.ly/1Lnyhh8

Disco kitty

To wrap up this section, you'll add a bit of custom behavior to your cat node. It's time for some sick dance moves!

Dance all the

moves!

You need to handle taps on the cat node, and you need to check if it's currently disco time. If it is, you'll make the cat "dance" for awhile. To expose the `isDiscoTime` property of `DiscoBallNode` to other classes, you'll need to add a static property.

In **DiscoBallNode.swift**, and the following propery:

```
static private(set) var isDiscoTime = false
```

Further, inside `didSet` for the instance property `isDiscoTime`, and below all of the other code in the `didSet` handler, add this line:

```
DiscoBallNode.isDiscoTime = isDiscoTime
```

This code will keep the static property `isDiscoTime` in sync with the instance property of the same name.

Now, each time the player taps on the cat node, you can check the static property on `DiscoBallNode` and see if there's a disco happening.

Open **CatNode.swift** and add a property to keep track of whether or not the cat is currently dancing:

```
private var isDoingTheDance = false
```

Now, append the following lines to `interact()`:

```
if DiscoBallNode.isDiscoTime && !isDoingTheDance {
  isDoingTheDance = true
  //add dance action
}
```

In `interact()`, you check if `DiscoBallNode.isDiscoTime` is on, and whether the cat is currently *not* dancing. When both conditions are fulfilled, it's dance time!

Wrapping up this method is as simple as adding a few actions to the cat node. First, replace `//add dance action` with this:

```
let move = SKAction.sequence([
  SKAction.moveByX(80, y: 0, duration: 0.5),
  SKAction.waitForDuration(0.5),
  SKAction.moveByX(-30, y: 0, duration: 0.5)
])
let dance = SKAction.repeatAction(move, count: 3)
```

The first action, `danceMove`, represents a single dance move: It moves the cat **80** points to the right, then waits half a second and moves the cat back **30** points.

The complete dance action, `dance`, repeats `danceMove` three times. When the action has finished running, the cat will effectively have moved to the right by **150** points.

This is exactly what you want, since the ultimate goal is to move the cat to the center of the screen and just over the bed.

Finally, you want to run the `dance` action, and when it completes, toggle the Boolean flag back to `false`. To get that working, add this bit of code just after the `let dance` line:

```
parent!.runAction(dance, completion: {
  self.isDoingTheDance = false
})
```

This runs the move action on the compound cat node. And that's it. You're ready to check out kitty's dance moves!

Build and run the game. Tap the disco ball a few times, and while the lights are on, tap on the cat to get him moving:

Can you figure out how to solve the level on your own? Give it a try!

Once you're over the center of the bed, you can make your way in:

When you're done with disco moves and fooling around, *dance* over to the next and final section of this chapter, where you'll turn this ride around and once more!

Shape nodes

A shape node lets you draw any kind of shape onscreen—from a simple circle or a rectangle, to any arbitrary shape you can define with a `CGPath`.

Speech bubbles are a great example of shape nodes used in games, because they need to have different widths or heights depending on the current phrase the character is speaking. Based on the amount of text that needs to fit in the bubble, you can easily create a smaller or a larger rectangle, like so:

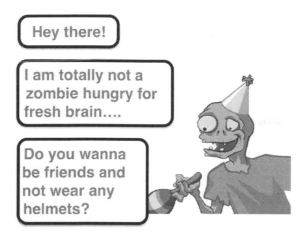

In fact, you've already used an SKShapeNode to draw a shape onscreen. In Chapter 2, "Manual Movement", you drew a rectangle onscreen to visualize the playable area:

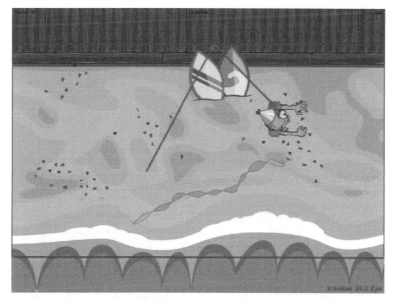

In this section of the chapter, you'll dive into that a little more. You'll learn how to set the stroke, color and width of the shape; how to make it hollow or filled; and finally, how to use a texture to make the shape look at home in the scene.

The final goal for this chapter is to add a dynamic hint arrow to show the player where to begin solving the level. Most games have hints or tutorials of some sort, and you'd like Cat Nap to be on par with them.

When you finish working through this section, you'll have a nice bouncing arrow floating next to the disco ball:

Adding a shape node

It's possible to add shape nodes in the scene editor, but the options for you to customize them are rather limited. Since you're a pro at developing custom nodes, you'll develop your own awesome node class for the hint arrow.

> **Node:** The shape node available in the scene editor's Object Library seems to be a bit buggy. For example, even if its textures render fine in the editor, when you run the project, the texture might be missing. For the time being, until Apple fixes the issue, use your own shape classes.

You'll still use the scene editor, but just to position a placeholder for your new node. Open **Level6.sks** and drag a new **color sprite** into the scene. It appears by default as a small red square, and that's good enough for a placeholder. You're going to hide the placeholder, anyway, so the player will never see it.

Before leaving the scene editor, adjust the node like so:

• Name **hint**, Position **(1300, 1200)**, Custom Class **HintNode**

Now, create a new file by choosing **File/New/File...** and selecting **iOS/Source/Cocoa Touch Class** for the file template. Name the new class **HintNode**, make it a subclass of

SKSpriteNode and click **Create**.

When Xcode automatically opens the file, replace the contents with the following:

```
import SpriteKit

class HintNode: SKSpriteNode, CustomNodeEvents {

  func didMoveToScene() {
    color = SKColor.clearColor()

  }
}
```

As soon as the node is added to the scene, you set its color to `clearColor()` and effectively make it fully transparent:

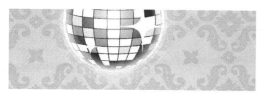

With the placeholder out of the way, you can create your own shape.

Shape node basics

First, you're going to try something simple. `SKShapeNode` has a number of convenience initializers that let you easily create the most commonly used shapes. You'll start with a simple rectangle with rounded corners.

In `didMoveToScene()`, and the following:

```
let shape = SKShapeNode(rectOfSize: size, cornerRadius: 20)
shape.strokeColor = SKColor.redColor()
shape.lineWidth = 4
addChild(shape)
```

Hey, that's easy! Here you create a shape node, which is a rectangle that fits into the current node's size and has rounded corners with a radius of **20** points. You configure the shape node to outline the shape with a 4-points thick red line, and add it onscreen.

A quick build and run shows you the result:

Looking good.

Try adjusting some more properties on your shape node by adding a few things to `didMoveToScene()`:

```
shape.glowWidth = 5
shape.fillColor = SKColor.whiteColor()
```

To make the outline a bit "fuzzier", you add a glow effect by increasing `glowWidth`, which defaults to `0`.

Finally, an easy win is to set `fillColor` and have Sprite Kit fill in the shape with a color automatically, like so:

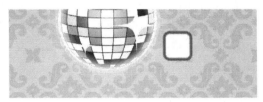

Before moving on to the real task at hand, watch how easy it is to change the shape of the node.

Find `SKShapeNode(rectOfSize: size, cornerRadius: 20)` and replace it with a call to another convenience initializer:

```
let shape = SKShapeNode(circleOfRadius: 120)
```

This will make your node a different shape, but all the rest of the properties you use to "beautify" it can remain the same.

Build and run to see how it looks now.

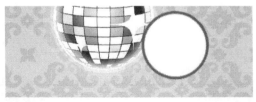

That's better. The path is now a circle.

I bet you're already asking, "Can't I just set my own custom path instead of using rectangles and circles?" Why yes, you can. Now that you've covered the basics, you're going to move on to working with custom shapes.

Adding the hint arrow

`SKShapeNode` includes a property named `path` that you can set to an arbitrary `CGPath`.

Then you can make the node draw anything you want.

You already worked with `CGPath` back in Chapter 9, "Beginning Physics", where you created a triangular shape for your triangle sprite's physics body.

Back then, you created this triangle in code: You started at the bottom-left corner, drew a line to the bottom-right corner, continued drawing to the top, and then back to where you started to close the shape.

Coming up with the precise coordinates to draw a triangle is a pleasant brain tease, but how about more complex shapes, like a star, a truck or a space station? Unless you're a geometry genius and calculate π for breakfast, finding the coordinates by hand might be a bit too much.

Luckily, there's a neat app named PaintCode that lets you draw with your mouse, and then translates your drawings into Swift code using `CGPath`. I used that app to prepare the code for the arrow shape, so you don't have to draw it yourself:

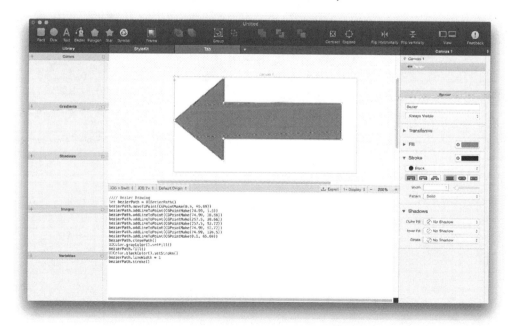

In PaintCode, the Swift code appears in the lower panel as you draw on the canvas. How cool is that!

For your Cat Nap arrow shape, you'll add a dynamic property on the `HintNode` class that will give you the arrow `CGPath`. With that said, add the following to `HintNode`:

```
var arrowPath: CGPath {
  let bezierPath = UIBezierPath()

  bezierPath.moveToPoint(CGPoint(x: 0.5, y: 65.69))
  bezierPath.addLineToPoint(CGPoint(x: 74.99, y: 1.5))
  bezierPath.addLineToPoint(CGPoint(x: 74.99, y: 38.66))
  bezierPath.addLineToPoint(CGPoint(x: 257.5, y: 38.66))
  bezierPath.addLineToPoint(CGPoint(x: 257.5, y: 92.72))
  bezierPath.addLineToPoint(CGPoint(x: 74.99, y: 92.72))
  bezierPath.addLineToPoint(CGPoint(x: 74.99, y: 126.5))
  bezierPath.addLineToPoint(CGPoint(x: 0.5, y: 65.69))
  bezierPath.closePath()

  return bezierPath.CGPath
}
```

Here, you create an empty `UIBezierPath` and execute a series of line-drawing instructions, which ultimately, when combined one after the other, draw an arrow.

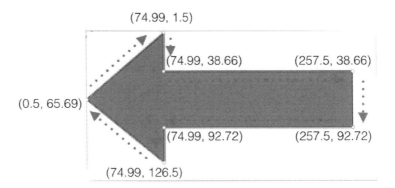

At the bottom of the method, you return the `CGPath` property on your bezier path object.

Now you have to get rid of all the test code you wrote. To do that, simply replace the complete `didMoveToScene()` method with this one:

```
func didMoveToScene() {
  color = SKColor.clearColor()

  let shape = SKShapeNode(path: arrowPath)
  shape.strokeColor = SKColor.grayColor()
  shape.lineWidth = 4
  shape.fillColor = SKColor.whiteColor()
  addChild(shape)
}
```

This code will get you started with a fresh, new arrow shape. This time around, you use a convenience initializer that takes a `CGPath` parameter, and you supply it with the path stored in your `arrowPath` property:

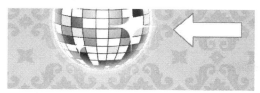

In this way, you can create any `CGPath` value and make `SKShapeNode` draw it onscreen. You can adjust the points of the path dynamically from your code, or even generate it on the fly based on the user's input.

There are a few, final touches you need to make, and then you'll be ready.

In `didMoveToScene()`, add this:

```
shape.fillTexture = SKTexture(imageNamed: "wood_tinted")
shape.alpha = 0.8
```

This simply makes the hint arrow a better fit for your scene; you fill it with a wooden texture and give it a bit of opacity:

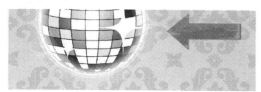

To quickly wrap up the level, add a few actions to the arrow to make it a bit more pleasant to the eye. Do so by adding these lines to `didMoveToScene()`:

```
let move = SKAction.moveByX(-40, y: 0, duration: 1.0)
let bounce = SKAction.sequence([
  move, move.reversedAction()
  ])
let bounceAction = SKAction.repeatAction(bounce, count: 3)

shape.runAction(bounceAction, completion: {
  self.removeFromParent()
})
```

This creates a bouncing animation action and runs it three times on the arrow node. When the action completes, you remove the node from the scene.

Build and run one last time, and enjoy your new hint arrow. Notice how it appears as the level begins, and then disappears after three bounces.

And that's a wrap!

You got to use the scene editor extensively, you learned about physics in Sprite Kit and how to create your own game worlds, you got to create complex physics-based mechanisms, and finally, you used fantastic picture frames, videos and custom shapes!

Now, it's time to move on and take the sleepy cat experience to the next frontier: the TV! In the next chapter, you'll add tvOS support to Cat Nap so the player to enjoy the game on the big screen.

And of course, you can always add more levels to Cat Nap on your own. Why not come back and revisit Cat Nap once you learn about all those exciting APIs from the chapters in the rest of the book?

But before moving on, there are two quick challenges waiting for you.

Challenges

Challenge 1: Hints all around!

Now that your HintNode is fully functional, you can add it to the other levels in Cat Nap. Consider how you added the node in the last level, and then add it to Level 1, as well:

And then to Level 2:

That should definitely make for more enjoyable gameplay! Can you think of other game levels where you could add this hint?

Challenge 2: fillColor meets fillTexture

One aspect of SKShapeNode not covered in this chapter is the relationship between fillColor and fillTexture. As you made your way through the chapter, it might have looked like only one of the two could be seen at any one time—as soon as you set the texture, you didn't see the white fill any more.

Indeed, the documentation for SKShapeNode says that once the texture is set, the value of fillColor is ignored. But that's not entirely true—you can use fillColor to tint the texture and produce an infinite number of differently colored textures.

In this challenge, you'll try that on your own.

Enable user interaction for the hint arrow, and each time the player taps on it, change the fillColor of the shape node. Keep an array of SKColor objects: red, yellow and orange colors. Upon each tap, pick a random color from the list and set it as the fill color.

I hope this challenge will make you feel like you're back in art class at school. What color would a blue texture mixed with a yellow fill color produce?

Chapter 13: Intermediate tvOS

By Marin Todorov

In this chapter, you're going to finish Cat Nap with a bang by putting it on the big screen in your living room! Or if you don't own an Apple TV, you'll simply use the Apple TV 1080p simulator. But, don't worry—that still counts. :]

In this chapter, you'll port the levels you have so far to run on the Apple TV, as well as add some new features. Of course, the main focus will be on porting the controls, so the player can use the Apple TV remote to play the game.

When you're finished working through this chapter, kitty will be ready to make his TV debut:

It may not be the red carpet, but close enough. Kitty would just scratch up the carpet anyway. :]

Note: This chapter begins where the previous chapter's Challenge 2 left off. If you were unable to complete the challenges or skipped ahead from an earlier chapter, don't worry—you can simply open the starter project from this chapter to pick up in the right place.

Adding a tvOS target

Back in Chapter 7, "Beginning tvOS", you set up a simple tvOS port for Zombie Conga. With Cat Nap, you'll take the same approach, but because the project is more complex, it will take a bit more effort.

The result, however, will be similar: you'll end up with two project targets, one for iOS to run on the iPhone and iPad, and another for tvOS to run on the Apple TV. The two targets will share the code that implements the gameplay, but each will have its own project settings.

Open Cat Nap in Xcode. Before you add an extra project target for Apple TV, you need to rename your existing assets catalog to make sure the one for the new target won't conflict with it. Rename Assets.xcassets to **Shared.xcassets**. Also, if you have a file named Game.xcassets, rename it to **SharedGame.xcassets**.

Then, select the project file in the project navigator to see the list of available project targets. At the bottom of the list, click the + button to add a new target:

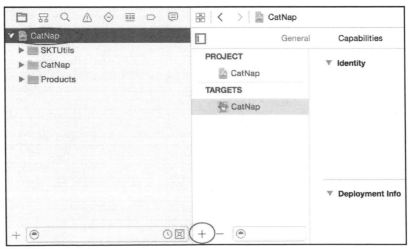

From the pop-up dialogue, choose **tvOS/Application/Game** as a project template:

Enter **CatNapTV** for **Product Name** and make sure the **Language** is **Swift** and the **Game Technology** is **Sprite Kit**. Then, click **Finish** to create the new target.

Xcode adds a new target for use on tvOS, as well as the needed project files, into a new folder named **CatNapTV**. So far, so good.

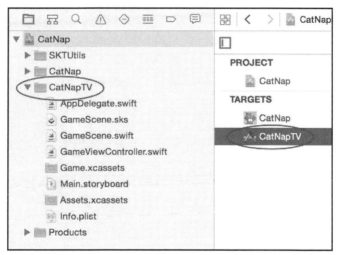

To begin testing Cat Nap on the Apple TV simulator, change the active project scheme to **CatNapTV/Apple TV 1080p**:

Build and run the project to make sure you're testing on the TV simulator; you'll see the default project template scene:

> **Note**: Remember, to see the Apple TV remote on the simulator, go to **Hardware \Show Apple TV Remote**.

Top-shelf image and 3D icons

Before delving into code, you'll finish setting up the Apple TV target by adding a tvOS top-shelf image, launch image and 3D icon.

Open **CatNapTV\Assets.xcassets** and click the item called **Launch Image**. In the resources for this chapter, you'll find a file named **CatNap_tvOS_LaunchImage.png**; drag this file into this slot.

Still in **Assets.xcassets**, expand **App Icon & Top Shelf Image** and then select the **Top Shelf Image** item. Drag the file from **CatNap_tvOS_TopShelf.png** file into this slot.

Finally, select **App Icon - Large** and make sure the Attributes Inspector is open. In Layers, click the **+** button once; there should be now four layers in total: Layer, Front, Middle and Back.

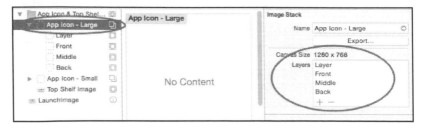

The layers in the list are ordered from front to back, so grab the four images from the **App Icon - Large** folder in the chapter resources and drop them, one by one, into the four slots under the big icon preview. Make sure the image names match the layer names. Once you've done that, you can hover with the mouse pointer over the preview to see the icon in 3D:

Now, select **App Icon - Small** from the assets list and repeat the same process for the smaller version of the game icon; you'll find the image files in the **App Icon - Small** folder in the chapter resources.

> **Note:** By iPhone standards, even the small TV icons are large. Just think: The small icon is 420x200 pixels, and the full screen resolution of the iPhone used to be 320x480!

Now, all Apple TV asset slots should be full:

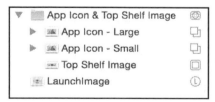

Build and run; then from Xcode, stop the program. You'll see the proper assets pop into your Apple TV simulator:

Good job! Next stop: Code Town. :]

Bringing the code to tvOS

You already know that Sprite Kit code runs on both iOS and tvOS without any changes necessary. Your only task is to configure the two project targets to share the code that drives the gameplay.

Look at all the files in your project's **CatNapTV** folder:

Open **AppDelegate.swift** and look inside—the code is the same as what you have in your iOS target **AppDelegate.swift**. The same goes for **GameScene.swift** and **GameViewController.swift**.

Since you worked on those files in previous chapters and added everything Cat Nap needs to run, you can simply reuse the files for your tvOS target.

With that in mind, select the following files in **CatNapTV** and delete them:

- **AppDelegate.swift**
- **GameScene.sks**

- **GameScene.swift**

- **GameViewController.swift**

You'll use their counterparts from the iOS target. In fact, you're going to use *all* of the files you created in your iOS target, except for the four items you now have remaining in **CatNapTV**.

But first, you need to add the iOS files to your tvOS target. Unfortunately, the only way to add them is to individually select each of the files in each of the folders.

Do that now. Select all of the necessary file groups in the bullet list below, and when you have each of them selected, make sure to tick the **CatNapTV** target checkbox in the Attribute Inspector:

Check the **CatNapTV** target for the following files:

- **CatNap/video/discolights-loop.mov**: the disco lights video;

- **CatNap/video/disco-sound.m4a**: the disco audio track;

- **CatNap/Scenes/*.sks**: all .sks files containing saved scenes;

- **CatNap/Sounds/*mp3**: all sound files;

- **CatNap/Nodes/*.swift**: if you separated your node classes in a folder, include all of them in the new target;

- **CatNap/*.swift**: all remaining Swift code files; make sure *not* to include other files in this folder;

- **SKTUtils/*.swift**: all Swift files from the SKTUtils library.

This should be all the files you've worked on for the iOS version of Cat Nap.

Build the project to see where you stand right now.

Xcode will attempt to build the project but then bail, reporting three errors—all of them located in **GameViewController.swift**:

- There is no shouldAutorotate() defined in UIViewController to overwrite, like you had in iOS;

- There is no prefersStatusBarHidden() defined in UIViewController;

- Finally, UIInterfaceOrientationMask is missing.

What Xcode tells you makes sense. On tvOS, UIViewController doesn't support rotation and therefore the tvOS version doesn't support rotation-related methods. Imagine if you tried to rotate your expensive 70" TV. :]

Further, the helper method related to hiding the status bar in iOS is missing—indeed, Apple TV doesn't show a status bar on top of the screen, either.

No worries. You can still keep those methods for the iOS version of Cat Nap.

From Xcode's main menu, select **File/New/File...** and select **iOS/Source/Swift File** for the file template. Name the new file **GameViewController+iOS.swift**. You'll use this file for all the iOS-only methods.

Replace the default import line `import Foundation` with this:

```
import UIKit

extension GameViewController {

}
```

Move the three methods that throw errors from **GameViewController.swift** into **GameViewController+iOS.swift**:

- **shouldAutorotate()**
- **supportedInterfaceOrientations()**
- **prefersStatusBarHidden()**

With **GameViewController+iOS.swift** open, look in the Attributes Inspector and make sure that *only* the CatNap target checkbox is ticked, like so:

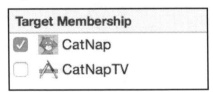

By excluding this file and separating all of the iOS-specific methods, you ensure that you don't have errors when building for tvOS. In fact, the Xcode errors have cleared, so build and run the game again:

You can hear the game music and the cat purring in the background, but it looks like you're missing all the textures. So there's one final step: select **CatNap/Shared.xcassets** and add it to the **CatNapTV** target.

This time around, everything looks purrfect!

Apple TV remote controls, Round 2

In Chapter 7, you learned how to track touches on the Apple TV remote's trackpad. That worked for Zombie Conga, but you need to do something different for Cat Nap, because players need to be able to precisely select the block they're about to destroy.

Your new controls also need to be different from what you have for the iOS game. For tvOS, you'll let players select the active elements in the scene one by one, until they decide which they want to interact with.

You'll also add an animation to the currently selected node, so that a player can clearly see which block she's about to destroy:

Once a player has selected her desired block, she'll be able to tap on the remote to interact with that node. Tapping on a block will destroy it; tapping on a spring will send kitty into the air.

You'll add this new control mechanism in three stages:

1. You'll fetch the list of all active items in the current level.

2. You'll let players loop over the list.

3. You'll observe for taps on the remote control and forward these events to the currently selected node.

TV controls, part 1: Who's up for some action?

It's time to add new code to the game!

Your first task is to find all the nodes in the current level that allow for user interaction. The best way to do that is to query all the children in the scene and find any that conform to `InteractiveNode`.

First of all, you want all the tvOS-specific code to be separate from your iOS-specific code. Earlier in this chapter, you enforced that by creating a class extension file and excluding that file from the tvOS target. Since that works well, you'll do something similar here.

This time, instead of excluding part of the functionality for Apple TV, you'll do the opposite—add part of the code, but only add it to the tvOS target.

Open **GameScene.swift** and toward the top of the file, add a new protocol:

```
protocol TVControlsScene {
  func setupTVControls()
}
```

`GameScene` will adhere to this protocol, but only on the Apple TV version of the game. To make that happen, you'll add a new file that defines an extension to `GameScene`, but you'll only add it to the tvOS project target.

Select your **CatNapTV** folder, and from Xcode's main menu, select **File/New/File...** and choose **tvOS/Source/Swift file** for the file template. Name the new file **GameScene +TV.swift**

While you have **GameScene+TV.swift** open, make sure that only the **CatNapTV** target is checked for the file's **Target Membership** in the Attributes Inspector:

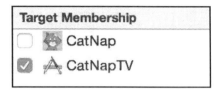

Now, replace the file contents with the following empty extension:

```swift
import SpriteKit

extension GameScene: TVControlsScene {

  func setupTVControls() {

  }
}
```

You define an extension of `GameScene` that adheres to the `TVControlsScene` protocol, and add a blank `setupTVControls()` method to make Xcode happy—and avoid compile errors.

The beauty of this configuration is that this extension only exists in the tvOS project target. That means you can simply check from your main `GameScene` file if `GameScene` adheres to `TVControlsScene`. This is a great way see if you're running on iOS or on tvOS. Then, you can set up the game controls accordingly.

Speaking of which, now is the perfect time to do that. Open **GameScene.swift** and add the following code to `didMoveToView(_:)`:

```swift
let scene = (self as SKScene)
if let scene = scene as? TVControlsScene {
  scene.setupTVControls()
}
```

You do a little trick with this code: First, you cast the current class instance of `GameScene` to a generic `SKScene` type; then, you check if the generic type is actually a `TVControlsScene`—this will only be true on a tvOS target.

If you're running on an Apple TV, you simply call setupTVControls(), which is where you'll put all the code that's only relevant to the user experience on tvOS. Good work so far!

Switch back to **GameScene+TV.swift**, because next, you're going to query the scene for active nodes—for example, nodes that have user interaction enabled.

First, add two variables just above the extension line but outside of the extension code:

```
private var activeNodes = [SKNode]()
private var currentNodeIndex = 0
```

activeNodes will contain the list of all active nodes in the current level, and currentNodeIndex is simply the index of the currently selected node in that list.

Now, add a new method to the extension:

```
func setupSelectableNodes() {
  activeNodes = []

  enumerateChildNodesWithName("//*", usingBlock: {node, _ in
    //check the node

  })
}
```

setupSelectableNodes() starts humbly, but it will achieve great things. :]

Here, you begin with an empty list of active nodes, and then you enumerate over all nodes in the scene. Remember, you used this technique in Chapter 10, "Intermediate Physics", to loop over all nodes in the scene and call their respective didMoveToScene() methods.

Next, replace //check the node with this:

```
if node is InteractiveNode && node.userInteractionEnabled {
  activeNodes.append(node)
}
```

This code checks if the current node accepts user touches and if it's a SKSpriteNode, in which case, you simply add it to activeNodes.

To see if setupSelectableNodes() is ready for prime time, add this line at the end of the method:

```
print(activeNodes)
```

Now, you need to call the method to see if it will find all active nodes in the current scene. Inside `setupTVControls()`, add the following:

```
setupSelectableNodes()
```

Build and run, and check the output console:

```
bed added to scene
cat added to scene
[<SKSpriteNode> name:'block' texture:[<SKTexture> 'wood_vert1' (120 x 340)] position:
{1024, 330} scale:{1.00, 1.00} size:{120, 340} anchor:{0.5, 0.5} rotation:0.00,
<SKSpriteNode> name:'block' texture:[<SKTexture> 'wood_vert1' (120 x 340)] position:
{1264, 330} scale:{1.00, 1.00} size:{120, 340} anchor:{0.5, 0.5} rotation:0.00,
<SKSpriteNode> name:'block' texture:[<SKTexture> 'wood_horiz1' (496 x 160)] position:
{1050, 580} scale:{1.00, 1.00} size:{496, 160} anchor:{0.5, 0.5} rotation:0.00,
<SKSpriteNode> name:'block' texture:[<SKTexture> 'wood_horiz1' (496 x 160)] position:
{1050, 740} scale:{1.00, 1.00} size:{496, 160} anchor:{0.5, 0.5} rotation:0.00,
<SKSpriteNode> name:'SKSpriteNode_11' texture:['nil'] position:{1589.284423828125,
430.941162109375} scale:{1.00, 1.00} size:{100, 100} anchor:{0.5, 0.5} rotation:0.00,
<SKSpriteNode> name:'cat_body' texture:[<SKTexture> 'cat_body' (238 x 214)] position:
{22, -112} scale:{1.00, 1.00} size:{238, 214} anchor:{0.5, 0.5} rotation:0.00]
```

You can see the details for all of the interactive blocks. If you're running the first level, there are four blocks, the hint arrow and the cat's body.

Before moving on, comment out the `print(activeNodes)` line to avoid output clutter in the console:

```
// print(activeNodes)
```

Now that you have all the blocks lined up, you can add the TV controls to let the player make a block selection.

TV controls, part 2: Stay in the loop

The Apple TV remote isn't meant for fine-grained, mouse-like control, and you can't touch objects directly like you can on your iPhone's screen.

Luckily, just like with all subclasses of `UIResponder`, you can assign gesture recognizers to your Sprite Kit view to recognize various gestures on the Apple TV remote touch surface, like swipes and taps. And gesture recognizers are a fantastic way to interact with Cat Nap.

As you saw in Chapter 7, "Beginning tvOS", tvOS forwards the user touches from the Apple TV remote to your Sprite Kit view. The same goes for working with gesture recognizers—you can create and add recognizers to the game view, and they'll work for touches coming from the Apple TV remote.

And what a better place to add the recognizers than `setupTVControls()`?

In **GameScene+TV.swift**, add the following to setupTVControls():

```
let swipeLeft = UISwipeGestureRecognizer(target: self,
  action: "didSwipeOnRemote:")
swipeLeft.direction = .Left
view!.addGestureRecognizer(swipeLeft)

let swipeRight = UISwipeGestureRecognizer(target: self,
  action: "didSwipeOnRemote:")
swipeRight.direction = .Right
view!.addGestureRecognizer(swipeRight)
```

With the code you just added, you create and attach two swipe gesture recognizers: one to detect swipes to the left and one to detect swipes to the right. Both recognizers invoke the same method, didSwipeOnRemote(_:), where you'll simply change the currently selected node to either the previous one or the next one.

Add the basics for didSwipeOnRemote(_:):

```
func didSwipeOnRemote(swipe: UISwipeGestureRecognizer) {
  guard activeNodes.count > 0 else {
    return
  }
}
```

First, this code checks to see if there are any active nodes. You probably don't expect to have any levels without any interactive blocks or other items, but this check is more for the end of a level, when all blocks have been destroyed and the player swipes by mistake.

Next, you need to update the current index based on the swipe direction. If the player swipes to the right, increase the index to select the next node; if the player swipes to the left, decrease the index.

Add the following code to the end of didSwipeOnRemote(_:):

```
var newIndexToSelect = currentNodeIndex

if (swipe.direction == .Right) {
  newIndexToSelect++
} else {
  newIndexToSelect--
}
```

This takes care of adjusting the index properly. However, you still need to deal with instances when the index goes beyond the bounds of the active node list. And you also need to let the player loop over the list.

Just after the `if` block you added, add the following:

```
if newIndexToSelect < 0 {
  newIndexToSelect = activeNodes.count-1
} else if newIndexToSelect > activeNodes.count-1 {
  newIndexToSelect = 0
}
```

Now, if the index goes below `0` or above the last index in the list, you change directions and turn the ride around, so to speak.

Finally, you need to select the node with the current index. To do that, add this line:

```
selectNodeAtIndex(newIndexToSelect)
```

As you know, you haven't yet created a method named `selectNodeAtIndex_:)`—and surely Xcode is already complaining about it.

Anything for you, Xcode!

Add the *missing* method to the class now:

```
func selectNodeAtIndex(index: Int) {
  guard activeNodes.count > 0 else {
    return
  }
}
```

There, are you happy, Xcode? You now have a method named `selectNodeAtIndex(_:)`, so settle down. :]

Just like the other method you added, this one begins with a `guard` statement to make sure you have active nodes in the scene.

Next, you're going to run a repeating animation to tint the currently selected node. You'll need two `SKAction` instances to build the tint animation.

Since you're about to run `selectCurrentNode(_:)` each time the player changes the selection, you'd like to create the actions once and then reuse them each time.

Scroll to the top of the file and add two private constants:

```
private let fadeOut = SKAction.fadeAlphaTo(0.5, duration: 0.5)
private let fadeIn = SKAction.fadeAlphaTo(1.0, duration: 0.5)
```

The former defines a fade-out animation, while the latter defines a fade-in animation. You won't fade the selected node until it's completely transparent, because that would look a bit awkward, so you fade it out until it's half opaque, then fade it back in to a 100% opacity.

Scroll back to selectNodeAtIndex(_:) and add:

```
activeNodes[index].runAction(
  SKAction.repeatActionForever(
    SKAction.sequence([fadeOut, fadeIn])
  )
)
```

Here, you access the currently selected node in activeNodes by using the index method parameter, and then you run the animation sequence on that node. This will make the current node fade in and fade out.

This is a great opportunity to finally see something happen onscreen.

To pre-select the first active node in the level, add this to setupTVControls():

```
selectNodeAtIndex(0)
```

This code simply selects the first node found by setupSelectableNodes().

Now, build and run. You'll see one of the blocks animate nicely and show the player which is the currently selected element in the scene:

And since you've already wired the swipe gesture recognizers, try swiping left and right on the Apple TV remote to see the result:

Of course, since you didn't write code to deselect the current node, they all become selected as you swipe through them—but you'll fix that in a moment.

You may also notice that the top block disappears on your first swipe-you'll fix that in the chapter's challenge.

Interacting with the Apple TV simulator

If you didn't read our previous tvOS chapter, you may be wondering how to interact with the Apple TV simulator. Don't worry - it's quite easy!

While you're running the Apple TV simulator, choose **Hardware/Show Apple TV Remote** from its main menu. This will bring up the Apple TV remote simulator window:

See that big empty area? That's the virtual remote trackpad. To simulate a swipe, hover the mouse just outside the area of the trackpad, then hold the **Option** key and swipe over the trackpad, releasing the Option key when you get to the end of the trackpad. It takes a bit of practice, but you'll get the hang of it in no time. :]

Deselecting nodes

By now, it's clear that you need to add some code to deselect nodes—otherwise the level quickly becomes a blinking mess.

At the bottom of `selectNodeAtIndex(_:)`, append the following:

```
if currentNodeIndex < activeNodes.count && index !=
currentNodeIndex,
  let node = activeNodes[currentNodeIndex] as? SKSpriteNode {
    node.removeAllActions()
    node.alpha = 1.0
}
```

First, you check if the currently selected node index is still within the bounds of the active nodes list. When could that be true? Well, if you destroy the last node in the list, its index will be bigger than the current last index. In that case, you won't need to deselect it—the node has already been destroyed!

The second condition in your `if` statement checks if the currently selected node is also the new node to select. This condition, which is a bit confusing at first, is `true` when the level first begins; the check ensures you don't stop the animation on the first block that gets selected by default.

If, on the other hand, the previously selected node is still in the scene, you remove all its running actions, thus stopping the tint animation. Then, you reset the `alpha` to `1.0` so the node no longer appears selected.

As a final touch, you need to update the current selection index, so add this line to the same method:

```
currentNodeIndex = index
```

Build and run, and you'll notice something a bit strange when you cycle through the blocks: There's one swipe that deselects the current block but doesn't select anything else. This happens because the hint arrow is present at the time you first run `setupSelectableNodes()`, but when it disappears after a bit, you still have a reference to it in `activeNodes`.

To quickly solve this issue, open **HintNode.swift** and remove `InteractiveNode` from the class declaration. This way, `setupSelectableNodes()` will skip over this node when it queries for active nodes in the scene.

That should fix cycling through the nodes, so you're ready to add some destructive action to the game!

There it goes again!
Meow!

TV controls, part 3: Taps for everyone!

In your iOS version of Cat Nap, each custom node handles its own taps. For example, when the player taps a certain spot on the screen, the node at that location receives a touchesEnded(_:withEvent:) message, and this method in turn calls interact().

However, on Apple TV, as you learned in Chapter 7, you don't get precise coordinates of the touches, and you can't rely on the player being able to tap precisely on a node on the scene.

But for Cat Nap, simply knowing that the player tapped on the remote is more than enough, since you added code to handle node selection on swipes. Therefore, whenever players tap on the remote, you already know which node they want to interact with. It seems like a simple tap gesture recognizer should suffice to complete the gameplay and have the game running on Apple TV in no time!

First, add a tap gesture recognizer to your Sprite Kit view. Open **GameScene+TV.swift** and add the following to setupTVControls():

```
let tap = UITapGestureRecognizer(target: self,
  action: "didTapOnRemote:")
view!.addGestureRecognizer(tap)
```

You've already added the recognizers for swiping left and right, and in the same manner, you add a simple tap recognizer to the scene's view.

To get started, add the basics for the function didTapOnRemote(_:):

```
func didTapOnRemote(tap: UITapGestureRecognizer) {
  guard activeNodes.count>0 else {
    return
  }
}
```

You still check for active nodes first.

Next, you need to cast the current node to `InteractiveNode` and call `interact()` on it. For this, append the following to `didTapOnRemote(_:)`:

```
if let node = activeNodes[currentNodeIndex] as? InteractiveNode
{
  node.interact()
}
setupSelectableNodes()
```

You use an `if let` construct to cast the current node, and then you call `interact()` on the selected node, which invokes the action for that node: blocks get destroyed, or in case of disco time, the cat dances, and so forth. In the end, you call `setupSelectableNodes()` because, as a result of calling `interact()`, there may be fewer nodes to cycle through.

With that, your swipe and tap recognizers are ready to go.

Build and run, and this time, you can play the game through.

The game looks absolutely gorgeous on the big screen! Using the Apple TV simulator is a bit difficult until you get used to it, but playing the game with the actual Apple TV remote is tons of fun.

Get ready to jump on the couch and fire up Cat Nap on your TV!

Challenges

You've already covered many tvOS concepts in this chapter, and the basic Cat Nap gameplay works pretty well on Apple TV. But there are a number of small things you can do to polish the game.

These challenges are optional. If you're eager to start working on the next game in the book, skip to the next chapter. If you can't get enough of our kitty and would like to improve Cat Nap's code further, read on!

Challenge 1: Polish all levels for Apple TV

Currently, Cat Nap is functional on the Apple TV, but there are four small details you can polish to improve its functionality.

1) Select the next node when one is destroyed

Now when you destroy a block, the selection disappears and that's it:

To keep the player going, you could automatically select the next node in the list of active nodes. You can implement this easily by checking if the number of active nodes has changed after calling `interact()` on the current one. If the number of active nodes has changed, you can simply call `selectNodeAtIndex(_:)` to select the next node.

The completed code chunk looks like this:

```
let originalCount = activeNodes.count

if let node = activeNodes[currentNodeIndex] as? InteractiveNode
{
  node.interact()
}
setupSelectableNodes()

if originalCount != activeNodes.count {
  selectNodeAtIndex(currentNodeIndex)
}
```

This code will adjust the selection each time the player destroys a block. You're welcome, player. :]

2) Remove the fade animation from the cat

Since the cat is sometimes the last active node in the scene, it's the one that remains selected when the player solves the level. That's why the kitty sometimes appears and disappears when he's supposed to be sleeping calmly in bed—it's just the animation loop continuing to run.

To fix this, you can simply remove all running actions on kitty whenever he falls into bed or onto the ground.

First, open **CatNode.swift** and scroll to curlAt(_:). Once there, add the following at the top:

```
removeAllActions()
alpha = 1.0
```

That should remove the selected node animation just before you load the curl up frame sequence.

Now in the same file, scroll to wakeUp() and add this at the top:

```
removeAllActions()
alpha = 1.0
```

This will remove the selection animation from the kitty before he falls over and onto the ground.

Now all is well:

3) Double taps or black magic?

You've built a great mechanism to handle touch events on an iPhone, an iPad and even on the Apple TV remote.

But there's still a problem: Your nodes are receiving `touchesEnded(_:withEvent:)` messages. In fact, if you do a specific kind of swipe on the Apple TV remote, you can confuse the game—big time.

Open Cat Nap Level 1 and do the swipe motion below on the remote. Make sure to stop your swipe at the end of the red line:

After you try it few times, you'll see something interesting happen: One of the blocks disappears even if you didn't tap to destroy it. It may not even be selected at the time.

This happens because if you do a swipe like the one above, you end your touch on the trackpad around the center of the screen. The remote forwards the touches to the responder chain, and that event ends up calling `touchesEnded(_:withEvent:)` on the block in the center of the screen.

It looks like you have to disable `touchesEnded(_:withEvent:)` on tvOS but still keep `userInteractionEnabled` on.

To achieve this, you'll use preprocessor macros. You'll mark all `touchesEnded(_:withEvent:)` methods on all interactive nodes as iOS-only methods, and Xcode won't compile these when you build your tvOS app.

Open **BlockNode.swift** and wrap touchesEnded(_:withEvent:) in a macro #if condition:

```
#if os(iOS)
override func touchesEnded(touches: Set<UITouch>, withEvent
event: UIEvent?) {
  super.touchesEnded(touches, withEvent: event)
  print("destroy block")
  interact()
}
#endif
```

This macro instructs Xcode to include this part of the source code only when building for iOS. When you build your tvOS app, it will be as if touchesEnded(_:withEvent:) never existed in your BlockNode class. This will solve the black magic node interaction.

To prevent the issue from happening throughout the game, go over CatNode, SpringNode, StoneNode, PictureNode and DiscoBallNode, and wrap touchesEnded(_:withEvent:) for each of those in an #if macro.

4) Adjusting the gameplay depending on the device

Cat Nap now works on both iPhone and iPad touch screens and with your Apple TV remote. The two versions of the game look exactly the same, but have different controls and input methods.

This inevitably results in discrepancies in the user experience between the different versions of the game. It happens when you port your Sprite Kit iOS game to OS X, and it happens when you port to Apple TV, as well.

One example of such a discrepancy in the user experience is in the last level, Level 6. When you play the game on your iPhone or iPad, you can tap the disco ball. Of course, when you do that, while you're in disco mode, you can also tap the cat to make him dance around.

On the other hand, when you play the game on your Apple TV, you have to cycle through all the blocks, and there are plenty in this level, to get to the disco ball. Then, after you make the long trek there, you have to tap the disco ball and cycle again through a number of blocks until you get to the cat.

Since you have to repeat that procedure a few times to solve the level, the players enjoying Cat Nap on an Apple TV might lose their motivation. Imagine they solve the level by doing all the necessary tapping and dancing (but not tap dancing!), and then move on to the next level, only to make a mistake and be sent back to the disco ball!

To keep players committed to this level on the Apple TV, it would be a good idea to adjust the level so that players can solve the puzzle faster.

For example, you can adjust the distance kitty moves with each dance routine. To do that, adjust the code like so:

```
#if os(iOS)
let move = SKAction.sequence([
  SKAction.moveByX(80, y: 0, duration: 0.5),
  SKAction.waitForDuration(0.5),
  SKAction.moveByX(-30, y: 0, duration: 0.5)
])
#endif
#if os(tvOS)
let move = SKAction.sequence([
```

```
  SKAction.moveByX(200, y: 0, duration: 0.5),
  SKAction.waitForDuration(0.5),
  SKAction.moveByX(-50, y: 0, duration: 0.5)
])
#endif
```

After you implement this code, try the level on your Apple TV or in the Apple TV simulator, and you'll see that now, the level is a lot more enjoyable.

Congratulations are in order!

You brought the complete Cat Nap game to Apple TV, and if you throw in a start menu, some extra levels and maybe some Game Center integration, the game is ready for prime time. Or should we say couch time! I hope you enjoyed working on this little game, and I hope you learned a lot about Sprite Kit along the way.

Now, on to your next adventure: Drop Charge!

Section III: Juice

In this section, you'll also learn how to take a good game and make it great by adding a ton of special effects and excitement – a.k.a. "juice."

In the process, you will create a game called Drop Charge, where you're a space hero with a mission to blow up an alien space ship - and escape with your life before it explodes. To do this, you must jump from platform to platform, collecting special boosts along the way. Just be careful not to fall into the red hot lava!

Chapter 14: Making Drop Charge

By Michael Briscoe

In this section of the book, you'll take what you've learned so far and use that knowledge to create an endless, platform jumper game named Drop Charge. You'll also learn how to take a game from good to great by adding "juice"—those special details that collectively make your game shine brightly among the pack.

You'll do all of this and more in multiple stages across the next four chapters:

1. **Chapter 14, Making Drop Charge**: You'll put together the basic gameplay using the scene editor and code, flexing the Sprite Kit muscles you've developed working through previous chapters.

2. **Chapter 15, State Machines**: You'll learn what state machines are and how to use them.

3. **Chapter 16, Particle Systems**: You'll learn how to use particle systems to create amazing special effects.

4. **Chapter 17, Juice Up Your Game**: You'll trick out your game with music, sound, animation, more particles and other special effects, experiencing for yourself the benefits of mastering the details.

When you're finished, Drop Charge will look like this:

In Drop Charge, you're a space hero with a mission to blow up an alien space ship - and escape with your life before it explodes. To do this, you must jump from platform to platform, collecting special boosts along the way. Just be careful not to fall into the red hot lava!

> **Note**: This chapter is optional; it is a review of what you have learned in the chapters so far. You should read this chapter if you'd like to get some additional practice while making a cool new game, but if you feel confident that you understand the material covered already, feel free to skip to the next chapter.

Getting started

As you've done in previous sections, start Xcode and create a new project with the **iOS \ Application \ Game** template. Enter **DropCharge** for the Product Name and verify that the Language is set to **Swift**, the Game Technology to **SpriteKit** and the Devices to **Universal**.

Drop Charge is designed to run in portrait mode. Therefore, click **DropCharge** in the Project Navigator, make sure the **General** tab is selected, click the **DropCharge** target and deselect the Landscape options listed in the **Device Orientation** section.

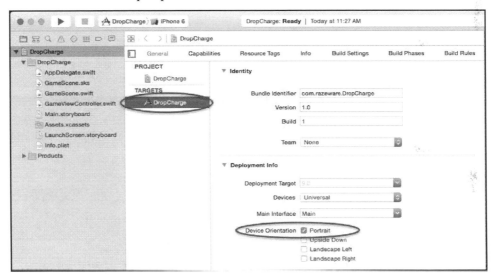

Also, open **Info.plist** and locate the **Supported interface orientations (iPad)** entry. Delete the entries for **Portrait (top home button)**, **Landscape (left home button)** and **Landscape (right home button)**.

Adding the art

In Xcode, open **Assets.xcassets** and delete the **Spaceship** entry. Then, select **AppIcon** and drag the appropriate icon from **starter\resources\icons** into each slot.

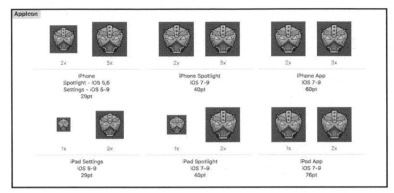

Finally, import the artwork you need for this game by dragging the files and folders from **starter\resources\images** into the left sidebar of **Assets.xcassets**.

> **Optional**: This would be a good point to set up your launch screen, if you'd like one. You can find the launch art in **starter\resources\images**. Refer to Chapter 1 if you need help.

Building the game world in the scene editor

Now that you've got your project set up and your art at hand, you're ready to start working in the scene editor. This section is a review of the material from Chapter 8, "Scene Editor".

The first step is to configure your scene for the appropriate mode, which in this case is portrait mode.

Configuring the scene

Open **GameScene.sks** and select the **Attributes Inspector**. Set the **Size** to **W: 1536** and **H: 2048**.

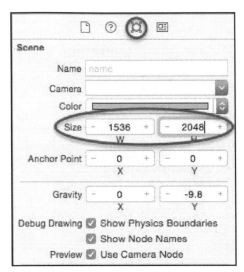

Remember, this is the standard scene size you are using for all games in this book, just in portrait mode instead of landscape mode.

From the **Object Library**, drag an **empty node** into the scene. Name this node **World** and set its position to **(768, 1024)**. All other nodes will be children of this node. This is a handy trick to use, because it will allow you to easily move all objects in the scene at once by moving the World node - which will be useful later on on when you implement a screen shake effect.

Next, drag another **empty node** into the scene. Name this node **Background**, and set its Parent to **World** and its Position to **(0, 0)**. You will add all backgrounds as descendants of this node, so that it will be easy to move all backgrounds at once by moving the Background node.

Add one last **empty node**. This time, name it **Overlay**. Set its Parent to **Background** and its Position to **(0, 0)**. This node will hold all of your background textures. The reason you are adding them to the Overlay node rather than directly to the Background node is that you will eventually be creating multiple copies of the Overlay node, in order to implement continuous scrolling backgrounds.

Adding the background sprites

Now for some pretty pictures. Because Drop Charge will scroll up and down as the game progresses, you're going to make a background composed of several textures. Later, in code, you'll duplicate the Overlay node to repeat the background as needed.

In the **Utilities Area**, select the **Media Library** and drag **bg_1** into the scene. Name this SKSpriteNode **bg1**, set its Parent to **Overlay**, its Position to **(0, -1024)** and its Anchor Point to **(0.5, 0.0)**.

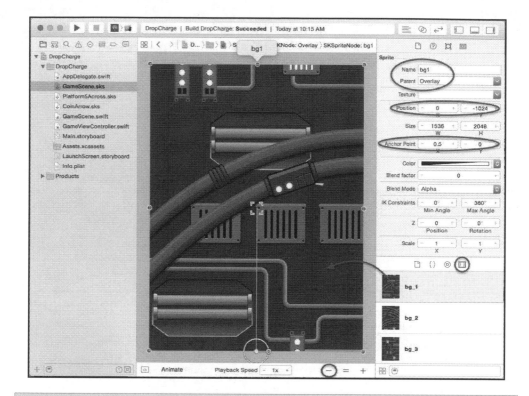

Note: While you're laying out the scene, the artwork will appear quite large. Remember, to better visualize your scene, you can zoom out by clicking the **minus (-)** button at the bottom-right of the scene editor.

Add the remaining two **bg** nodes to the **Overlay** node with the following settings:

Media	Name:	Position		Anchor Point	
		X:	Y:	X:	Y:
bg_2	bg2	0	1024	0.5	0
bg_3	bg3	0	3072	0.5	0

Note: Setting the anchor point to the center-bottom of the SKSpriteNode aids in positioning the stacked background, because you can simply add the texture's height to the y-position for each additional texture.

To make the background a little more interesting you'll add some decorations. Add the **midground** sprites to the **Overlay** node using the following settings:

Media	Name:	Position		Z Position:
		X:	Y:	
midground_1	m1	0	0	1
midground_2	m2	0	1690	1
midground_3	m3	0	3088	1
midground_4	m4	0	4726	1

Your complete background node will look like this:

How's that for a payoff? Build and run to see your progress.

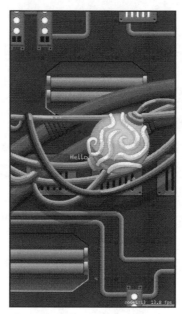

You've finished the background. That can only mean it's time to work on the foreground!

Adding the foreground sprites

Begin by adding another **empty node** to your scene. Name it **Foreground**, set its Parent to **World**, its Position to **(0, 0)** and its Z Position to **2**. Here you are continuing your strategy of using an empty node to represent a "layer" of your game, this time for objects in the foreground like the title text, player, and bomb.

From the Media Library, add four sprites to the **Foreground** node using these settings:

Media	Name:	Position		Scale		Z Position:
		X:	Y:	X:	Y:	
DropCharge_title	Title	0	410	1	1	1
Ready	Ready	0	0	0	0	1
player01_jump_1	Player	0	-460	1	1	3
bomb_1	Bomb	25	-417	1	1	1

Here's how you'll use these sprites:

- **Title** is the game's title, which you'll display until the player taps the screen to start.
- **Ready** is what you'll display once the game has loaded and is ready to play.

- **Player** is the space marine—the player's avatar.

- **Bomb** is what the space marine will drop to explode the alien spaceship and get the action started!

Next, you're going to add your last foreground node: the lava.

Lava is the enemy! It continuously rises as your marine strives for escape. The player must avoid falling in the lava, or risk a smouldering end.

From the Object Library, drag a **Color Sprite** into the scene. In Chapter 16, you'll attach an awesome particle system to this sprite, but you'll keep it simple for now. Name the sprite **Lava**, set its Parent to **Foreground**, its Position to **(0, -1024)**, its Size to **W: 1536** and **H: 2048**, its Anchor Point to **(0.5, 1)** and its Z Position to **4**. Also, change the Color to **orange** and set its Opacity to **75%**.

Build and run to make sure you're still on track.

The lava is calmly resting just off-screen, waiting to be agitated by a bomb blast.

You're almost ready to start coding, but you don't want to leave your hero hanging in midair with a lit bomb behind him. You need some platforms—and as extra incentive to get him jumping, some shiny coins.

Creating platforms

To keep your players coming back, the game should be different every time they play. Later in this chapter, you'll add code that will randomly place platforms and coins in the level as your player moves up the screen. You could create your platform configurations entirely in code, but it's a lot easier—and more fun—to do it in the scene editor!

Control-click on your **DropCharge** folder, select **New Group**, and rename the group to **Scene Files**. You'll be creating lots of these, so it will be nice to keep them organized.

Control-click your new **Scene Files** group and select **New File**. Select the **iOS\Resource \SpriteKit Scene** template and click **Next**. Save your scene as **Platform5Across.sks**.

Set the scene's size to **W: 900** and **H: 200**. Now drag a **Color Sprite** from the Object Library, name it **Overlay**, set its Position to **(450, 100)** and set its Size to **W: 900** and **H: 200**. This sprite is merely a container, so you don't need to see it; therefore, set its Opacity to **0%**.

> **Note**: You're using an `SKSpriteNode` here because you want to get the overlay node's exact dimensions, keeping the spacing between platforms consistent.

For this node, you want five platforms evenly spaced across the scene. Start by dragging **platform01** from the Media Library. Set its Name to **p1**, its Parent to **Overlay** and its Position to **(-360, 0)**.

This time, you're also going to add a physics definition to the sprite, because you want the player to interact with the platform rather than just fall through it.

Scroll the Attributes Inspector down until you see the **Physics Definition** heading. Choose **Bounding Rectangle** for the Body Type and make sure to **uncheck** Dynamic, Allows Rotation, Pinned and Affected By Gravity. Set the Category Mask to **2** (the bit flag for a platform), the Collision Mask to **0**, the Field Mask to **0** and the Contact Mask to **1** (the bit flag for the player).

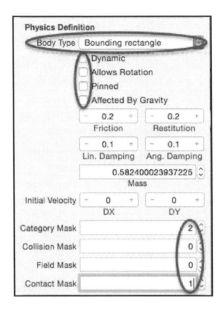

Now that you have the first platform set up, click on **p1** and **duplicate (Command-D)** it four times with the following changes:

Name:	Position	
	X:	Y:
p2	-180	0
p3	0	0
p4	180	0
p5	360	0

When you're done, your platform scene will look like this:

Creating coins

Now you're going to create some coins to give the marine a boost, and then you'll write some code.

This coin node will consist of five coins in an arrow pattern. As you did before, create a new file in your **Scene Files** group with the **iOS\Resource\SpriteKit Scene** template. This time, name it **CoinArrow.sks** and set the scene size to **W: 900** and **H: 600**.

Drag a **Color Sprite** from the Object Library and name it **Overlay**. Set its Position to **(450, 300)**, its Size to **W: 900** and **H: 600**, and its Opacity to **0%**.

Now from the Media Library, drag **powerup05_1** into the scene. Set its Name to **c1**, its Parent to **Overlay** and its Position to **(-360, -200)**.

Under Physics Definition, choose **Bounding Circle** for the Body Type. Also, **uncheck** Dynamic, Allows Rotation, Pinned and Affected By Gravity. Set the Category Mask to **8** (the bit flag for a coin), the Collision Mask to **0**, the Field Mask to **0** and the Contact Mask to **1** (the bit flag for the player).

With that done, click on **c1** and **duplicate (Command-D)** it four times with the following changes:

Name:	Position	
	X:	Y:
c2	-180	0
c3	0	200
c4	180	0
c5	360	-200

Your finished coin arrow scene will look like this:

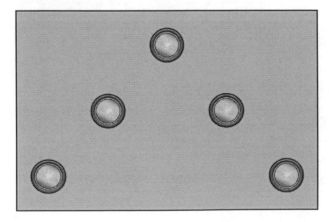

You're done with the scene editor—for now. It's time to get coding!

Writing the gameplay code

In this section, you'll implement Drop Charge's basic gameplay by:

1. Adding randomized platforms and coins;

2. Implementing touch events to drop the bomb;

3. Adding physics and collision detection so the marine can jump on platforms and collect coins;

4. Implementing code to read the device accelerometer data to steer the marine;

5. Creating methods to handle the camera node so that it follows the player sprite;

6. Implement code to get the lava flowing;

7. Adding code to continuously repeat the background, platforms and coins;

Most of these things you've done before, so crack your knuckles and let's get started!

Adding platforms

Your hero is still floating in midair! Put some platforms under his feet to give the guy a rest—he'll need it when he finds out his ship's about to explode.

Mwahahahaha...

Begin by dragging **SKTUtils** into the project navigator. Verify **Copy items if needed**, **Create groups**, and the **DropCharge** target are selected, and click **Finish**. You'll be using these utilities here to generate random numbers.

Open **GameScene.swift**. Delete everything and replace it with the following:

```
import SpriteKit

class GameScene: SKScene {

  // MARK: - Properties
  var bgNode = SKNode()
  var fgNode = SKNode()
  var background: SKNode!
  var backHeight: CGFloat = 0.0
  var player: SKSpriteNode!
```

```
    var platform5Across: SKSpriteNode!
    var coinArrow: SKSpriteNode!
    var lastItemPosition = CGPointZero
    var lastItemHeight: CGFloat = 0.0
    var levelY: CGFloat = 0.0

    override func didMoveToView(view: SKView) {
      setupNodes()
    }

    func setupNodes() {
      let worldNode = childNodeWithName("World")!
      bgNode = worldNode.childNodeWithName("Background")!
      background = bgNode.childNodeWithName("Overlay")!.copy()
        as! SKNode
      backHeight = background.calculateAccumulatedFrame().height
      fgNode = worldNode.childNodeWithName("Foreground")!
      player = fgNode.childNodeWithName("Player") as! SKSpriteNode
      fgNode.childNodeWithName("Bomb")?.runAction(SKAction.hide())
    }

}
```

These properties will hold the nodes and platform overlays you set up in the scene editor. There are also properties here to hold the background height, and keep track of the last platform's position, height and current position, making it possible for the game logic to properly position future platforms in a random manner once gameplay begins.

setupNodes() loads the children nodes from the **World** node into their respective properties, calculates the height of the background, and it also hides the **Bomb** node.

Note that when you retrieve the Overlay node (containing the background images) from the scene file, you use copy() to make a new copy of the node.

Now implement the methods that load and create the platforms:

```
// MARK: Platform/Coin overlay nodes.

func loadOverlayNode(fileName: String) -> SKSpriteNode {
  let overlayScene = SKScene(fileNamed: fileName)!
  let contentTemplateNode =
    overlayScene.childNodeWithName("Overlay")
  return contentTemplateNode as! SKSpriteNode
}

func createOverlayNode(nodeType: SKSpriteNode, flipX: Bool) {
  let platform = nodeType.copy() as! SKSpriteNode
  lastItemPosition.y = lastItemPosition.y +
    (lastItemHeight + (platform.size.height / 2.0))
  lastItemHeight = platform.size.height / 2.0
```

```
    platform.position = lastItemPosition
    if flipX == true {
      platform.xScale = -1.0
    }
    fgNode.addChild(platform)
  }

  func createBackgroundNode() {
    let backNode = background.copy() as! SKNode
    backNode.position = CGPoint(x: 0.0, y: levelY)
    bgNode.addChild(backNode)
    levelY += backHeight
  }
```

Let's review this method by method:

1. `loadOverlayNode()` takes the name of a scene file (such as **Platform5Across**) and looks for a node called "Overlay" inside, and then returns that node. Remember that you created an "Overlay" node in both of your scenes so far, and all the platforms/ coins were children of this.

2. `createOverlayNode()` positions the new overlay node right above where any previous overlay node was placed. It also has a parameter to flip the node along its x-axis (wihch you will use later to add more variability into the level).

3. `createBackgroundNode()` makes a copy of the background and places it right above the current background. You will use this to keep the background continuously cycling.

Add these lines to `setupNodes()` to load the overlays:

```
platform5Across = loadOverlayNode("Platform5Across")
coinArrow = loadOverlayNode("CoinArrow")
```

Next, add the following code immediately after `setupNodes()`:

```
func setupLevel() {
  // Place initial platform
  let initialPlatform = platform5Across.copy() as! SKSpriteNode
  var itemPosition = player.position
  itemPosition.y = player.position.y -
    ((player.size.height * 0.5) +
      (initialPlatform.size.height * 0.20))
  initialPlatform.position = itemPosition
  fgNode.addChild(initialPlatform)
  lastItemPosition = itemPosition
  lastItemHeight = initialPlatform.size.height / 2.0
}
```

This method places the platform right below the player, and updates `lastItemPosition` and `lastItemHeight` appropriately.

Finally, add this line to `didMoveToView(_:)`:

```
setupLevel()
```

Now give your game a build and run.

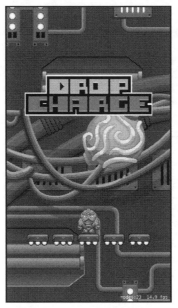

Nice work! Your hero is standing his ground, looking like a boss—for now.

More platforms!

But you want more than one set of platforms in your level—and what about those coins? Add the following method after `createOverlayNode(_:flipX:)`:

```
func addRandomOverlayNode() {
  let overlaySprite: SKSpriteNode!
  let platformPercentage = 60
  if Int.random(min: 1, max: 100) <= platformPercentage {
    overlaySprite = platform5Across
  } else {
    overlaySprite = coinArrow
  }
  createOverlayNode(overlaySprite, flipX: false)
}
```

This bit of code generates a random number and adds a platform 60% of the time; otherwise, it adds the arrow of coins. Later, as a challenge, you'll build on this method to add other platform and coin configurations.

Now, Add these lines to the bottom of `setupLevel()`:

```
// Create random level
levelY = bgNode.childNodeWithName("Overlay")!.position.y +
backHeight
while lastItemPosition.y < levelY {
  addRandomOverlayNode()
}
```

This continuously calls `addRandomOverlayNode()` to fill up content equal to the background's height.

Build and run. You'll see something like this (your screen might look slightly different):

Dropping the bomb

Your hero looks a little bored—let's give him some motivation to get jumping!

Still working inside **GameScene.swift**, add the following property:

```
var isPlaying: Bool = false
```

This Boolean keeps track of whether or not the user is playing the game. Next, add the following methods:

```
// MARK: - Events

override func touchesBegan(touches: Set<UITouch>, withEvent
event: UIEvent?) {
  if !isPlaying {
    bombDrop()
  }
}
```

```
func bombDrop() {
  let scaleUp = SKAction.scaleTo(1.25, duration: 0.25)
  let scaleDown = SKAction.scaleTo(1.0, duration: 0.25)
  let sequence = SKAction.sequence([scaleUp, scaleDown])
  let repeatSeq = SKAction.repeatActionForever(sequence)
  fgNode.childNodeWithName("Bomb")!.runAction(SKAction.unhide())
  fgNode.childNodeWithName("Bomb")!.runAction(repeatSeq)
  runAction(SKAction.sequence([
    SKAction.waitForDuration(2.0),
    SKAction.runBlock(startGame)
    ]))
}

func startGame() {
  fgNode.childNodeWithName("Title")!.removeFromParent()
  fgNode.childNodeWithName("Bomb")!.removeFromParent()
  isPlaying = true
}
```

You're already familiar with touch events from Chapter 2, "Manual Movement". Here you only need `touchesBegan(_:withEvent:)` to monitor for a screen tap. Once you detect a touch, this method checks to make sure gameplay hasn't already started, and if it hasn't, calls `bombDrop()` to animate the bomb and start the game.

Build and run and you'll see the bomb pulse breifly then disappear, along with the title.

Getting physical

If there was a bomb behind you, wouldn't you get moving real fast? Your hero needs to be a lot more physical. Let's fix that by configuring **GameScene.swift** to handle some basic physics.

In this section, you'll practice the skills you developed in Chapters 9, 10, and 11 - the three chapters on Sprite Kit physics. If at any point you get confused about what you're doing, please review those chapters.

Insert this method just below `setupLevel()`:

```
func setupPlayer() {
  player.physicsBody = SKPhysicsBody(circleOfRadius:
    player.size.width * 0.3)
  player.physicsBody!.dynamic = false
  player.physicsBody!.allowsRotation = false
  player.physicsBody!.categoryBitMask = 0
  player.physicsBody!.collisionBitMask = 0
}
```

This configures the physics properties for your `player` node, aka your hero. Now add this line to `didMoveToView(_:)` to call `setupPlayer()`:

```
setupPlayer()
```

Since `player` now has a `physicsBody` let's turn it on when the game starts. Add the following line to `startGame()`:

```
player.physicsBody!.dynamic = true
```

Build and run to see what happens.

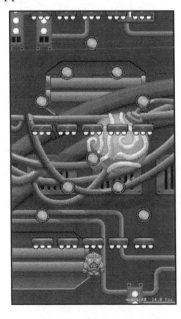

Oops! It looks like your marine is a bit clumsy—falling off the platform like that. Help him out by giving him a boost with the following methods:

```
func setPlayerVelocity(amount:CGFloat) {
  let gain: CGFloat = 1.5
  player.physicsBody!.velocity.dy =
    max(player.physicsBody!.velocity.dy, amount * gain)
}

func jumpPlayer() {
  setPlayerVelocity(650)
}

func boostPlayer() {
  setPlayerVelocity(1200)
}

func superBoostPlayer() {
  setPlayerVelocity(1700)
}
```

These methods set the vertical velocity of the `player` nodes physics body, giving him thrust. When the marine lands on a platform or collides with a coin, `jumpPlayer()` will fire. You'll use `boostPlayer()` when the player collects a special coin.

Add a call to `superBoostPlayer()` at the start of the game when the bomb explodes, by adding this line to `startGame()`:

```
superBoostPlayer()
```

Now give your game a build and run.

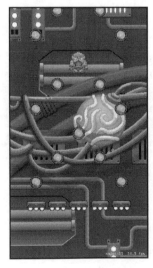

He goes up—and he comes down! Your marine needs to know about those coins and platforms, before he becomes lava food.

Collision detection

First, add the following `struct` definition between the `import` statements and the `class` declaration:

```
struct PhysicsCategory {
  static let None: UInt32              = 0
  static let Player: UInt32            = 0b1       // 1
  static let PlatformNormal: UInt32    = 0b10      // 2
  static let PlatformBreakable: UInt32 = 0b100     // 4
  static let CoinNormal: UInt32        = 0b1000    // 8
  static let CoinSpecial: UInt32       = 0b10000   // 16
  static let Edges: UInt32             = 0b100000  // 32
}
```

Here you define the various physics categories for collision detection. This is why earlier in the scene editor you set the platform's category to 2, the coin's category to 8, and both of them to register a contact with 1 (the player).

Next, change the `class` declaration to read as follows:

```
class GameScene: SKScene, SKPhysicsContactDelegate {
```

Then add this line to `didMoveToView(_:)`:

```
physicsWorld.contactDelegate = self
```

This declares your class as a delegate for `SKPhysicsContactDelegate`, and sets the delegate to the scene.

Now implement this method in **GameScene.swift**:

```
func didBeginContact(contact: SKPhysicsContact) {
  let other = contact.bodyA.categoryBitMask ==
    PhysicsCategory.Player ? contact.bodyB : contact.bodyA
  switch other.categoryBitMask {
  case PhysicsCategory.CoinNormal:
    if let coin = other.node as? SKSpriteNode {
      coin.removeFromParent()
      jumpPlayer()
    }
  case PhysicsCategory.PlatformNormal:
    if let _ = other.node as? SKSpriteNode {
      if player.physicsBody!.velocity.dy < 0 {
        jumpPlayer()
      }
    }
  }
```

```
    default:
        break;
    }
}
```

This method handles collision detection and how it affects the player in various circumstances. Now when the marine makes contact with the platforms and coins, he'll get that boost he needs to get moving. There's just one more thing to do first.

In `setupPlayer()` change the line that reads:

```
player.physicsBody!.categoryBitMask = 0
```

To the following:

```
player.physicsBody!.categoryBitMask = PhysicsCategory.Player
```

This is to make sure `didBeginContact(_:)` can differentiate between the `player` node and other game objects.

Go ahead and do a build and run.

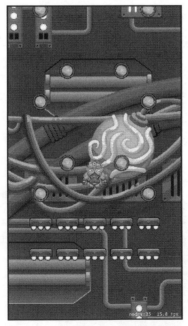

Yay! Now your hero is grabbing coins and bouncing happily off of the platforms.

> **Note**: Note there is a chance that your hero could get stuck offscreen based on the configuration of your random coins and platforms. If this happens, build and run again until you verify that you see the bouncing working.

Using Core Motion to steer the player

You're going to use a framework called Core Motion to control your marine.

Core Motion is the framework responsible for receiving and processing motion data from device hardware, including both accelerometer and gyro-based data. In the games you created in earlier chapters of this book, you controlled your player sprites with touch events. In Drop Charge, you'll control the marine by tilting your device right or left.

Core Motion is beyond the scope of this book, but it's easy to set up and will be quite useful in controlling your marine's movement.

Begin by adding this import statement just below import SpriteKit in **GameScene.swift**:

```
import CoreMotion
```

Add these properties:

```
let motionManager = CMMotionManager()
var xAcceleration = CGFloat(0)
```

Here you're declaring an instance of the CMMotionManager() that you'll poll for motion data, and adding a variable to track the accelerometer.

Next, implement setupCoreMotion(), just after setupPlayer():

```
func setupCoreMotion() {
  motionManager.accelerometerUpdateInterval = 0.2
  let queue = NSOperationQueue()
  motionManager.startAccelerometerUpdatesToQueue(queue,
withHandler:
  {
    accelerometerData, error in
    guard let accelerometerData = accelerometerData else {
      return
    }
    let acceleration = accelerometerData.acceleration
    self.xAcceleration = (CGFloat(acceleration.x) * 0.75) +
      (self.xAcceleration * 0.25)
  })
}
```

This method sets up the motionManager to periodically check the accelerometer and update the xAcceleration variable based on how much the user is tilting the device right or left. You'll use the xAcceleration property in the updatePlayer() method that you'll add shortly.

Add this line to didMoveToView(_:), just before physicsWorld.contactDelegate...:

```
setupCoreMotion()
```

Finally implement the updatePlayer() method:

```
func updatePlayer() {
  // Set velocity based on core motion
  player.physicsBody?.velocity.dx = xAcceleration * 1000.0

  // Wrap player around edges of screen
  var playerPosition = convertPoint(player.position,
    fromNode: fgNode)
  if playerPosition.x < -player.size.width/2 {
    playerPosition = convertPoint(CGPoint(x: size.width +
      player.size.width/2, y: 0.0), toNode: fgNode)
    player.position.x = playerPosition.x
  }
  else if playerPosition.x > size.width + player.size.width/2 {
    playerPosition = convertPoint(CGPoint(x:
      -player.size.width/2, y: 0.0), toNode: fgNode)
    player.position.x = playerPosition.x
  }
}
```

This updates the velocity of the player's physics body based on the xAcceleration property you set based on the accelerometer. Note it multiplies the value by 1000 - this felt right through trial and error. This also contains some code to wrap the player around the edges of the screen.

You'll call updatePlayer() continuously to steer your marine; to do that you'll need to override the scenes update(_:) method:

```
override func update(currentTime: NSTimeInterval) {
  updatePlayer()
}
```

Build and run - but this time be sure to use an actual device, as Core Motion isn't supported in the iOS Simulator.

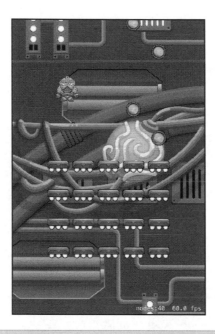

> **Note:** For more information about Core Motion, visit Apple's iOS Developer Library: http://apple.co/1F4DjCH. I highly recommend you acquaint yourself with this framework because it's often handy to add accelerometer-based input into your games.

Camera tracking

Now that you've got the marine jumping, you may have noticed that he frequently moves out of view. To fix that, you'll add an `SKCameraNode` and some methods, to track the hero as he jumps his way to safety. This is a review of the material from Chapter 5, "Camera".

Begin by adding this to **GameScene.swift**, where the rest of the properties are:

```
let cameraNode = SKCameraNode()
```

Next, add the following lines to `setupNodes()`:

```
addChild(cameraNode)
camera = cameraNode
```

These lines add the `SKCameraNode` to the scene, and sets its `camera` property.

Implement the camera methods:

```
// MARK: - Camera

func overlapAmount() -> CGFloat {
  guard let view = self.view else {
    return 0
  }
  let scale = view.bounds.size.height / self.size.height
  let scaledWidth = self.size.width * scale
  let scaledOverlap = scaledWidth - view.bounds.size.width
  return scaledOverlap / scale
}

func getCameraPosition() -> CGPoint {
  return CGPoint(
    x: cameraNode.position.x + overlapAmount()/2,
    y: cameraNode.position.y)
}

func setCameraPosition(position: CGPoint) {
  cameraNode.position = CGPoint(
    x: position.x - overlapAmount()/2,
    y: position.y)
}

func updateCamera() {
  // 1
  let cameraTarget = convertPoint(player.position,
    fromNode: fgNode)
  // 2
  var targetPosition = CGPoint(x: getCameraPosition().x,
    y: cameraTarget.y - (scene!.view!.bounds.height * 0.40))

  // 3
  let diff = targetPosition - getCameraPosition()
  // 4
  let lerpValue = CGFloat(0.05)
  let lerpDiff = diff * lerpValue
  let newPosition = getCameraPosition() + lerpDiff

  // 5
  setCameraPosition(CGPoint(x: size.width/2, y: newPosition.y))
}
```

The `overlapAmount()`, `getCameraPosition()`, and `setCameraPosition()` methods are the same methods you used in Zombie Conga, to get around the current bug with Sprite Kit's camera handling at the time of writing this chapter.

As for `updateCamera()`, let's review this section by section:

1. The player's position is relative to it's parent (`fgNode`), so you use this method to convert the position to scene coordinates.

2. Set the target camera position to the player's Y position less 40% of the scene's height, since we want to see what's coming ahead of the player.

3. Calculate the difference between the target camera position, and its current position.

4. Rather than updating the camera straight to the target, move the camera 5% toward the target. This will make the camera appear to take a while to catch up to the player when the player moves quickly, for a cool effect. This technique is also known as a linear interpolation, or "lerp" for short.

5. Set the camera to the new target position.

Now add the following line to the bottom of `didMoveToView(_:)`:

```
setCameraPosition(CGPoint(x: size.width/2, y: size.height/2))
```

This code will center the camera. To make sure that the camera is tracking your hero at all times, add this line to the top of `update(_:)`:

```
updateCamera()
```

Build and run to see how the camera tracks the hero, always keeping him onscreen.

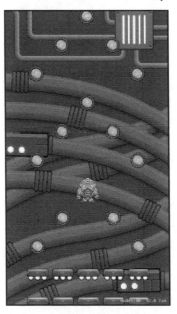

> **Note**: You may notice if you jump far enough, the background disappears! Don't worry, you'll fix that soon.

Let the lava flow

You've almost all of the gameplay for Drop Charge in place. It's time to set the antagonist—lava—into motion.

Begin by adding this property to **GameScene.swift**:

```
var lava: SKSpriteNode!
```

Then add this line to `setupNodes()`:

```
lava = fgNode.childNodeWithName("Lava") as! SKSpriteNode
```

You use this property to hold your "Lava" node that you set up in the scene editor. Now add the following method:

```
func updateLava(dt: NSTimeInterval) {
  // 1
  let lowerLeft = CGPoint(x: 0, y: cameraNode.position.y -
    (size.height / 2))
  // 2
  let visibleMinYFg = scene!.convertPoint(lowerLeft, toNode:
    fgNode).y
  // 3
  let lavaVelocity = CGPoint(x: 0, y: 120)
  let lavaStep = lavaVelocity * CGFloat(dt)
  var newPosition = lava.position + lavaStep
  // 4
  newPosition.y = max(newPosition.y, (visibleMinYFg - 125.0))
  // 5
  lava.position = newPosition
}
```

Here's what's going on with `updateLava(_:)`:

1. This calculates the lower left position of the viewable part of the screen. Since the (y) position is changing constantly, you are subtracting the height of the scene from the camera's current (y) position.

2. The Lava's parent (`fgNode`) position is relative to `lowerLeft`, so you convert the position to scene coordinates.

3. Here you are defining a base velocity for the lava, then multiplying the velocity by the current time step, and adding it to lava's position.

4. The `max` method returns the highest (y) position between `newPosition` and a position slightly below the visible area of the screen. This keeps the lava in sync with the camera position; otherwise it would fall behind as the hero climbs his way up.

5. Finally, you set the lava's position to the calculated `newPosition`.

Next, add this method:

```
func updateCollisionLava() {
  if player.position.y < lava.position.y + 90 {
    boostPlayer()
  }
}
```

This pseudo collision detector doesn't actually detect contact between the lava and player nodes, but rather compares their proximity to each other. If the marine falls too close to the lava, he'll jump up as if his feet are afire!

Now you need to modify the camera to accommodate the lava. Scroll back to updateCamera() and add these lines just after var targetPosition...:

```
let lavaPos = convertPoint(lava.position, fromNode: fgNode)
targetPosition.y = max(targetPosition.y, lavaPos.y)
```

Also within updateCamera(), change lerpValue to:

```
let lerpValue = CGFloat(0.2)
```

These modifications get the current lava position and compares it to the camera target; choosing the larger of the two values. This keeps the lava from appearing higher than the middle of the screen.

Before you build and run let's properly set up your update(_:) method. Start by adding the following properties:

```
var lastUpdateTimeInterval: NSTimeInterval = 0
var deltaTime: NSTimeInterval = 0
```

Then replace update(_:) with:

```
override func update(currentTime: NSTimeInterval) {
  // 1
  if lastUpdateTimeInterval > 0 {
    deltaTime = currentTime - lastUpdateTimeInterval
  } else {
    deltaTime = 0
  }
  lastUpdateTimeInterval = currentTime
  // 2
  if paused { return }
  // 3
  if isPlaying == true {
    updateCamera()
    updatePlayer()
    updateLava(deltaTime)
    updateCollisionLava()
```

```
    }
  }
```

Here's a quick overview:

1. `currentTime` is a relatively large number and can be unwieldy for some methods that use a time step, such as your `updateLava(_:)` method. So `deltaTime` is calculated to a much more manageable fraction.

2. Next you check to see if the scene is paused, and if so, exit the method.

3. Then check to see if the game is playing, and if it is, call your update methods, including your new lava methods.

Now go ahead and build and run, and play your game for a bit. Everything is looking great! You've got some hot lava, the marine is collecting coins and jumping from platform, to platform, then—hey! Houston we've got a problem!

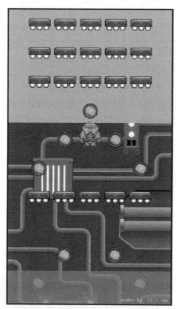

Repeating the background, coins and platforms

You've got one more method to add. To make this game a continuous platform jumper, there should be a never ending supply of coins and platforms.

Implement the following method in **GameScene.swift**:

```
func updateLevel() {
  let cameraPos = getCameraPosition()
  if cameraPos.y > levelY - (size.height * 0.55) {
    createBackgroundNode()
    while lastItemPosition.y < levelY {
      addRandomOverlayNode()
    }
  }
}
```

This tracks the camera's position and adds a new background node, as well as a random platform or coin overlay node when needed. Now call it by adding this line to `update(_:)`:

```
updateLevel()
```

One more thing

The marine needs a little more pop in his jump now that everything is properly set up. Scroll to `setPlayerVelocity(_:)` and change `gain` to:

```
let gain: CGFloat = 2.5
```

Now that you've completed most of the basic gameplay for Drop Charge, build and run to see everything you've accomplished.

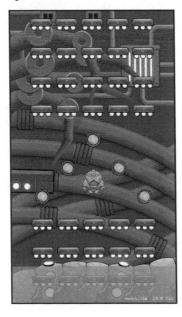

Congratulations - you now have the core gameplay for Drop Charge complete, and have reviewed everything you've learned about Sprite Kit so far!

Now that you have a solid understanding of the basics of Sprite Kit, it's time to move onto some new techniques, such as state machines, particle systems, and adding Juice. By the time you've done the next three chapters, you'll take this basic gameplay and make it shine!

Challenges

You only created two object overlays for Drop Charge: a standard five-across platform and an arrow pattern of coins. It would be a lot more interesting if your game had a variety of platform and coin patterns.

You're going to practice what you've learned on your own by creating additional object overlays. This mission is divided into four challenges. As you begin to work through them, keep in mind that each object has its own physics category to differentiate itself in `didBeginContact(_:)`.

And remember, if you get stuck with any of these challenges, you can find the solutions in the resources for this chapter. But give them your best shot first!

Challenge 1: Create a five-across breakable platform

In Drop Charge, there will be platforms that break when the marine lands on them. Using the **block_break01** art from the Media Library, create a **Break5Across.sks** file. Don't worry about making the platform break—you'll do that in the next chapter.

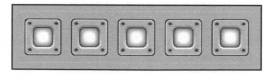

Challenge 2: Create a "special" coin arrow

When your hero collects a "special" coin, you want him to get a bigger boost! Using the **powerup01_1** art from the Media Library, create a **CoinSArrow.sks** file, making only the top coin "special".

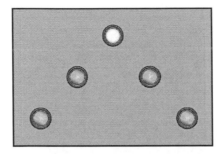

Important: Be sure to name your special coins "special", as certain methods will look for this name in Chapter 17, "Juice Up Your Game".

Challenge 3: Create additional platform and coin patterns

- **PlatformArrow.sks**: an arrow pattern of five standard platforms.

- **PlatformDiagonal.sks**: a diagonal pattern of five standard platforms.

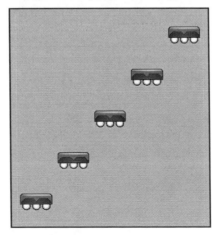

- **BreakArrow.sks**: an arrow pattern of five breakable platforms.

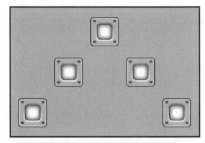

- **BreakDiagonal.sks**: a diagonal pattern of five breakable platforms.

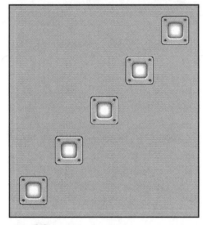

- **Coin5Across.sks**: a pattern of five coins across.

- **CoinDiagonal.sks**: a diagonal pattern of five coins.

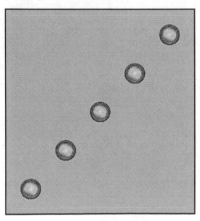

- **CoinCross.sks**: a cross pattern of nine coins. Make five coins horizontal and five vertical—no need to duplicate the center coin.

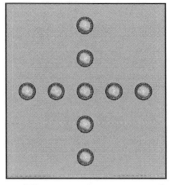

- **CoinS5Across.sks**: a pattern of five coins across, two of them special coins.

- **CoinSDiagonal.sks**: a diagonal pattern of five coins, two of them special.

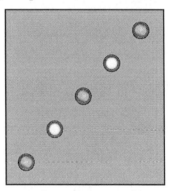

- **CoinSCross.sks**: a cross pattern of nine coins just like the standard coin cross, but include three special coins in the horizontal bar.

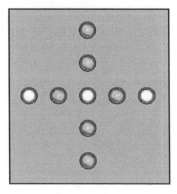

- **Optional**: Can you think of other interesting platform/coin patterns for your game? Using what you learned, come up with your own pattern!

> **Hint:** You can save yourself a bit of work by duplicating and renaming existing **.sks** files from the finder and using them as the basis for your new ones.

Challenge 4: Add code for new overlay objects

Now that you've created additional platform and coin overlays, update **GameScene.swift** to use the new objects.

Here are a few hints:

- Add properties to hold your SKSpriteNode overlays.

- Load the overlays from setupNodes().

- Update addRandomOverlayNode() to accommodate the new overlays. Use logic statements to choose regular platforms 75% of the time and breakable platforms for the remaining 25%. Do the same for regular coins versus special coins.

- Update didBeginContact(_:) to add a new case for .CoinSpecial that boosts the player (rather than jumping the player).

- Update didBeginContact(_:) to add a new case for .PlatformBreakable that is just like .PlatformNormal except it also removes the platform from the game.

If you get this working, congratulations; you have truly mastered the material so far in this book!

In the next chapter, you'll learn about **state machines**—what they are and how useful they can be in keeping your code organized. You'll also expand Drop Charge's gameplay by adding code to accommodate the game ending—in other words, what happens when the player succumbs to the lava!

Chapter 15: State Machines

By Michael Briscoe

Drop Charge is starting to come together! In the previous chapter, you built the game's UI and level objects using the scene editor. You also added the code for most of the basic gameplay. In this chapter, you'll further enhance the game while learning about **state machines**.

Most gameplay logic is governed by the current **state** of the game. For example, if the game is in the "main menu" state, the player shouldn't move, but if the game is in the "action" state, it should.

In a simple app, you could manage the state by using Boolean variables inside the update loop. So far, this is the approach you've taken in Drop Charge with the `isPlaying` variable.

But as a game grows, `update(_:)` can develop convoluted logic and become difficult to maintain. By using a state machine, you can better organize your code as your game becomes more complex.

Simply put, a **state machine** manages a group of states, with a single current state and a set of rules for transitioning between states. As the state of the game changes, the state machine will run methods upon exiting the previous state and entering the next. These methods cans be used to control gameplay from within each state. After a successful state change, the machine will then execute the current state's update loop.

Many games have multiple state machines. You could use a state machine to control the hero's animation, the behavior of an enemy sprite and even the game's user interface. To better understand this concept, you'll create a state machine to manage the UI for Drop Charge, as pictured here:

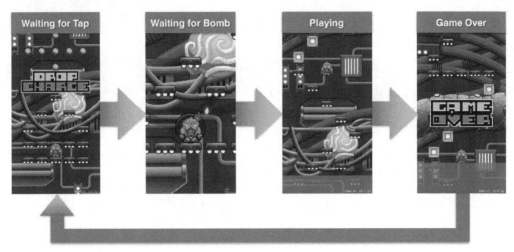

How State Machines work

Apple introduced the **GameplayKit** framework in iOS 9, which has built-in support for state machines and makes working with them easy. You'll learn more about GameplayKit later in this book, but for now, you'll use two of its many classes: the GKStateMachine and GKState classes.

To add a state machine to your game, first think about the various states that you would want to manage. In Drop Charge you have four—Waiting for Tap; Waiting for Bomb; Playing; and Game Over.

For each state, you'll subclass GKState. Within your custom class, you define state-specific behavior by overriding these four methods:

- didEnterWithPreviousState(_:): Executes when the state machine transitions into the state. The previous state is passed in here, so you can apply any logic based on the previous state.

- isValidNextState(_:): This method returns a Boolean to your state machine to indicate whether it's allowed to transition into the next state. If this returns false the state machine will ignore the request to change states.

- updateWithDeltaTime(_:): Executes periodically while the state machine is in this state. This is where you would perform actions that take place over time, such as controlling player movement or updating the camera.

- willExitWithNextState(_:): This method is called when the state machine transitions out of the state. The next state is passed in, so you can apply logic based on the next state.

After creating your GKState subclasses, you create an instance of GKStateMachine and initialize it with an array of your state objects. GKStateMachine has the following properties and methods available:

- currentState: This is a read-only property that returns the state machines current state. A state machine can only be in one state at a time.

- canEnterState(_:): Use this method to check whether you can transition into a specified state.

- enterState(_:): Call this to transition into the specified state. This is what you'll use to switch from state to state.

- updateWithDeltaTime(_:): Generally, you'll call this from within your scenes update(_:) method. The state machine will in turn call this method on its currentState to perform periodic actions.

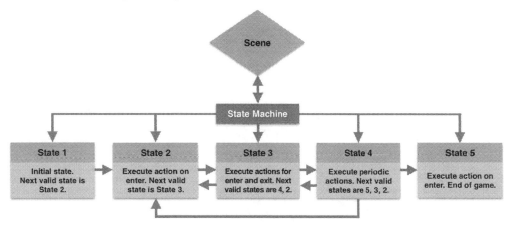

Now that you've got some state machine knowledge under your belt, it's time to put it into practice.

> **Note:** This chapter begins where the previous chapter's Challenge 4 left off. If you were unable to complete the challenges or skipped ahead from an earlier chapter, don't worry—simply open the starter project from this chapter to pick up where the previous chapter left off.

Getting started

Let's take a closer look at the four states you're going to define for Drop Charge:

1. **Waiting for Tap**: The game is waiting for user interaction. Once the player taps the screen, you transition to the Waiting for Bomb state.

2. **Waiting for Bomb**: You play a short animation of the bomb pulsing and then transition to the Playing state.

3. **Playing**: Drop Charge enters the main gameplay loop. If the player falls into the lava three times, you transition to the Game Over state.

4. **Game Over**: In this state, you stop the gameplay and display the "Game Over" sprite. When the user taps the screen, you transition back to the Waiting for Tap state.

The Game Over state means that Drop Charge will no longer be the game that never ends. Not even a fancy space suit can protect the hero from the lava anymore!

Throughout the rest of this chapter, you'll implement each state in turn. Pay attention, because when you're done, you'll be challenged to create your own state machine!

State 1: Waiting for Tap

This is your game's initial state. Its job is to display the "READY" message and wait for the user to tap the screen.

In Xcode, open either your **DropCharge** project or the starter project found in **projects \starter\DropCharge**.

Remember, to create a state machine, you first need to define your states by subclassing GKState.

Select **File\New\File...** from the main menu. Choose the **iOS\Source\Cocoa Touch Class** template and click **Next**. Enter **WaitingForTap** for the Class, **GKState** for the Subclass and **Swift** for the Language, click **Next** and then **Create**.

In the new file, replace the import UIKit line with this:

```
import SpriteKit
import GameplayKit
```

To use the GameplayKit framework, you first need to import it. You'll also be using SpriteKit, so you import that, as well.

Next, add the following code after the class declaration:

```
unowned let scene: GameScene

init(scene: SKScene) {
  self.scene = scene as! GameScene
  super.init()
}
```

You add a property to hold a reference to GameScene. This property gets initialized when you create an instance of this state, so that WaitingForTap can interact with the state machine and the scene.

Next, override didEnterWithPreviousState(_:):

```
override func didEnterWithPreviousState(previousState: GKState?)
{
  let scale = SKAction.scaleTo(1.0, duration: 0.5)
  scene.fgNode.childNodeWithName("Ready")!.runAction(scale)
}
```

Once this state is active, GKState will run this method. This is a good place to display the "READY" sprite you created in the last chapter, indicating that the game has loaded.

Now open **GameScene.swift** and add this import statement to the top of the file:

```
import GameplayKit
```

Then add the following code to your class properties:

```
lazy var gameState: GKStateMachine = GKStateMachine(states: [
    WaitingForTap(scene: self)])
```

By defining this variable, you've effectively created the state machine for Drop Charge. Notice that you're initializing GKStateMachine with an array of GKState subclasses. Well, just the one subclass for now—you'll add more later.

Now set the state by adding this code to didMoveToView(_:):

```
gameState.enterState(WaitingForTap)
```

To see what you've done so far, build and run!

Once the game is loaded and the `WaitingForTap` game state is active, the "READY" prompt appears.

State 2: Waiting for Bomb

This state will display the bomb animation and then transition to the `Playing` state.

Repeat the process for creating a new **GKState** subclass, this time naming it **WaitingForBomb**. Replace its contents with the following code:

```
import SpriteKit
import GameplayKit

class WaitingForBomb: GKState {
  unowned let scene: GameScene

  init(scene: SKScene) {
    self.scene = scene as! GameScene
    super.init()
  }

  override func didEnterWithPreviousState(
    previousState: GKState?) {
    if previousState is WaitingForTap {

      // Scale out title & ready label
      let scale = SKAction.scaleTo(0, duration: 0.4)
```

```
        scene.fgNode.childNodeWithName("Title")!.runAction(scale)
        scene.fgNode.childNodeWithName("Ready")!.runAction(
          SKAction.sequence(
            [SKAction.waitForDuration(0.2), scale]))

        // Bounce bomb
        let scaleUp = SKAction.scaleTo(1.25, duration: 0.25)
        let scaleDown = SKAction.scaleTo(1.0, duration: 0.25)
        let sequence = SKAction.sequence([scaleUp, scaleDown])
        let repeatSeq = SKAction.repeatActionForever(sequence)
        scene.fgNode.childNodeWithName("Bomb")!.runAction(
          SKAction.unhide())
        scene.fgNode.childNodeWithName("Bomb")!.runAction(
          repeatSeq)
    }
  }
}
```

When Drop Charge enters this state, `didEnterWithPreviousState(_:)` will animate the title sprite and the "READY" message off of the screen, and start the bomb animation.

Open **GameScene.swift** and replace your `gameState` variable declaration with this:

```
lazy var gameState: GKStateMachine = GKStateMachine(states: [
    WaitingForTap(scene: self),
    WaitingForBomb(scene: self)
    ])
```

You add your new state to the state machine.

Next, replace `touchesBegan(_:withEvent:)` with the following:

```
override func touchesBegan(touches: Set<UITouch>, withEvent
event: UIEvent?) {
  switch gameState.currentState {
  case is WaitingForTap:
    gameState.enterState(WaitingForBomb)

  default:
    break
  }
}
```

This bit of code switches game states, depending on the current state, when the user taps the screen.

While you're here, delete `bombDrop()` and `startGame()`, since you're going to move these actions into your state machine.

One more bit of business and you're done with this state. Open **WaitingForTap.swift** and implement the following method:

```
override func isValidNextState(stateClass: AnyClass) -> Bool {
  return stateClass is WaitingForBomb.Type
}
```

This method tells your state machine that `WaitingForTap` can only transition to certain valid states—in this case, Waiting For Bomb. This "rule" prevents the game from accidentally transitioning to the wrong state. It wouldn't be fair to send your player to the `GameOver` state on the first tap. ;]

ZERO
STARS!1!!

Build and run. Now, when you touch the screen, you'll see a bomb pulsing behind your hero—forever! If the suspense is too much for you, move quickly to the next section.

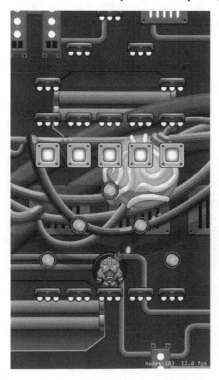

State 3: Playing

This state is where all the action takes place. Drop Charge will enter the gameplay loop and check to see if the hero has fallen into the lava. If the hero collides with the lava three times, the state machine will transition to the `GameOver` state.

Like before, create a new **GKState** subclass. This time, name it **Playing** and replace its contents with the following code:

```
import SpriteKit
import GameplayKit

class Playing: GKState {
  unowned let scene: GameScene

  init(scene: SKScene) {
    self.scene = scene as! GameScene
    super.init()
  }
}
```

There's nothing new going on here, but you'll be adding to this class in a moment.

Now switch back to **WaitingForBomb.swift** and add these methods:

```
override func isValidNextState(stateClass: AnyClass) -> Bool {
  return stateClass is Playing.Type
}

override func willExitWithNextState(nextState: GKState) {
  if nextState is Playing {
    scene.fgNode.childNodeWithName("Bomb")!.removeFromParent()
  }
}
```

In the familiar first method, you define the next valid state. You execute `willExitWithNextState(_:)` when the game transitions to `Playing`. That's a good time to do a little cleanup, so you remove the bomb sprite from the scene. In the next chapter, you'll do something more exciting with the bomb by adding an explosion.

Open **GameScene.swift** and update the `gameState` variable to add your new state:

```
lazy var gameState: GKStateMachine = GKStateMachine(states: [
    WaitingForTap(scene: self),
    WaitingForBomb(scene: self),
    Playing(scene: self)
    ])
```

Now scroll down to `touchesBegan(_:withEvent:)` and add the following just below gameState.enterState(WaitingForBomb):

```
// Switch to playing state
self.runAction(SKAction.waitForDuration(2.0),
  completion:{
    self.gameState.enterState(Playing)
})
```

This action makes sure the game switches to the Playing state after a couple of seconds of the bomb animation.

Switch back to **Playing.swift** and add the following:

```
override func didEnterWithPreviousState(previousState: GKState?)
{
  if previousState is WaitingForBomb {
    scene.player.physicsBody!.dynamic = true
    scene.superBoostPlayer()
  }
}
```

Build and run, tap the screen, and watch as the game enters the Playing state. Let the fun begin!

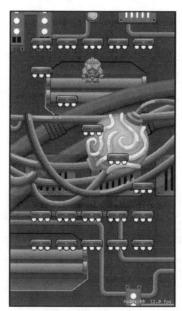

Updating the gameplay

OK, so it's not much fun yet. You still need to add the method calls to update the hero, camera, lava and so forth.

Before you added game states, you made those calls in the scene's update(_:). Now you're going to pass them on to the state machine.

Still in **Playing.swift**, implement this new method:

```
override func updateWithDeltaTime(seconds: NSTimeInterval) {
  scene.updateCamera()
  scene.updateLevel()
  scene.updatePlayer()
  scene.updateLava(seconds)
  scene.updateCollisionLava()
}
```

The updateWithDeltaTime(_:) method is similar to your scenes update(_:) method, as it gets called periodically. Since this is the games Playing state, this is where you'll call the update methods for gameplay.

Switch back to **GameScene.swift** and change update(_:) as follows:

```
override func update(currentTime: CFTimeInterval) {
  if lastUpdateTimeInterval > 0 {
    deltaTime = currentTime - lastUpdateTimeInterval
  } else {
    deltaTime = 0
  }
  lastUpdateTimeInterval = currentTime
  if paused { return }
  gameState.updateWithDeltaTime(deltaTime)
}
```

This calls the state machine's updateWithDeltaTime(_:), which in turn calls the same method on the current state. Now you're seeing the real power of state machines!

To make the switch to your state machine complete, scroll to the top and remove the isPlaying variable from your properties.

Build and run. The game plays much as it did before you started this chapter, but this time with much more manageable code, thanks to the state machine.

 I am head
of state!

State 4: Game Over

So far, you've been playing an endless game, suffering no consequences when the hero falls into the lava. The GameOver state will fix that.

Create one more **GKState** subclass and name it—you've guessed it—**GameOver**. Replace its contents with the following:

```
import SpriteKit
import GameplayKit

class GameOver: GKState {
  unowned let scene: GameScene

  init(scene: SKScene) {
    self.scene = scene as! GameScene
    super.init()
  }

  override func didEnterWithPreviousState(previousState:
GKState?) {
    if previousState is Playing {
      scene.physicsWorld.contactDelegate = nil
      scene.player.physicsBody?.dynamic = false

      let moveUpAction = SKAction.moveByX(0,
        y: scene.size.height/2, duration: 0.5)
      moveUpAction.timingMode = .EaseOut
      let moveDownAction = SKAction.moveByX(0,
        y: -(scene.size.height * 1.5), duration: 1.0)
      moveDownAction.timingMode = .EaseIn
      let sequence = SKAction.sequence(
        [moveUpAction, moveDownAction])
      scene.player.runAction(sequence)

      let gameOver = SKSpriteNode(imageNamed: "GameOver")
      gameOver.position = scene.getCameraPosition()
      gameOver.zPosition = 10
      scene.addChild(gameOver)
    }
  }

  override func isValidNextState(stateClass: AnyClass) -> Bool {
    return stateClass is WaitingForTap.Type
  }
}
```

When Drop Charge enters the GameOver state, you turn off the game's physics and create an action to animate the hero offscreen. Then you create the "Game Over" sprite and add it to the scene.

Now switch back to **Playing.swift** and implement the following method:

```
override func isValidNextState(stateClass: AnyClass) -> Bool {
   return stateClass is GameOver.Type
}
```

As you may remember, this method tells the `Playing` state that it can only transition to certain valid states—in this case, only Game Over.

Open **GameScene.swift** and update your `gameState` variable to add the new state to your state machine:

```
lazy var gameState: GKStateMachine = GKStateMachine(states: [
    WaitingForTap(scene: self),
    WaitingForBomb(scene: self),
    Playing(scene: self),
    GameOver(scene: self)
    ])
```

Now add a new property to track your hero's number of lives:

```
var lives = 3
```

To decrement the hero's lives after a collision with the lava, change `updateCollisionLava()` as follows:

```
func updateCollisionLava() {
   if player.position.y < lava.position.y + 90 {
      boostPlayer()
      lives--
      if lives <= 0 {
         gameState.enterState(GameOver)
      }
   }
}
```

When your hero touches the lava, you decrement his lives by 1. If the number of lives is less than or equal to 0, then you transition to the `GameOver` state.

Finishing touches

One last thing and your state machine will be complete!

Replace your `touchesBegan(_:withEvent:)` with the following:

```
override func touchesBegan(touches: Set<UITouch>, withEvent
event: UIEvent?) {
   switch gameState.currentState {
```

```
  case is WaitingForTap:
    gameState.enterState(WaitingForBomb)
    // Switch to playing state
    self.runAction(SKAction.waitForDuration(2.0),
      completion:{
        self.gameState.enterState(Playing)
    })

  case is GameOver:
    let newScene = GameScene(fileNamed:"GameScene")
    newScene!.scaleMode = .AspectFill
    let reveal = SKTransition.flipHorizontalWithDuration(0.5)
    self.view?.presentScene(newScene!, transition: reveal)

  default:
    break
  }
}
```

Now when the player taps the screen, touchesBegan(_:withEvent:) will check which state the game is in using a switch statement:

- If gameState is WaitingForTap then enter the WaitingForBomb state, run the bomb animation for two seconds, then enter the Playing state.

- If gameState is GameOver then reload GameScene which effectively resets the state machine to WaitingForTap.

Build and run to see your finished state machine in action!

Drop Charge now feels much like a complete game. Through your state machine, you've added an opening bomb animation, losing criteria and a game over sequence, so users can experience your game from start to finish. More importantly, your code is now much better organized, which will make it easier to manage as you begin to add your "juice"!

Challenges

There's only one challenge this time, but it's one of the most challenging you've had in the book so far and requires mastery of this chapter's material.

It will be tough, but we believe in you! :]

As always, if you get stuck you can find the solution in the resources for this chapter--but give it your best shot first!

Challenge 1: A heroic state machine

Can you think of another object in your game that could benefit from a state machine?

What about the space marine? The space marine can be alive, in the process of dying (running the bounce up and down actions when you hit the lava), or dead. It would also be nice to keep track of whether the space marine is currently jumping or falling, so you can play the appropriate animations in later chapters.

In this chalenge, you'll practice what you've learned by creating a state machine to manage your hero's behavior. Here's a flow chart of what the player state machine should do:

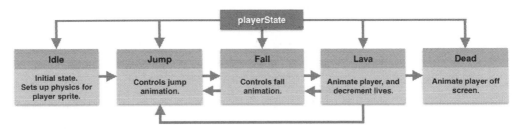

Here are some hints to get you started:

- Create an GKStateMachine named **playerState** with five GKState subclasses. You can use the **WaitingForTap.swift** file as a basic template.

- **Idle** will be the player's initial state. Move the code to set up the physics for the player sprite into this state . Remove setupPlayer() from **GameScene.swift**.

- **Jump** will control the jump animation. Just add the init() and isValidNextState(_:) methods for now; you'll add more to this state later. Also add a `didEnterWithPreviousState(_:)` method with printing out the name of the state for debugging purposes.

- **Fall** will control the fall animation. Just add the `init()` and `isValidNextState(_:)` methods for now; you'll add more to this state later. Also add a `didEnterWithPreviousState(_:)` method with printing out the name of the state for debugging purposes.

- **Lava** will control what happens when the player touches the lava. Set this state within `updateCollisionLava()` in **GameScene.swift**. Move the code that boosts the player and decrements his lives into this state.

- **Dead** will control what happens when the player has lost all his lives. Also set this state within `updateCollisionLava()`, just before setting `gameState` to `GameOver`. Move the code that animates the player offscreen into this state.

Within the **GameScene.swift** file:

- Don't forget to add your state machine to the properties!

- Enter the `Idle` state in `didMoveToView()`.

- You'll need to add code to `updatePlayer()` to check the player's y-velocity and set the state to `Fall` or `Jump`.

Build and run, and the game should work as usual, but now nicely refactored (along with some print statements when you jump or fall).

Over the next two chapters you will flesh out the `playerState` with additional code as you add more "juice".

In the next chapter, you'll learn about **particle systems**, and how they can be used to create stunning visual effects like explosions and smoke—and lava!

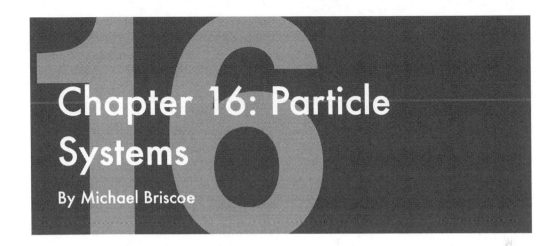

Chapter 16: Particle Systems

By Michael Briscoe

Nothing can "juice" up your game quite like a particle system.

Particle systems such as this spectacular explosion are an easy way to create a variety of special effects in your games. Here are just a few of the things you can simulate with a particle system:

Smoke	Water	Fog
Star Fields	Snow	Rain
Fire	Explosions	Fireworks
Sparks	Blood	Bubbles

And this is only the beginning. It's impossible to imagine all you could do with a particle system, and it pays to be creative. For instance, say you want to simulate subatomic particles emanating from a rip in the space-time continuum. That's easy!

What makes particle systems so great? Without a particle system, to achieve a special effect like the explosion above, you'd have to resort to traditional frame-by-frame animation techniques. This would require several images taking up significant texture space and memory—not to mention be tedious to create—and the results might not look very realistic. In a particle system, the effects are created with a small image texture and a configuration file, greatly reducing memory requirements. This allows for real-time editing and rendering, resulting in greater realism.

In this chapter, you'll continue preparing Drop Charge for its juice-up by using particle systems to create three dazzling special effects. You'll learn how to implement particle systems programmatically, as well as by using the Xcode editor.

> **Note**: This chapter begins where the previous chapter's challenge left off. If you were unable to complete the challenge or skipped ahead from an earlier chapter, don't worry—simply open the starter project for this chapter to pick up where the previous chapter left off.

How do particle systems work?

Before you start coding, it's important to know how particle systems work, both in theory and within Sprite Kit.

Particle systems in theory

A single particle in Sprite Kit is simply two triangles put together to create a square or quad. This quad is then textured, colored and rendered to the screen. For example, here's a raindrop depicted as a particle:

During each frame, the particle system looks at each individual particle it owns and advances it according to the system's configuration. For example, the configuration might say, "Move each particle between 2-10 pixels toward the bottom of the screen." You can see the effects of this configuration in the following diagram:

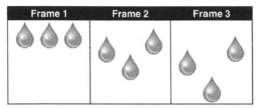

When it's initialized, a particle system will typically create a cache of particles known as the **particle pool**. When it's time for a new particle to be born, the particle system will obtain an available particle from its particle pool, set the initial values of the new particle and then add it to the rendering queue.

When the particle has reached the end of its life, the system will remove it from the render queue and return it to the particle pool, to be used at a later time.

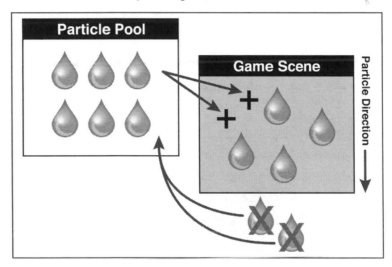

Particle systems in practice

Sprite Kit makes it incredibly easy to create and use particle systems by giving you a special node named `SKEmitterNode`, the sole purpose of which is to make particle systems and render them as quickly as possible.

This section will give you a quick overview of how to use particle systems in Sprite Kit. You'll begin by reading through this information without doing anything in Xcode. This will likely get you excited to try it out for yourself. Later in the chapter, you'll do just that.

To use an `SKEmitterNode` programmatically, you simply declare an instance of the node and configure its properties, like so:

```
let rainTexture = SKTexture(imageNamed: "Rain_Drop.png")
let emitterNode = SKEmitterNode()
emitterNode.particleTexture = rainTexture
emitterNode.particleBirthRate = 80.0
emitterNode.particleColor = SKColor.whiteColor()
emitterNode.particleSpeed = -450
emitterNode.particleSpeedRange = 150
emitterNode.particleLifetime = 2.0
emitterNode.particleScale = 0.2
emitterNode.particleScaleRange = 0.5
emitterNode.particleAlpha = 0.75
emitterNode.particleAlphaRange = 0.5
emitterNode.position = CGPoint(x: CGRectGetWidth(frame) / 2, y:
CGRectGetHeight(frame) + 10)
emitterNode.particlePositionRange = CGVector(dx:
CGRectGetMaxX(frame), dy: 0)
addChild(emitterNode)
```

For now, don't worry about what these properties mean—you'll learn about them shortly. To see the effects of this code, open and run the **Rain** project included in the **starter\examples** folder.

You can also use Xcode's built-in editor to visually create and configure a particle system:

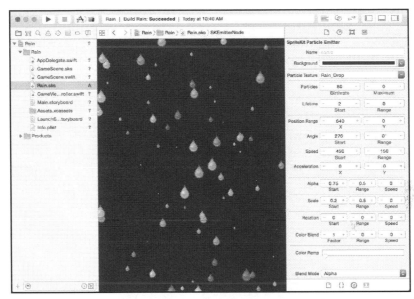

To do this, you simply create a new file with the **iOS\Resource\SpriteKit Particle File** template, resulting in an **.sks** file that you can edit with the built-in particle emittor editor.

Then, in code, you create an SKEmitterNode with the file, like this:

```
let rainEmitter = SKEmitterNode(fileNamed: "Rain.sks")!
rainEmitter.position = CGPoint(x: 320, y: 960)
addChild(rainEmitter)
```

This visual editor is super convenient, because it lets you visualize the particle system in real time as you tweak its properties, making it quick and easy to get the exact effects you want.

There's much more to discover, but it's time to begin to learn by doing. You'll create your first particle system for Drop Charge by implementing an SKEmitterNode programmatically. Later, you'll create additional effects using the visual editor.

Programmatic particle systems

Wouldn't it be great if the bomb in Drop Charge actually exploded instead of just winking off the screen? In this section, you'll get your first taste of particle systems by creating an explosion at the start of the game. You'll create it programmatically to help you understand what's going on behind the scenes.

Open your **DropCharge** project in Xcode. If you've skipped ahead, you can open the project located in **starter**.

Sprite Kit renders every particle displayed onscreen using a single texture attached to the particle system. This texture can be anything you wish, giving you great freedom to customize the look of your particles.

From the project navigator, open the **Assets.xcassets** file. Drag the **spark.png** file from **starter\resources** into the left sidebar. This is a white circular image that you will tint orange, and create a ton of copies of to look like an explosion.

Now that you have a texture, you can create the particle system.

Core properties of particle systems

Open **GameScene.swift** and implement the following method:

```swift
func explosion(intensity: CGFloat) -> SKEmitterNode {
  let emitter = SKEmitterNode()
  let particleTexture = SKTexture(imageNamed: "spark")

  emitter.zPosition = 2
  emitter.particleTexture = particleTexture
  emitter.particleBirthRate = 4000 * intensity
  emitter.numParticlesToEmit = Int(400 * intensity)
  emitter.particleLifetime = 2.0
  emitter.emissionAngle = CGFloat(90.0).degreesToRadians()
  emitter.emissionAngleRange = CGFloat(360.0).degreesToRadians()
  emitter.particleSpeed = 600 * intensity
  emitter.particleSpeedRange = 1000 * intensity
  emitter.particleAlpha = 1.0
  emitter.particleAlphaRange = 0.25
  emitter.particleScale = 1.2
  emitter.particleScaleRange = 2.0
  emitter.particleScaleSpeed = -1.5
  emitter.particleColor = SKColor.orangeColor()
  emitter.particleColorBlendFactor = 1
  emitter.particleBlendMode = SKBlendMode.Add
  emitter.runAction(SKAction.removeFromParentAfterDelay(2.0))

  return emitter
}
```

This method creates, configures and returns an `SKEmitterNode` based on an "intensity factor" representing how strong you would like the explosion, allowing you to reuse this method to add additional explosions later in the game. You first create a new `SKEmitterNode` and an `SKTexture`. Then, after setting the emitter's `zPosition`, you set these properties:

- **particleTexture** is the texture to use for each particle, and probably the most important property to set. The default value is `nil`, and if you don't set a texture, the emitter uses a colored rectangle to draw the particle.

- **particleBirthRate** is the rate at which the emitter generates the particles per second. It defaults to 0.0. If you leave the birth rate at 0.0, the emitter won't generate any particles. In your method above, you set the `particleBirthRate` to a high value of `4000` so that the emitter generates its particles very quickly, creating an explosive effect.

- **numParticlesToEmit** is the number of particles the emitter will generate before stopping. The default value is 0, which means the emitter will generate an endless stream of particles. You want this emitter to stop after generating a few particles.

- **particleLifetime** is the duration of time, in seconds, each particle is active. The default value is 0.0, and if you don't change this, the emitter won't generate any particles.

- **emissionAngle** is the angle from which the particles are emitted. The default value is 0.0, which is straight down. In your method, you set the particles to initially emit straight up. Controlling the emission angle can be useful when you want to create effects like fountains or geysers, where the water should move up the screen before slowing and falling back down the screen, as if affected by gravity.

- **emissionAngleRange** randomizes the emission angle plus or minus half the range value. This is really useful when simulating explosions. The default value is 0.0. By setting it to 360°, you give the explosion a more realistic round shape.

- **particleSpeed** is the initial speed for a new particle in points per second. The default value is 0.0. In your method, you scale the speed to create explosions of varying intensity.

- **particleSpeedRange** randomizes the particle speed, plus or minus half the range value. The default value is 0.0. This property is especially important for simulating turbulence, without which your explosion would look like an 'O'.

- **particleAlpha** is the average starting alpha value for each particle, and thus determines the transparency of your particles. The default value is 1.0, which is fully opaque.

- **particleAlphaRange** randomizes the particle alpha, plus or minus half the range value. The default value is 0.0, which makes some of the particles slightly transparent.

- **particleScale** is the scale at which the emitter renders each particle. The default value is 1.0, which means the emitter renders the texture for each particle at the texture's full size. Values greater than 1.0 scale up the particles while values less than 1.0 scale them down.

- **particleScaleRange** randomizes the particle scale plus or minus half the range value. The default value is 0.0, which varies the size of your particles for a more convincing explosion.

- **particleScaleSpeed** is the rate at which a particle's scale factor changes per second. The default value is 0.0. In your method, you use a negative number so that the particles quickly shrink and wink out of sight.

- **particleColor** is the color the emitter blends with the particle texture using the `particleColorBlendFactor` (see below). The default value is `SKColor.clearColor()`. In your method, you set this to orange so that the particles look more like fire and sparks.

- **particleColorBlendFactor** is the amount of color the emitter applies to the texture when rendering each particle. It defaults to 0.0, which means the emitter uses the color of the texture and blends none of the color specified in `particleColor`. A value greater than 0.0 blends the texture color with the `particleColor` using the defined `particleBlendMode` (see below).

- **particleBlendMode** is the blending mode used to blend particles with the other colors onscreen. The default value is `SKBlendModeAlpha`, which means that the particles and other objects are blended by multiplying the particles' alpha value. In your method, you set the blend mode to `SKBlendModeAdd`, which adds the particles' and objects' colors together—making the particles seem to give off light.

After setting the emitter's properties, you attach an action to remove the emitter after a two-second delay. The method then returns the configured emitter node.

As you can see, there are a lot of properties you can set on an `SKEmitterNode`—and there are even more you'll learn about very soon.

Now that you have a method that can create and configure a particle system, add one to your scene to see what it looks like.

Open **WaitingForBomb.swift**. Within `willExitWithNextState(_:)`, find this line:

```
scene.fgNode.childNodeWithName("Bomb")!.removeFromParent()
```

And replace it with the following code:

```
let bomb = scene.fgNode.childNodeWithName("Bomb")!
let explosion = scene.explosion(2.0)
explosion.position = bomb.position
scene.fgNode.addChild(explosion)
bomb.removeFromParent()
```

This bit of code grabs a reference to the bomb sprite and creates an explosion particle system. Then, it places the explosion at the bomb's position, adds the particle system to the scene and removes the bomb sprite.

Build and run to see this in action.

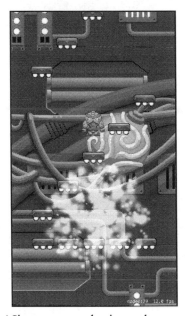

Now that's an explosive start! I'm sure you don't need any more convincing that particle systems can really juice up your game!

Advancing the simulation in time

At times, your particle system simulations will need to start from some point in the future, as in the case of a star field or weather. In other words, you may want the simulation to begin with a screen full of stars, rain or snowflakes—not wait for them to slowly fall from the top of the screen.

To demonstrate this, open and run the **Starfield** project located in **starter\examples**. Notice that it takes a few seconds for the screen to fill with stars.

Not very convincing, is it?

Still in the **Starfield** project, open **GameScene.swift** and add the following line to didMoveToView(_:), just after setting the emitter position but before adding the emitter to the scene:

```
emitter.advanceSimulationTime(15)
```

This property sets the start time of the particle system ahead by 15 seconds, effectively filling the sky with stars.

Build and run to see the difference.

Now you see a screen full of stars, as if you were traveling on a starship at warp speed! Any time you want to advance a particle system to a point beyond its initial state, you'll find this method handy.

More core properties of particle systems

There are a number of other core particle system properties. Here's a list of what's available:

> **Note:** Unless stated otherwise, all of these properties default to 0.

- **particleZPosition**: The starting z-position for each particle.
- **particleColorRed/Green/Blue/AlphaSpeed**: The rate at which each color component changes per second, per particle.
- **particleColorBlendFactorSpeed**: The rate at which the blend factor changes per second.
- **xAcceleration**: The amount of x-acceleration to apply to the velocity of each particle. This property is useful for simulating wind.

- **yAcceleration**: The amount of y-acceleration to apply to the velocity of each particle. This property is useful for simulating gravity.

- **particleRotation**: The starting rotation to apply to each particle.

- **particleRotationSpeed**: The rate at which the amount of rotation should change over one second.

- **particleSize**: The initial size of each particle. It defaults to `CGSizeZero`, causing the particle to use the assigned texture size as its initial size. If you haven't assigned a texture to your particle, you must set this property to a non-empty size or you won't see anything.

- **particleScaleSpeed**: The rate at which to modify the particle scale over one second.

- **particleAlphaSpeed**: The rate at which to modify the particle alpha value over one second.

- **targetNode**: This lets you render particles as if they belong to another node. It's an important property that you can use to create some unique effects. You'll learn more about this property later.

Range properties

There is another set of properties on `SKEmitterNode` designed to allow you to add random variance to a related property. You've seen examples of this already, when you used `emissionAngleRange`, `particleSpeedRange`, `particleAlphaRange` and `particleScaleRange` to add random values to the explosion emitter. Without these properties, your explosion would look more like an electric candle flame.

These range properties are very important when you're trying to simulate real world objects and phenomena. By adding a bit of randomness to the way your system generates particles, you're introducing *turbulence* and adding realism to your effects.

Here are other properties that can have random variance:

- **particleLifetimeRange**: Use this to randomize the lifetime of each particle, meaning some particles will live longer than other particles.

- **particlePositionRange**: This starts every particle in a random position. It defaults to (0.0, 0.0), meaning all particles originate from the same position.

- **particleRotationRange**: Use this to randomize the initial rotation of each particle.

- **particleColorRed/Green/Blue/AlphaRange**: This creates each particle with random red/green/blue/alpha component values, according to the range.

- **particleColorBlendFactorRange**: This randomizes the initial blend factor for each particle.

Keyframe properties

There are four properties on SKEmitterNode that provide a very cool technique referred to as **key framing**. Instead of varying the property between a single value and a random range, the idea with key frames is to change a property to several specific values over time.

For example, there is a keyframe property on SKEmitterNode of type SKKeyframeSequence named particleColorSequence:

```
var particleColorSequence: SKKeyframeSequence?
```

To use a keyframe property, you first initialize it and then add one or more keyframes. Each keyframe has two properties:

- **value**: This is the value the property takes when this keyframe occurs. particleColorSequence expects an SKColor instance for the value, such as SKColor.yellowColor(). Other properties may expect different types of values.

- **time**: This is the time the keyframe occurs within the lifetime of the particle, with a value ranging from 0 (the moment the particle is created) to 1 (the moment the particle is destroyed). For example, if the lifetime of a particle is 10 seconds and you specify 0.25 for time, the keyframe would occur at 2.5 seconds.

Give key framing a shot by using the particleColorSequence to make the explosion more lifelike.

Switch back to your **DropCharge** project and open **GameScene.swift**. Add the following code to explosion(_:), before the return statement:

```
let sequence = SKKeyframeSequence(capacity: 5)
sequence.addKeyframeValue(SKColor.whiteColor(), time: 0)
sequence.addKeyframeValue(SKColor.yellowColor(), time: 0.10)
sequence.addKeyframeValue(SKColor.orangeColor(), time: 0.15)
sequence.addKeyframeValue(SKColor.redColor(), time: 0.75)
sequence.addKeyframeValue(SKColor.blackColor(), time: 0.95)
emitter.particleColorSequence = sequence
```

Also **remove** the emitter.particleColor = SKColor.orangeColor() line, as you no longer need it.

The code you just added does the following:

1. It creates an SKKeyframeSequence and initializes it with a capacity of 5, since you'll be adding five color keyframes.

2. It adds an SKColor.whiteColor() when the particle is first generated.

3. It adds an SKColor.yellowColor() when 10% of the particle's life has passed.

4. It adds an SKColor.orangeColor() when 15% of the particle's life has passed. This is the dominant color.

5. It adds an SKColor.redColor() when 75% of the particle's life has passed.

6. It adds an SKColor.blackColor() just before the particle is destroyed.

Build and run to see your modified explosion.

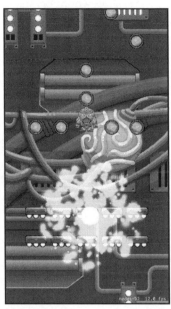

The explosion starts out brighter than before and then fades away to glowing embers. It's a subtle effect, but remember, adding juice is all about the details—especially the subtle ones!

There are three other properties that support keyframe sequences:

- **particleColorBlendFactorSequence**: This allows you to accurately control the blend factor applied to each particle during its lifetime.

- **particleScaleSequence**: Using this sequence allows you to scale each particle up and down multiple times during its lifetime.

- **particleAlphaSequence**: The sequence gives you full control over each particle's alpha channel during its lifetime.

Sequence properties

There are two important properties to mention for SKKeyframeSequence: the interpolationMode and the repeatMode.

The interpolationMode property specifies how to calculate the values for times between each keyframe. The available `interpolationMode` values are:

- **Linear**: This mode calculates the interpolation values linearly. This is the default mode.

- **Spline**: This mode calculates the interpolation values using a spline, which gives the effect of easing at the start and end of a keyframe sequence. If you were to scale a particle with this mode, then the scaling would begin slowly, pick up speed and then slow down until coming to the end of the sequence, providing a smooth transition.

- **Step**: This mode does *not* interpolate the time values between keyframes. It simply calculates the value as that of the most recent keyframe.

The `repeatMode` property specifies how to calculate values if they're outside of the keyframes defined in the sequence. It's possible to define keyframes from 0.0 all the way to 1.0, but you don't have to; you could have a keyframe that runs from 0.25 to 0.75. In that case, the `repeatMode` property defines what values to use from 0.0 to 0.25 and from 0.75 to 1.0. The available `SKRepeatMode` values are:

- **Clamp**: This mode clamps the value to the range of time values found in the sequence. If, for example, the last keyframe in a sequence had a time value of 0.5, any time from 0.5 to 1.0 would return the last keyframe value. This is the default mode.

- **Loop**: This mode causes the sequence to loop. If, for example, the last keyframe in a sequence had a time value of 0.5, any time from 0.5 to 1.0 would return the same value as from 0.0 to 0.5.

Visually-created particle systems

Now that you've got a big explosion to start the game, let's heat up the lava! This time, you're going to create the lava particle system within Xcode's particle emitter editor.

Creating an SKS file

Adding particle systems programmatically is not your only option. Sprite Kit also supports an Xcode file type named an SKS file. This file allows you to store all of the necessary settings for a particle system in a single file as part of your project, so you can take full advantage of the built-in Xcode editor, as well as of easy loading and saving via `NSCoding`.

OK! It's time to create a new group to hold all of your particle systems. With **GameScene.swift** highlighted, select **File\New\Group** from the main menu. Name this group **Particles** and click Enter to confirm.

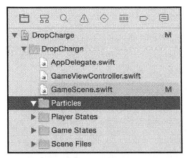

With the **Particles** group highlighted, select **File\New\File...** from the main menu. Select **iOS\Resource\SpriteKit Particle File**.

Click **Next**. On the next screen, you'll see a drop-down that contains a number of different particle templates.

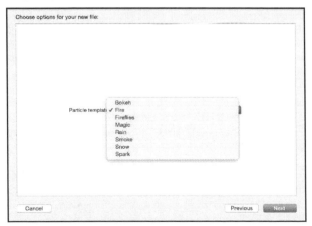

These templates give you a handy starting point from which to create your own particles. The items in the list are common particle configurations that you can adapt to your own needs. The following images show what each template looks like:

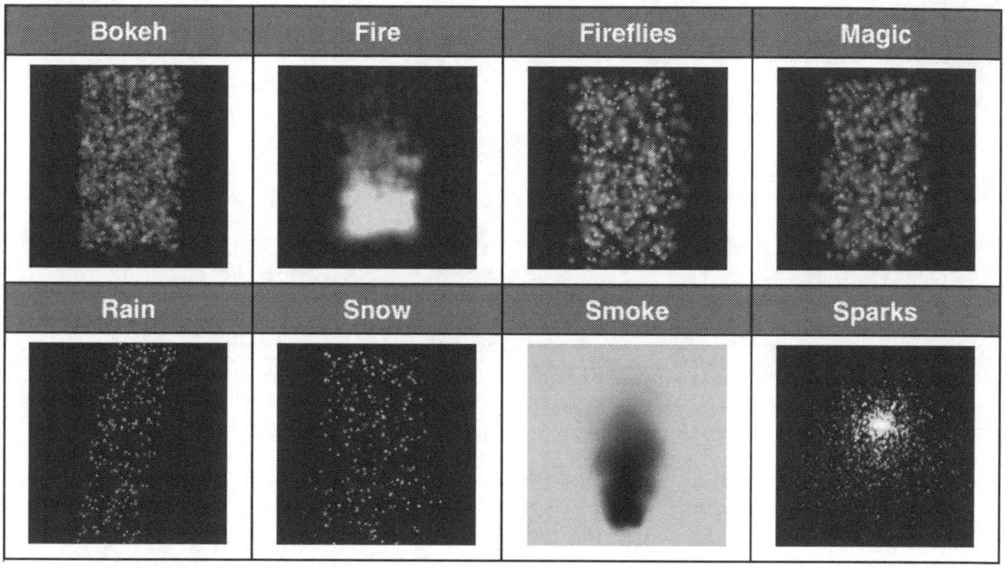

Bokeh	Fire	Fireflies	Magic

Rain	Snow	Smoke	Sparks

Generally you should choose whichever is closest to the effect you're trying to make and then tweak it from there. Although you could use any of these templates to get started on the lava, fire is the closest thing to lava, so select the **Fire** template from the list.

Click **Next** once more and enter **Lava** for the file name.

> **Note:** When you add your first particle file to a project, Xcode automatically adds a second file, **spark.png**, alongside it. This image file is the default texture for all particle templates built into Xcode, apart from one: the Bokeh template has its own default image called **bokeh.png**. You don't have to use this texture for your particle system. If you want to use your own texture, simply add it to your project and select it in the Xcode particle emitter editor (see below).

The Xcode particle emitter editor

Not all properties of an SKEmitterNode are configurable through Xcode's built-in particle editor—those that aren't include the sequence properties for scale, blend factor and alpha—but the most important ones are. To access the editor, select **Lava.sks** and verify that the Attributes Inspector is visible on the right:

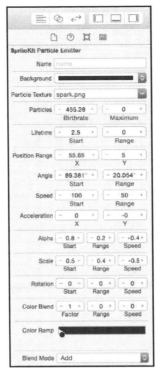

Feel free to take a moment to play around with the settings in the inspector to see how the particle system behaves in response.

Notice the **Particle Texture** property? It's set to use the default texture file, **spark.png**. This is where you would set the texture to one of your own, if you desired.

Making lava

The best way to begin making lava is by changing the color of the template. The default color is close to what you want, but you'll get a softer lava effect if the color ramps up from black to a reddish-orange glow.

Locate the **Color Ramp** property in the editor and click on the color stop at the left of the color selection panel. This will display a standard OS X color picker. Change the color in the picker and watch the color of the particles change.

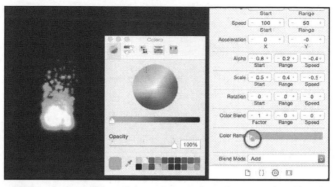

Select the **Color Sliders** tab in the color picker and make sure that the drop-down shows **RGB Sliders**. Now set the first color stop to **black** by setting the red, green and blue sliders all to **0**. The color ramp in the editor is actually editing the emitter's `particleColorSequence`. You're going to add two more stops (keyframes) to the sequence.

Click at about the **25%** mark of the color ramp to create a new color stop. Enter **99** for the red value, **50** for the green and **0** for the blue. Next, click at the end of the color ramp to create another color stop. Enter **219** for the red value, **66** for the green and **0** for the blue.

Your color ramp will look something like this:

With the color sequence set, you can start to edit the shape, speed and position of the emitter. At the top of the particle editor pane, find **Particles Birthrate** and change the value to **50** with a **Maximum** of **0**. Then set **Lifetime Start** to **1.5** with a **Range** of **0**.

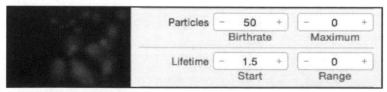

This causes the emitter to generate 50 particles per second, with each particle living for 1.5 seconds. To optimize performance, you want to keep the number of particles as low as possible to get the effect you want. So 50 particles per second * 1.5 seconds of lifetime per particle means only about 75 particles will be onscreen at one time.

For now, set **Position Range X** to **128** and **Y** to **0**. You'll change this in code later.

Change **Angle** to **90** with a **Range** of **360**. This causes the particles to emit from every direction.

Next, set the **Speed Start** and **Range** to **0**. Lava is thick and slow, so you don't need any speed here.

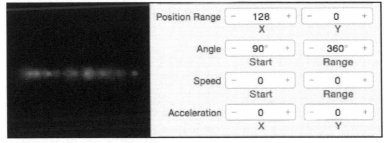

Now, set **Alpha Start** to **1** with a **Range** of **0.2** and a **Speed** of **-0.2**. The particles will start with an opacity between 80–100% and then fade out slowly.

Finally, give your lava some mass by setting **Scale Start** to **9** with a **Range** and **Speed** of **0**. Your particle system is beginning to look a lot more like hot lava!

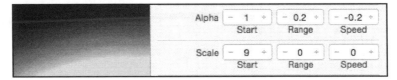

Loading an SKS file

The SKEmitterNode is fully NSCoding-compliant, making the loading process simple. When you edit and save a particle system using Xcode, your SKS file will be updated and included in the app bundle, ready to be deployed to a device. To load a particle system in code, simply initialize an SKEmitterNode with the name of the SKS file.

Now that you've configured your lava particle system, it's time to see it in action. Switch to **GameScene.swift** and implement the following method:

```
func setupLava() {
  lava = fgNode.childNodeWithName("Lava") as! SKSpriteNode
  let emitter = SKEmitterNode(fileNamed: "Lava.sks")!
  emitter.particlePositionRange = CGVector(dx: size.width *
1.125, dy: 0.0)
  emitter.advanceSimulationTime(3.0)
  emitter.zPosition = 4
  lava.addChild(emitter)
}
```

First, you grab a reference to the lava SKSpriteNode that you created in the scene editor; you're going to attach the emitter to this.

Then you create an SKEmitterNode, providing the filename of the SKS file you created.

The next line sets the `particlePositionRange` property so that particles are generated along the entire width of the screen, with a little overlap.

Next, you advance the simulation time so your lava is extra hot! You set the `zPosition` to 4 so the lava covers everything else.

Finally, you add the emitter to the lava `SKSpriteNode`.

Now scroll to `setupNodes()` and find this line:

```
lava = fgNode.childNodeWithName("Lava") as! SKSpriteNode
```

Replace that line with a call to set up your lava particle system:

```
setupLava()
```

While you're at it, modify `updateCollisionLava()` to better accommodate your particle system. Update the first line to:

```
if player.position.y < lava.position.y + 180 {
```

This places the marine a little higher above the lava in it's collision. Without this modification, the marine sinks a little too far into the lava before his boost.

Build and run to see your particle system SKS file!

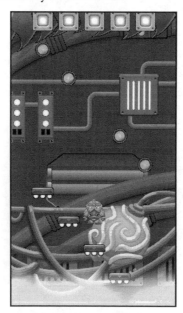

Wow! That's some hot lava!

Note: Be sure to test on an actual device rather than the simulator, as particle systems do not perform well on the simulator.

Continuous and play-once systems

So far, you've created two particle systems for Drop Charge: a bomb explosion and a lava pit. The explosion you created in code is an example of a **play-once** system, which generates particles until it reaches a designated number, at which point, it stops. The lava system, on the other hand, **continuously** emits particles.

The difference is in the **Particles: Maximum** setting, or the `numParticlesToEmit` property in code. Remember, if this property is set to 0, the particles will emit continuously, and any number greater than 0 will only render the specified number of particles. For the rest of this chapter, you'll be creating a few play-once particle systems.

Where there's fire, there's smoke

When the space hero collides with the lava, he jumps up vigorously—as we all would if we were game heroes! That works, but wouldn't it be cool to make the collision a bit more obvious by giving him a hot foot?

Highlight the **Particles** group in the project navigator and select **File\New\File...** from the main menu. Select **iOS\Resource\SpriteKit Particle File**, and then select **Spark** from the list of templates and click **Next**. Name the file **SmokeTrail.sks** and click **Create**.

You now have a new particle file you can edit. Notice the spark template emits particles continuously. For this effect, you only want the smoke to last for a second or two. To accomplish this, start by setting **Particles Birthrate** to **200** and **Maximum** to **200**. Then set **Lifetime Start** to **1** and **Range** to **0.5**.

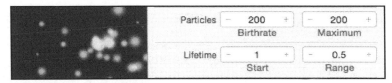

Set both the **Position Range X** and the **Position Range Y** to **24**. Set **Angle** to **0** and **Angle Range** to **360**. These settings give your smoke a little turbulence.

Now to slow things down a bit, set **Speed Start** to **50** and **Range** to **100**. Smoke tends to float, so remove the gravity effect by setting both **Acceleration X** and **Y** to **0**.

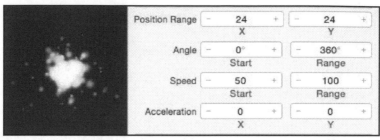

You want the smoke particles to start fairly large, then shrink and fade out. To do this, set **Alpha Start** to **1**, **Range** to **0** and **Speed** to **-0.25**. Then set **Scale Start** to **1.6**, **Range** to **1** and **Speed** to **-2**.

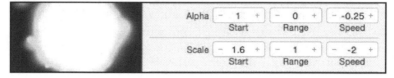

Next, you'll color your particles gray so that together, they look more like smoke. Begin by setting **Color Blend Factor** to **1** and **Range** to **1**. This will apply random values of color to the existing texture color. Now click on the left-most color stop on the **Color Ramp** to bring up the color picker, and set **Red**, **Green** and **Blue** all to **100**.

Click at about the 75% mark to create a new color stop, and set **Red**, **Green** and **Blue** to **177**.

Finally, create a third color stop at the right-most edge of the color ramp and set **Red**, **Green** and **Blue** to **255**. Lastly, you don't want the smoke to glow, so set **Blend Mode** to **Alpha**.

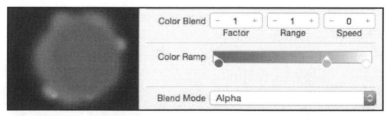

You have your smoke particles, so it's time to set them loose. Switch back to **GameScene.swift**. You'll be creating another trail effect for your hero later, so add these helper methods:

```
func addTrail(name: String) -> SKEmitterNode {
  let trail = SKEmitterNode(fileNamed: name)!
  player.addChild(trail)
  return trail
}

func removeTrail(trail: SKEmitterNode) {
```

```
    trail.numParticlesToEmit = 1
    trail.runAction(SKAction.removeFromParentAfterDelay(1.0))
}
```

The first method helps by creating an SKEmitterNode with the specified SKS file and attaching it to the player sprite. It then returns the SKEmitterNode, so that you can clean it up later by passing it to removeTrail(_:).

Now within the **Player States** group, open **Lava.swift** and add the following code to the top of didEnterWithPreviousState(_:):

```
let smokeTrail = scene.addTrail("SmokeTrail")
scene.runAction(SKAction.sequence([
  SKAction.waitForDuration(3.0),
  SKAction.runBlock() {
  self.scene.removeTrail(smokeTrail)
  }
  ]))
```

You create a smoke trail particle system, add it to the player, and after three seconds, remove it. Since you only want the smoke trail effect when the player enters the Lava state, you only need to add the code to this file.

Build and run, and let the hero fall into the lava.

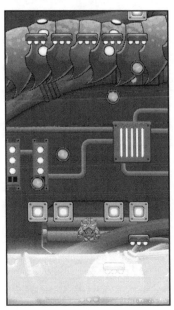

Hey, what's going on? Where's the smoke? The particle system is there, but it's behind the player sprite, and there are no forces influencing the trajectory of the particles.

Targeted particle systems

Imagine you're traveling in a car with the windows rolled up, holding a smoke grenade. The smoke would stay contained within the car, probably making it hard to see and breathe! Observers watching your car pass by wouldn't see any smoke streaming from behind. Once you rolled down the window, though, air would rush in and out of the car, pulling the smoke out with it.

Something similar is going on with your particle system. You need to tell the emitter that there's a world outside of the sprite to which it's attached.

SKEmitterNode has a property called targetNode that allows you to set the node that renders the emitter's particles. The initial properties of new particles are based on the emitter, but in future frames, the particles are treated as children of the target node.

Go back to **GameScene.swift** and add the following line to addTrail(_:), right before adding the emitter to player:

```
trail.targetNode = fgNode
```

Now build and run. Each time your hero touches the lava, a trail of smoke will appear!

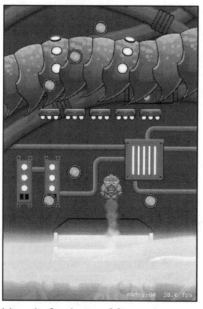

Congratulations! Besides adding hefty doses of fire and smoke to Drop Charge, you've developed your understanding of particle systems and their usefulness. You've learned how to create particle systems and configure their properties, both programmatically and within the Xcode editor, and how to load them and deploy them in your game.

But probably what's made the biggest impression is the dramatic effect these systems can have on your player's experience—and this is just the beginning. In the next chapter get ready to make this game even sweeter - through the power of Juice! :]

Challenges

Now it's time to practice creating particle systems on your own. With each challenge, you'll create a particle system for your game using Xcode's particle emitter editor.

If you get lost or feel stuck, have a look at the particle system SKS files in the **challenge \particles** folder. But most importantly, have fun and feel free to experiment!

Challenge 1: Collecting normal coins effect

Create a **CollectNormal.sks** particle file to use when the player sprite collides with the normal coins. It should be a play-once system similar to your explosion. There is a **Star.png** texture located in **challenge\resource** for your use.

Challenge 2: Collecting special coins effect

Create a **CollectSpecial.sks** particle file to use when the player sprite collides with the special coins. It should be similar to the CollectNormal system, but slightly bigger and with more energy.

Challenge 3: Breaking platform effect

Create a **BrokenPlatform.sks** particle file to use when the player sprite lands on a breakable platform. Use the **block_break01_piece01** texture that's already included in the DropCharge project. It should be a short, play-once particle system.

Challenge 4: Player trail effect

Create a **PlayerTrail.sks** particle file to use when the player sprite is jumping. This should be similar to the smoke trail system. Use the **Star.png** texture and give it a bluish color.

> **Note**: Don't worry about adding the code to spawn these particle effects yet; you'll handle that in the next chapter.

Chapter 17: Juice Up Your Game

By Michael Briscoe

Pop quiz: What's the difference between a good game and a *great* game? Why does one game delight its players while another is greeted with indifference? Why do some games have raving fans and stellar reviews? And what is the magical potion named "polish" that you're supposed to sprinkle on your games to make them awesome?

The answer is all in the details.

Great games are filled to the brim with droves of details that are often so subtle you might not even consciously notice them while you're playing. Polishing a game means paying attention to these details. Don't stop developing once your game reaches a playable state, and don't rush it to the App Store. Push your game further. Spice it up! Add polish!

"Juice" is a special type of polish that is easy and fun to add, and serves to bring joy and exuberance to your game. When a game is *juicy*, it feels alive—every interaction between the player and the game world results in a stimulating response.

For example, when two objects collide, you shouldn't just see it happen on the screen— that collision should look so convincing that you can almost *feel* it in your body. Playing a juicy game is a visceral experience.

No Juice   With Juice

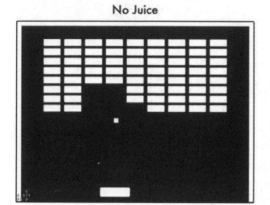 

The great thing about juice is that you don't need to have a large art budget or hire expensive consultants with impressive resumes. Instead, you can use simple animation effects—like scaling, rotation and movement, particle effects, music and sound effects. Most of these things are already in your toolkit; others, like music and sound effects, you can find online or create with free or inexpensive software. This is wonderful news for programmers like you and me!

On their own, none of these effects are terribly exciting, but when combined, every interaction within the game world results in a cascade of visual and audible feedback that keeps players coming back for more. That is what it means to make your game *juicy*.

In this chapter, you'll take Drop Charge and juice it up by adding a myriad of details to it. Although it's a good game now, adding juice will make it totally awesome!

Note: This chapter begins where the previous chapter's challenge left off. If you were unable to complete the challenge or skipped ahead from an earlier chapter, don't worry—simply open the starter project for this chapter to pick up where the previous chapter left off.

Three steps to juice up your game

Juicing up your game is like performing a magic trick: The results may look impressive to an unsuspecting audience, but it's really just slight of hand. Fortunately, you don't need to go to a school of witchcraft and wizardry and study for years just to become a master of special effects.

Before you begin randomly adding effects, you need to know where to apply them. If you add them arbitrarily or without consideration, your game runs the risk of confusing and distracting players.

But there's good news! You simply need to follow this three-step algorithm to plan your game's effects:

1. **List the actors**: First, make a list of all of the objects that play a role in your game, often called the **actors**. For example, the space hero and a platform object are two of your actors.

2. **List the interactions**: Second, make a list of the interactions that exist between the actors. For example, the hero collides with a coin to collect it. An object can also perform interactions with itself, like moving or changing state. For example, the hero could be moving upwards, or falling.

3. **Add effects to interactions**: Finally, add as many effects to these interactions as you can. This is what makes the player feel like they're making magic as they play. For example, in the previous chapter, when you created the smoke trail effect to mark the hero's collision with the lava, you were adding juice.

Simple enough, right? Good. Now it's time to carry out steps 1 and 2 with Drop Charge. Then later, you'll repeatedly apply step 3.

Step 1: The actors

First, who or what are the actors in Drop Charge?

- **The hero**: Your space hero, frantically jumping to escape his exploding ship.
- **Normal platforms**: The hero's immediate destination and a place to rest.

- **Breakable platforms**: Fragile platforms that break when the hero lands on them, providing very little respite from his escape.

- **Normal coins**: These help the hero by providing a boost to his upward movement.

- **Special coins**: These provide a greater boost to the hero, propelling him closer to safety.

- **Lava**: The hero must avoid the rising lava at all costs or risk a serious hot foot!

- **Background**: This includes the scrolling images of the ship's machinery and vents. The images serve no real purpose in the game, other than to make it look more interesting.

- **The screen itself**: The game world is the container for all of the other actors.

- **Gameplay rules**: Certain gameplay rules might cause interesting things to happen. For example, in Drop Charge, if the marine falls in the lava three times, he dies, and the game is over.

- **The player**: Yes, the player is an actor in the game, too. In fact, the player has the most important role! In this game, the hero is the player's avatar.

Step 2: The interactions

Now that you've identified the gameplay actors, what interactions exist between them?

Here's a partial list:

- **The hero interacts with platforms**, as when he rests or jumps up the screen.

- **The hero interacts with coins**, as when he collects and destroys coins for a speed boost.

- **The hero interacts with the lava**, as when he gets a boost and a hot foot, or maybe even dies.

- **The hero interacts with the game world**, as when he performs an action like jumping, falling or changing direction.

- **The player interacts with the screen**, as when she moves the device or taps the screen.

- **A game rule interacts with the game world**, as when the "game over" conditions are satisfied.

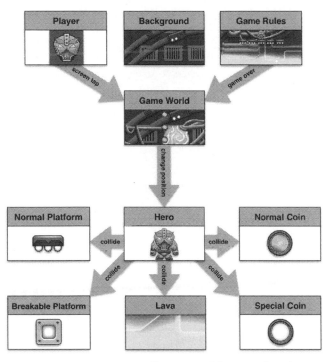

All of these interactions are opportunities for juice—like ripe fruit hanging from a tree, just waiting for you to pluck and squeeze. But what effects should you use?

Step 3: Five basic special effects

Here are the five basic effects you can use to add juice to your game:

1. **Music and sound effects**: Snappy music and sound effects can set the mood of your game and enhance your visual effects.

2. **Frame animation**: Animating the texture of your sprite to further convey an action or movement can have a dramatic impact.

3. **Particle systems**: You've already seen how adding particle effects, like explosions and smoke, can add high-octane juice.

4. **Screen effects**: Shaking and/or flashing the entire game world more deeply engages the player and conveys a sense of urgency.

5. **Sprite effects**: You can change a node's size, rotation, color and transparency to create interesting effects and enhance visual cues.

All of these effects can be temporary or permanent, immediate or animated, performed by themselves or—and this is where the magic happens—in combination with other effects. When you add a bunch of these effects together, you can make the entire screen jump and bounce. That's when things get juicy!

You can add most of these effects with a simple SKAction. That's the wonderful thing about these effects—they're incredibly simple to program, so adding them to your game is a quick win. Be warned, however: Once you start adding special effects, it's hard to stop!

Getting started

Open your **DropCharge** project. If you're skipping ahead, you can find the project in **starter\DropCharge**.

Once you have your project open, drag the **starter\resources\sounds** folder to the Xcode project navigator to import them. Make sure **Copy items if needed**, **Create Groups**, and the **DropCharge** target is checked. Once you're done, you should see them in your project navigator:

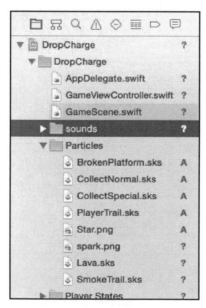

Music and sound effects

Have you ever watched an action movie with the sound turned off? Besides the obvious fact that you can't hear the dialog, the visuals seem a little flat and sometimes confusing. It's well established that music plays an important part in setting the tone and pace of a film, and sound effects can enhance or exaggerate realism. You can use this same concept to add juice to your game.

Drop Charge seems a little tepid without sound. To fix that, you'll start by adding music.

Open **GameScene.swift** and add this variable to your properties:

```
var backgroundMusic: SKAudioNode!
```

With iOS 9, Apple gave Sprite Kit a new node, the **SKAudioNode**, which makes it easy to play sound files from within your game. What used to take several lines of code can now be done in two!

Add this helper method to **GameScene.swift**:

```
func playBackgroundMusic(name: String) {
  if backgroundMusic != nil {
    backgroundMusic.removeFromParent()
  }

  backgroundMusic = SKAudioNode(fileNamed: name)
  backgroundMusic.autoplayLooped = true
  addChild(backgroundMusic)
}
```

The first part of this method checks to see if you've already added the `backgroundMusic` node to the scene, and if so, removes it. Next, you initialize an `SKAudioNode` with the file name passed into the method, setting its `autoplayLooped` property. Then, you add the node to your scene.

Because you set the `autoplayLooped` to `true`, your music file will automatically play once it's added to the scene; it will repeat until you remove it. Now you need to call this method with a sound file.

Scroll to `didMoveToView(_:)` and add this line:

```
playBackgroundMusic("SpaceGame.caf")
```

Build and run Drop Charge. If all went well, you'll hear a jazzy little tune welcoming you to the game.

Creating a change of pace

Your space hero seems a little laid back at the moment, chillin' to some tunes. But when that bomb drops, things get crazy real fast! This seems like a good time to switch to more frenetic music.

Open the **Playing.swift** state file and add this line to
didEnterWithPreviousState(_:), within the if statement:

```
scene.playBackgroundMusic("bgMusic.mp3")
```

This code executes when the game enters the Playing state, replacing the calmer music
with a more frantic beat. Build and run to hear the results. Don't forget, you'll need to
start the gameplay to hear the music change.

Not bad, but you can juice it up even move by adding some background noise. Go back
to **GameScene.swift** and add this variable to the properties:

```
var bgMusicAlarm: SKAudioNode!
```

Then, modify playBackgroundMusic(_:) by adding the following code just after
backgroundMusic.removeFromParent():

```
if bgMusicAlarm != nil {
  bgMusicAlarm.removeFromParent()
} else {
  bgMusicAlarm = SKAudioNode(fileNamed: "alarm.wav")
  bgMusicAlarm.autoplayLooped = true
  addChild(bgMusicAlarm)
}
```

When the game enters the Playing state and makes the call to
playBackgroundMusic(_:), backgroundMusic is no longer nil. From there, you
check to see if bgMusicAlarm is nil. If it is, you initialize it and add bgMusicAlarm to
the scene.

Now open **GameOver.swift** and add this code to didEnterWithPreviousState(_:),
just after if previousState is Playing {:

```
scene.playBackgroundMusic("SpaceGame.caf")
```

This changes the background music to the original music, and since the bgMusicAlarm
variable isn't nil, playBackgroundMusic(_:) will remove it from the scene, silencing
the alarm sound.

Build and run and notice a cool alarm sound effect as you play the game, and that the
game reverts back to the peaceful music on game over.

Adding sound effects

You've got background music, and it's just as easy to add accompanying sound effects.
Switch back to **GameScene.swift** and add these constants to the class properties:

```
let soundBombDrop = SKAction.playSoundFileNamed("bombDrop.wav",
  waitForCompletion: false)
let soundSuperBoost = SKAction.playSoundFileNamed("nitro.wav",
  waitForCompletion: false)
let soundTickTock = SKAction.playSoundFileNamed("tickTock.wav",
  waitForCompletion: false)
let soundBoost = SKAction.playSoundFileNamed("boost.wav",
  waitForCompletion: false)
let soundJump = SKAction.playSoundFileNamed("jump.wav",
  waitForCompletion: false)
let soundCoin = SKAction.playSoundFileNamed("coin1.wav",
  waitForCompletion: false)
let soundBrick = SKAction.playSoundFileNamed("brick.caf",
  waitForCompletion: false)
let soundHitLava =
SKAction.playSoundFileNamed("DrownFireBug.mp3",
  waitForCompletion: false)
let soundGameOver =
SKAction.playSoundFileNamed("player_die.wav",
  waitForCompletion: false)

let soundExplosions = [
  SKAction.playSoundFileNamed("explosion1.wav",
    waitForCompletion: false),
  SKAction.playSoundFileNamed("explosion2.wav",
    waitForCompletion: false),
  SKAction.playSoundFileNamed("explosion3.wav",
    waitForCompletion: false),
  SKAction.playSoundFileNamed("explosion4.wav",
    waitForCompletion: false)
  ]
```

You define a series of SKAction constants, each of which will load and play a sound file. Because you define these actions before you need them, they are preloaded into memory, which prevents the game from stalling when you play the sounds for the first time. You also create an array of explosion sound effects that you'll use to play a random boom.

Open **WaitingForBomb.swift** and add these lines to didEnterWithPreviousState(_:), right after running repeatSeq on the bomb:

```
scene.runAction(scene.soundBombDrop)
scene.runAction(SKAction.repeatAction(scene.soundTickTock,
count: 2))
```

When the game enters the WaitingForBomb state, it will play bombDrop.wav, followed by tickTock.wav, before transitioning to the Playing state.

But no bomb would be complete with an Earth-shattering *kaboom*, right? Add this line to willExitWithNextState(_:), after the line that removes the bomb from the scene:

```
scene.runAction(scene.soundExplosions[3])
```

Build and run to hear the bomb tick, with a huge explosion!

Things are already getting juicy!

It's time to add the sound effects for when the player collides with the coins and platforms. Open **GameScene.swift** and scroll to `didBeginContact(_:)`. Replace the `switch` statement with the following:

```
switch other.categoryBitMask {
case PhysicsCategory.CoinNormal:
  if let coin = other.node as? SKSpriteNode {
    coin.removeFromParent()
    jumpPlayer()
    runAction(soundCoin)
  }
case PhysicsCategory.CoinSpecial:
  if let coin = other.node as? SKSpriteNode {
    coin.removeFromParent()
    boostPlayer()
    runAction(soundBoost)
  }
case PhysicsCategory.PlatformNormal:
  if let _ = other.node as? SKSpriteNode {
    if player.physicsBody!.velocity.dy < 0 {
      jumpPlayer()
      runAction(soundJump)
    }
  }
case PhysicsCategory.PlatformBreakable:
  if let platform = other.node as? SKSpriteNode {
    if player.physicsBody!.velocity.dy < 0 {
      platform.removeFromParent()
      jumpPlayer()
      runAction(soundBrick)
    }
  }
default:
  break
}
```

`didBeginContact(_:)` is pretty much the same, except you add the `playSoundFileNamed` actions you defined earlier. Now, when the hero makes contact with the platforms and coins, the game plays a nice and juicy sound effect.

Give it a go! Build and run, and listen to the sweet sound (effects) when you hit platforms and coins.

Final sound effects

Lastly, you'll add sounds effects for when the marine collides with the lava and when the game reaches the "game over" state.

Open **Lava.swift** and add this to the top of `didEnterWithPreviousState(_:)`:

```
scene.runAction(scene.soundHitLava)
```

Switch to **Dead.swift** and add this to `didEnterWithPreviousState(_:)`, just after `scene.player.runAction(sequence)`:

```
scene.runAction(scene.soundGameOver)
```

Both of the lines you've added simply play their respective sound files after the marine collides with the lava or enters the dead state.

Build and run. Play your game for a bit, and then play it again—but this time, with the sound muted. Notice how the interactions between your game actors are enhanced by the simple addition of sound. But you're just getting started with the juice!

Frame animation

Now you're going to get a bit more visual by adding texture animation.

At the moment, the game objects in Drop Charge seem a little static, and the coins blend in with the background. You can fix that by animating the textures of SKSpriteNode.

You can do this in code with SKAction.animateWithTextures(_:timePerFrame:), or you can set up animation actions visually in Xcode's scene editor. For Drop Charge, you'll take advantage of both methods.

Creating actions visually

To save yourself some work, you'll create two new scenes to act as animation references for all the other coin overlays.

As you've done before, create a new file in your **Scene Files** group with the **iOS \Resource\SpriteKit Scene** template. Name this scene **Coin.sks**.

Now from the Media Library, drag **powerup05_1** into the scene. Set its Name to **Overlay**, and its Position to **(0, 0)**.

Under Physics Definition, choose **Bounding Circle** for the Body Type. Also, **uncheck** Dynamic, Allows Rotation, Pinned and Affected By Gravity. Set the Category Mask to **8** (the bit flag for a coin), the Collision Mask to **0**, the Field Mask to **0** and the Contact Mask to **1** (the bit flag for the player).

Make sure the Utilities Area is visible on the right and that the Attributes Inspector is selected. From the Object Library, drag an **AnimateWithTextures action** toward the scene; the action editor will expand if it's not already visible. Drop the action on **Overlay** within the action editor.

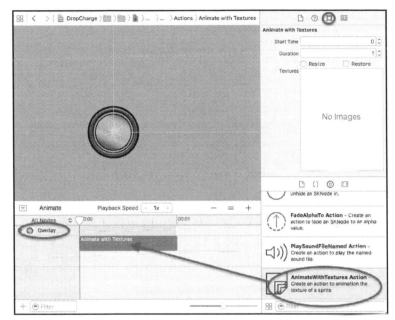

Within the Utilities Area, switch to the Media Library and drag and drop **powerup05_1** through **powerup05_6** into the **Textures** attribute. Set the **Duration** to **0.5**.

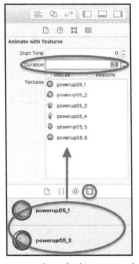

You can preview your animation action by clicking on the **Animate** button at the top of the action editor. The toolbar will turn blue, and the Animate button will change to **Layout**, as your animation begins to play.

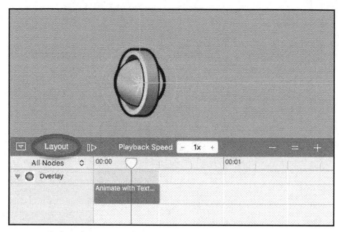

The coin animation only cycles once, but you can do better than that by making the coin rotate repeatedly. Luckily, you can specify how the action loops along its timeline.

Editing from the timeline

Click the **Animate with Textures** action to select it, and hover your cursor over the action. If your cursor is near the middle of the action, it appears as a hand, indicating you can move the entire action to another location within the timeline. If you move the cursor to the edges of the action, it will appear as a bar with arrows pointing to the left and right, indicating you can scale the action duration over time by dragging its edges.

Get a feel for how this works by dragging the action to a new location. Next, try scaling its duration over several seconds. Click on **Animate** to preview your action to see how it's changed. When you're finished, make sure to return your action to the beginning of the timeline and its duration to 0.5.

Click on the **circular arrow** icon on the bottom-left of the action to bring up the **Looping** pop-up. You could use this pop-up to set a finite number of loops by clicking on the plus (+) and minus (-) buttons, but you want this action to loop over and over, so click on the **loop forever** icon on the left—it looks like a sideways 8. Notice how the action representation in the timeline has changed to reflect its looping status.

Click the **Animate** button to watch your coin spin continuously.

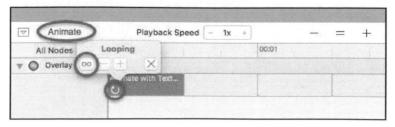

Now that you have your coin reference scene, you'll also need one for the *special* coin. As you did before, create a new scene and name it **CoinSpecial.sks**. This time drag the blue coin, **powerup01_1**, into the scene. Set its Name to **Overlay**, and its Position to **(0, 0)**.

Under Physics Definition, choose **Bounding Circle** for the Body Type. Also, **uncheck** Dynamic, Allows Rotation, Pinned and Affected By Gravity. Set the Category Mask to **16** (the bit flag for a special coin), the Collision Mask to **0**, the Field Mask to **0** and the Contact Mask to **1**.

Repeat the process for adding an **AnimateWithTextures action**. Be sure to use the **powerup01_1** through **powerup01_6** textures. Set the **Duration** to **0.5**, and the **Looping** property to infinity.

Using coin references

Your coin is spinning, so how do you get the rest of them going? It would be tedious to repeat what you just did for the rest of the coins–not to mention all the coins in all the other scene files.

You could use some new iOS 9 features, such as **action references** or **reference nodes**; but at the time of this writing these features were a bit buggy. For now, you'll have to swap out the old static coins for the new animated ones—in code.

Start by opening **GameScene.swift** and add the following variables to the class properties:

```
var coinRef: SKSpriteNode!
var coinSpecialRef: SKSpriteNode!
```

These variables will hold references to the two coin scenes you just created. Now add this code to **setupNodes()** just after breakDiagonal...:

```
coinRef = loadOverlayNode("Coin")
coinSpecialRef = loadOverlayNode("CoinSpecial")
```

Just like the platform nodes, you're loading the *overlay* node into your reference properties. Next, implement this new method just below loadOverlayNode(_:):

```
func loadCoinOverlayNode(fileName: String) -> SKSpriteNode {
  // 1
  let overlayScene = SKScene(fileNamed: fileName)!
  let contentTemplateNode =
    overlayScene.childNodeWithName("Overlay")
  // 2
  contentTemplateNode!.enumerateChildNodesWithName("*",
    usingBlock: {
    (node, stop) in
    let coinPos = node.position
```

```
    let ref: SKSpriteNode
    // 3
    if node.name == "special" {
      ref = self.coinSpecialRef.copy() as! SKSpriteNode
    } else {
      ref = self.coinRef.copy() as! SKSpriteNode
    }
    // 4
    ref.position = coinPos
    contentTemplateNode?.addChild(ref)
    node.removeFromParent()
  })
  // 5
  return contentTemplateNode as! SKSpriteNode
}
```

Here's what this function is doing:

1. First it loads a scene file, then sets `contentTemplateNode` to the "Overlay" node.

2. Next, it enumerates through all of the children in the overlay node.

3. If a node named "special" is found, then make a copy of the `coinSpecialRef` node, otherwise copy the `coinRef` node.

4. Position and add the new animated coin node, then remove the old static one.

5. Finally, return the overlay `SKSpriteNode`.

Now that you have the `loadCoinOverlayNode(_:)` method, let's put it to use.

Scroll to `setupNodes()` and replace these lines:

```
coin5Across = loadOverlayNode("Coin5Across")
coinDiagonal = loadOverlayNode("CoinDiagonal")
coinCross = loadOverlayNode("CoinCross")
coinArrow = loadOverlayNode("CoinArrow")
coinS5Across = loadOverlayNode("CoinS5Across")
coinSDiagonal = loadOverlayNode("CoinSDiagonal")
coinSCross = loadOverlayNode("CoinSCross")
coinSArrow = loadOverlayNode("CoinSArrow")
```

With the following:

```
coin5Across = loadCoinOverlayNode("Coin5Across")
coinDiagonal = loadCoinOverlayNode("CoinDiagonal")
coinCross = loadCoinOverlayNode("CoinCross")
coinArrow = loadCoinOverlayNode("CoinArrow")
coinS5Across = loadCoinOverlayNode("CoinS5Across")
coinSDiagonal = loadCoinOverlayNode("CoinSDiagonal")
coinSCross = loadCoinOverlayNode("CoinSCross")
coinSArrow = loadCoinOverlayNode("CoinSArrow")
```

Instead of using the `loadOverlayNode()` as before, you are now using `loadCoinOverlayNode()` to load the coins. You've saved yourself a ton of work by stripping away all the old stationary coins, and replacing them with brand new spinning ones—all at runtime!

Build and run to see your animation action and coin references, at work in the game.

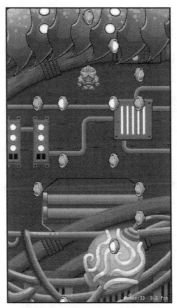

Whether or not you're a space marine, those coins now look a lot more enticing.

Animation actions in code

It's fun and easy to visually create animation actions in the scene editor. It's also great for looping animation, or for animation that occurs at finite points along a timeline.

But what if you want the animation to occur when triggered by specific actions, such as when your brave space hero is jumping? That's when it makes more sense to create those animation actions in code.

In this section, you're going to add some animation to the space marine himself. To do this, open **GameScene.swift** and add the following variables to the class properties:

```
var animJump: SKAction! = nil
var animFall: SKAction! = nil
var animSteerLeft: SKAction! = nil
var animSteerRight: SKAction! = nil
var curAnim: SKAction? = nil
```

These are empty `SKAction` variables that you'll initialize in just a moment. But before you do, add these two helper methods:

```
func setupAnimWithPrefix(prefix: String,
  start: Int,
  end: Int,
  timePerFrame: NSTimeInterval) -> SKAction {
    var textures = [SKTexture]()
    for i in start..<end {
      textures.append(SKTexture(imageNamed: "\(prefix)\(i)"))
    }
    return SKAction.animateWithTextures(textures,
      timePerFrame: timePerFrame)
}

func runAnim(anim: SKAction) {
  if curAnim == nil || curAnim! != anim {
    player.removeActionForKey("anim")
    player.runAction(anim, withKey: "anim")
    curAnim = anim
  }
}
```

The first method loads several textures into an array. Then, it creates an `animateWithTextures` action using the `textures` and the `timePerFrame` for its parameters.

The second method does the following:

- It checks to see if there's a current animation and if there is, makes sure it's not the same as the input animation.

- If the animation passes these tests, then the method removes any running animation actions.

- Then the method runs the input animation action, `anim`.

- Finally, the method sets the `curAnim` to the input `anim`, so you can properly track it.

Scroll to `didMoveToView(_:)` and add these lines to initialize your animation actions:

```
animJump = setupAnimWithPrefix("player01_jump_",
  start: 1, end: 4, timePerFrame: 0.1)
animFall = setupAnimWithPrefix("player01_fall_",
  start: 1, end: 3, timePerFrame: 0.1)
animSteerLeft = setupAnimWithPrefix("player01_steerleft_",
  start: 1, end: 2, timePerFrame: 0.1)
animSteerRight = setupAnimWithPrefix("player01_steerright_",
  start: 1, end: 2, timePerFrame: 0.1)
```

Now that you've created your player animations, it's time to put them to use. Open **Jump.swift** and add this method:

```
override func updateWithDeltaTime(seconds: NSTimeInterval) {
  if abs(scene.player.physicsBody!.velocity.dx) > 100.0 {
    if (scene.player.physicsBody!.velocity.dx > 0) {
      scene.runAnim(scene.animSteerRight)
    } else {
      scene.runAnim(scene.animSteerLeft)
    }
  } else {
    scene.runAnim(scene.animJump)
  }
}
```

Because you want the Jump state to track the hero during his jump cycle, you use updateWithDeltaTime(_:). This checks the player sprite's horizontal velocity and plays the appropriate animation action for the Jump state.

Open **Fall.swift**. There's only one animation for falling, so for this state, replace didEnterWithPreviousState(_:) with the following:

```
override func didEnterWithPreviousState(previousState: GKState?)
{
  scene.runAnim(scene.animFall)
}
```

There's only one thing left to do before testing this. Switch back to **GameScene.swift** and add this line to update(_:):

```
playerState.updateWithDeltaTime(deltaTime)
```

This ensures the Jump state executes its updateWithDeltaTime(_:), so it can change the hero's jump animation.

Build and run to see Drop Charge in all its animated glory!

Things are really starting to get juicy, but you're going to take it up another notch by adding particle systems.

Particle effects

It's time to put those particle systems you created in the last chapter to use, starting with a motion trails effect for the hero. This will enhance the illusion that he's moving quickly, eager to escape the ship.

For this effect, you want to temporarily turn off the trails when the hero has his hot foot. To do that, you need a reference to the player trail's `SKEmitterNode`.

Open **GameScene.swift** and add this variable to the class properties:

```
var playerTrail: SKEmitterNode!
```

Next, switch to **Idle.swift** and add this line to `didEnterWithPreviousState(_:)`:

```
scene.playerTrail = scene.addTrail("PlayerTrail")
```

Here, you use the `addTrail(_:)` method you created for adding the smoke trail, passing in the the PlayerTrail filename.

Build and run to see the hero's speedy motion trail.

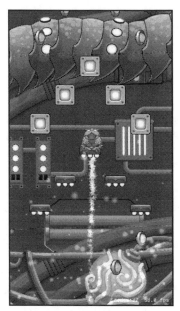

When the hero hits the lava, you currently can't see the smoke trail because the motion trail covers it.

To fix that, open **Lava.swift** and add the following line to the top of didEnterWithPreviousState(_:):

```
scene.playerTrail.particleBirthRate = 0
```

The particleBirthRate emitter property from the last chapter comes in handy here, stopping the flow of particles just before you add the smoke trail.

Next, open **Jump.swift** and replace didEnterWithPreviousState(_:) with the following code:

```
override func didEnterWithPreviousState(previousState: GKState?)
{
  if previousState is Lava {
    return
  }
  if scene.playerTrail.particleBirthRate == 0 {
    scene.playerTrail.particleBirthRate = 200
  }
}
```

In the first part of this method, you check to make sure the last player state wasn't Lava. If it was, you skip the rest. If the previous state wasn't Lava, then you restore the playerTrail birthrate to 200, provided it's not 0.

Build and run. Now you'll see the motion and smoke trails playing nicely together.

Random explosions

Let's step up the chaos factor and add more juice by creating random explosions in the background to enhance the sense of the ship disintegrating.

Start by opening **GameScene.swift** and adding these variables to the class properties:

```
var timeSinceLastExplosion: NSTimeInterval = 0
var timeForNextExplosion: NSTimeInterval = 1.0
```

You'll use these properties to track when to add your random explosions.

Next, add the following method just above `explosion(_:)`:

```
func createRandomExplosion() {
  // 1
  let cameraPos = getCameraPosition()
  let screenSize = self.view!.bounds.size

  let screenPos = CGPoint(x: CGFloat.random(min: 0.0,
    max: cameraPos.x * 2.0), y: CGFloat.random(min:
    cameraPos.y - screenSize.height * 0.75,
    max: cameraPos.y + screenSize.height))
  // 2
  let randomNum = Int.random(soundExplosions.count)
  runAction(soundExplosions[randomNum])
  // 3
  let explode = explosion(0.25 * CGFloat(randomNum + 1))
  explode.position = convertPoint(screenPos, toNode: bgNode)
  explode.runAction(SKAction.removeFromParentAfterDelay(2.0))
  bgNode.addChild(explode)
}
```

Here's what you do in this method:

1. First, you get the camera position and generate a random position within the viewable part of the game world.

2. Next, you get a random number to play a random sound effect from the `soundExplosions` array.

3. Finally, you create an explosion with a random intensity. Then you set its position, removing it after two seconds, and add it to the background node of the game world.

Before you can see your explosions, you need to do a couple more things.

First, add this method just below `updateCollisionLava()`:

```
func updateExplosions(dt: NSTimeInterval) {
  timeSinceLastExplosion += dt
  if timeSinceLastExplosion > timeForNextExplosion {
    timeForNextExplosion = NSTimeInterval(CGFloat.random(min:
```

```
        0.1, max: 0.5))
    timeSinceLastExplosion = 0

    createRandomExplosion()
  }
}
```

This method checks periodically to see when to set off an explosion by comparing the last explosion time with a randomly chosen time in the future. When that time is reached, the method fires `createRandomExplosion()`.

Lastly, open **Playing.swift** and add this method to `updateWithDeltaTime(_:)`:

```
scene.updateExplosions(seconds)
```

Build and run.

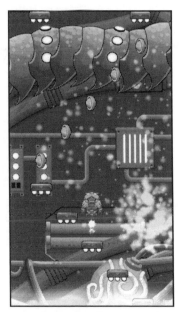

Woo-hoo! Everything's better with lots of explosions.

Power-up particles

There's another actor interaction that's begging for an effect: when the hero collides with the coins. Right now, the coins simply disappear from the screen and give him a boost. Wouldn't it be cool to add particles to the mix?

Open **GameScene.swift** and start by adding this helper method:

```
func emitParticles(name: String, sprite: SKSpriteNode) {
  let pos = fgNode.convertPoint(sprite.position, fromNode:
    sprite.parent!)
  let particles = SKEmitterNode(fileNamed: name)!
  particles.position = pos
  particles.zPosition = 3
  fgNode.addChild(particles)
  particles.runAction(SKAction.removeFromParentAfterDelay(1.0))
  sprite.runAction(SKAction.sequence([SKAction.scaleTo(0.0,
    duration: 0.5), SKAction.removeFromParent()]))
}
```

This method takes a filename and a sprite node, does all the work of creating and positioning your particle system and then removes the sprite.

Now, scroll to didBeginContact(_:) and make the following changes to the switch statement:

Within case PhysicsCategory.CoinNormal:, replace this line:

```
coin.removeFromParent()
```

With this line:

```
emitParticles("CollectNormal", sprite: coin)
```

Do the same within case PhysicsCategory.CoinSpecial: but replacing with this line:

```
emitParticles("CollectSpecial", sprite: coin)
```

While you're there, add the particle system for contact with the breakable platforms.

Within case PhysicsCategory.PlatformBreakable:, replace this line:

```
platform.removeFromParent()
```

With this line:

```
emitParticles("BrokenPlatform", sprite: platform)
```

Game over, man

How about a big explosion when the game ends? The bigger the better, right? Open **GameOver.swift** and add the following code to didEnterWithPreviousState(_:):

```
let explosion = scene.explosion(6.0)
explosion.position = gameOver.position
explosion.zPosition = 11
scene.addChild(explosion)
scene.runAction(scene.soundExplosions[3])
scene.screenShakeByAmt(200)
```

This code creates a large explosion and positions it over the gameOver sprite, complete with screen shake and sound effects.

Build and run to see your juicy power-ups, platforms, and particle mayhem!

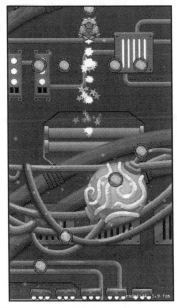

You'll see sparks and rubble flying everywhere!

Screen effects

You've juiced things up with sound, animation and particles, so it's time to turn to screen effects, which can really bring things to life by affecting the entire game world. For Drop Charge, you'll implement a **screen shake** to simulate transient spatial movement similar to an earthquake—or in your case, a *shipquake*!

Open **GameScene.swift** and add this constant to the class properties:

```
let gameGain: CGFloat = 2.5
```

You'll learn more about this constant later.

Next, add the following helper method:

```
func screenShakeByAmt(amt: CGFloat) {
  // 1
  let worldNode = childNodeWithName("World")!
  worldNode.position = CGPoint(x: size.width / 2.0, y:
    size.height / 2.0)
  worldNode.removeActionForKey("shake")
  // 2
  let amount = CGPoint(x: 0, y: -(amt * gameGain))
  // 3
  let action = SKAction.screenShakeWithNode(worldNode, amount:
    amount, oscillations: 10, duration: 2.0)
  // 4
  worldNode.runAction(action, withKey: "shake")
}
```

This method does the following:

1. It grabs a reference to the world node, *resets* its position and removes any previous "shake" actions. This code makes sure that only one screen shake action is running at a time—preventing pandemonium!

2. It creates a `CGPoint` based on the input `amount`. You only want the screen to shake vertically, so you set `x:` to `0`.

3. It creates a `screenShakeWithNode` action that oscillates the world node 10 times by the input amount, over two seconds.

4. Using the "shake" key, the method executes the action on the world node so that subsequent calls to the method can remove it.

> **Note**: `screenShakeWithNode` is a custom `SKAction` that's included with SKUtils. You can learn more about this action and other useful screen effects by taking a look at the **SKAction+SpecialEffects.swift** file.

Now you need to put this helper method to use. Juicing up the bomb explosion is a good way to start!

Open **WaitingForBomb.swift** and add this line to the end of `willExitWithNextState(_:)`, within the `if` statement:

```
scene.screenShakeByAmt(100)
```

Build and run. You'll see just how much shaking the screen can invigorate the game.

Shake, shake, shake

Let's sprinkle more juicy screen-shaking throughout the game. Open the **Lava.swift** player state file and add this to `didEnterWithPreviousState(_:)`:

```
scene.screenShakeByAmt(50)
```

The next time the player hits the lava, she'll really know it!

Next, open **GameScene.swift** and add this line to `boostPlayer()`:

```
screenShakeByAmt(40)
```

Now the screen will shake a little when the hero collects a special coin.

Lastly, juice up `createRandomExplosion()` by adding this code:

```
if randomNum == 3 {
  screenShakeByAmt(10)
}
```

Because it's possible to overuse the screen shake effect, you only shake the screen a small amount, and only with the largest explosion. You don't want to make the player queasy!

Build and run Drop Charge to admire your controlled chaos.

Sprite effects

There are a lot of sprite properties and actions you can use to achieve a variety of effects. For example, often games will change a sprite's scale to convey a sense of elasticity, like that of a bouncing ball, or change its color to indicate a transition to a new mode.

In the first section of this chapter, you added an alarm sound to create a sense of urgency. Now you'll juice that up by adding an oscillating red-light effect.

Open **GameScene.swift** and add the following variable to the class properties:

```
var redAlertTime: NSTimeInterval = 0
```

Your red-light effect will use this to track its oscillation.

Next, add this helper method:

```
func isNodeVisible(node: SKSpriteNode, positionY: CGFloat) ->
Bool {
  if !cameraNode.containsNode(node) {
    if positionY < getCameraPosition().y * 0.25 {
      return false
    }
  }
  return true
}
```

You'll use this method to determine if a node is visible within the game world. This will help with performance and memory management, as you don't want unused objects taking up valuable resources.

Now add this method:

```
func updateRedAlert(lastUpdateTime: NSTimeInterval) {
  // 1
  redAlertTime += lastUpdateTime
  let amt: CGFloat = CGFloat(redAlertTime) * π * 2.0 / 1.93725
  let colorBlendFactor = (sin(amt) + 1.0) / 2.0
  // 2
  for bg in bgNode.children {
    for node in bg.children {
      if let sprite = node as? SKSpriteNode {
        let nodePos = bg.convertPoint(sprite.position,
          toNode: self)
        // 3
        if isNodeVisible(sprite, positionY: nodePos.y) == false
        {
          sprite.removeFromParent()
        } else {
          sprite.color = SKColorWithRGB(255, g: 0, b: 0)
```

```
                    sprite.colorBlendFactor = colorBlendFactor
                }
              }
            }
          }
        }
```

Here's what's going on in this method:

1. This part of the code calculates the oscillation of color to apply to each background sprite.

2. Here, you loop to iterate through all of the background nodes in the game world.

3. If the node isn't visible, you remove it to free up resources; otherwise, you set its color to red and blend it according to the amount you calculated in step 1.

Since this effect is generated over time, you need to add it to your game's update loop.

Open **Playing.swift** and add this line to updateWithDeltaTime(_:):

```
scene.updateRedAlert(seconds)
```

Bouncing platforms

Finally, you're going to add a method to make the platforms bounce when the player lands on them. As if things weren't sketchy enough for our poor space marine!

Implement the following code in **GameScene.swift**:

```
func platformAction(sprite: SKSpriteNode, breakable: Bool) {
  let amount = CGPoint(x: 0, y: -75.0)
  let action = SKAction.screenShakeWithNode(sprite,
    amount: amount, oscillations: 10, duration: 2.0)
  sprite.runAction(action)

  if breakable == true {
    emitParticles("BrokenPlatform", sprite: sprite)
  }
}
```

This method takes a sprite node, and uses the custom screenShakeWithNode(_:amoount:oscillations:duration:) action to vertically shake the platform. It then checks to see if the platform is breakable, and if so, calls emitParticles(_:sprite:).

Next, scroll to didBeginContact(_:) and replace the case statements for PhysicsCategory.PlatformNormal and PhysicsCategory.PlatformBreakable to the following:

```
case PhysicsCategory.PlatformNormal:
  if let platform = other.node as? SKSpriteNode {
    if player.physicsBody!.velocity.dy < 0 {
      platformAction(platform, breakable: false)
      jumpPlayer()
      runAction(soundJump)
    }
  }
case PhysicsCategory.PlatformBreakable:
  if let platform = other.node as? SKSpriteNode {
    if player.physicsBody!.velocity.dy < 0 {
      platformAction(platform, breakable: true)
      jumpPlayer()
      runAction(soundBrick)
    }
  }
```

When the `player` sprite makes contact with either the normal or breakable platforms, `platformAction(_:breakable:)` is now called to bounce the platform.

Finishing touches

Before you build and run, you need to do some cleanup and a performance tweak.

First, scroll to `updateLevel()`. Once there, add the following lines of code:

```
// remove old nodes...
for fg in fgNode.children {
  for node in fg.children {
    if let sprite = node as? SKSpriteNode {
      let nodePos = fg.convertPoint(sprite.position, toNode:
self)
      if isNodeVisible(sprite, positionY: nodePos.y) == false {
        sprite.removeFromParent()
      }
    }
  }
}
```

Like the code you used in the red-light effect, this code iterates through all of the platforms and coins in the scene and removes any obsolete objects. This avoids runaway memory usage - like a pile of offscreen cat ladies in Zombie Conga.

Now for one last tweak. Modify `setPlayerVelocity(_:)` as follows:

```
func setPlayerVelocity(amount:CGFloat) {
  player.physicsBody!.velocity.dy =
    max(player.physicsBody!.velocity.dy, amount * gameGain)
}
```

This moves the hard-coded `gain` property to the `gameGain` property you created earlier - this will make it easier to tweak later on in one of the challenges.

Build and run your game, and behold the abundance of juice!

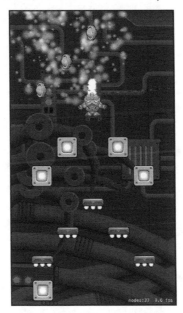

Challenges

Putting what you've learned into practice, here are a couple of challenges for you.

As always, you can find solutions to these challenges in the **challenge** folder—but believe in yourself and try your very best first. Good luck!

Challenge 1: Create a "squash and stretch" effect

Create a effect that squashes and stretches the player sprite, enhancing his visual motion. This is a common technique used in traditional animation, where an object compresses as it hits the ground, then extend as it bounces up. Here are some hints to get you going:

- Create a `squashAndStretch` action property made up of a sequence of scale actions that squash and then stretch the player sprite.

- Use a scale factor of about 15%.

- The duration of each action should be relatively short.

- Use the EaseInEaseOut timing mode.

- Run the action on the player sprite within the Jump, Fall and Lava player states.

Challenge 2: Port Drop Charge to tvOS

Earlier in this book, you learned about making your game run on tvOS. Use your new skills to port Drop Charge to AppleTV! Here are some things to keep in mind:

- You'll have to create a new **GameScene.sks** file to accommodate the AppleTV's landscape orientation. Try using a scene size of 1536x864. This matches the width of your background art, yet retains the Apple TV's aspect ratio. SpriteKit will automatically scale the scene to match the screen.

- tvOS does not support Core Motion, so use something like touchesMoved(_:withEvent:) to steer the hero. You'll also need to use compiler logic in several places to prevent compiler errors. For example:

```
#if os(iOS)
   import CoreMotion
#endif
```

- Adjust the gameGain constant to a lower number to keep the hero onscreen.

Where to go from here?

In this chapter, you learned about the concept of "juice" and how it can make a good game great. Now you have the tools: the three-step process to juice up your game and the five basic special effects.

For some ideas of more ways to add Juice to your game, check out Ray's AltConf talk on the matter here: http://bit.ly/1FViSbC

Also, check out what other developers are doing with their games. Make a list of the things you like about them. The best thing about adding juice is that you're only limited by your imagination!

Section IV: GameplayKit

In this section, you'll learn how to use iOS 9's new GameplayKit to improve your game's architecture and reusability, along with adding pathfinding and basic game AI.

In the proces, you'll create a fun tower defense game called Dino Defense where you construct a perfect defense to save your village from an onslaught of angry dinosaurs!

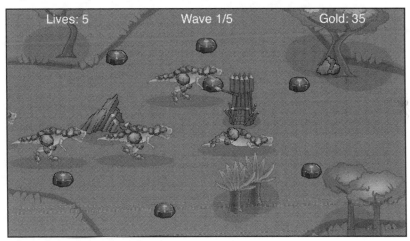

Chapter 18: Entity-Component System

Chapter 19: Pathfinding

Chapter 20: Agents, Goals and Behaviors

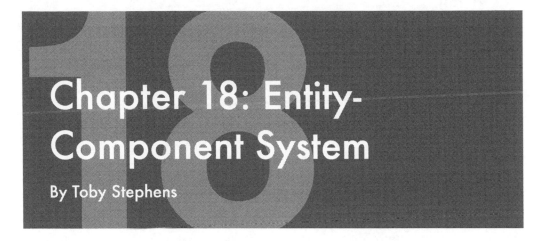

Chapter 18: Entity-Component System

By Toby Stephens

In the next few chapters, you're going to learn about a cool new framework introduced in iOS 9 called **GameplayKit**. In the process, you're going to develop a tower defense game named **Dino Defense**.

In tower defense games, the player must place towers on a map to stop invading enemies from reaching her home base. In Dino Defense, hoards of dinosaurs are attacking the player's village, and it's up to the player to defend the townsfolk from the onslaught.

Here's what the finished game will look like:

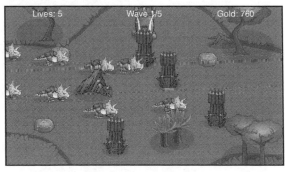

You'll build this game across the next three chapters:

- **Chapter 18, Entity-Component System:** You are here! You'll learn all about modeling your game's objects using the new GKEntity and GKComponent objects provided with GameplayKit, and you'll use what you've learned to implement your first dinosaur and tower.

- **Chapter 19, Pathfinding:** You'll use GameplayKit's pathfinding features to move your dinosaurs across the scene, avoiding obstacles and towers.

- **Chapter 20, Agents, Goals and Behaviors:** Finally, you'll add a second dinosaur to your game that will use a `GKAgent` with `GKGoal` and `GKBehavior` objects to move across the scene as a more organic alternative to pathfinding.

Get ready to get prehistoric!

Getting started

The purpose of the chapters in this section of the book is to take a deep dive into some of GameplayKit's features. To keep focused on GameplayKit, this chapter includes a starter project that already contains a lot of the Sprite Kit code required to get you to a point where you can implement the entities and components.

The starter project takes care of loading the game scene, the win and lose scenes and an initial ready scene. It prepares the background music for you, and manages a HUD for displaying the player's gold, remaining lives and the approaching wave of dinosaurs. This should all be review from previous chapters in this book.

To begin, launch Xcode and open the **DinoDefense.xcodeproj** project located in the **projects/starter/** folder for this chapter.

Build and run. You'll briefly see a loading screen with the Dino Defense logo before being presented with the ready scene.

Tapping right now won't do much—you'll see to that later.

There are two things in particular that are important to understand about this project: game layers, and texture atlases.

Game layers

The starter project contains a single scene in which the entire game plays, implemented in **GameScene.sks** and **GameScene.swift**.

The scene is split into a number of top-level nodes that comprise logical layers of the game, one on top of the other. You can see those layers in this diagram:

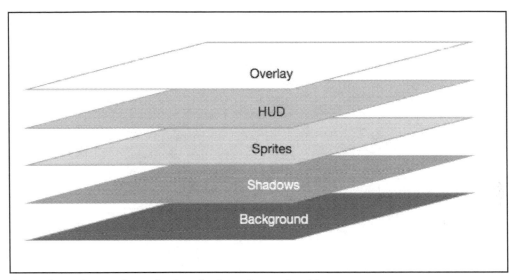

Open **GameScene.sks** and take a look at the top-level layers:

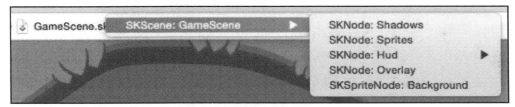

The layers are set up as follows, from background to foreground:

- **Background:** This layer is a sprite node with the texture for the background of your game. It's also the layer on which you'll be placing nodes for the possible tower locations.

- **Shadows:** This is a special layer for all the shadows of your game sprites. It's important that each shadow is always under the sprites—even the sprites that don't possess that particular shadow.

- **Sprites:** Sitting above the shadows layer is the sprites layer. This is where you'll add your dinosaurs, towers and obstacles—the key game objects.

- **HUD:** This is a node for displaying game information to the player, such as the gold available to build towers.

- **Overlay:** You'll use the top-level layer to display in-game menus, such as the win and lose screens.

Texture atlases

Up until this point in the book, you have stored the images for your game in Sprite Kit's asset catalog. When you do this, Sprite Kit automatically organizes your images into a set of **texture atlases**.

A texture atlas is basically one big image that contains all your other images as sub-images - this is done to improve your game's performance. For example, here's what your texture atlas might look like for Cat Nap:

An alternative to using Sprite Kit's asset catalog is to save your images inside folders with an **.atlas** extension. If you do this, Sprite Kit will create a texture atlas for each folder name.

This is the approach that Dino Defnense takes. If you take a look at the **ArtAndSounds** folder, you will see several folders with an **.atlas** extension:

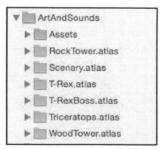

The advantage of manually specifying the texture atlases this way is that you can have images with the same filename in different texture atlases. For example, the dinosaurs in this game all have images for walk animations that go from **Walk__01.png** to **Walk__30.png**. Because they are in different texture atlases, the names to not conflict.

Sprite Kit provides a class called SKTextureAtlas that allows you to load a texture atlas and retrieve a texture from it (along with other operations like enumerationg all textures). Here's an example of using it:

```
let textureAtlas = SKTextureAtlas(named: "T-Rex")
let walkTexture = textureAtlas.textureNamed("Walk__01.png")
```

You will be using this later in the chapter to retrieve textures to use for the sprites in this game.

At this point, feel free to take a peek through the rest of the project to get a feel for what's inside. Once you're feeling good, keep reading to start your tour of GameplayKit!

Introducing GameplayKit

When writing a complex game, it's important to plan a good architecture for the game's many elements. If you've developed a game before, I'm sure you've sat down with a pen and paper and thought about each of the components in the game—mapping those components to an object hierarchy.

For example, with the tower defense game that you're about to write, you'll have enemies (dinosaurs), towers (wood and rock) and a number of other game objects (projectiles for the towers, obstacles in the scene). Thinking about code reusability, you might plan your object model to look something like this:

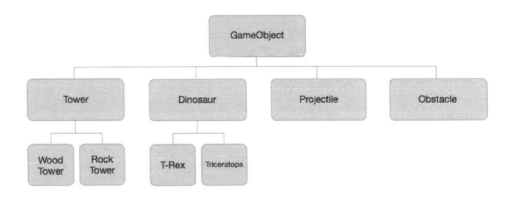

The GameObject might contain code to render itself, determine the objects' physics and other generic functions that apply to each game object. The Tower class might provide extra information for towers, and the Wood and Rock tower classes might provide functionality pertaining to the individual towers.

Assume for a moment that the Tower class contains code for aiming at and attacking enemies. Now, imagine that your game expands and a new dinosaur—a particularly aggressive `Raptor` class—is allowed to attack the towers, rather than the typical passive behavior.

If you wanted to reuse the attacking code for rate of attack, damage and so forth, then you would have to move that attacking code up the class hierarchy to the `GameObject` class for the new `Raptor` subclass to use it. You would then have to explicitly tell your game that T-Rex and Triceratops dinosaurs can't attack towers.

Now imagine this process of moving code up to the `GameObject` layer continues as you develop your game. Eventually, your `GameObject` class will become a bloated class full of switches. A new way of modeling these concepts is clearly required—enter GameplayKit.

Entity-Component system

One of the key features of GameplayKit is its Entity-Component system. This architecture enables you to design your object model based on what the game objects *do* as opposed to what they *are*.

There are two basic steps:

1. First, you create a **component** class for each thing you want your objects to do (such as appear on the screen, display a shadow, or shoot).

2. Then, you create an **entity** classs for each type of object in your game, and add any components you would like to the entity.

Let's see how this will work in Dino Defense. Your game will have two tower types:

• **Wood Towers** fire arrows at the dinosaurs. They fire rapidly, but don't do much damage.

• **Stone Towers** fire rocks at the dinosaurs, doing more damage and slowing the dinosaurs down.

The dinosaurs featured in your game are:

• **T-Rex**: A slow-moving dinosaur.

• **Triceratops**: A faster dinosaur, with less health than the T-Rex.

• **T-Rex Boss**: A T-Rex with a substantial amount of health.

The towers will fire projectiles at the dinosaurs when they're in range, and there will be obstacles for the dinosaurs to avoid scattered throughout the scene. Taking all these game objects into account, the Entity-Component model you're going to implement looks like this:

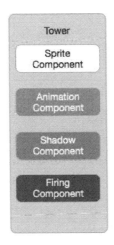

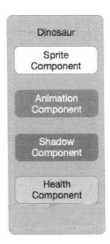

Since all of the actual code for executing each of the pieces of functionality is in the components, the entities are relatively small implementations, and you can reuse the component code by simply adding the component to the entity.

Each of the components has a specific piece of functionality that it's responsible for providing:

- The **sprite component** renders the entity to the scene. This is a Sprite Kit game, so the sprite component will use an SKSpriteNode to place the entity in the scene.

- The **animation component** is responsible for loading the entity's animations and providing an easy way to switch animations.

- The **shadow component** creates a shadow SKSpriteNode of a given size that you can place under the entity's sprite component node.

- The **firing component** contains all of the functionality associated with the tower attacks.

- Finally, the **health component** renders an entity's health above it in the form of a health bar. It redraws the health bar when the entity takes damage.

GameplayKit's Entity-Component System

Now that you understand the entity-component system architecture, let's take a look at how it works in GameplayKit.

There are two classes you need to override to use GameplayKit's entity-component system:

- **GKComponent**: You override this class for each component you want to add to your game (such as a sprite component). Often a component will perform periodic processing in its `updateWithDeltaTime(_:)` method.

- **GKEntity**: You override this class for each entity you want to add to your game (such as a dinosaur component). You then add various components to the entity (like a sprite component, animation component, shadow component, and health component).

Here's a diagram of what this will look like for the first two entities you'll add to the game:

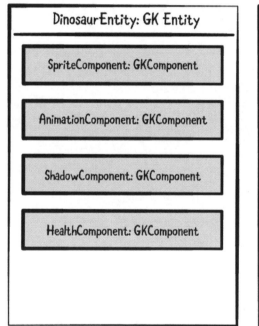
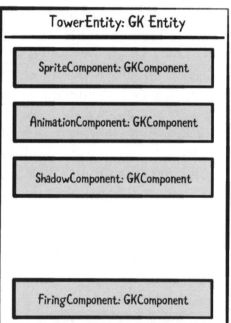

Basically, you will create several subclasses of `GKComponent` for various behavior you want your entities to have, and then creating a `GKEntity` subclass for each entity, which is basically a collection of components.

It's a different way of thinking, but it makes your code much cleaner and more flexible. Let's give it a try!

Your first component

Let's get started by adding your first component: a component to render a sprite to the scene.

In the project navigator, create a new group named **Components**, and add a new Swift source file to the group named **SpriteComponent.swift**.

Replace the contents of the file with the following:

```swift
import SpriteKit
import GameplayKit

class EntityNode: SKSpriteNode {
  weak var entity: GKEntity!
}

class SpriteComponent: GKComponent {

  // A node that gives an entity a visual sprite
  let node: EntityNode

  init(entity: GKEntity, texture: SKTexture, size: CGSize) {
    node = EntityNode(texture: texture,
      color: SKColor.whiteColor(), size: size)
    node.entity = entity
  }

}
```

The `EntityNode` class is a simple subclass of `SKSpriteNode` that contains a reference to the `GKEntity` that it represents. This is so you can get back to the `GKEntity` from the `SKSpriteNode`, should you wish.

The `SpriteComponent` is a very simple class that does nothing more than gives an entity a representation in a Sprite Kit scene via an `SKSpriteNode`. To use `SpriteComponent`, you simply have to initialize it with your `GKEntity` subclass, give it a texture to use, and then add its node to your scene. Let's do that next.

Your first entity

In the Xcode project navigator, create a new group named **Entities**, and add a new Swift source file to the group named **DinosaurEntity.swift**.

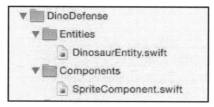

Add the following to **DinosaurEntity.swift**:

```
import UIKit
import GameplayKit
import SpriteKit

enum DinosaurType: String {
  case TRex = "T-Rex"
  case Triceratops = "Triceratops"
  case TRexBoss = "T-RexBoss"
}
```

This first adds some imports you need. To implement the dinosaur `GKEntity`, you need to import GameplayKit. You'll also be using Sprite Kit and some UIKit elements so you'll need those frameworks as well.

`DinosaurType` is a simple enumeration of the three dinosaur types that you'll have in your completed game. Later, you'll add to this enum so it also provides type-specific dinosaur information, like health and movement speed.

Now, add the following to define your dinosaur entity class:

```
class DinosaurEntity: GKEntity {

  // 1
  let dinosaurType: DinosaurType
  var spriteComponent: SpriteComponent!

  // 2
  init(dinosaurType: DinosaurType) {
    self.dinosaurType = dinosaurType
    super.init()

    // 3
    let size: CGSize
    switch dinosaurType {
    case .TRex, .TRexBoss:
      size = CGSizeMake(203, 110)
```

```
    case .Triceratops:
        size = CGSizeMake(142, 74)
    }

    // 4
    let textureAtlas = SKTextureAtlas(named:
dinosaurType.rawValue)
    let defaultTexture =
textureAtlas.textureNamed("Walk__01.png")

    // 5
    spriteComponent = SpriteComponent(entity: self,
        texture: defaultTexture, size: size)
    addComponent(spriteComponent)
  }

}
```

There's a lot here, so let's review this section-by-section:

1. These are two properties to store the type of the dinosaur, and keep a reference to the `SpriteComponent` you will add to this entity.

2. Here you declare the initializer and store the type of the dinosaur.

3. Here you determine the size of the dinosaur, based on the type of the dinosaur.

4. This starter project comes with a different texture atlas for each type of dinosaur in the game. Here you find the appropriate texture atlas based on the type of the dinosaur, and pick out the default sprite to use.

5. Finally, you create the `SpriteComponent` and call `addComponent()` (a built-in method of `GKEntity`) to add the component to the entity.

Now that you've created your component and entity, you can add them to the scene and see this in action!

Adding an entity to the scene

Next, open **GameScene.swift** and add this new method:

```
func addDinosaur(dinosaurType: DinosaurType) {
  // TEMP — Will be removed later
  let startPosition = CGPointMake(-200, 384)
  let endPosition = CGPointMake(1224, 384)

  let dinosaur = DinosaurEntity(dinosaurType: dinosaurType)
  let dinoNode = dinosaur.spriteComponent.node
  dinoNode.position = startPosition
```

```
    dinoNode.runAction(SKAction.moveTo(endPosition, duration: 20))

    addEntity(dinosaur)
}
```

Here, you create an instance of the `DinosaurEntity` and position the `SpriteComponent` node at the start position.

Your implementation of this function will change as you continue through the chapters of this section of the book. Right now, this function creates start and end points for your dinosaur and moves the dinosaur from one to the other using an `SKAction`. In the next chapter, you'll remove this and use pathfinding to let the dinosaur make its way across the scene.

Right now Xcode is warning you that the `addEntity()` method does not exist. You'll fix this next, but first add this property to the top of the class to keep track of all of the entities in the game:

```
var entities = Set<GKEntity>()
```

Then, add the missing method:

```
func addEntity(entity: GKEntity) {
  // 1
  entities.insert(entity)

  // 2
  if let spriteNode = entity.componentForClass(
    SpriteComponent.self)?.node {

    addNode(spriteNode, toGameLayer: .Sprites)

    // TODO: More here!
  }
}
```

This method does two things:

1. Adds the entity to the set you created earlier.

2. This checks to see if there is a `SpriteComponent`, and if so adds its node to the `.Sprites` layer of the game. This method is meant to work for any `GKEntity` you may add to the game, even ones that might not have a `SpriteComponent`, which is why you write it this way.

One last step! In `startFirstWave()`, add the following:

```
addDinosaur(.TRex)
```

You're good to go! Build and run, and tap to start.

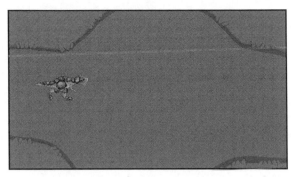

Congratulations, you have created your first entity and component! Let's review what you did:

1. You created a subclass of `GKComponent` to handle rendering a sprite (`SpriteComponent`).

2. You created a subclass of `GKEntity` for the dinosaur (`DinosaurEntity`). This contains just one component for now--the `SpriteComponent`--but you will add more components shortly.

3. You created an instance of the `DinosaurEntity`, and added the node of it's sprite component to the scene (along with running an action to make it move).

You might not be too impressed yet, as this looks like more code than you'd typically have to write to make a sprite move across the screen, but you'll begin to see the benefits as you continue to make components and reuse code in your game.

Let's continue working on the dinosaur by adding another component - one for his shadow.

The shadow component

In your **Components** group in the project navigator, create a new Swift source file named **ShadowComponent.swift**.

Replace the contents of **ShadowComponent.swift** with the following:

```
import Foundation
import GameplayKit
import SpriteKit

class ShadowComponent: GKComponent {

  let node: SKShapeNode

  init(size: CGSize, offset: CGPoint) {
```

```
        node = SKShapeNode(ellipseOfSize: size)
        node.fillColor = SKColor.blackColor()
        node.strokeColor = SKColor.blackColor()
        node.alpha = 0.2
        node.position = offset
    }
}
```

This is a simple class that uses SKShapeNode to draw a semi-transparent black oval shape to represent a shadow, as you learned how to do in Chapter 12, "Crop, Video, and Shape Nodes."

Now that you've created your component, you need to add it to your entity. To do this, open **DinosaurEntity.swift** and add this property:

```
var shadowComponent: ShadowComponent!
```

This creates a handy reference to the ShadowComponent you're about to add to the entity. Next, add this code to the end of init(dinosaurType:):

```
let shadowSize = CGSizeMake(size.width, size.height * 0.3)
shadowComponent = ShadowComponent(size: shadowSize,
  offset: CGPointMake(0.0, -size.height/2 + shadowSize.height/
2))
addComponent(shadowComponent)
```

This creates an instance of ShadowComponent, positions it below the sprite, and adds it to the entity.

There's one final step - you need to add the shape node to the scene so it appears. To do this, open **GameScene.swift** and add the following inside addEntity(:) right after the "TODO" comment:

```
// 1
if let shadowNode = entity.componentForClass(
  ShadowComponent.self)?.node {

  // 2
  addNode(shadowNode, toGameLayer: .Shadows)

  // 3
  let xRange = SKRange(constantValue: shadowNode.position.x)
  let yRange = SKRange(constantValue: shadowNode.position.y)
  let constraint = SKConstraint.positionX(xRange, y: yRange)
  constraint.referenceNode = spriteNode
  shadowNode.constraints = [constraint]
}
```

Let's review this section by section:

1. Checks to see if there is a `ShadowComponent` on this entity. Remember, in the future not all entities will have shadows.

2. If a shadow exists, it adds it to the shadows layer.

3. This applies a constraint to make the shadow follow the movement of the dinosaur sprite, as you learned in Chapter 11, "Advanced Physics".

Build and run, and you should now see a shadow underneath your T-Rex:

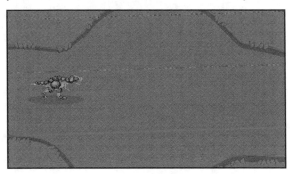

Things are getting ferocious!

The animation component

Let's create one more component for the dinosaur - a component to make him animated!

Start by creating another Swift source file in the **Components** group and name it **AnimationComponent.swift**.

Replace the contents of the file with the following:

```swift
import SpriteKit
import GameplayKit

enum AnimationState: String {
  case Idle = "Idle"
  case Walk = "Walk"
  case Hit = "Hit"
  case Dead = "Dead"
  case Attacking = "Attacking"
}
```

This enumeration provides a list of the possible animation states in which your game objects can be. The `String` raw value is used in the file name when loading the animations. For example, `Walk` frames are named Walk__01, Walk__02 and so forth.

Now add the following:

```
struct Animation {
    let animationState: AnimationState
    let textures: [SKTexture]
    let repeatTexturesForever: Bool
}
```

This simple struct represents everything you need to know about a particular animation. Each animation will have an `AnimationState` from the enumeration you just defined, an array of textures for the frames of the animation, and a Boolean dictating whether or not the animation repeats continuously.

For the `AnimationComponent` itself, add the following code:

```
class AnimationComponent: GKComponent {
    // 1
    let node: SKSpriteNode

    // 2
    var animations: [AnimationState: Animation]

    // 3
    private(set) var currentAnimation: Animation?

    // 4
    init(node: SKSpriteNode, textureSize: CGSize,
        animations: [AnimationState: Animation]) {

        self.node = node
        self.animations = animations
    }
}
```

There's quite a lot here, so take a look at each section in turn:

1. The animations need an `SKSpriteNode` on which to set the texture.

2. This is a store of the available animations in this component.

3. This is the current active animation.

4. This is a custom initializer that stores the `SKSpriteNode` on which to run the animation, and sets the available animations.

Remember from earlier in this chapter that you'll load the frames of each animation from a texture atlas, using the `SKTextureAtlas` class. To do this, add the following to the `AnimationComponent` class:

```
class func animationFromAtlas(atlas: SKTextureAtlas,
  withImageIdentifier identifier: String,
  forAnimationState animationState: AnimationState,
  repeatTexturesForever: Bool = true) -> Animation {

  let textures = atlas.textureNames.filter {
    $0.hasPrefix("\(identifier)_")
    }.sort {
      $0 < $1
    }.map {
      atlas.textureNamed($0)
  }

  return Animation(
    animationState: animationState,
    textures: textures,
    repeatTexturesForever: repeatTexturesForever
  )
}
```

This method takes an image identifier for the animation, such as `Walk`, and loads the frames of the animation from the provided texture atlas. It then returns an `Animation` struct for the `AnimationState`.

Now that the `AnimationComponent` class has a class method to load the animations for a given atlas and `AnimationState`, and an initializer that takes the available animations, you need to provide an action that will actually run the animation on the node.

Add the following to the class:

```
private func runAnimationForAnimationState(
  animationState: AnimationState) {

  // 1
  let actionKey = "Animation"
  // 2
  let timePerFrame = NSTimeInterval(1.0 / 30.0)

  // 3
  if currentAnimation != nil &&
    currentAnimation!.animationState == animationState
{ return }

  // 4
  guard let animation = animations[animationState] else {
    print("Unknown animation for state \
(animationState.rawValue)")
    return
  }

  // 5
  node.removeActionForKey(actionKey)
```

```
    // 6
    let texturesAction: SKAction
    if animation.repeatTexturesForever {
      texturesAction = SKAction.repeatActionForever(
          SKAction.animateWithTextures(
            animation.textures, timePerFrame: timePerFrame))
    }
    else {
      texturesAction = SKAction.animateWithTextures(
        animation.textures, timePerFrame: timePerFrame)
    }

    // 7
    node.runAction(texturesAction, withKey: actionKey)

    // 8
    currentAnimation = animation
  }
```

There's a lot going on here, but it's actually pretty simple stuff. Take a look:

1. To be able to remove the existing animation, if there is one, you need a key for the animation running on the node.

2. The animation frames in this game have been created to run at 30 frames per second.

3. Here you check that, if there's an existing animation, it's a different state than the one that's being requested. If this method is called with the same animation as the one that is currently running, then there's nothing to do.

4. This is a simple guard against requesting an `AnimationState` that doesn't exist for this component.

5. You remove the existing animation, if there is one.

6. This is where you create the animation `SKAction`. It will either be a repeating animation such as `Walk`, or a single animation such as `Dead`.

7. You run the action on the node.

8. You store the current animation as the new animation.

You see, while it's a lot of code, it's straightforward enough.

To set the next `AnimationState`, you'll make a request to the `AnimationComponent`, and the `AnimationComponent` will update the animation on the next call to its `updateWithDeltaTime(_:)`.

Add this property to `AnimationComponent`:

```
  var requestedAnimationState: AnimationState?
```

This will be the requested animation.

Now, add the following updateWithDeltaTime(_:) override to
AnimationComponent:

```
override func updateWithDeltaTime(deltaTime: NSTimeInterval) {
  super.updateWithDeltaTime(deltaTime)

  if let animationState = requestedAnimationState {
    runAnimationForAnimationState(animationState)
    requestedAnimationState = nil
  }
}
```

With each frame update, the AnimationComponent checks to see if an
AnimationState has been requested; if one has, it runs the animation and resets the
requestedAnimationState.

It turns out that updateWithDeltaTime(_:) on your components is not called
automatically; you need to write some code to do that. To understand how this works,
let's discuss one last piece of Sprite Kit's entity-component system:
GKComponentSystem.

GKComponentSystem

GKComponentSystem is a class that contains all of the components of a particular type in
your game. For example, you can make a GKComponentSystem that contains all of the
animation components in your game.

This is handy because then you can call the update methods on all instances of a
component at the same time. It's often handy in games to know that processing for a
single "system" (like animation) happens at a known time in your game loop.

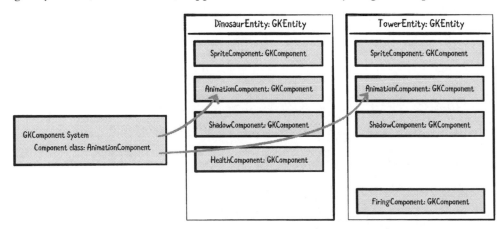

Let's see how this works by creating a GKComponentSystem to track your animation
components and call their update methods at the same time. Open **GameScene.swift**

and add the following property:

```
lazy var componentSystems: [GKComponentSystem] = {
  let animationSystem = GKComponentSystem(
    componentClass: AnimationComponent.self)
  return [animationSystem]
}()
```

This creates an instance of `GKComponentSystem` to track all instances of the `AnimationComponent` you just created. You could create other component systems for your sprite and shadow components, but they don't have update methods so there is no need.

Next in `addEntity(_:)`, just after you add the entity to your entities set, add the following:

```
for componentSystem in self.componentSystems {
  componentSystem.addComponentWithEntity(entity)
}
```

This loops through the array of component systems you just created (currently, only the animation component system) and adds the entity to that system. If the entity has any aniation components, the component system will keep track of it.

Fianlly, to do the actual update, add the following to the end of `update(_:)`:

```
for componentSystem in componentSystems {
  componentSystem.updateWithDeltaTime(deltaTime)
}
```

Now, with every frame, you update each of the component systems. This means that when you request an animation from the `AnimationComponent`, the animation component will run the animation on the next frame.

You're almost done - you just need to add your new animation component to your dinosuar entity!

Adding to your entity

Open **DinosaurEntity.swift** and add this property to the top of your class:

```
var animationComponent: AnimationComponent!
```

This keeps track of the animation component you're about to create.

Remember, when you initialize the `AnimationComponent`, you need to provide the animations—an array of your `Animation` structs. To load the animations for the dinosuar, add the following method:

```
func loadAnimations() -> [AnimationState: Animation] {
  let textureAtlas = SKTextureAtlas(named:
dinosaurType.rawValue)
  var animations = [AnimationState: Animation]()

  animations[.Walk] = AnimationComponent.animationFromAtlas(
    textureAtlas,
    withImageIdentifier: "Walk",
    forAnimationState: .Walk)
  animations[.Hit] = AnimationComponent.animationFromAtlas(
    textureAtlas,
    withImageIdentifier: "Hurt",
    forAnimationState: .Hit,
    repeatTexturesForever: false)
  animations[.Dead] = AnimationComponent.animationFromAtlas(
    textureAtlas,
    withImageIdentifier: "Dead",
    forAnimationState: .Dead,
    repeatTexturesForever: false)

  return animations
}
```

Now that you have a function for loading the animations, you can add the
AnimationComponent to the entity.

Add the following to the bottom of init(dinosaurType:):

```
animationComponent = AnimationComponent(node:
spriteComponent.node, textureSize: size, animations:
loadAnimations())
addComponent(animationComponent)
```

Here, you create the AnimationComponent, providing the sprite node to animate and
also the array of animations. This way, the animation node takes care of the animation,
and the sprite component node takes care of the position of the entity in the scene.

Theres one last step. Add this line to the bottom of addDinosaur(_:) to set the initial
animation:

```
dinosaur.animationComponent.requestedAnimationState = .Walk
```

Build and run, and see your dino strut in style!

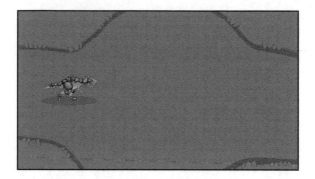

Reusing components

Now you're going to see the true power of the Entity-Component model by reusing the components you created in a tower entity.

Create a new Swift source file in your **Entities** group named **TowerEntity.swift**, and replace the contents of the file with the following:

```swift
import UIKit
import SpriteKit
import GameplayKit

enum TowerType: String {
  case Wood = "WoodTower"
  case Rock = "RockTower"

  static let allValues = [Wood, Rock]
}
```

Just as with the `DinosaurEntity`, you create an enum to provide a tower type. The `TowerType` will contain more information about each of the towers as you continue to build your game.

Now, add the class:

```swift
class TowerEntity: GKEntity {

  let towerType: TowerType
  var spriteComponent: SpriteComponent!
  var shadowComponent: ShadowComponent!
  var animationComponent: AnimationComponent!

  init(towerType: TowerType) {
    // Store the TowerType
    self.towerType = towerType
```

```
    super.init()

    let textureAtlas = SKTextureAtlas(named: towerType.rawValue)
    let defaultTexture = textureAtlas.textureNamed("Idle__000")
    let textureSize = CGSizeMake(98, 140)

    // Add the SpriteComponent
    spriteComponent = SpriteComponent(entity: self,
      texture: defaultTexture, size: textureSize)
    addComponent(spriteComponent)

    // Add the ShadowComponent
    let shadowSize = CGSizeMake(98, 44)
    shadowComponent = ShadowComponent(size: shadowSize,
      offset: CGPointMake(0.0,
        -textureSize.height/2 + shadowSize.height/2))
    addComponent(shadowComponent)

    // Add the AnimationComponent
    animationComponent = AnimationComponent(node:
spriteComponent.node,
      textureSize: textureSize, animations: loadAnimations())
    addComponent(animationComponent)

  }

}
```

This is exactly the same thing you did for DinosaurEntity, and like DinosaurEntity, you'll need to provide a function for loading the animations.

Add the following to your class:

```
func loadAnimations() -> [AnimationState: Animation] {
  let textureAtlas = SKTextureAtlas(named: towerType.rawValue)
  var animations = [AnimationState: Animation]()

  animations[.Idle] = AnimationComponent.animationFromAtlas(
    textureAtlas,
    withImageIdentifier: "Idle",
    forAnimationState: .Idle)
  animations[.Attacking] =
AnimationComponent.animationFromAtlas(
    textureAtlas,
    withImageIdentifier: "Attacking",
    forAnimationState: .Attacking)

  return animations
}
```

This function is almost identical to the one in DinosaurEntity, except that the animations are for the Idle and Attacking states.

And that's it! You created an SKEntity subclass for your towers and added all the required components. You can see the power behind the Entity-Component model here. You didn't have to create a new renderer or code a shadow generator or animation functions for the TowerEntity—they're all available to you, for free, as the same code you created for the DinosaurEntity.

To add a tower to your scene, open **GameScene.swift** and add the following function:

```
func addTower(towerType: TowerType) {
  // TEMP - Will be removed later
  let position = CGPointMake(400, 384)

  let towerEntity = TowerEntity(towerType: towerType)
  towerEntity.spriteComponent.node.position = position
  towerEntity.animationComponent.requestedAnimationState = .Idle
  addEntity(towerEntity)
}
```

In the next chapter, you'll position the towers at points determined by the player, but for the moment, you've added the tower to a hard-coded position in the scene. Just like with the dinosaur, you've set the position of the SpriteComponent node and requested the .Idle animation, before adding the entity to the scene.

Finally, to make the call to add the tower to the scene, simply add the following line to startFirstWave():

```
addTower(.Wood)
```

Build and run.

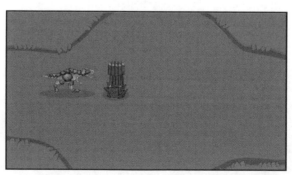

You now have a shiny new wood tower in your scene, and for a relatively small amount of extra code. The entity is reusing all the functionality provided by your components. Pretty neat, huh? :]

Now that you've seen how awesome components are, why not create another two.

Firing component

At the moment, your tower just sits there and very politely lets the dinosaur run past. That's not entirely to plan, and so it's time to give your tower some firepower.

Your two tower types, Wood and Rock, will fire projectiles at the dinosaurs at different rates. As the rate of fire is determined by the tower type, the `TowerType` enum is an excellent place to put this property.

Open **TowerEntity.swift** and add the following property to the `TowerType` enum:

```
var fireRate: Double {
  switch self {
    case Wood: return 1.0
    case Rock: return 1.5
  }
}
```

The Wood towers will fire twice per second, and the Rock towers will fire once per second.

Each of the towers will also do a different amount of damage to the dinosaurs, so add another property to `TowerType` for the damage inflicted:

```
var damage: Int {
  switch self {
    case Wood: return 20
    case Rock: return 50
  }
}
```

The wooden arrows that the Wood tower fires do 20 points of damage, while a dinosaur will receive 50 points of damage from a rock in the face!

It would also be cool if the towers had different ranges, so add another property to `TowerType`:

```
var range: CGFloat {
  switch self {
    case Wood: return 200
    case Rock: return 250
  }
}
```

The arrows from the Wood towers fly a little farther than the rocks from the Rock towers.

The `FiringComponent` will use these stored properties to launch projectiles at a target dinosaur.

Create a new Swift source file in your **Components** group named
FiringComponent.swift, and replace the code inside with the following:

```swift
import SpriteKit
import GameplayKit

class FiringComponent: GKComponent {

  let towerType: TowerType
  let parentNode: SKNode
  var currentTarget: DinosaurEntity?
  var timeTillNextShot: NSTimeInterval = 0

  init(towerType: TowerType, parentNode: SKNode) {
    self.towerType = towerType
    self.parentNode = parentNode
  }

}
```

Here, you create your new `GKComponent` subclass and give it the following properties:

- **towerType**: This identifies the tower type that's doing the firing, so you can get the firing rate, damage done and the range of the tower.

- **parentNode**: This is the tower's `SpriteComponent` node and is used to add the projectile node as a child.

- **currentTarget**: This is an optional target `DinosaurEntity` for the tower. The tower won't always have a target—only when a dinosaur is in range.

- **timeTillNextShot**: Based on the firing rate of the tower, this holds the time interval before the tower's next shot.

You've got the start of a firing component here, but before you can implement the firing of the projectile, you're going to need a projectile entity. The projectile will need its own sprite in the scene, and this is sounding very much like a `GKEntity` subclass with a `SpriteComponent`.

Create a new Swift source file in the **Entities** group named **ProjectileEntity.swift**, and replace the contents of the file with this:

```swift
import SpriteKit
import GameplayKit

class ProjectileEntity: GKEntity {

  var spriteComponent: SpriteComponent!

  init(towerType: TowerType) {
    super.init()
```

```
    let texture = SKTexture(imageNamed:
      "\(towerType.rawValue)Projectile")
    spriteComponent = SpriteComponent(entity: self,
      texture: texture, size: texture.size())
    addComponent(spriteComponent)
  }

}
```

This should all look very familiar. You create a new `GKEntity` subclass and given it your `SpriteComponent`. By attaching the correct projectile sprite as a child to the `SpriteComponent` node, you finish the new entity in just a few lines of code. Now you can get back to firing this projectile from the `FiringComponent`.

Firing projectiles

Open **FiringComponent.swift**.

Since the firing of the projectile is a timed feature, the logic will go in the component's `updateWithDeltaTime(_:)` function, much like the change of animation in the `AnimationComponent`.

Add the following function override:

```
override func updateWithDeltaTime(seconds: NSTimeInterval) {
  super.updateWithDeltaTime(seconds)

  guard let target = currentTarget else { return }

  timeTillNextShot -= seconds
  if timeTillNextShot > 0 { return }
  timeTillNextShot = towerType.fireRate
}
```

Remember that `GameScene` calls `updateWithDeltaTime(_:)` every frame. So every frame, you check to see if you have a valid `currentTarget`. If not, you simply return.

If you have a valid target, you take the delta time from the `timeTillNextShot` and see if the result is greater than zero—which indicates there's still time to wait until the next shot is fired. If `timeTillNextShot` is 0 or less, then you reset `timeTillNextShot`, and you're ready to take the shot. That's what you need to code now.

At the end of `updateWithDeltaTime(_:)`, add the following code:

```
// 1
let projectile = ProjectileEntity(towerType: towerType)
let projectileNode = projectile.spriteComponent.node
projectileNode.position = CGPointMake(0.0, 50.0)
parentNode.addChild(projectileNode)

// 2
let targetNode = target.spriteComponent.node
projectileNode.rotateToFaceNode(targetNode, sourceNode:
parentNode)

// 3
let fireVector = CGVectorMake(targetNode.position.x -
parentNode.position.x, targetNode.position.y -
parentNode.position.y)

// 4
let soundAction = SKAction.playSoundFileNamed("\
(towerType.rawValue)Fire.mp3", waitForCompletion: false)
let fireAction = SKAction.moveBy(fireVector, duration: 0.4)
let removeAction = SKAction.runBlock { () -> Void in
  projectileNode.removeFromParent()
}
let action = SKAction.sequence([soundAction, fireAction,
removeAction])
projectileNode.runAction(action)
```

Take a look at each of these steps in turn:

1. You create an instance of the `ProjectileEntity` and position the node toward the top of the tower, before adding it as a child to the parent node.

2. You get the target node from the target's `SpriteComponent` and rotate the projectile to face it.

3. You get the vector for the translation between the parent node's position and the position of the target, so that you can move the projectile along the correct line to the target.

4. You put together an `SKAction` series to play a fire sound, move the projectile to the target and finally, remove the projectile when it's hit something. Then, you run the action on the projectile node.

It's time to add the `FiringComponent` to the `TowerEntity`.

Open **TowerEntity.swift** and add the following property:

```
var firingComponent: FiringComponent!
```

Now, initialize the property by adding this to the bottom of `init(towerType:)`:

```
firingComponent = FiringComponent(towerType: towerType,
  parentNode: spriteComponent.node)
addComponent(firingComponent)
```

Again, this should be very familiar. You add a `FiringComponent` property and initialize it with the tower type and the parent node: the tower's `SpriteComponent` node.

There are still a few steps to complete before the tower will fire, the first of which is to set the tower's current target when a dinosaur is in range. To do that, you're going to check the distance between all of the dinosaurs and all of the towers in your scene. If you spot any dinosaurs within range of a tower, you'll choose the dinosaur that's closest to its destination as a priority.

The best place to do this check is after the scene has updated each frame. In an `SKScene`, this is in `didFinishUpdate()`. So, open **GameScene.swift** and add the following override:

```
override func didFinishUpdate() {
  let dinosaurs: [DinosaurEntity] = entities.flatMap { entity in
    if let dinosaur = entity as? DinosaurEntity {
      return dinosaur
    }
    return nil
  }

  let towers: [TowerEntity] = entities.flatMap { entity in
    if let tower = entity as? TowerEntity {
      return tower
    }
    return nil
  }
}
```

After every frame update, this function gets an array of the dinosaurs in the scene and a separate array of the towers. For each tower, you're going to use a function named `distanceBetween(_:nodeB:)`—provided in the `Utils` class that's been added the starter project—to determine if any of the dinosaurs are in range.

Add this to the bottom of `didFinishUpdate()`:

```
for tower in towers {
  // 1
  let towerType = tower.towerType
  // 2
  var target: DinosaurEntity?
  // 3
  for dinosaur in dinosaurs.filter({
    (dinosaur: DinosaurEntity) -> Bool in
    distanceBetween(tower.spriteComponent.node, nodeB:
      dinosaur.spriteComponent.node) < towerType.range}) {
```

```
    // 4
    if let t = target {
      if dinosaur.spriteComponent.node.position.x >
         t.spriteComponent.node.position.x {
        target = dinosaur
      }
    } else {
      target = dinosaur
    }

  }

  // 5
  tower.firingComponent.currentTarget = target
}
```

For each tower in the scene, you perform the following steps:

1. You store the tower type; this is what you use to get the range of the tower.

2. You keep track of the target; this is optional because there might not be any targets in range.

3. Next, you filter the dinosaurs to get those that are in range, and then loop through these dinosaurs.

4. For each dinosaur that's in range of the tower, you check to see which is the farthest across the scene—that is, which has the highest `position.x` value.

5. Finally, you set the target on the firing component for the tower.

You're almost set; there's just one more step.

As with the `AnimationComponent`, `updateWithDeltaTime(_:)` in the `FiringComponent` won't be called unless the component is part of the component system registered in the scene. So, add a new `GKComponentSystem` for the `FiringComponent` to the `componentSystems` dynamic property, like this:

```
lazy var componentSystems: [GKComponentSystem] = {
  let animationSystem = GKComponentSystem(
    componentClass: AnimationComponent.self)
  let firingSystem = GKComponentSystem(componentClass:
FiringComponent.self)
  return [animationSystem, firingSystem]
}()
```

Build and run.

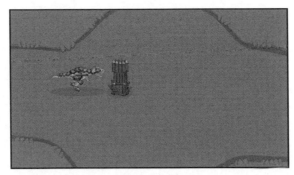

As the dinosaur gets within range of the tower, the tower begins to fire its wooden projectiles into the dinosaur. Pew pew!

Congratulations - this is starting to look like a real tower defense game, and you've learned a lot about GameplayKit's Entity-Component system in the process. Keep reading if you'd like a challenge to practice what you've learned - or skip forward to the next chapter, where you'll learn about another great feature in GameplayKit: Pathfinding!

Challenges

There's just one challenge in this chapter, and it's to add one more component to your game: a health bar component for the dinosaur.

As always, if you get stuck, you can find solutions in the resources for this chapter—but give it your best shot first!

Challenge 1: Health component

At this point, the wooden stakes from the Wood tower are bouncing right off the dinosaur without causing so much as a scratch. It's time to give the dinosaur a world of hurt.

These invincible dinosaurs need to respect the international gaming laws by using a health bar. You're going to create a simple `SKShapeNode` that displays a green bar above the dinosaur to indicate how much health it has remaining. The bar won't be visible until the dinosaur has taken damage.

Create your final new Swift source file in your **Components** group and name it **HealthComponent.swift**.

Replace the code inside with the following:

```
import SpriteKit
import GameplayKit

class HealthComponent: GKComponent {

  let fullHealth: Int
  var health: Int
  let healthBarFullWidth: CGFloat
  let healthBar: SKShapeNode

  init(parentNode: SKNode, barWidth: CGFloat,
    barOffset: CGFloat, health: Int) {

    self.fullHealth = health
    self.health = health

    healthBarFullWidth = barWidth
    healthBar = SKShapeNode(rectOfSize:
      CGSizeMake(healthBarFullWidth, 5), cornerRadius: 1)
    healthBar.fillColor = UIColor.greenColor()
    healthBar.strokeColor = UIColor.greenColor()
    healthBar.position = CGPointMake(0, barOffset)
    parentNode.addChild(healthBar)

    healthBar.hidden = true
  }

}
```

The `HealthComponent` stores the current health and the full health, and draws an `SKShapeNode` whose size represents the amount of health remaining as a proportion of the full health. The bar is attached to a parent node as a child. The parent node will be the `SpriteComponent` node of the `DinosaurEntity` that's been targeted by the tower.

The `HealthComponent` needs to know how to take damage and display it. It also seems like the logical place to play a sound when the damage is done. So, add this `SKAction` property to the `HealthComponent` class to let it play a sound when the projectile hits the dinosaur:

```
let soundAction = SKAction.playSoundFileNamed("Hit.mp3",
  waitForCompletion: false)
```

Now, add this function to let the `HealthComponent` respond to damage:

```
func takeDamage(damage: Int) -> Bool {
  health = max(health - damage, 0)

  healthBar.hidden = false
  let healthScale = CGFloat(health)/CGFloat(fullHealth)
```

```
    let scaleAction = SKAction.scaleXTo(healthScale, duration:
 0.5)
    healthBar.runAction(SKAction.group([soundAction,
 scaleAction]))
    return health == 0
 }
```

Here, you reduce the current health value by the provided amount of damage taken. The health value can't go any lower than zero. You then make sure the health bar is visible, and scale the health bar down using an SKAction to make it a smooth transition. When scaling back the health bar, you also play the sound of the dinosaur being hit.

To initialize the HealthComponent, you're going to need to know the dinosaur's starting health value. Since each dinosaur has a different health value, it makes sense for this property to be in the DinosaurType enum. So, open **DinosaurEntity.swift** and add this property to DinosaurType:

```
var health: Int {
  switch self {
    case .TRex: return 60
    case .Triceratops: return 40
    case .TRexBoss: return 1000
  }
}
```

Here, you set the Triceratops to be slightly weaker than the T-Rex. That T-Rex Boss looks tough, doesn't it? More from him later. ;]

Your challenge is to add the your new health component to the dinosaur entity. To do this, you'll need to do 2 steps:

1. Add a healthComponent property to DinosaurEntity.

2. Initialize and add the healthComponent in init(dinosaurType:). Make it as wide as the dino, and appear above the dino.

Now your dinosaurs have a health bar; all that's left is to apply the damage when the projectile hits the dinosaur. Since the FiringComponent is responsible for all of this violence, that's the best place to force the HealthComponent to take damage. So, open **FiringComponent.swift**.

At the bottom of updateWithDeltaTime(_:), you have an SKAction series to play the fire sound and animate the projectile. Add the following action just before you create the removeAction:

```
let damageAction = SKAction.runBlock { () -> Void in
  target.healthComponent.takeDamage(self.towerType.damage)
}
```

Then, add the damage action to the sequence, just before the removeAction, like this:

```
let action = SKAction.sequence([soundAction, fireAction,
  damageAction, removeAction])
```

Build and run.

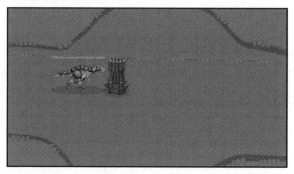

Now, when the projectile hits the dinosaur, you can see the health bar appear and take damage from each shot.

If you made it this far, congratulations! In this chapter, you learned how the Entity-Component model can help to split your code into groups of functionality that you can share between game objects without needing to rewrite any of the code. A great example is the SpriteComponent, which works for dinosaurs, towers, projectiles and—spoiler alert—in the next chapter, obstacles.

The component systems that you update during the update cycle in the scene also provide an excellent way to trigger actions on your components, like the rate-controlled firing on the FiringComponent.

This is a great beginning for your Dino Defense game. In the next chapter, you'll implement pathfinding, so your dinosaurs can avoid the towers and any other obstacles in the scene. You'll also give the player the means to place her towers and try to stop those pesky little—no, wait... BIG—dinosaurs!

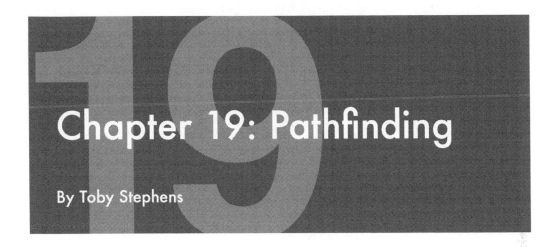

Chapter 19: Pathfinding

By Toby Stephens

In the previous chapter, you used GameplayKit's Entity-Component system to build the object model for a tower defense game named Dino Defense. By the end of the chapter, you had all the entities and components you needed to move a rampaging dinosaur across the game scene and attack it from a tower firing wooden stakes.

One very noticeable issue with what you've created so far is that the dinosaur walks straight through the tower without a care in the world. I think you'll agree, the dinosaur's AI could use work!

In this chapter, you're going to use the pathfinding functionality provided by GameplayKit to let the dinosaur walk around your towers and other obstacles you'll add to the game. But lest you think you're giving the dinosaur a path to an easy victory, you'll also add features to let players construct and place towers on their own. This war is just getting started!

Yes, there's a lot of fun coming up, but first, you'll take a brief look at the pathfinding APIs provided by GameplayKit.

Pathfinding in GameplayKit

For your dinosaurs to navigate a path across the game scene, they'll need to be aware of any obstacles in their way, such as towers, rocks and trees. To catalog these obstacles, GameplayKit provides a GKGraph, which is a collection of locations in the scene. You can deal with this collection of locations in one of two ways, depending on which is the best fit for your particular game: You can use either grid-based or obstacle-based paths.

Grid-based pathfinding

When the pathfinding is based on a playable grid, you can use a GKGraph subclass named GKGridGraph to provide a list of *valid* locations on a two-dimensional grid. The entities are only allowed to travel between the specified grid locations.

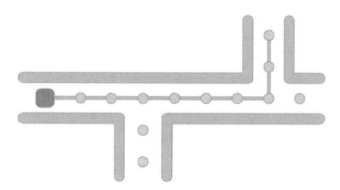

A good example of where you would use this kind of pathfinding is in Pac-Man, the classic arcade game. Valid locations, specified using GKGridGraphNodes, would be the paths on which Pac-Man and the ghosts can run. Locations on the grid occupied by walls would be invalid, and wouldn't be added to the GKGridGraph.

Obstacle-based pathfinding

When your pathfinding needs to be less controlled and the entities need to avoid obstacles while moving across an open field, you can use a GKGraph subclass named GKObstacleGraph.

In GKObstacleGraph, you provide a collection of *invalid* polygons that specify the shapes of the obstacles in the scene.

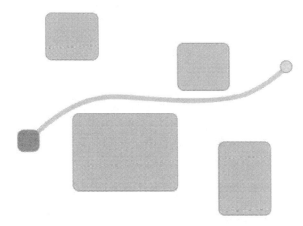

Given that the dinosaurs in Dino Defense are running across open terrain and avoiding your towers, this is the pathfinding API you'll use.

You'll create a GKObstacleGraph and add polygons to it representing the bounds of your towers and other game obstacles. Then, GameplayKit will create the dinosaur path using a sequence of valid positions that avoids the obstacles provided in the GKObstacleGraph.

When you add new towers to the game, GameplayKit will recalculate the paths based on the dinosaurs' current positions.

Tower obstacles

> **Note**: The next several pages of this chapter explain how to implement the ability for the player to place towers into the game. This is a review of material from previous chapters.
>
> If you are here to learn about GameplayKit pathfinding, we recommend you skip ahead to the "Creating an obstacle graph" section later in this chapter, where we will have a starter project waiting for you.
>
> But if you'd like some review or to learn how to let the player place the towers, keep reading! :]

The first obstacles you're going to add to your obstacle graph will be the towers. This would be a good time to enable the player to place the towers on her own.

To do that, you're going to give the player a number of possible tower placement positions in the scene. If the player selects one of these placement nodes, she'll be able to choose which tower she wishes to build, and the little elves inside the CPU will build the tower. :]

Open **GameScene.sks**.

Do you recall the discussion of game layers from the previous chapter?
The .Background layer is the logical place to put your tower placement nodes. So, start by locating the **TowerPlaceholder.png** in the Media Library.

Now, drag the **TowerPlaceholder** image into the scene and make the following changes to the sprite node in the Attributes Inspector:

• Set the **Name** to **Tower_01**.

• Set the **Parent** to **Background**.

• Set the **Position** to **(600, 400)**.

• Set the **Z Position** to **1** to ensure the image is always on top of the background texture.

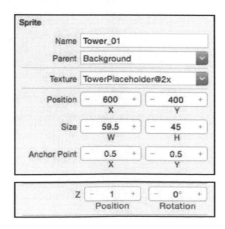

You'll use the name of the node later, when you test to find out which node the player has selected.

Add seven more **TowerPlaceholder** nodes to the scene, making the following changes in the Attributes Inspector:

1. Name **Tower_02**, Parent **Background**, Position **(140, 240)**, Z Position **1**
2. Name **Tower_03**, Parent **Background**, Position **(280, 550)**, Z Position **1**
3. Name **Tower_04**, Parent **Background**, Position **(400, 160)**, Z Position **1**
4. Name **Tower_05**, Parent **Background**, Position **(512, 580)**, Z Position **1**
5. Name **Tower_06**, Parent **Background**, Position **(528, 480)**, Z Position **1**
6. Name **Tower_07**, Parent **Background**, Position **(750, 480)**, Z Position **1**
7. Name **Tower_08**, Parent **Background**, Position **(780, 260)**, Z Position **1**

> **Note**: As a shortcut, try duplicating one of the tower placeholders with Option-D and then change the name and position.

When you're done, your scene will look like this:

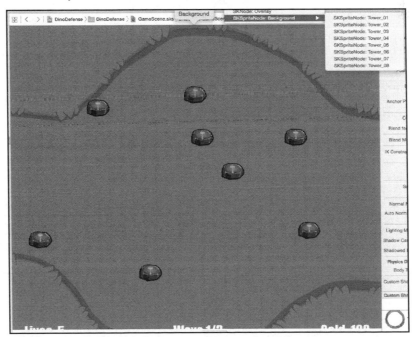

Build and run.

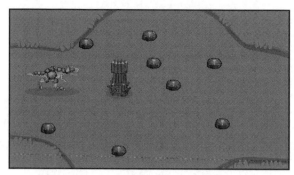

You can see the tower selector nodes you created, sitting on the playing field.

When the player taps on one of these nodes, she needs to see the available tower types so she can choose which tower to build. The starter project includes a simple node that you'll use to show a tower type for selection.

Open **TowerSelector.sks** and take a look.

The scene file provides an image of the tower type and also a label to tell the player how much the tower will cost. Cost? Yes, in your completed game, the player will have to pay gold to build each tower. You'll deal with the mechanics behind paying for towers in the next chapter, but for now, you need to give each tower a cost.

Open **TowerEntity.swift** and add the following dynamic property to the TowerType enum:

```
var cost: Int {
  switch self {
    case Wood: return 50
    case Rock: return 85
  }
}
```

Those rock towers sure pack a punch, but they'll cost the player more than the wood towers.

OK, now that you have a cost for each of your tower types, you can get back to the tower selector node. You're going to create the class that displays the tower selector in the scene file.

Create a new Swift source file in your project named **TowerSelectorNode.swift**.

Replace the contents of the file with the following:

```
import SpriteKit

class TowerSelectorNode: SKNode {

  var costLabel: SKLabelNode {
    return self.childNodeWithName("CostLabel") as! SKLabelNode
  }

  var towerIcon: SKSpriteNode {
    return self.childNodeWithName("TowerIcon") as! SKSpriteNode
  }

  override init() {
    super.init()
  }

  required init?(coder aDecoder: NSCoder) {
    super.init(coder: aDecoder)
  }

}
```

This is an `SKNode` subclass and represents the `MainNode` in **TowerSelector.sks**. The node has child nodes for the tower cost label and the tower image, named `CostLabel` and `TowerIcon`, respectively. You create dynamically stored properties for both of these nodes, so you can access them when you set the tower type for each instance of `TowerSelectorNode`.

Now, add the following method that will set the tower type on the selector node:

```
func setTower(towerType: TowerType) {
  // Set the name and icon
  towerIcon.texture = SKTexture(imageNamed: towerType.rawValue)
  towerIcon.name = "Tower_Icon_\(towerType.rawValue)"

  // Set the cost
  costLabel.text = "\(towerType.cost)"
}
```

Taking a tower type, you set the correct tower image and also show the correct cost of the tower in the `costLabel`. You also name the `towerIcon`, so you can identify the tower type of the icon later, when you handle tower type selection.

Tower selector animations

It would be cool if, when you show the tower selectors to the player, the selectors spun out to different positions around the tower placement node. Depending on the number of tower types, you could position the tower selectors in a circle:

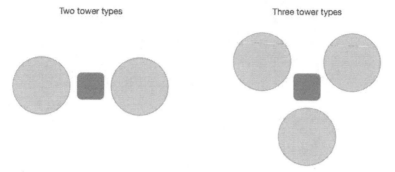

To implement this, your `TowerSelectorNode` needs to know the angle on the circle at which to position itself. Add the `angle` argument to `setTower(_:)` so that it looks like this:

```
func setTower(towerType: TowerType, angle: CGFloat) {
```

To spin the `TowerSelectorNode` out to the correct angle, you're going to create, show and hide animations using actions. Add the following properties to the `TowerSelectorNode` class:

```
var showAction = SKAction()
var hideAction = SKAction()
```

To define these actions, add the following to the bottom of `setTower(_:angle:)`:

```
self.zRotation = 180.degreesToRadians()

let rotateAction = SKAction.rotateByAngle(
  180.degreesToRadians(),
  duration: 0.2)

let moveAction = SKAction.moveByX(
  cos(angle) * 50,
  y: sin(angle) * 50,
  duration: 0.2)

showAction = SKAction.group([rotateAction, moveAction])
hideAction = showAction.reversedAction()
```

The tower selector is initially rotated through 180 degrees, and then the `rotateAction` rotates the node back into the correct position when you show the tower selector to the user. The `moveAction` will move the node to its correct position on the circle around the tower placement node, based on the provided angle.

The `showAction` combines the rotation and translation. The `hideAction` is simply the reverse.

To invoke the actions, add the following functions to the class:

```
func show() {
  self.runAction(showAction)
}

func hide(completion: () -> ()) {
  self.runAction(SKAction.sequence([
    hideAction, SKAction.runBlock(completion)]))
}
```

So you can remove the tower selector node from the game scene, the hide function takes a completion closure that runs after the `hideAction` has finished.

To make use of these new tower selectors, you need to create them in your game scene. Open **GameScene.swift** and add a property for these tower selectors, as follows:

```
var towerSelectorNodes = [TowerSelectorNode]()
```

You need to create one of these selector nodes per tower type. Create a function to do this by adding this code to the `GameScene` class:

```
func loadTowerSelectorNodes() {
  // 1
  let towerTypeCount = TowerType.allValues.count

  // 2
  let towerSelectorNodePath: String = NSBundle.mainBundle()
    .pathForResource("TowerSelector", ofType: "sks")!
  let towerSelectorNodeScene =
NSKeyedUnarchiver.unarchiveObjectWithFile(
    towerSelectorNodePath) as! SKScene
  for t in 0..<towerTypeCount {
    // 3
    let towerSelectorNode =
(towerSelectorNodeScene.childNodeWithName(
      "MainNode"))!.copy() as! TowerSelectorNode
    // 4
    towerSelectorNode.setTower(TowerType.allValues[t],
      angle: ((2*π)/CGFloat(towerTypeCount)*CGFloat(t))
    // 5
    towerSelectorNodes.append(towerSelectorNode)
  }
}
```

Take a closer look at what's going on here:

1. You get the number of tower types, so you can calculate the position of each tower selector node as it's arranged in the diagram above.

2. You get the `TowerSelector` scene from the scene file.

3. For each tower type, you make a copy of the `MainNode` from the `TowerSelector` scene.

4. You set the tower type on the `TowerSelectorNode` and also the angle at which the node will be placed around the circle.

5. Finally, you append the node to the `TowerSelectorNode` array you just defined.

Call this function as part of the scene setup by adding the following to `didMoveToView(_:)`, just after the call to `super.didMoveToView(view)`:

```
loadTowerSelectorNodes()
```

Selecting a tower

You've loaded all of the selector nodes for the tower types you have in the game, so you're ready to show them to the player when she taps a tower placement node.

First, remove the tower you temporarily placed in your scene by *deleting* the following line from `startFirstWave()`:

```
addTower(.Wood)
```

To track the player's tower placement activities, add the following properties to the class:

```
var placingTower = false
var placingTowerOnNode = SKNode()
```

`placingTower` tells you whether the player is placing a tower, and `placingTowerOnNode` stores the tower placement node onto which the player is placing the tower.

Next, add a function to show the tower selectors:

```
func showTowerSelector(atPosition position: CGPoint) {
  // 1
  if placingTower == true {return}
  placingTower = true

  // 2
  self.runAction(SKAction.playSoundFileNamed("Menu.mp3",
```

```
waitForCompletion: false))

  for towerSelectorNode in towerSelectorNodes {
    // 3
    towerSelectorNode.position = position
    // 4
    gameLayerNodes[.Hud]!.addChild(towerSelectorNode)
    // 5
    towerSelectorNode.show()
  }
}
```

1. If the player is already placing a tower, then there's nothing to do here.

2. The starter project came with a sound effect for opening and closing the tower selectors, so use it. ;]

3. For each tower selector node, you set the position to the touch position passed to the function. The tower selector nodes will spin out from this point.

4. You add the tower selector nodes to the .Hud game layer. This means you're placing it *above* the other nodes in the game, which is what you want for game UI elements.

5. You call the show() function you wrote to spin the tower selector nodes into view.

Now, add a function to hide the tower selector nodes. Add this code:

```
func hideTowerSelector() {
  if placingTower == false { return }
  placingTower = false

  self.runAction(SKAction.playSoundFileNamed("Menu.mp3",
waitForCompletion: false))

  for towerSelectorNode in towerSelectorNodes {
    towerSelectorNode.hide {
      towerSelectorNode.removeFromParent()
    }
  }
}
```

This is almost identical to showTowerSelector(atPosition:), with the obvious exception that this is now hiding the tower selector.

Note the closure you pass to the hide function on your tower selector nodes. As discussed earlier, this is so you can wait for the hide animation to complete before removing the node from its parent node—that is, before removing the tower selector node from the .Hud layer.

Displaying the menu

To see all of this in action, you're going to need to respond to the player's touch on a tower placement node. So, add the following to the *bottom* of touchesBegan(_:withEvent:):

```
let touchedNodes: [SKNode] =
self.nodesAtPoint(touch.locationInNode(self)).flatMap { node in
  if let nodeName = node.name where nodeName.hasPrefix("Tower_")
  {
    return node
  }
  return nil
}
```

Here, you go through the nodes located at the position of the player's touch. You use a flatmap on the array of SKNodes returned from nodesAtPoint(_:) to only include nodes with names that start with "Tower_" in the resulting touchedNodes array.

Now that you have an array that only contains tower placement nodes, you can check to see if the player actually touched any of these nodes. Add the following:

```
if touchedNodes.count == 0 {
  hideTowerSelector()
  return
}
```

You check to see if the player did, in fact, touch a tower placement node; if not, you hide the tower selector if it needs hiding, and return.

So, what if the player *did* touch a tower placement node? Continue touchesBegan(_:withEvent:) by adding the following:

```
let touchedNode = touchedNodes[0]

if placingTower {
  hideTowerSelector()
}
else {
  placingTowerOnNode = touchedNode
  showTowerSelector(atPosition: touchedNode.position)
}
```

Here, you take the first touched node. You shouldn't ever have more than one node here, because that would mean you had more than one tower placement node at the same position in the game scene. If you're already placing a tower, you hide the tower selector; if you aren't placing a tower yet, you store the tower selector node that was touched and show the tower selector.

Build and run, and when you start the game, touch one of the tower placement nodes.

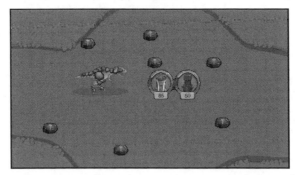

The tower selector nodes spin out from the point you touched. Now this is starting to feel more like a game!

Placing a tower

What about selecting and placing a tower? Well, to add a tower to a specified position in the scene, you need to make some changes to addTower(_:).

In addTower(_:), *remove* the temporary line you added to set the position of the tower:

```
let position = CGPointMake(400, 384)
```

And change addTower(_:) so that it takes a position parameter, like this:

```
func addTower(towerType: TowerType, position: CGPoint) {
```

Now, add the following to the *top* of addTower(_:position:):

```
placingTowerOnNode.removeFromParent()
self.runAction(SKAction.playSoundFileNamed("BuildTower.mp3",
waitForCompletion: false))
```

You remove the tower placement node from the game, because a tower has been placed on top of it. You also play the build tower sound effect provided in the starter project.

To finish placing the tower, you need to check which tower type the player has selected. This will be on a touch event again, so head back to touchesBegan(_:withEvent:).

Inside the if placingTower statement, at the point where you call hideTowerSelector(), add the following *directly above* that line:

```
let touchedNodeName = touchedNode.name!

if touchedNodeName == "Tower_Icon_WoodTower" {
  addTower(.Wood, position: placingTowerOnNode.position)
}
else if touchedNodeName == "Tower_Icon_RockTower" {
  addTower(.Rock, position: placingTowerOnNode.position)
}
```

If placingTower is true, then you now check to see if one of the tower icons in the tower selector node has been touched. If it has, then you know which tower the player selected, and you can place the tower before hiding the tower selector.

Build and run, and try building a tower again.

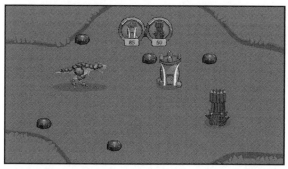

The player can now select which type of tower she wishes to build!

Run the game again, and this time, make sure you build a tower on the center placement node so that it's in the path of the dinosaur.

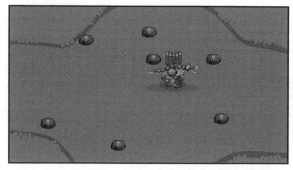

The dinosaur walks right through the tower. Hey, this chapter was supposed to be about pathfinding, right? Right!

Creating an obstacle graph

> **Note**: If you skippead ahead from earlier in this chapter, you can continue with the **starter_towers** project in the resources for this chapter. This is the same as where you left off the game in the previous chapter, with the added feature of tower selection and placement.

It's time to create a GameplayKit obstacle graph into your game!

To do this, open **GameScene.swift** and add the following property to your `GameScene` class:

```
let obstacleGraph = GKObstacleGraph(obstacles: [], bufferRadius:
    32)
```

You create a `GKObstacleGraph` as described above. At the moment, there are no obstacles, so you provide an empty array. The `bufferRadius` in the initializer is the distance by which your entities will avoid the obstacles when GameplayKit calculates the path. The larger the number, the wider the berth the dinosaurs will give your obstacles.

Adding towers to the obstacle graph

Next, you need to add your towers to your obstacle graph.

Recall that the obstacle graph is going to contain a collection of polygons that define the areas where the dinosaurs can't go. The polygon obstacle for a tower needs to be a shape around its base. Fortunately, you already have something that defines a shape around the tower's base: the `ShadowComponent`.

You're going to let the `ShadowComponent` define a polygon obstacle. That way, any entity that has the `ShadowComponent` can also have a polygon obstacle for the obstacle graph. Clever, right?

Open **ShadowComponent.swift** and add this new property:

```
let size: CGSize
```

Set it in `init(size:offset:)`:

```
self.size = size
```

Then add the following method to the class:

```
func createObstaclesAtPosition(position: CGPoint) ->
[GKPolygonObstacle] {
  let centerX = position.x + node.position.x
  let centerY = position.y + node.position.y
  let left = float2(CGPointMake(centerX - size.width/2,
centerY))
  let top = float2(CGPointMake(centerX, centerY + size.height/
2))
  let right = float2(CGPointMake(centerX + size.width/2,
centerY))
  let bottom = float2(CGPointMake(centerX, centerY -
size.height/2))
  var vertices = [left, bottom, right, top]

  let obstacle = GKPolygonObstacle(points: &vertices, count: 4)
  return [obstacle]
}
```

Here, you create a simple diamond-shaped polygon with four sides based on the shape of the shadow node. This will provide an effective and efficient obstacle for the pathfinding.

Note: The more complex the polygon used in the obstacle, the longer it will take to calculate the path. This is because more complex shapes require more computation from the pathfinding algorithms.

Now, open **GameScene.swift** so you can make use of this polygon obstacle.

To add an polygon obstacle to the obstacle graph, implement the following function:

```
func addObstaclesToObstacleGraph(newObstacles:
[GKPolygonObstacle]) {
  obstacleGraph.addObstacles(newObstacles)
}
```

This simply takes an array of GKPolygonObstacles and adds them to the obstacle graph.

To create an obstacle and add it to the obstacle graph when you build a tower, add the following to the *end* of addTower(_:position:):

```
addObstaclesToObstacleGraph(

  towerEntity.shadowComponent.createObstaclesAtPosition(position))
```

You take the new tower entity's shadow component, create a polygon obstacle from the shadow and add it to the graph.

At present, your dinosaur ignores the obstacle graph because it's following a simple `SKAction.moveTo(_:duration:)` path and not using GameplayKit's pathfinding. It's time to sort this out.

Moving an entity with pathfinding

Create a new function to use pathfinding. In **GameScene.swift**, add the following:

```
func setDinosaurOnPath(dinosaur: DinosaurEntity, toPoint point:
CGPoint) {
  let dinosaurNode = dinosaur.spriteComponent.node

  // 1
  let startNode = GKGraphNode2D(
    point: vector_float2(dinosaurNode.position))
  obstacleGraph.connectNodeUsingObstacles(startNode)

  // 2
  let endNode = GKGraphNode2D(point: vector_float2(point))
  obstacleGraph.connectNodeUsingObstacles(endNode)

  // 3
  let pathNodes = obstacleGraph.findPathFromNode(
    startNode, toNode: endNode) as! [GKGraphNode2D]


  // 4
  obstacleGraph.removeNodes([startNode, endNode])
}
```

This is the core of your obstacle graph's functionality. The graph needs to know about the start and end positions—represented as `GKGraphNode2D` objects—so it can calculate a valid path between them.

1. You add the dinosaur's start position to the obstacle graph.

2. Then, you add the dinosaur's target end position to the obstacle graph, based on the value passed into this method.

3. Using the nodes you just added, you calculate a valid path between the start and end nodes. The resulting path is a collection of `GKGraphNode2D` objects that provide the positions of each of the points the dinosaur will visit along its path.

4. Finally, you clean up the obstacle graph by removing the start and end nodes.

The last step is to use this path to create an `SKAction` sequence to move the dinosaur between the points on the path. To do that, you first need to give the dinosaur a speed— as mentioned in the last chapter, dinosaur types will move at different speeds.

Open **DinosaurEntity.swift** and add the following dynamic property to the
DinosaurType enum:

```
var speed: Float {
  switch self {
    case .TRex: return 100
    case .Triceratops: return 150
    case .TRexBoss: return 50
  }
}
```

These values represent the relative speed of each dinosaur. Who knew the mighty
Triceratops was so nimble! ;]

Go back to **GameScene.swift** and implement the SKAction sequence that will move the
dinosaur along the path. Add the following to the end of
setDinosaurOnPath(_:toPoint:):

```
// 1
dinosaurNode.removeActionForKey("move")

// 2
var pathActions = [SKAction]()
var lastNodePosition = startNode.position
for node2D in pathNodes {
  // 3
  let nodePosition = CGPoint(node2D.position)
  // 4
  let actionDuration =
    NSTimeInterval(lastNodePosition.distanceTo(node2D.position)
      / dinosaur.dinosaurType.speed)
  // 5
  let pathNodeAction = SKAction.moveTo(
    nodePosition, duration: actionDuration)
  // 6
  pathActions.append(pathNodeAction)
  lastNodePosition = node2D.position
}
// 7
dinosaurNode.runAction(SKAction.sequence(pathActions), withKey:
"move")
```

Here you place the dinosaur on the path provided by the obstacle graph. There's a lot
going on, and it's really important, so take a close look at the steps:

1. You could be updating this dinosaur's path while it's already moving—say, if the
    player adds a new tower—so you clear all the existing actions first.

2. You're going to create an SKAction for each step of the path and store them in an
    array to be animated in sequence.

3. A node on a path is a GKGraphNode2D object that holds a position as a vector_float2. For each node, you need to convert the position into a CGPoint so you can use it in an SKAction.moveTo(_:duration:) initializer.

4. The duration of the SKAction for each step of the path is determined by the distance between the nodes and also the speed of the dinosaur, which you defined moments ago in the DinosaurType enum.

5. Using the target position for this step, and the duration of the action, you create the SKAction to move the dinosaur to the next node on the path.

6. You add this action to the array.

7. Finally, you run the array of move actions on the dinosaur as a sequence, thereby setting the dinosaur off on its path.

Right now, to move across the screen, the dinosaur still uses the temporary SKAction you wrote in the last chapter. You're going to replace that with your new setDinosaurOnPath(_:toPoint:) function.

Remove the following line from addDinosaur(_:):

```
dinoNode.runAction(SKAction.moveTo(endPosition, duration: 20))
```

And replace it with this:

```
setDinosaurOnPath(dinosaur, toPoint: endPosition)
```

Before you see all of this at work in your game, you need to ensure you recalculate the dinosaur's path when you add towers to the game. To do this, add the following method:

```
func recalculateDinosaurPaths() {
  // 1
  let endPosition = CGPointMake(1224, 384)

  // 2
  let dinosaurs: [DinosaurEntity] = entities.flatMap { entity in
    if let dinosaur = entity as? DinosaurEntity {
      if dinosaur.healthComponent.health <= 0 {return nil}
      return dinosaur
    }
    return nil
  }

  // 3
  for dinosaur in dinosaurs {
    setDinosaurOnPath(dinosaur, toPoint: endPosition)
  }
}
```

There are only three steps:

1. This is the same end position you use when adding the dinosaur.

2. You go through the dinosaur entities in the scene and get all those that have health remaining. Dead dinosaurs don't move much. ;]

3. For each dinosaur, you redetermine its path using `setDinosaurOnPath(_:toPoint:)`.

Now, simply call this function whenever you add a tower to the scene. Add the following line to the *end* of `addTower(_:position:)`:

```
recalculateDinosaurPaths()
```

OK, let's take it for a spin. Build and run, and put your tower on the same central placement node as before.

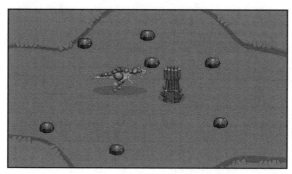

The dinosaur now avoids the tower on its path to rampaging the player's village, mwuahaha!

Congratulations, you've now learned the basics of GameplayKit's pathfinding system. Keep reading for some more practice, or skip forward to the next chapter where you'll use GameplayKit's Agents, Goals, and Behavior system to add some basic artificial intelligence into your game.

Challenges

This chapter has two challenges - one to get practice adding additional types of obstacles, and one to fix an annoying bug you may have noticed while testing your game with the z-ordering of sprites.

If you get stuck, you can find solutions in the resources for this chapter—but to get the most from this book, give these your best shot before you look!

Challenge 1: More obstacles

Now that you're calculating your dinosaur's path using your obstacle graph, it's time to add some non-tower obstacles to the scene to make it a little more interesting. To do that, you're going to create a new `ObstacleEntity`.

Your new `ObstacleEntity` will have a `SpriteComponent` so it can be rendered to the scene, and a `ShadowComponent` so it can have a shadow *and* be used in the obstacle graph.

To place obstacles in the scene, you'll position them in the **GameScene.sks** scene file, in the `.Sprites` layer. Then, when Sprite Kit creates an `ObstacleEntity` in the GameScene, the entity will use its obstacle node in the scene file as a reference.

First of all, add some obstacles to the `GameScene`.

Open **GameScene.sks**. In the Media Library, find the **Stone1.png** sprite:

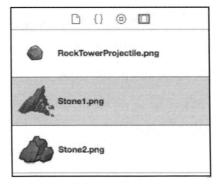

Drag the sprite into the scene and make the following changes to the sprite node in the Attributes Inspector:

- Set the **Name** to **Obstacle_Rock01**.
- Set the **Parent** to **Sprites**.
- Set the **Position** to **(250, 400)**.

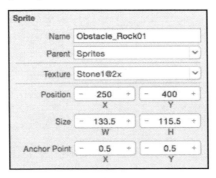

This obstacle will definitely get in the dinosaur's way! Add some more obstacles, using these settings:

1. Sprite **Tree2b**, Name **Obstacle_Tree01**, Parent **Sprites**, Position **(125, 640)**

2. Sprite **Tree2b**, Name **Obstacle_Tree02**, Parent **Sprites**, Position **(800, 620)**

3. Sprite **Stone2**, Name **Obstacle_Rock02**, Parent **Sprites**, Position **(826, 528)**

4. Sprite **Tree2**, Name **Obstacle_Tree03**, Parent **Sprites**, Position **(900, 600)**

5. Sprite **Tree3b**, Name **Obstacle_Tree04**, Parent **Sprites**, Position **(880, 180)**

6. Sprite **Tree3**, Name **Obstacle_Tree05**, Parent **Sprites**, Position **(950, 150)**

7. Sprite **Tree1**, Name **Obstacle_Bush01**, Parent **Sprites**, Position **(635, 240)**

8. Sprite **Tree1**, Name **Obstacle_Bush02**, Parent **Sprites**, Position **(585, 220)**

Your scene now looks like this:

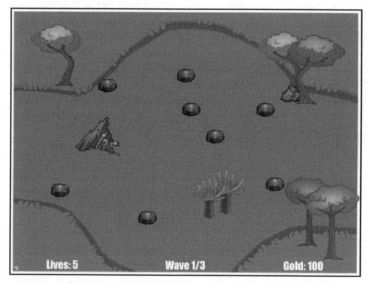

This is really starting to look good! Each of these new obstacles will simply be a placeholder for an `ObstacleEntity`. You're going to grab each of the obstacles in turn and create an `ObstacleEntity`, then you'll remove the placeholder from the scene and replace it with the `SpriteComponent` node of your `ObstacleEntity`.

First off, create a new Swift source file in your **Entities** group and name it **ObstacleEntity.swift**. Replace the contents of the file with the following:

```
import SpriteKit
import GameplayKit

class ObstacleEntity: GKEntity {
```

```
// 1
var spriteComponent: SpriteComponent!
// 2
var shadowComponent: ShadowComponent!

// 3
init(withNode node: SKSpriteNode) {
  super.init()

  // 4
  spriteComponent = SpriteComponent(entity: self, texture:
node.texture!, size: node.size)
  addComponent(spriteComponent)

  // 5
  let shadowSize = CGSizeMake(node.size.width*1.1,
node.size.height * 0.6)
  shadowComponent = ShadowComponent(size: shadowSize, offset:
CGPointMake(0.0, -node.size.height*0.35))
  addComponent(shadowComponent)

  // 6
  spriteComponent.node.position = node.position
  node.position = CGPointZero
  spriteComponent.node.addChild(node)
  }
}
```

That's a lot of code—in fact, it's *all* of the ObstacleEntity code—but it should be very familiar to you from the previous chapter. However, here's the breakdown so you can be clear on each step:

1. ObstacleEntity needs a SpriteComponent so it can be added to the scene.

2. ObstacleEntity also needs a ShadowComponent to have a shadow, as well as the polygon obstacle you can get from the shadow.

3. You initialize the ObstacleEntity with a sprite node from the scene. These are the sprite nodes you just added to the scene file.

4. You instantiate the SpriteComponent.

5. You instantiate the ShadowComponent using the sprite node's size as a guide.

6. Finally, you add the existing sprite node as a child to the SpriteComponent node, so that it looks exactly like it does in your scene file—only now, with all the added benefits of being an ObstacleEntity.

To add each `ObstacleEntity` to the scene, open **GameScene.swift** and add a new method:

```
func addObstacle(withNode node: SKSpriteNode) {
  // 1 - Store nodes's position

  // 2 - Remove node from parent

  // 3 - Create obstacle entity

  // 4 - Add obstacle entity to scene

  // 5 - Create obstacles from shadow component

  // 6 - Add obstacles to obstacle graph
}
```

Your challenge is to implement each of the commented lines in this method. Here are some hints on each line:

1. You're going to add the obstacle at the same position as the sprite node in your scene file. So, you get the position of the supplied node.

2. Since you're going to add the sprite component node of the new `ObstacleEntity` to the scene, you need to remove the placeholder you put in the scene file.

3. You create the `ObstacleEntity`.

4. You add the entity to the scene.

5. You take the polygon obstacle from the obstacle's shadow component.

6. You add the obstalce to the obstacle graph, using the helper method you wrote earlier.

Once you get this working, all that's left is to call this function for each of the obstacles in the scene when you first load the scene.

Add the following to `didMoveToView(_:)`, just *after* your call to `loadTowerSelectorNodes()`:

```
let obstacleSpriteNodes = self["Sprites/Obstacle_*"] as!
[SKSpriteNode]
for obstacle in obstacleSpriteNodes {
  addObstacle(withNode: obstacle)
}
```

Here, you get all the obstacle nodes from the scene and call `addObstacle(withNode:)` for each one.

Build and run.

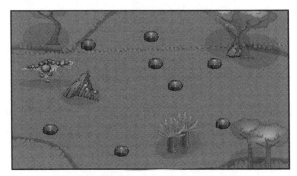

All the obstacles are in the scene, with shadows. They're also clearly taking part in the pathfinding, as the dinosaur is avoiding that rock at the start.

Run again, and add some towers to the scene. You'll see that you can get the dinosaur to take some long paths around your obstacles and towers!

Challenge 2: Z-positions of sprites

Sometimes the dinosaur walks in front of a tower, but the node still appears below the tower in the rendering order:

This happens because you haven't explicitly set the z-positions of all the sprites in the `.Sprites` layer, so Sprite Kit is assigning them randomly.

It's important to fix that. The desirable z-position for a sprite is directly related to the sprite's y-position—the closer the sprite is to the bottom of the screen, the farther forward its z-position should be. You can use this information to determine if a sprite should be above another sprite.

In **GameScene.swift**, add the following to the *end* of `didFinishUpdate()`:

```
// 1
let ySortedEntities = entities.sort {
  let nodeA = $0.0.componentForClass(SpriteComponent.self)!.node
  let nodeB = $0.1.componentForClass(SpriteComponent.self)!.node
  return nodeA.position.y > nodeB.position.y
}

// 2
var zPosition = GameLayer.zDeltaForSprites
for entity in ySortedEntities {
  // 3 — Get the entity's sprite component

  // 4 — Get the sprite component's node

  // 5 — Set the node's zPosition to zPosition

  // 6 — Increment zPosition by GameLayer.zDeltaForSprites

}
```

1. This sorts all the entities in the scene by their `position.y` values.

2. You set an initial z position and loop through the sorted entities.

Your challenge is to implement lines 3-6, given the comments above. When you're done, build and run again.

Your dinosaur is now always where it should be—in front of the towers it's below in the scene.

If you made it this far, congratulations - you now have a firm understanding of

GameplayKit's pathfinding feature!

In this chapter, you created an obstacle graph for your scene and used it to calculate the path for your dinosaur. You gave the player the ability to add towers to the scene, making sure to update the dinosaur's path whenever the player adds a new tower.

The pathfinding introduced in this chapter uses GameplayKit's `GKObstacleGraph`, producing a path for your dinosaur using the nodes of the graph. In the next chapter, you're going to use an entirely different set of GameplayKit tools to move the Triceratops dinosaurs along their path—agents, goals and behaviors!

With these tools, you'll see how you can give your pathfinding a more fluid and organic feel, thereby completing your new blockbuster game.

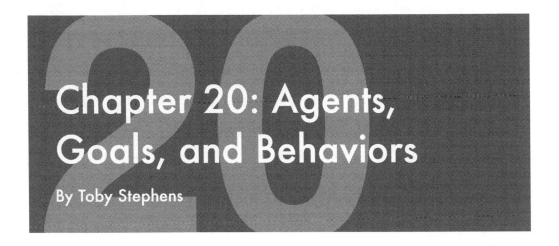

Chapter 20: Agents, Goals, and Behaviors

By Toby Stephens

In the last chapter, you used GameplayKit's awesome pathfinding tools to make your T-Rex attack the player's base while avoiding obstacles and towers along the way. The pathfinding works well, but in this chapter, you're going to use a different set of GameplayKit tools to move your other dinosaur type—the Triceratops.

Leading scientists in paleontological research have suggested that the walking pattern exhibited by the common T-Rex would have been in straight lines between several distinct points along a path, whereas the Triceratops would have moved in a more organic and goal-focused way.

OK, that's a lie. No such research exists. ;]

But to demonstrate another fantastic feature of GameplayKit, you're going to model the movement of the Triceratops using something called an **agent**. GameplayKit's agent system, with its associated goal and behavior classes, makes it easy for you to give your game entities goals, and have them seek them out with basic artificial intelligence.

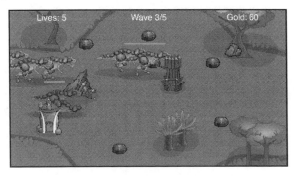

> **Note**: This chapter begins where the previous chapter's challenge 2 left off. If you were unable to complete the challenges or skipped ahead from an earlier chapter, don't worry—simply open the starter project from this chapter's resources to pick up in the right place.

GameplayKit agents, goals, and behaviors

In the previous chapter, you learned how to make a node follow a path from point A to point B, avoiding obstacles along the way. You can think of this as having a single goal for your node: follow a pre-determined path.

This is great for many games, but what if you want more than one goal at a time? For example, maybe you want to follow a path while staying in formation with other enemies at the same time.

This is what Agents, Goals, and Behaviors are all about. Let's take a look at each in turn:

Goals allow you to specify a set of goals that may influence a node's movement, such as:

- **Moving to a new position;**

- **Avoiding obstacles;**

- **Staying on a path;**

- **Moving as a flock.**

You create goals in GameplayKit by using different initializers of `GKGoal`, similar to how you create actions in SpriteKit by using different initializers of `SKAction`. Here's what it looks like:

```
let goal1 = GKGoal(toReachTargetSpeed: agent.maxSpeed)
let goal2 = GKGoal(toAvoidObstacles: obstacles,
maxPredictionTime: 0.5)
let goal3 = GKGoal(toFollowPath: path, maxPredictionTime: 0.5,
  forward: true)
```

Behaviors are a collection of goals. For each goal, you can set a "weight" of how important it is.

Here's what that looks like:

```
let behavior = GKBehavior()
behavior.setWeight(0.5, forGoal: goal1)
behavior.setWeight(1.0, forGoal: goal2)
behavior.setWeight(1.0, forGoal: goal3)
```

Finally, **agents** are a subclass of `GKComponent`. When `updateWithDeltaTime(_:)` updates the agent every frame, it evaluates each of the goals making up the current behavior and update variables on the agent like position and speed appropriately. Here's what that looks like:

```
// Do this inside an entity
let agent = GKAgent2D()
agent.maxSpeed = 100.0
agent.maxAcceleration = 200.0
agent.mass = 0.1
agent.radius = Float(size.width * 0.5)
agent.behavior = behavior
agent.delegate = self
addComponent(agent)
```

Note that agents do not set the position of your sprite directly; you are responsible for implementing a delegate method to set your sprite's position to the agent's position.

In short, a collection of goals informs a behavior, which drives an agent to move an entity. Make that your mantra for this chapter. ;]

Using a combination of goals to move to a target position, stay on a path and avoid obstacles, your Triceratops will have an agent that dictates its movement in the scene. This allows you to create more complex movement behavior, quite easily.

Adding an agent

Open DinoDefense where you left it off in the previous chapter's challenge 2 (or load the starter project for this chapter).

The first thing to do is add a `GKAgent2D` subclass to your `DinosaurEntity`. `GKAgent2D` is itself a subclass of `GKAgent`—it takes the abstract mass, speed and acceleration properties of `GKAgent` and makes them more applicable and accessible for a 2D game scene by translating those properties into position, rotation and velocity.

Open **DinosaurEntity.swift** and add the following new class:

```
class DinosaurAgent: GKAgent2D {
}
```

You subclass `GKAgent2D`, in case you wish to add any agent logic to `DinosaurAgent`. You won't be adding anything to this subclass in this tutorial, but it makes sense to future-proof your design.

Next, make `DinosaurAgent` accessible by adding the property to the `DinosaurEntity` class:

```
var agent: DinosaurAgent?
```

You make this an optional since you will only have an agent set for Triceratops dinosaurs.

Add the following to the end of `init(dinosaurType:)`:

```
if dinosaurType == .Triceratops {
  agent = DinosaurAgent()
  agent!.maxSpeed = dinosaurType.speed
  agent!.maxAcceleration = 200.0
  agent!.mass = 0.1
  agent!.radius = Float(size.width * 0.5)
  agent!.behavior = GKBehavior()
  addComponent(agent!)
}
```

If the `dinosaurType` of this `DinosaurEntity` is Triceratops, then you create the `DinosaurAgent` and set the properties of the agent:

- **maxSpeed** comes from the `dinosaurType` and tells the agent that this is as fast as the entity can move within the scene.

- **maxAcceleration** describes how quickly the Triceratops can reach its maximum speed.

- **mass** affects how quickly the Triceratops responds to goals that change its speed or direction.

- **behavior** is the default behavior for this agent—it has no goals and so the agent has no motivation to move the entity.

You then add the agent component to the `DinosaurEntity` components. Remember from earlier in this chapter that an agent is a subclass of `GKComponent`.

Adding behaviors and goals

To give your agent-driven dinosaurs a purpose in life, you're now going to create a behavior that will set them on their attacking path toward the player's base.

Create a new group in the project navigator named **Behaviors**.

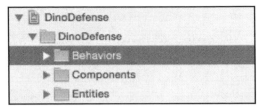

In this new group, create a new Swift source file named **DinosaurPathBehavior.swift** and replace the contents of the file with this:

```
import Foundation
import GameplayKit

class DinosaurPathBehavior: GKBehavior {
}
```

In this `GKBehavior` subclass, you're going to provide a factory function to create a `GKBehavior` for your `DinosaurAgent`. The behavior will contain these `GKGoals`:

- **Reach a maximum speed;**
- **Avoid obstacles;**
- **Follow a path;**
- **Stay on the path as closely as possible.**

To create these goals, your factory function will need to know the following:

- The path as calculated from the obstacle graph you created in the last chapter;
- The obstacles that make up the obstacle graph as `GKPolygonObstacle` objects.

So, in your `DinosaurPathBehavior` class, define the following function:

```
static func pathBehavior(forAgent agent: GKAgent,
    onPath path: GKPath,
    avoidingObstacles obstacles: [GKPolygonObstacle])
    -> DinosaurPathBehavior {

    let behavior = DinosaurPathBehavior()
    return behavior

}
```

Now that you have the `GKPath` and `GKPolygonObstacle` array available in your function, you can create your goals.

To add goals to a behavior, you need to give the goals a weighted value. The `weight` value tells the behavior just how much the individual goal should affect the decisions being made. A goal with a `weight` of `0.0` will have no effect on the decisions made by the behavior, while other `weight` values are taken into account relative to the `weight` values of the other goals in the behavior. You will use values for `weight` up to a maximum value of `1.0`, which will be reserved for the most important goals.

Since staying on the path is far more important than the dinosaur reaching its top speed, the target speed goal will have a `weight` of `0.5`.

Add the following to `pathBehavior(forAgent:onPath:avoidingObstacles)`, before you return the behavior:

```
behavior.setWeight(0.5,
   forGoal: GKGoal(toReachTargetSpeed: agent.maxSpeed))
```

Here, you create a `GKGoal` for the behavior to reach a target speed, which in this case is the `maxSpeed` you defined earlier in `DinosaurAgent`. You also set the goal to have a `weight` of `0.5`, as discussed above.

Now, add the following goal to help the behavior avoid obstacles:

```
behavior.setWeight(1.0,
   forGoal: GKGoal(toAvoidObstacles: obstacles,
maxPredictionTime: 0.5))
```

This is an important goal; you don't want your dinosaurs bumping into things, so you give it a `weight` of `1.0`. This goal uses the `GKPolygonObstacle` array you provided in the function. `maxPredictionTime` is the maximum amount of time between updates to the behavior for this goal. This means the behavior will wait a maximum of `0.5` seconds before checking again for obstacles in its way.

The final goal for this behavior relates to pathfinding. Add the following two goals:

```
behavior.setWeight(1.0,
   forGoal: GKGoal(toFollowPath: path, maxPredictionTime: 0.5,
   forward: true))
behavior.setWeight(1.0,
   forGoal: GKGoal(toStayOnPath: path, maxPredictionTime: 0.5))
```

These two goals each perform a distinct task: `toFollowPath` motivates the behavior to keep the agent facing `forward` on the path, while `toStayOnPath` influences the behavior to keep the agent within the radius of the path. Together, the two goals ensure that the dinosaur will walk the path and head the correct way between the nodes on the path.

That completes your `DinosaurPathBehavior`. Now you're going to add it to your dinosaurs.

Setting a behavior on an agent

Making a dinosaur behave—easier said than done?

Well, it actually is pretty easy thanks to GameplayKit. Now that you've defined the behavior, you simply have to set the behavior on the `DinosaurAgent` for it to tow the line.

Open **GameScene.swift** and find setDinosaurOnPath(_:toPoint:).

It's only the Triceratopses that are going to use the `DinosaurAgent` to move, and so logically, only the T-Rex and the T-Rex Boss are going to use your existing pathfinding code. At the bottom of setDinosaurOnPath(_:toPoint:), locate the line:

```
dinosaurNode.removeActionForKey("move")
```

Replace the code from that line until the end of the method with the following:

```
switch dinosaur.dinosaurType {
case .TRex, .TRexBoss:

  dinosaurNode.removeActionForKey("move")

  var pathActions = [SKAction]()
  var lastNodePosition = startNode.position
  for node2D in pathNodes {

    let nodePosition = CGPoint(node2D.position)

    let actionDuration =

NSTimeInterval(lastNodePosition.distanceTo(node2D.position) /
        dinosaur.dinosaurType.speed)

    let pathNodeAction = SKAction.moveTo(
      nodePosition, duration: actionDuration)

    pathActions.append(pathNodeAction)
    lastNodePosition = node2D.position
  }

  dinosaurNode.runAction(SKAction.sequence(pathActions),
withKey: "move")

case .Triceratops:
  if pathNodes.count > 1 {
    let dinosaurPath = GKPath(graphNodes: pathNodes, radius:
32.0)
    dinosaur.agent!.behavior =
DinosaurPathBehavior.pathBehavior(
```

```
        forAgent: dinosaur.agent!,
        onPath: dinosaurPath,
        avoidingObstacles: obstacleGraph.obstacles)
    }
}
```

You use the existing pathfinding code only for the `.TRex` and `.TRexBoss` dinosaurs; for the `.Triceratops` dinosaur type, you create a `GKPath` from the `pathNodes` and set the behavior on the agent using the path and the obstacles from the `obstacleGraph`. Now the Triceratops dinosaurs have a behavior that will drive their agents to move them along the path to the target positions.

At the start of the chapter, you learned that `GKAgent` objects are updated by `updateWithDeltaTime(_:)` as part of the update cycle in the scene. Back in Chapter 18, "Entity-Component System", you added `GKComponentSystem` objects to your scene for each of the components that requires updates every frame.

Look at the `componentSystems` property in your `GameScene` class, and you can see the component systems for the `AnimationComponent` and the `FiringComponent`, which you added in Chapter 18.

Now, add a third component system to the dynamic property, as follows:

```
let agentSystem = GKComponentSystem(componentClass:
DinosaurAgent.self)
```

Then, add it to the returning array, like this:

```
return [animationSystem, firingSystem, agentSystem]
```

Now, the `DinosaurAgent` will also update itself every frame. Once it does, the agent will move along the path according to the goals in its behavior.

This doesn't yet do anything to the actual entity in the game—you need to link the two together so that updates to the agent are rendered in the game scene, and updates to the position of the entity can be applied to the position of the agent. To do this, first you need to make `DinosaurEntity` conform to the `GKAgentDelegate` protocol.

Implementing GKAgentDelegate

`GKAgentDelegate` is a protocol that synchronizes the agent's state with its corresponding entity—in this case, `DinosaurEntity`. The protocol provides two events triggered by the agent's update function. These events are:

- **agentWillUpdate(_:):** tells the delegate the agent is about to perform its next update.

- **agentDidUpdate(_:):** tells the delegate the agent has updated itself.

When the agent is about to update itself, the entity needs to set the position on the agent so that their positions match. After the agent has performed the update, and has therefore moved according to its behavior, the agent needs to set the position of the entity.

Open `DinosaurEntity` and add the `GKAgentDelegate` protocol to the class:

```
class DinosaurEntity: GKEntity, GKAgentDelegate {
```

Now, add the following functions to update the agent and entity positions, before and after the agent update:

```
func agentWillUpdate(agent: GKAgent) {
    self.agent!.position = float2(x:
Float(spriteComponent.node.position.x),
      y: Float(spriteComponent.node.position.y))
}

func agentDidUpdate(agent: GKAgent) {
    let agentPosition = CGPoint(self.agent!.position)
    spriteComponent.node.position = CGPoint(x: agentPosition.x,
      y: agentPosition.y)
}
```

In `agentWillUpdate(_:)`, you set the position of the agent to equal the position of the entity's `SpriteComponent` node.

In `agentDidUpdate(_:)`, the agent has performed its update, and has its new position on the path, so you update the position of the entity's `SpriteComponent` node to equal the position of the agent.

To set the agent's delegate, add the following line to `init(dinosaurType:)`, just *after* you create the `DinosaurAgent`:

```
agent!.delegate = self
```

That's it. You now have a dinosaur that uses the GameplayKit agent, behavior and goals model to motivate it to move across the scene.

To see it in action, open **GameScene.swift** and *replace* this line in `startFirstWave()`:

```
addDinosaur(.TRex)
```

With this line:

```
addDinosaur(.Triceratops)
```

Build and run.

When you start the game, you'll see your Triceratops confidently pick its way across the scene, avoiding the obstacles and towers as it goes. See how much smoother the path is for the Triceratops than it was for the T-Rex? That's the behavior at work trying to keep the Triceratops on the path, while it obeys the agent's other behavioral goals.

Note: For the rest of this chapter, you're going to implement the remaining gameplay and interface elements of Dino Defense. It's pretty cool stuff, but if you only wanted to learn about agents, goals and behaviors, feel free to skip these sections and go right to the challenge at the end. The dinosaurs will forgive you!

A musical interlude

That was a lot of new information to take on board—you deserve a small break! Before you look at adding more dinosaurs to the game, why not give the player a musical backdrop to their battle? All great games have great music, and there's some great music included in the starter project.

But here's the sweet part—to get that music pumping, you just have to add the following line to the end of `didMoveToView(_:)`:

```
startBackgroundMusic()
```

The rest is already done for you, so this truly is a moment of light relief in your code writing.

If you wish, open **GameSceneHelper.swift** and take a look at `startBackgroundMusic()`. It uses an `AVAudioPlayer` instance to play an MP3 file from your project bundle on repeat.

So, build and run, sit back, and enjoy the Dino Defense score. ;]

Attack waves

OK, break time is over—back to the dinosaurs.

Right now, sending one dinosaur on a solo mission to attack the base doesn't give the player much of a challenge. It's time to send out those dinos in numbers, in a series of waves. You're going to create a wave manager that handles sending out waves of different numbers of dinosaurs straight at the player's defenses—a kind of dinosaur general.

Create a new Swift source file named **Waves.swift**.

Each wave is going to contain only one type of dinosaur. The wave will send a fixed number of dinosaurs across the scene, a certain number of seconds apart. To define a wave, create the following struct in **Waves.swift**:

```
struct Wave {
    let dinosaurCount: Int
    let dinosaurDelay: Double
    let dinosaurType: DinosaurType
}
```

The wave manager will have an array of these `Wave` objects that it will issue. Define the `WaveManager` class by adding the following to **Waves.swift**:

```
class WaveManager {
    var currentWave = 0
    var currentWaveDinosaurCount = 0

    let waves: [Wave]
}
```

Note: At this point, Xcode will complain that `WaveManager` has no initializers; you'll fix this momentarily.

The `currentWave` property holds the current index of the active wave. `currentWaveDinosaurCount` tells you how many dinosaurs from this wave are currently in the game scene. You'll set it when the wave starts, and decrement it when a dinosaur is killed or reaches the base. The `waves` property holds the array of `Waves`.

Every time the `WaveManager` is ready to send a new wave, you'll execute a closure that you'll specify in `GameScene`. There will be another closure for the `WaveManager` to execute when it wants to send out a new dinosaur.

Add properties for these two closures to `WaveManager`:

```
let newWaveHandler: (waveNum: Int) -> Void
let newDinosaurHandler: (mobType: DinosaurType) -> Void
```

Now, provide `WaveManager` with an initializer, as follows:

```
init(waves: [Wave],
  newWaveHandler: (waveNum: Int) -> Void,
  newDinosaurHandler: (dinosaurType: DinosaurType) -> Void) {
    self.waves = waves
    self.newWaveHandler = newWaveHandler
    self.newDinosaurHandler = newDinosaurHandler
}
```

You can now create a `WaveManager` by providing an array of `Waves`, and callback closures for new waves and dinosaurs. Do that now.

Open **GameScene.swift** and add the following property to `GameScene`:

```
var waveManager: WaveManager!
```

At the end of `didMoveToView(_:)`, add the following to define your waves for the game:

```
let waves = [Wave(dinosaurCount: 5, dinosaurDelay: 3,
dinosaurType: .TRex),
  Wave(dinosaurCount: 8, dinosaurDelay: 2,
dinosaurType: .Triceratops),
  Wave(dinosaurCount: 10, dinosaurDelay: 2,
dinosaurType: .TRex),
  Wave(dinosaurCount: 25, dinosaurDelay: 1,
dinosaurType: .Triceratops),
  Wave(dinosaurCount: 1, dinosaurDelay: 1,
dinosaurType: .TRexBoss)]
```

You've defined waves for your game in this sequence:

- Five T-Rexs with a 4-second gap between each dinosaur;
- Eight Triceratopses with a 2-second gap between each dinosaur;
- 10 T-Rexs with a 2-second gap between each dinosaur;
- 25 Triceratopses with a 1-second gap between each dinosaur;
- The final fight—a single T-Rex Boss!

To initialize the `WaveManager`, add the following to the end of `didMoveToView(_:)`:

```
waveManager = WaveManager(waves: waves,
  newWaveHandler: { (waveNum) -> Void in
    self.runAction(SKAction.playSoundFileNamed("NewWave.mp3",
      waitForCompletion: false))
  }, newDinosaurHandler: { (dinosaurType) -> Void in
    self.addDinosaur(dinosaurType)
})
```

The `WaveManager` initializer takes the `Waves` array and also two closures:

- `newWaveHandler` is a closure that the `WaveManager` will call when it wants to start a new wave. Here, you simply play a sound to tell the player a new wave of dinosaurs is about to begin.

- `newDinosaurHandler` is a closure that the `WaveManager` will call when it wants to send out a new dinosaur. Here, you call `addDinosaur(_:)` to add a new dinosaur of the specified type to the scene.

Sending out waves

Open **Waves.swift** and add the following function to the `WaveManager` class:

```
func startNextWave() -> Bool {
  // 1
  if waves.count <= currentWave {
    return true
  }

  // 2
  self.newWaveHandler(waveNum: currentWave+1)

  // 3
  let wave = waves[currentWave]
  // 4
  currentWaveDinosaurCount = wave.dinosaurCount
  for m in 1...wave.dinosaurCount {
    // 5
    delay(wave.dinosaurDelay * Double(m), closure: { () -> () in
      self.newDinosaurHandler(mobType: wave.dinosaurType)
    })
  }

  // 6
  currentWave++

  // 7
  return false
}
```

This function kicks off the `WaveManager` and sends in the first wave of dinosaurs. Every time a wave of dinosaurs is cleared—either by the player killing them all or by the dinosaurs making it to the player's base—you call the function again. If `startNextWave()` is called when there are still more waves to come, then it will return `false`. If there are no waves left, the function will return `true`.

Take a closer look at the steps in this function:

1. If there are no more waves left to deliver, then the player has won the game and the function returns `true`.

2. You execute the `newWaveHandler` closure, as this is a new wave.

3. You get the current `Wave` from the array.

4. You determine how many dinosaurs there are in this wave.

5. For each dinosaur in the wave, you execute the `newDinosaurHandler` closure, delaying each call by an increasingly longer time based on the `dinosaurDelay`.

6. You increment the `currentWave` so the `WaveManager` is ready to send out the next wave.

7. You just kicked off a new wave—it's not game over yet, so return `false`.

To kick off the next wave whenever all of the dinosaurs in the current wave have been dealt with, the `WaveManager` needs to know when to decrement the `currentWaveDinosaurCount`.

Add the following function:

```
func removeDinosaurFromWave() -> Bool {
  if --currentWaveDinosaurCount <= 0 {
    return startNextWave()
  }
  return false
}
```

The `GameScene` can now tell the `WaveManager` when a dinosaur has been killed or has made it to the base. `removeDinosaurFromWave()` calls `startNextWave()` if all of the dinosaurs from the current wave have been removed. It will also return `true` or `false`, depending on whether the last wave has finished—informing `GameScene` whether or not the player has won the game.

To send out the first attacking wave, open **GameScene.swift** and locate `startFirstWave()`. Then, *replace* this line:

```
addDinosaur(.Triceratops)
```

With this line:

```
waveManager.startNextWave()
```

Build and run.

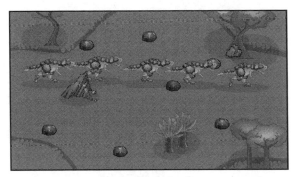

When the game starts, the trumpets announce the first wave and a proud flock of five T-Rexs begin their assault on the player's base camp.

You've deployed your first wave of dinosaurs—well done!

Randomizing the start position

At the moment, every dinosaur begins at exactly the same position when it's added to the scene, so the wave takes the form of a straight line of dinosaurs moving through the player's territory. It's time to randomize the start position a little so it isn't so easy for the player to predict their paths.

In `addDinosaur(_:)`, change `startPosition` to a `var`, like this:

```
var startPosition = CGPointMake(-200, 384)
```

Now that the `startPosition` is a variable and not a constant, you can change its y-value to a random value within a certain range. Do so by adding the following just below the declaration of `startPosition`:

```
startPosition.y = startPosition.y +
(CGFloat(random.nextInt()-10)*10)
```

Here, you randomize `startPosition.y` by adding a random float between `-100.0` and `100.0`. The `random` object is defined in the `GameSceneHelper` class and uses another GameplayKit tool to generate a random number between 1 and 20. You'll take a closer look at the GameplayKit randomization tools in Chapter 22, "Randomization".

Build and run, and this time, you'll see the dinosaurs come across the scene in a much less predictable pattern.

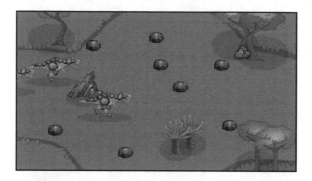

Removing dinosaurs from the wave

No matter how many arrows or stones the player's towers shoot into the dinosaurs, they simply refuse to die. You need to fix that before you can get the `WaveManager` to send in the second wave of dinosaurs.

When one of the dinosaurs dies, you'll play a death animation and sound effect, and then remove the entity from the scene. When the dinosaur reaches the base, you simply need to remove it from the scene without the death animation.

Open **DinosaurEntity.swift** and add the following function:

```
func removeEntityFromScene(death: Bool) {
  if death {
    // Set the death animation
    animationComponent.requestedAnimationState = .Dead
    let soundAction = SKAction.playSoundFileNamed(
      "\(dinosaurType.rawValue)Dead.mp3",
      waitForCompletion: false)
    let waitAction = SKAction.waitForDuration(2.0)
    let removeAction = SKAction.runBlock({ () -> Void in
      self.spriteComponent.node.removeFromParent()
      self.shadowComponent.node.removeFromParent()
    })
    spriteComponent.node.runAction(SKAction.sequence(
      [soundAction, waitAction, removeAction]))
  }
  else {
    spriteComponent.node.removeFromParent()
    shadowComponent.node.removeFromParent()
  }
}
```

This function takes a Boolean that specifies whether the entity is being removed from the scene because it died or simply because it reached the end of the scene.

If the dinosaur died, then you play the death sound for the correct dinosaur type and request the `.Dead` animation. After giving the animation two seconds to play out, you remove the entity's sprite and shadow from the scene.

If the dinosaur hasn't died, then you simply remove the sprite and shadow from the scene.

The best place to determine whether a dinosaur has died or reached the base is at the end of every frame update in the game scene.

Open **GameScene.swift** and add the following to didFinishUpdate(), just *before* you sort the entities by y-position:

```
for dinosaur in dinosaurs {
  if dinosaur.healthComponent.health <= 0 {
    dinosaur.removeEntityFromScene(true)
    entities.remove(dinosaur)
  }
  else if dinosaur.spriteComponent.node.position.x > 1124 {
    dinosaur.removeEntityFromScene(false)
    entities.remove(dinosaur)
  }
}
```

You go through the dinosaurs in the scene and check each one to see if it has any remaining health. If it doesn't, then you call removeEntityFromScene(true). If the dinosaur still has health, then you check to see if it's reached the player's base at the edge of the scene. If it has, then you call removeEntityFromScene(false). In both cases, you remove the dinosaur from the array of GKEntity objects in the scene, as you're now done with that dinosaur.

Build and run, and construct enough towers to take out a dinosaur.

When the dinosaur dies, you'll hear its death rattle as it collapses to the ground. You'll watch with amusement, though, as it continues on its path. You need a way to stop it dead in its tracks—pun intended!

Add the following function to **GameScene.swift**:

```
func stopDinosaurMoving(dinosaur: DinosaurEntity) {
  switch dinosaur.dinosaurType {
  case .TRex, .TRexBoss:
    let dinosaurNode = dinosaur.spriteComponent.node
    dinosaurNode.removeActionForKey("move")
  case .Triceratops:
    dinosaur.agent!.maxSpeed = 0.1
  }
}
```

This function checks the dinosaur type and stops the dinosaur from moving.

- .TRex and .TRexBoss dinosaurs move along a path dictated by a series of actions, so stopping them is simply a matter of removing all actions on the SpriteComponent node.

- .Triceratops dinosaurs move along a path in response to the goals in their behaviors, so the best way to stop them is by setting the speed on their SKAgent to zero.

> **Note:** At the time of writing, setting a maxSpeed to 0.0 on a GKAgent causes the sprite to disappear from the scene, so you're actually using 0.1—that's pretty slow. ;]

Head back to where you were just working in didFinishUpdate() and add this line *just before **both*** times you call removeEntityFromScene(_:):

```
stopDinosaurMoving(dinosaur)
```

If the dinosaur has no remaining health or has reached the end of the scene, you stop it in its tracks.

Before testing this, also make sure you get a second wave of dinosaurs once the first wave of dinosaurs are dead. Inside the if statement where you check to see if the dinosaur has zero health, add the following code:

```
let win = waveManager.removeDinosaurFromWave()
if win {
  stateMachine.enterState(GameSceneWinState.self)
}
```

If the dinosaur dies, you remove it from the current wave in the WaveManager, checking to see if the player has killed the last dinosaur in the game. If all the dinosaurs are dead, then you set the `GameSceneWinState` in the game's state machine, and the player has won the game.

Inside the second `if`, where you check to see if the dinosaur has reached the end of the scene, add the following:

```
waveManager.removeDinosaurFromWave()
```

Since removing a dinosaur because it's reached the player's base can never mean the player has won the game, there's no need to check the returned Boolean.

Now that the `WaveManager` knows when dinosaurs have exited the scene, it will start the second wave as soon as the first has finished.

Build and run, and construct enough towers to take out all the dinosaurs in the first wave.

When the dinosaurs die, they now stop and behave like dead dinosaurs. As the last of the dinosaurs from the first wave is dispatched, you hear the trumpets announce the second wave, and the Triceratopses begin their stampede.

The HUD

Your game is now progressing through the waves of dinosaurs, so it would be useful for the player to know which wave she's up against and how many waves are left. To convey this information, you'll show the HUD elements that are already available in the `.HUD` layer of your game scene.

These are the labels in the .HUD layer for each of these game elements:

1. The number of lives the player's base has left. This will start at 5, and every time a dinosaur reaches the base, it will decrement by a certain amount per dinosaur type.

2. The current wave and the total number of waves.

3. The amount of gold the player has available for building towers.

The `.HUD` labels for each of these elements is initially hidden from the player. To make them visible when the player starts the game, add the following to the end of `startFirstWave()`:

```
baseLabel.runAction(SKAction.fadeAlphaTo(1.0, duration: 0.5))
waveLabel.runAction(SKAction.fadeAlphaTo(1.0, duration: 0.5))
goldLabel.runAction(SKAction.fadeAlphaTo(1.0, duration: 0.5))
```

You run an `SKAction` on each of the labels; this action fades the labels into the scene over a period of 0.5 seconds.

You haven't yet implemented the base lives or the cost of a tower, but you can now update the wave label every time there's a new wave.

Find where you initialize the `WaveManager`. Inside the `newWaveHandler` closure, add the following:

```
self.waveLabel.text = "Wave \(waveNum)/\(waves.count)"
```

Now, when the `WaveManager` calls the `newWaveHandler` at the start of each wave, you update the `waveLabel` to display the current and total number of waves.

Build and run.

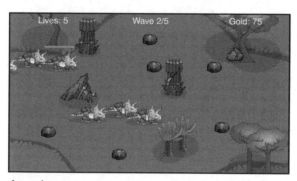

The HUD now displays the correct current wave number and tells the player there will be a total of five waves.

Decrementing lives

It's time to deal with the next element in the HUD: the number of lives of the player's base.

As you can see, the player starts the game with five lives. Every time a dinosaur reaches the base, you'll decrement the number of lives remaining. However, to make it more interesting, each dinosaur type will inflict a different amount of damage to the base.

Open **DinosaurEntity.swift** and add the following to the `DinosaurType` enum:

```
var baseDamage: Int {
  switch self {
  case .TRex: return 2
  case .Triceratops: return 1
  case .TRexBoss: return 5
  }
}
```

The Triceratops is a little weaker than the T-Rex, but that Boss can take out the player's base in one hit!

To implement this lives system, you need to decrement the number of base lives by the dinosaur's `baseDamage` value whenever the dinosaur reaches the base.

You already have a check for when a dinosaur has reached the base, so open **GameScene.swift** and go to `didFinishUpdate()`. In the `if` statement where you check to see if the dinosaur has passed an x-position of `1124`, find this line:

```
waveManager.removeDinosaurFromWave()
```

Directly below this line, add the following:

```
//1
baseLives -= dinosaur.dinosaurType.baseDamage
// 2
updateHUD()
// 3
self.runAction(baseDamageSoundAction)

// 4
if baseLives <= 0 {
  stateMachine.enterState(GameSceneLoseState.self)
}
```

1. Here, you reduce the `baseLives` by the amount of damage done by the dinosaur type.

2. The `GameSceneHelper` class contains a function called `updateHUD()` that updates the base lives and gold labels to show their current values.

3. `GameSceneHelper` also contains `SKAction` sound effects for things like damage to the base, winning the game and losing the game.

4. If `baseLives` has reached zero, the game is over and the player has lost, so tell the game's state machine to change to the `GameSceneLoseState`.

Build and run, and let at least one of the dinosaurs reach the player's base at the far right side of the screen.

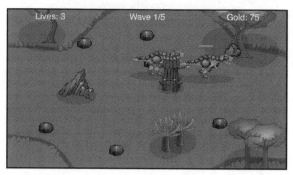

The dinosaur roars as it attacks the base, and the number of base lives decreases by the correct amount, based on the type of dinosaur that made it to the base.

Paying for towers

Dino Defense now looks and feels like a complete game! But as it stands, it's pretty easy to destroy the dinosaurs—you have endless resources with which to build towers. It's a good idea to begin making your players pay for all those defenses. That will certainly improve the game's balance.

Towers will be paid for with gold. Players begin with 75 gold pieces, and you'll award more gold for defeating dinosaurs.

You already gave towers a cost in the previous chapter. Now you need to define how much gold to award the player for killing each dinosaur type.

Open **DinosaurEntity.swift** and add the following to the `DinosaurType` enum:

```
var goldReward: Int {
  switch self {
  case .TRex: return 10
  case .Triceratops: return 5
  case .TRexBoss: return 50
  }
}
```

You award the player twice as much gold for killing a T-Rex as for killing a Triceratops. Killing the Boss will earn the player a big bag of shiny gold coins.

Open **GameScene.swift** and add the following code to the *top* of `addTower(_:position:)`:

```
if gold < towerType.cost {
    self.runAction(SKAction.playSoundFileNamed("NoBuildTower.mp3",
waitForCompletion: false))
    return
}
```

You check to see if the player has enough gold to afford the tower she's trying to build. If she doesn't have enough gold, you play a sound to give her an audible cue, and return from the function without building the tower.

Directly after you make this check in `addTower(_:position:)`, add the following:

```
gold -= towerType.cost
updateHUD()
```

You've established that the player can afford the tower, so now you decrement the cost of the tower from the player's gold reserves. Then, you update the HUD to show the new amount of available gold.

To award gold for a dinosaur kill, go to `didFinishUpdate()` and find the point at which you check to see if a dinosaur's health has been reduced to zero. Inside that `if` statement, just *after* you remove the dinosaur from the `entities` array, add the following:

```
gold += dinosaur.dinosaurType.goldReward
updateHUD()
```

In the same way as you reduce the gold when the player builds a tower, you increase the amount of available gold when the player kills a dinosaur. Then, you update the HUD just as you did before.

Build and run, and start building towers.

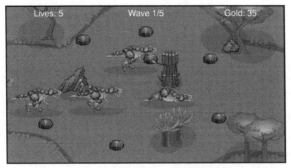

As you buy towers, the amount of gold shown in the HUD becomes lower and lower. Every time you kill a dinosaur, you get a little bit of gold back.

Playing the game, you quickly run out of available gold, and suddenly the location of your first tower is of vital importance. That's a much better game balance! Now, it's a real challenge for the player.

Continue playing the game and see if you can win. It's pretty difficult, right? I think you may have pushed the game balance a little bit against the player now, but you have one last thing to add to your gameplay that might just tip back the scales.

Slow down effect

When you first learned about the Dino Defense gameplay, you read about the different tower types and how the projectiles from the rock towers would do more than inflict damage on the dinos—they would also slow them down. You're going to implement that now by giving each tower type a `slowFactor` that will determine just how much a dinosaur's speed will drop when it's hit by projectiles from that tower type.

Open **TowerEntity.swift** and add the following to the `TowerType` enum:

```
var slowFactor: Float {
  switch self {
    case Wood: return 1
    case Rock: return 0.5
  }
}
```

A `slowFactor` of `1.0` means the projectile has no effect on the dinosaur's speed, whereas a `slowFactor` of `0.0` means it stops the dinosaur completely. The wood tower doesn't slow dinosaurs and so has a `slowFactor` of `1`. The rock tower, with a `slowFactor` of `0.5`, slows the dinosaurs to half their speed.

So you can quickly check if a tower slows a dinosaur, add the following to the `TowerType` enum:

```
var hasSlowingEffect: Bool {
  return slowFactor < 1.0
}
```

This is a simple convenience function that returns `true` if the `slowFactor` is less than `1.0`, telling you that the tower does indeed slow down dinosaurs.

When a dinosaur slows down, you'll reduce its speed, of course, but you're also going to highlight the dinosaur's sprite with a blue tint.

Open **DinosaurEntity.swift** and add the following function to the `DinosaurEntity` class:

```
func slowed(slowFactor: Float) {
  animationComponent.node.color = SKColor.cyanColor()
  animationComponent.node.colorBlendFactor = 1.0
  switch dinosaurType {
  case .TRex, .TRexBoss:
    spriteComponent.node.speed = CGFloat(slowFactor)
  case .Triceratops:
    agent!.maxSpeed = dinosaurType.speed * slowFactor
  }
}
```

First, you add the blue tint to the `AnimationComponent` node. Then, you adjust the speed of the dinosaur, depending on the dinosaur type.

- `.TRex` and `.TRexBoss` dinosaurs use actions to move along their paths, so you adjust their speeds by changing the `speed` on the `SpriteComponent` node, which affects all actions running on that node.

- `.Triceratops` dinosaurs use goals in their agent's behavior to move, so simply adjusting the `maxSpeed` of their agent will slow them down.

After it slows down a dinosaur, the rock tower is going to see if it can hit any other dinosaurs in its range before it hits the same dinosaur again. This is so the rock tower can slow down multiple dinosaurs if they're in range, thereby giving the player a fighting chance.

Track this state by adding the following property to the `DinosaurEntity` class:

```
var hasBeenSlowed = false
```

Now, add this to the *top* of `slowed(_:)`:

```
hasBeenSlowed = true
```

You now have a Boolean that will tell you whether or not the tower has already slowed down a dinosaur.

Since it's the tower's `FiringComponent` that damages the dinosaur, this is a logical place to also slow down the dinosaur, if necessary. Open **FiringComponent.swift** and locate `damageAction` in `updateWithDeltaTime(_:)`.

`damageAction` is an `SKAction` that executes a closure block. Inside the closure for `damageAction`, add the following:

```
if self.towerType.hasSlowingEffect {
  target.slowed(self.towerType.slowFactor)
}
```

All that remains is to change the targeting logic of rock towers—or indeed, any tower types that have a slowing effect.

Open **GameScene.swift** and go to didFinishUpdate(). At the point where you check which dinosaurs are in range of your towers, *replace* the following lines:

```
if dinosaur.spriteComponent.node.position.x >
  t.spriteComponent.node.position.x {
  target = dinosaur
}
```

With these lines:

```
if towerType.hasSlowingEffect {
  if !dinosaur.hasBeenSlowed && t.hasBeenSlowed {
    target = dinosaur
  }
  else if dinosaur.hasBeenSlowed == t.hasBeenSlowed
    && dinosaur.spriteComponent.node.position.x >
      t.spriteComponent.node.position.x {
      target = dinosaur
  }
}
else if dinosaur.spriteComponent.node.position.x >
  t.spriteComponent.node.position.x {
  target = dinosaur
}
```

Instead of simply checking which dinosaur is the furthest down the path, now you check to see if there's a dinosaur in range that hasn't been slowed. If you find one, it takes precedence as a target. If both dinosaurs have already been slowed, the one furthest along on the path takes priority as a target.

Build and run, and at some point, build a rock tower to slow down those rampaging dinos.

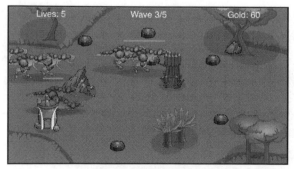

That rock tower certainly packs a punch, and with its new slowing effect, it could just about tip the balance in the player's favor.

Try to beat your new game with a combination of rock and wood towers—and watch out for that T-Rex Boss, as he can take a lot of punishment!

Congratulations! Using some of GameplayKit's great features, you've created a fully functioning tower defense game:

- In the first chapter, you learned how to use entities and components to design your game to reuse functionality. You separated key game object functions into components and used those components in your game entities without having to rewrite any of the code.

- In the chapter after that, you used GameplayKit's pathfinding tools to move your T-Rex dinosaur across the scene, avoiding obstacles and towers along the way.

- And finally, in this chapter, you used agents, goals and behaviors to move your Triceratops dinosaurs along their paths. They avoided the obstacles and towers in your scene by obeying the goals set in your pathfinding behavior.

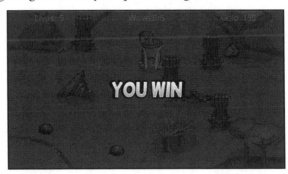

But you're not quite done yet... a game like this deserves to be seen on a bigger screen!

Challenges

There's only one challenge for this chapter, and it's a great one. One of the main things we want to see developers like yourself create with this book are games for AppleTV, so why not take on this challenge and convert your tower defense game to tvOS?

Challenge 1: Dino Defense TV

Dino Defense would play beautifully on a TV screen. Your challenge is to add a tvOS target to your Dino Defense project and get this game up and running on AppleTV.

This book has a whole section devoted to developing games for AppleTV, so you should have everything you need, but here are a few tips regarding gameplay:

- Tapping a tower selector node isn't going to be an effective way to play the game with the AppleTV remote. Instead, how about having a highlighted tower selector node in the scene and switching the highlighted node with a swipe on the remote.

• With a tower selector node highlighted, a tap on the remote should bring up the tower selection interface. Then, swiping right could give the player a wood tower, and swiping left a rock tower.

As always, our implementation of the challenge is available with the source code for this chapter, but no cheating—and good luck. ;]

Section V: Advanced Topics

In this section, you'll delve into some more advanced topics like procedural level generation, GameplayKit randomization, and game controllers.

In the proccs, you'll create a tile-based dungeon crawler called Delve where you try to guide your miner through a rock-elemental infested dungeon.

Chapter 21: Tile Map Games

Chapter 22: Randomization

Chapter 23: Procedural Levels

Chapter 24: Game Controllers

Chapter 21: Tile Map Games

By Neil North

Tile map games are a great way to create large scale games with minimal device memory usage. Instead of creating artwork for an entire world, the environment is broken down into small square images; this lets you build your world with smaller images, called tiles, rather than having to use one giant continuous image.

But memory management isn't the only reason you may want to consider using a tile map design for your game. Here are just a few more:

- **Less artwork required**: With a little bit of creativity, you can create numerous beautiful environments from a rather small set of tiles. You get all of the benefits of smaller builds and smaller memory imprints, plus you require less work from the artist.

- **Easier to create and scale levels**: You can add extra levels, and extend existing levels, usually without requiring any new artwork. If you need to adjust the distance between a jump or fine-tune the layout, no problem!

- **Ability to procedurally generate levels**: Pre-built levels are great, but if you want to generate levels using software algorithms, tile maps make this process easy.

- **Ability to dynamically change levels**: A lot of popular **build-and-wait**-style games let you change the game world by adding new buildings or growing resources. Developers often use tile maps for this style of game because of how easy it is to modify them.

- **Works great with GameplayKit**: Using `GKGridGraph` and pathfinding, you can create impressive board games and other games with grid-based movement.

- **It's awesome!**: No game design principle has withstood the test of time as strongly as tile map level design. It's used successfully in a massive catalog of 2D games and has huge nostalgic appeal.

So, what's the catch?

At the time of writing this chapter, the Sprite Kit scene editor, built into Xcode, doesn't do a great job of supporting tile map levels; it's time consuming to lay out the tiles, and the resulting .sks file isn't anywhere near as efficient as a basic text file with tile code.

However, there are plenty of good alternatives to the scene editor, and you'll be exploring some of the best ones as you build the mini-game for the next few chapters, **Delve**.

Introducing Delve

Grab your mining pick and prepare to *delve* into a mystical dungeon. The objective of the game is to reach the stairs that descend to the next level.

Think that sounds easy?

Well, it would be—except for the fact that you need to get out before your hero runs out of health. But, even that's a challenge: Your health deteriorates over time, and hordes of dark magic rock golems aren't happy that you're invading their dungeon. As you make your way through their world, the angry golems will try to stop you.

You will build this game across the next four chapters, in stages:

- **Chapter 21, Tile Map Games**: You are here! In this chapter, you will learn techniques for building tile map levels, including how to create a fully functional tile map game.

- **Chapter 22, Randomization**: Take advantage of the new GameplayKit class GKRandom to generate the game world.

- **Chapter 23, Procedural Levels**: Remove some of the random aspects of the level generation to make the process more predictable, but still an adventure into the unknown.

- **Chapter 24, Game Controllers**: This game is perfect for external game controllers;

you'll be adding a tvOS target and exploring how to use the Apple TV remote as a game controller.

By the end of these chapters, you'll have learned some advaned game creation techniques, and will have made a fun new dungeon crawler!

Getting started

I have created a starter project for you to use, which you can find in the resources for this chapter under **starter\Delve**.

Although you're going to build the game from scratch, the starter project contains groups that you'll use to build the game and keep things organized.

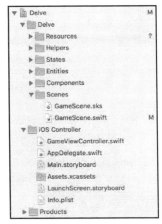

After you open the project, drag the **Tiles.atlas** folder from **starter\Resources** into the **Resources** group in Xcode.

This texture atlas contains all the tiles you'll use to build the levels for Delve.

Take a moment to review the tiles within the texture atlas and create a quick mental plan for your first level.

Each tile is more than a decoration—it fulfills a specific function:

- **Floor**: This is the space on which the hero and the enemies move.

- **Wall**: An impassible object. Walls can be used to create corridors, rooms and paths. You need to give consideration as to how much space the characters need in order to move through their world.

- **Triggers**: The level may contain tiles or objects that *do something* when the characters step onto or over them. For example, a special tile may exist at the end of a level, or a collectible health enhancement may sit on top of a tile.

> **Note**: Tiles can be layered, so you can place a collectible object on a floor tile.

Starting the level builder

In your project, inside the **Helpers** group, create a new Swift file named **LevelHelper.swift**.

You'll use this class to prepare levels before they're passed to the scene.

Replace the contents of the file with the following:

```
import SpriteKit
import GameplayKit

struct tileMap {

}
```

This imports the frameworks you need for this class. It also sets the basis for your tile map struct.

Now you need to define exactly what tiles you wish to support in your game. This includes walls and floors, but it can also include hero and enemy spawn locations as well as other triggers, like health objects.

Include this enum above your struct:

```
enum tileType: Int {
  case tileAir = 0
  case tileWall = 1
  case tileWallLit = 2
  case tileGround = 3
  case tileStart = 4
  case tileEnd = 5
  case tileEnemy = 6
  case tileFood = 7
```

```
    }
```

This is a simple enumeration that includes a value for each type of tile you will add into Delve.

You also need a way to inform the game scene what type of tile you need and where to build it. To do this, add the following protocol above your struct:

```
protocol tileMapDelegate {
    func createNodeOf(type type:tileType, location:CGPoint)
}
```

Now, your `tileMap` struct has to track its delegate. Add the following line inside your struct:

```
var delegate: tileMapDelegate?
```

There are a few more instance variables you need for your tile map. Below the delegate variable, add this:

```
//1
var tileSize = CGSize(width: 32, height: 32)
//2
var tileLayer: [[Int]] = Array()
//3
var mapSize = CGPoint(x: 5, y: 5)
```

Each variable has its own purpose:

1. **Tile Size**: Tile maps are made up of tiles of equal size; this variable holds the sprite size for each tile on the tile map.

2. **Tile Layer**: The `tileLayer` variable holds an array, also known as a two-dimensional (2D) array. The first part of the array stores the row information; the second part stores the column information as an `Int`. That integer relates directly to the `tileType` enum.

3. **Map Size**: The `mapSize` variable holds the total number of columns and rows in the tile map.

Excellent! You've created all of the attributes you need to define the tile map's layout. Now, you just need to implement the logic to lay them out!

Creating a basic level

The `tileLayer` variable is currently empty. That's fine if you're appending its contents by column, then by row, but what if you want to support other ways of constructing the tile map? In that case, you need to be able to update it.

Under your instance variables and within `tileMap`, add the following:

```
mutating func generateLevel(defaultValue: Int) {
  var columnArray:[[Int]] = Array()

  repeat {
    var rowArray:[Int] = Array()
    repeat {
      rowArray.append(defaultValue)
    } while rowArray.count < Int(mapSize.x)
    columnArray.append(rowArray)
  } while columnArray.count < Int(mapSize.y)
  tileLayer = columnArray
}
```

The `defaultValue` variable passed into the function defines the tile map you're creating. This number directly relates to your `tileType` enum.

The `repeat` loops go through each column of each row and append the `defaultValue`. Then, the `tileLayer` variable is updated with the new tile map.

To see how this tile map looks, go to **GameScene.swift** and insert the following instance variable inside the class:

```
var worldGen = tileMap()
```

Now, add this function below the other functions, within that same class:

```
func setupLevel() {
  worldGen.generateLevel(0)
  print(worldGen.tileLayer)
}
```

You'll use this function to generate the level each time the game is loaded; therefore, you need to call this function in `didMoveToView(_:)`. Do that now by adding this line to `didMoveToView(_:)`:

```
setupLevel()
```

Now, build and run the game. Keep an eye on your debug output; it should read:

```
[[0, 0, 0, 0, 0], [0, 0, 0, 0, 0], [0, 0, 0, 0, 0], [0, 0, 0, 0, 0],
[0, 0, 0, 0, 0]]
```

Each group of five numbers is your row of column values. Since you passed zero into `generateLevel(_:)`, all of the tiles have been assigned the default value.

Show me the level!

To visualize the level for you, `GameScene` needs to implement the delegate of your level helper.

Update the class line to read as follows:

```
class GameScene: SKScene, tileMapDelegate {
```

Then, add this function below your other functions:

```
func createNodeOf(type type:tileType, location:CGPoint) {
  let atlasTiles = SKTextureAtlas(named: "Tiles")

  switch type {
  case .tileGround:

    break
  case .tileWall:

    break
  case .tileWallLit:

    break
  case .tileStart:

    break
  case .tileEnemy:

    break
  case .tileEnd:

    break
  case .tileFood:

    break
  default:
    break
  }
}
```

When your LevelHelper struct is ready to build the level, it will tell its delegate to add a tile of tileType at a specified location. It will use this switch statement to determine which tile to load. You'll come back to this switch statement soon.

But first, *replace* the setupLevel() function with this one:

```
func setupLevel() {
  worldGen.generateLevel(3)
  worldGen.presentLayerViaDelegate()
}
```

The number passed in has changed from 0 to 3; 3 is the ground tile. You removed the print statement and replaced it with a function the helper will use to tell its delegate what to do.

Now, head back to **LevelHelper.swift** and implement `presentLayerViaDelegate()` under your current functions—all still within the `tileMap` struct:

```
//MARK: Setters and getters for the tile map

//MARK: Level creation

//MARK: Presenting the layer

func presentLayerViaDelegate() {
  for (indexr, row) in tileLayer.enumerate() {
    for (indexc, cvalue) in row.enumerate() {
      if (delegate != nil) {
        delegate!.createNodeOf(type: tileType(rawValue:
cvalue)!,
          location: CGPoint(
            x: tileSize.width * CGFloat(indexc),
            y: tileSize.height * CGFloat(-indexr)))
      }
    }
  }
}
```

In `presentLayerViaDelegate()`, you loop through each row, and then each column, using `for-in` loops. Since you also need the index for each value to pinpoint its position on the tile map, you use `.enumerate()` to return a tuple containing the index and the value.

Once you have the indices of the row and the column for your value, you have everything you need to tell the `GameScene` what to do.

To calculate the tile position, you simply multiply the tile size by its column and row indices.

A later part of this chapter will refer to the `MARK:` comments to show you where to add additional code.

Head back to **GameScene.swift**, locate the `.tileGround` case statement in `createNodeOf(type: location:)`, and add this code:

```
let node = SKSpriteNode(texture:
atlasTiles.textureNamed("Floor1"))
node.size = CGSize(width: 32, height: 32)
node.position = location
node.zPosition = 1
addChild(node)
```

The code above sets some key properties for the node and then adds it to the scene.

OK—there are a few more things you need to do before you can build and run the game:

1. You still need to set the delegate;

2. You need an implementation of the scene's camera node so you can see your tiles.

Adding a camera node

In **GameScene.swift**, navigate to the bottom of the class and add the following code just below the other functions:

```
//MARK: camera controls

func centerCameraOnPoint(point: CGPoint) {
  if let camera = camera {
    camera.position = point
  }
}

func updateCameraScale() {
  if let camera = camera {
    camera.setScale(0.44)
  }
}
```

These two functions update the location and set the scale of the camera.

You're almost done. Now, you need to implement the camera in `didMoveToView(_:)`. Replace the existing function, in its entirety, with the following:

```
override func didMoveToView(view: SKView) {

  //Delegates
  worldGen.delegate = self

  //Setup Camera
  let myCamera = SKCameraNode()
  camera = myCamera
  addChild(myCamera)
  updateCameraScale()

  //Gamestate
  setupLevel()
}
```

First, you assign the delegate. Then, you set up the camera node and add it to the scene. Finally, you call the function that updates the camera's scale. And, of course, you call `setupLevel()`.

At the bottom of `createNodeOf(type:location:)`, add the following:

```
centerCameraOnPoint(location)
```

That's it! Now you can build and run to see your five-by-five grid of floor tiles.

Crafting a tile-based level

Your level helper class is almost ready to generate a base level and tell its delegate to do something with each tile type at a specific location on the scene.

Go back to **LevelHelper.swift**; you're going to expand this functionality to generate more specific tile maps.

Under `//MARK: Setters and getters for the tile map`, add the following functions:

```
//1
mutating func setTile(position position:CGPoint, toValue:Int) {
  tileLayer[Int(position.y)][Int(position.x)] = toValue
}

//2
func getTile(position position:CGPoint) -> Int {
  return tileLayer[Int(position.y)][Int(position.x)]
}

//3
func tilemapSize() -> CGSize {
  return CGSize(width: tileSize.width * mapSize.x, height:
tileSize.height * mapSize.y)
}
```

These three functions each have their own purpose:

1. Suppose you wanted to change the value at row 3, column 2 to 5. You could access it directly by using `tileLayer[3][2] = 5`; however, by setting up this function to handle the interaction, you can potentially expand upon its functionality later—for example, if you need to guard certain tiles.

2. This function lets you retrieve the value of a point by providing a `CGPoint`.

3. This is useful when trying to calculate the bounds of the tile map environment, because it obtains/returns the total size of the tile map.

Return to **GameScene.swift** and locate the instance variable at the top of the class. Update that variable, and add a few more variables, too:

```
//World generator
var worldGen = tileMap()

//Layers
var worldLayer = SKNode()
var guiLayer = SKNode()
var enemyLayer = SKNode()
var overlayLayer = SKNode()
```

Soon, you'll add a lot more content to the game world, and these layers will help you manage them.

Now, it's time to add the layers. In `didMoveToView(_:)`, below the camera setup, add the following:

```
//Config World
addChild(worldLayer)
camera!.addChild(guiLayer)
guiLayer.addChild(overlayLayer)
worldLayer.addChild(enemyLayer)
```

You add the `worldLayer` and `enemyLayer` to the scene. You add the `guiLayer` and `overlayLayer` to the camera so they'll move wherever the camera moves.

Scroll down to `createNodeOf(type:location:)` and modify the case statement for `.tileWall` so it reads as follows:

```
case .tileWall:
  let node = SKSpriteNode(texture:
atlasTiles.textureNamed("Wall1"))
  node.size = CGSize(width: 32, height: 32)
  node.position = location
  node.zPosition = 1
  node.name = "wall"
  worldLayer.addChild(node)
  break
```

You added the ground tile to the worldLayer, and now you implement a wall tile in the same way.

To test your wall tile, use setTile(position:toValue:) by adding the following line to setupLevel(), between generating the base map and presenting the map:

```
worldGen.setTile(position: CGPoint(x: 0, y: 0), toValue: 1)
```

When you're done, the new method will look like this:

```
func setupLevel() {
  worldGen.generateLevel(3)

  //Add
  worldGen.setTile(position: CGPoint(x: 0, y: 0), toValue: 1)

  worldGen.presentLayerViaDelegate()
}
```

Now build and run, and you'll have a wall tile in the first column of the first row.

Manually setting the type of each tile isn't the most efficient way to create a level. Luckily, there are ways to pre-build levels—take a look!

Pre-building a level

In **GameScene.swift**, navigate back to setupLevel() and update it as follows:

```
func setupLevel() {

  //Update
  worldGen.generateLevel(0)
```

```
    //Add
    worldGen.generateMap()

    worldGen.presentLayerViaDelegate()
}
```

Now you need to implement the new `generateMap()` function.

Head back to **LevelHelper.swift** and add the following code after `//MARK: Level creation`:

```
mutating func generateMap() {
    //Template Level
    let template =
    [
      [1, 1, 1, 1, 1],
      [1, 3, 3, 3, 1],
      [1, 3, 3, 3, 1],
      [1, 3, 3, 3, 1],
      [1, 1, 3, 1, 1]
    ]

    //Set tiles based on template
    for (indexr, row) in template.enumerate() {
        for (indexc, cvalue) in row.enumerate() {
            setTile(position: CGPoint(x: indexc, y:indexr), toValue:
cvalue)
        }
    }
}
```

Every tile in the game is assigned by the template. The position of the number in the template relates to the position of the tile; once again, the numbers relate directly to the type of tile.

The wall tiles are surrounding the ground tiles like in a room. In this setup, there's a gap in the wall in the bottom row to represent a doorway or path to the next room.

Build and run the game to see your tile map. It looks just as you'd expect from the template.

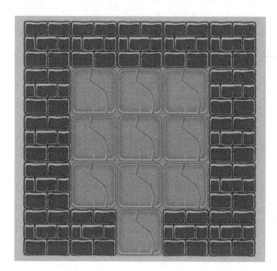

Implementing the state machine

Now that you can create and display your tile maps, it's time to *delve* into building the actual game. First, you'll need to put your game's structure in place.

As you learned in Chapter 15, "State Machines", state machines are a feature in iOS 9's new GameplayKit framework that make it easy to handle different behaviors for your game world—or your characters—depending on the current state of the game.

For Delve, you're going to implement the following game states:

- **Initial**: When the game starts, it loads the level and assets.

- **Active**: The game is playable and all timers—and the game loop—are running.

- **Paused**: All timers, animations and game functions stop until the state returns to active.

- **Limbo**: All controls are disabled; however, the game is still active.

- **Win**: Provides a game over screen if you win; increments the level or difficulty and restarts the scene in its initial state.

- **Loss**: Provides a game over screen if you lose; restarts the level in its initial state without altering the game progress.

Inside the **States** group, create a new Swift file named **GameState.swift**.

Replace the default file contents with the following code:

```swift
import Foundation
import GameplayKit
import SpriteKit

//1
class GameSceneState: GKState {
  unowned let levelScene: GameScene
  init(scene: GameScene) {
    self.levelScene = scene
  }
}

//2
class GameSceneInitialState: GameSceneState {

}

class GameSceneActiveState: GameSceneState {

}

class GameScenePausedState: GameSceneState {

}

class GameSceneLimboState: GameSceneState {

}

class GameSceneWinState: GameSceneState {

}

class GameSceneLoseState: GameSceneState {

}
```

1. The `GameSceneState` class acts as a base class and inherits from `GKState`. As the class is initialized, it stores a pointer to the instance of `GameScene` to which it's attached.

2. Each state inherits its functionality from the base `GameSceneState`. This is where you'll add your behaviors for each state.

> **Note**: You can split each class into its own file, if you wish. But since this game won't have a lot of state information, it's perfectly fine to leave it in a single file.

Go back to **GameScene.swift** and add the following code, just below the layer variables:

```
//State Machine
lazy var stateMachine: GKStateMachine = GKStateMachine(states: [
  GameSceneInitialState(scene: self),
  GameSceneActiveState(scene: self),
  GameScenePausedState(scene: self),
  GameSceneLimboState(scene: self),
  GameSceneWinState(scene: self),
  GameSceneLoseState(scene: self)
  ])
```

This creates your state machine and adds all of the states you've just created to it.

The compiler will complain about not finding GKStateMachine; that's because you haven't imported GameplayKit. Do that now by adding the import statement at the top of the file:

```
import GameplayKit
```

In didMoveToView(_:), update the Gamestate section by *removing* setupLevel() and *replacing* it with the line below:

```
stateMachine.enterState(GameSceneInitialState.self)
```

This causes the state machine to enter GameSceneInitialState on game startup.

When you added the state, you removed the instruction to build the level. You need to re-add this instruction to **GameState.swift**.

Update the GameSceneInitialState class as follows:

```
class GameSceneInitialState: GameSceneState {
  override func didEnterWithPreviousState(previousState:
GKState?) {
    levelScene.setupLevel()

    //Scene Activity
    levelScene.paused = false //to be changed later
  }
}
```

> **Note**: Code entered in didEnterWithPreviousState(_:) will run whenever the state machine enters this state. In this case, setupLevel() will run when the scene enters the GameSceneInitialState.

Build and run to verify everything still works. Although it looks exactly the same, in reality, it's not—it's structurally superior!

This game needs a hero

A level isn't exciting without a character, especially a hero, exploring it. You'll be using GameplayKit's Entity-Component system to implement a fully animated character.

> **Note**: This section is review of Chapter 18, "Entity-Component System". If you feel like you understand this material well, feel free to skip ahead to the "Moving the hero" section, where we will have a starter project waiting for you. But if you'd like some review, keep reading!

First, you'll need some artwork for your character. Drag the **player.atlas** folder from **starter\Resources** into the **Resources** group in Xcode.

Your player entity is going to need a few components:

- **Sprite Component**: An entity by itself has no visual presence in your scene. This component takes care of adding a sprite node to the scene.

- **Animation Component**: The character will have idle and walking animations facing in four directions. This component handles all of the animation logic and provides the animated character for the sprite component.

- **Movement Component**: This component handles the player movement. On iOS devices, the main movement input will be updates via the accelerometer. In a later chapter, you'll add support for game controllers, so you need to make sure this component is flexible enough to receive inputs from different sources.

When designing the sprite and animation components, keep in mind that other entities within your game will use them, too.

Inside the **Entities** group, add a new Swift file named **PlayerEntity.swift**. Replace the contents of the file with the following:

```
import SpriteKit
import GameplayKit

class PlayerEntity: GKEntity {

}
```

Right now, this class doesn't do a whole lot.

After implementing each component, you can add its functionality to the entity. That's the beauty of the Entity-Component architecture—it's truly modular.

Creating the sprite component

Inside the **Components** group, add a new Swift file named **SpriteComponent.swift**. Replace the contents of the file with the following:

```
import SpriteKit
import GameplayKit

// 1
class EntityNode: SKSpriteNode {
  weak var entity: GKEntity!
}

class SpriteComponent: GKComponent {

  // 2
  let node: EntityNode

  // 3
  init(entity: GKEntity, texture: SKTexture, size: CGSize) {
    node = EntityNode(texture: texture,
      color: SKColor.whiteColor(), size: size)
    node.entity = entity
  }

}
```

Here's what's going on:

1. Your sprite component is attached to the entity; the node also needs a connection to the entity or else it won't be able to identify itself as belonging to an entity. This subclass of `SKSpriteNodeNode` adds an entity property.

2. This is the entity node that will be added to your scene.

3. Upon initializing the component, you set the entity property of the node that's

linked to the component.

That's all the code you need for your sprite entity.

Now, go back to **PlayerEntity.swift** and add the following code within the class:

```
var spriteComponent: SpriteComponent!
```

This is a property for the sprite component you're about to create.

Directly below your instance variable, add this initializer:

```
override init() {
  super.init()

  let texture = SKTexture(imageNamed: "PlayerIdle_12_00.png")
  spriteComponent = SpriteComponent(entity: self, texture:
texture,
    size: CGSize(width: 25, height: 30))
  addComponent(spriteComponent)
}
```

You initialize the sprite component and provide a link to the entity. Then you add the component to the entity.

Adding the hero to the scene

You need a place to give the hero his debut. Take a trip back to **LevelHelper.swift** and update the template to spawn the character in the middle:

```
let template =
  [
    [1, 1, 1, 1, 1],
    [1, 3, 3, 3, 1],
    [1, 3, 4, 3, 1],
    [1, 3, 3, 3, 1],
    [1, 1, 3, 1, 1]
  ]
```

With that out of the way, open **GameScene.swift**. Start by adding a new property to the top of the class, underneath the `stateMachine` property:

```
//ECS
var entities = Set<GKEntity>()
```

You will use this to store all entities added to the scene in a set. This lets you keep track of the entities and also holds a strong pointer to each entity so it isn't released earlier than expected.

Each object added from an entity has a few standard places it needs to be set up. To avoid complications, its worth implementing a function to handle entity creation. Add this function just below `createNodeOf(type:location:)`:

```
func addEntity(entity: GKEntity) {
  //1
  entities.insert(entity)

  //2
  if let spriteNode =
    entity.componentForClass(SpriteComponent.self)?.node {

    worldLayer.addChild(spriteNode)

  }
}
```

Take a look at what this function does:

1. You add the entity to the set of entities for the scene.

2. You add the node from the sprite component to the scene, on the correct layer.

Finally, go to `createNodeOf(type:location:)` and scroll to the `.tileStart` case; update it with the following:

```
//1
let node = SKSpriteNode(texture:
atlasTiles.textureNamed("Floor1"))
node.size = CGSize(width: 32, height: 32)
node.position = location
node.zPosition = 1
worldLayer.addChild(node)

//2
let playerEntity = PlayerEntity()
let playerNode = playerEntity.spriteComponent.node
playerNode.position = location
playerNode.name = "playerNode"
playerNode.zPosition = 50
playerNode.anchorPoint = CGPointMake(0.5, 0.2)

//3
addEntity(playerEntity)
```

When `.tileStart` is detected, here's what happens:

1. The tile location still needs a ground tile, so you place one down first.

2. You create the entity and update the sprite component's node information.

3. You pass the entity to `addEntity(:_)`.

Now build and run; your hero will be visible at the spawn point:

Creating the animation component

Next let's add a component to make your sprite animated.

Begin by creating a file called **AnimationComponent.swift** inside the **Components** group. Replace the contents of the file with the following:

```swift
import SpriteKit
import GameplayKit

struct Animation {
    let animationState: AnimationState
    let textures: [SKTexture]
    let repeatTexturesForever: Bool
}

class AnimationComponent: GKComponent {

}
```

You'll use the animation struct to represent each individual animation. This struct lets the game pre-load the animation to avoid frame rate issues while the game is running.

From here onwards, you'll be adding a lot more enums and game settings. To make things easier, you can create a file to hold all of these global constants—which, incidentally, will clear up the error you're seeing in Xcode.

Create a new Swift file inside the **Helpers** group named **GameSettings.swift**. Replace the contents of the file with the following code:

```
import Foundation
import SpriteKit

//1
enum AnimationState: String {
    case Idle_Down = "Idle_12"
    case Idle_Up = "Idle_4"
    case Idle_Left = "Idle_8"
    case Idle_Right = "Idle_0"
    case Walk_Down = "Walk_12"
    case Walk_Up = "Walk_4"
    case Walk_Left = "Walk_8"
    case Walk_Right = "Walk_0"
    case Die_Down = "Die_0"
}

//2
enum LastDirection {
    case Left
    case Right
    case Up
    case Down
}
```

These settings provide the following:

1. This is a list of all the possible animations. The string values correspond with the names of the textures. In the strings, each number beside the action word represents a direction. Right is 0, Up is 4, Left is 8, and Down is 12.

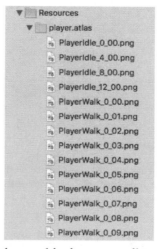

2. If the hero is walking, and then suddenly stops walking, it will return to an idle

animation. You're tracking the direction of movement to make sure the idle animation is facing the same direction as the walking animation.

Return to **AnimationComponent.swift** and add the following instance variables and initializer:

```
//1
static let actionKey = "Action"
static let timePerFrame = NSTimeInterval(1.0 / 20.0)

//2
let node: SKSpriteNode
//3
var animations: [AnimationState: Animation]
//4
private(set) var currentAnimation: Animation?

//5
var requestedAnimationState: AnimationState?

//6
init(node: SKSpriteNode, textureSize: CGSize,
  animations: [AnimationState: Animation]) {
  self.node = node
  self.animations = animations
}
```

Take a look at what's happening in that code block:

1. These are the default name and frame rate settings for the `Animation SKAction`.

2. This is the node that you are animating (the one from the sprite component).

3. This is the collection of all animations that have been set up in the current instance of the animation component.

4. This property defines which animation is currently running.

5. This property lets the scene, entity or another component notify this component that the animation is about to change. The change will then be picked up by this component's `updateWithDeltaTime(_:)` function.

6. The `init()` initializes the component.

The component will need to be capable of updating the current animation regularly. If a character is walking through a dungeon, it's likely to change direction frequently, and a delayed animation can make the character look rather silly.

To run a new animation, implement the following after your initializer:

```
private func runAnimationForAnimationState(animationState:
AnimationState) {
  //1
  if currentAnimation != nil &&
    currentAnimation!.animationState == animationState
{ return }

  //2
  guard let animation = animations[animationState] else {
    print("Unknown animation for state \
(animationState.rawValue)")
    return
  }

  //3
  node.removeActionForKey(AnimationComponent.actionKey)

  //4
  let texturesAction: SKAction

  if animation.repeatTexturesForever {
    texturesAction = SKAction.repeatActionForever(
      SKAction.animateWithTextures(animation.textures,
        timePerFrame: AnimationComponent.timePerFrame))
  } else {
    texturesAction =
SKAction.animateWithTextures(animation.textures,
      timePerFrame: AnimationComponent.timePerFrame)
  }

  //5
  node.runAction(texturesAction, withKey:
AnimationComponent.actionKey)

  //6
  currentAnimation = animation
}
```

Here's the breakdown:

1. You check if the animation state requested is the same as the current animation state. If both animation states are the same, you do nothing, since the animation is already running. If you revert to a new animation state every frame, then you'll only ever see the first frame of each animation.

2. You make sure the requested animation is supported by the entity.

3. Then, you remove the current animation from the node.

4. Next, you set up the new animation using SKAction to either play once, or repeat until removed.

5. You add the animation to the node.

6. Finally, you set the `currentAnimation` property to the current animation.

Since the update function is called via the game loop, you'll need to check if a new animation has been requested. To do so, add the following code below the new function you just added.

```
override func updateWithDeltaTime(deltaTime: NSTimeInterval) {
  super.updateWithDeltaTime(deltaTime)

  if let animationState = requestedAnimationState {
    runAnimationForAnimationState(animationState)
    requestedAnimationState = nil
  }
}
```

If a new animation state is requested, then you call `runAnimationForAnimationState(_:)`.

There's one last thing your animation component needs: a way to take a texture atlas and create an animation using the `Animation` struct you added at the top of this component.

Add this function below the last function you added:

```
class func animationFromAtlas(atlas: SKTextureAtlas,
withImageIdentifier identifier: String, forAnimationState
animationState: AnimationState, repeatTexturesForever: Bool =
true) -> Animation {

  let textures = atlas.textureNames.filter {
    $0.containsString("\(identifier)_")
  }.sort {
    $0 < $1
  }.map {
    atlas.textureNamed($0)
  }

  return Animation(
    animationState: animationState,
    textures: textures,
    repeatTexturesForever: repeatTexturesForever
  )
}
```

This code filters the texture atlas for files that contain the identifier string for the animation. It then sorts the frames into numerical order and constructs them into an animation using the `Animation` struct.

Head back to **PlayerEntity.swift** and add this instance variable under the
spriteComponent variable:

```
var animationComponent: AnimationComponent!
```

Here, you just make sure the component exists.

Now, in the initializer, add the following code after you initialize the spriteComponent
variable:

```
animationComponent = AnimationComponent(node:
spriteComponent.node,
   textureSize: CGSizeMake(25,30), animations: loadAnimations())
addComponent(animationComponent)
```

There's an Xcode error that loadAnimations() is missing, so let's add that now. Add
this function after your initializer:

```
func loadAnimations() -> [AnimationState: Animation] {
  let textureAtlas = SKTextureAtlas(named: "player")
  var animations = [AnimationState: Animation]()

  animations[.Walk_Down] =
AnimationComponent.animationFromAtlas(
    textureAtlas,
    withImageIdentifier: AnimationState.Walk_Down.rawValue,
    forAnimationState: .Walk_Down)
  animations[.Walk_Up] = AnimationComponent.animationFromAtlas(
    textureAtlas,
    withImageIdentifier: AnimationState.Walk_Up.rawValue,
    forAnimationState: .Walk_Up)
  animations[.Walk_Left] =
AnimationComponent.animationFromAtlas(
    textureAtlas,
    withImageIdentifier: AnimationState.Walk_Left.rawValue,
    forAnimationState: .Walk_Left)
  animations[.Walk_Right] =
AnimationComponent.animationFromAtlas(
    textureAtlas,
    withImageIdentifier: AnimationState.Walk_Right.rawValue,
    forAnimationState: .Walk_Right)

  animations[.Idle_Down] =
AnimationComponent.animationFromAtlas(
    textureAtlas,
    withImageIdentifier: AnimationState.Idle_Down.rawValue,
    forAnimationState: .Idle_Down)
  animations[.Idle_Up] = AnimationComponent.animationFromAtlas(
    textureAtlas,
    withImageIdentifier: AnimationState.Idle_Up.rawValue,
    forAnimationState: .Idle_Up)
```

```
    animations[.Idle_Left] =
AnimationComponent.animationFromAtlas(
    textureAtlas,
    withImageIdentifier: AnimationState.Idle_Left.rawValue,
    forAnimationState: .Idle_Left)
  animations[.Idle_Right] =
AnimationComponent.animationFromAtlas(
    textureAtlas,
    withImageIdentifier: AnimationState.Idle_Right.rawValue,
    forAnimationState: .Idle_Right)

  return animations
}
```

As mentioned, the character has four walking and four idle states. You'll cover switching between them when you implement the movement component. Right now, you must be itching to build and run—but first, you need to add the character to the scene.

Adding the component system

Remember from Chapter 18, "Entity-Component System", that in order to call the update method on your components you need to create a GKComponentSystem, add the component to it, then call updateWithDeltaTime(_:) on the component system.

To do this, open **GameScene.swift** and add these new properties below the existing entities property:

```
//1
var lastUpdateTimeInterval: NSTimeInterval = 0
let maximumUpdateDeltaTime: NSTimeInterval - 1.0 / 60.0
var lastDeltaTime: NSTimeInterval = 0

//2
lazy var componentSystems: [GKComponentSystem] = {
  let animationSystem = GKComponentSystem(componentClass:
AnimationComponent.self)
  return [animationSystem]
}()
```

Here's a quick explanation of the code you just added:

1. You store information about the delta time so it can be calculated in the game loop.

2. You add your animation component to a component system.

> **Note**: If you aren't sure if you need to add your component to a component system, have a look at its structure; if it adopts an updateWithDeltaTime(_:) loop, consider adding it to a component system to perform the loop.

At the top of update(_:), add this code to calculate the delta time, or the number of seconds between the last update and this one:

```
//Calculate delta time
var deltaTime = currentTime - lastUpdateTimeInterval
deltaTime = deltaTime > maximumUpdateDeltaTime ?
  maximumUpdateDeltaTime : deltaTime
lastUpdateTimeInterval = currentTime
```

Next, in update(_:), add this code after the delta time calculation:

```
//Update all components
for componentSystem in componentSystems {
  componentSystem.updateWithDeltaTime(deltaTime)
}
```

This performs an updateWithDeltaTime(_:) for each component in the component system.

Next, add this to the bottom of addEntity(_:):

```
for componentSystem in self.componentSystems {
  componentSystem.addComponentWithEntity(entity)
}
```

For each component associated with the entity, you add it to a component system if one exists for that type of component.

Finally, go to createNodeOf(type:location:) and scroll to the .tileStart case; add this line right before you call addEntity():

```
playerEntity.animationComponent.requestedAnimationState
= .Walk_Down
```

This sets the intial animation to the walking animation.

Now build and run to see your hero strut in style!

Moving the hero

> **Note**: If you skipped ahead from earlier in this chapter, you can continue with the **starter\Delve_Hero** project in the resources for this chapter. This has the hero entity and two components to display and animate the sprite.

It's time for this explorer to begin exploring. Begin by creating a new Swift file inside your **Components** group named **PlayerMoveComponent.swift**.

Replace the contents of the file with the following:

```
import SpriteKit
import GameplayKit

class PlayerMoveComponent: GKComponent {

  //1
  var movement = CGPointZero
  //2
  var lastDirection = LastDirection.Down

  //3
  var spriteComponent: SpriteComponent {
    guard let spriteComponent =
entity?.componentForClass(SpriteComponent.self) else
{ fatalError("A MovementComponent's entity must have a
spriteComponent") }
    return spriteComponent
  }

  //4
  var animationComponent: AnimationComponent {
    guard let animationComponent =
entity?.componentForClass(AnimationComponent.self) else
{ fatalError("A MovementComponent's entity must have an
animationComponent") }
    return animationComponent
  }

}
```

Most of this is likely familiar to you by now:

1. As mentioned earlier, you should design the movement component to accept multiple data sources. The simplest way to do that is by providing a CGPoint to represent the current direction of movement. No matter what control source you use, it will be able to convert the movement instructions to a CGPoint.

2. You store the last direction of movement to let the player fall back to an idle state while maintaining the direction the character is currently facing.

3. You need a link to the sprite component to update its `position` based on the calculated movement of the character.

4. You also need a link to the animation component to update its state between walking and idle, as well as the direction of the animation.

> **Note**: Note you look up the sprite and animation components up dynamically here. An alternative would be to pass references to these components in the initializer, but this is more flexible.

Under the instance variables, add this function:

```
override func updateWithDeltaTime(seconds: NSTimeInterval) {
  super.updateWithDeltaTime(seconds)

}
```

Great! Now, you need to fill that function with all of the relevant calculations to move the character and update the animations.

Start by calculating and setting the new position of the sprite node. Do this by adding the following at the bottom of the function:

```
//Update player position
let xMovement =
  ((movement.x * CGFloat(seconds)) *
playerSettings.movementSpeed)
let yMovement =
  ((movement.y * CGFloat(seconds)) *
playerSettings.movementSpeed)
spriteComponent.node.position = CGPoint(
  x: spriteComponent.node.position.x + xMovement,
  y: spriteComponent.node.position.y + yMovement)
```

For each of the x- and y-axes, you find the product of the movement property for that axis, the delta time and the movement speed. Combined, these three properties give you the character's movement.

At this point, you'll see an error message because you haven't yet implemented a movement speed setting. You need to do that now.

Go to **GameSettings.swift** and add the following:

```
struct playerSettings {

  //Player
  static let movementSpeed: CGFloat = 320.0

}
```

Revisit **PlayerEntity.swift** and add this instance variable, right below the others:

```
var moveComponent: PlayerMoveComponent!
```

In the initializer for the entity, add the `moveComponent` declaration right below the other component declarations:

```
moveComponent = PlayerMoveComponent()
addComponent(moveComponent)
```

Tilt to move

This is a good point to implement the controls for your game. In this chapter, you'll use accelerometer controls.

Head over to **GameScene.swift**. Once there, you need to import Core Motion, so add the `import` statement at the top of the file. Because Core Motion is only available on iOS (and later you will make this game work on tvOS), you need to use the `#if os(iOS)` macro:

```
#if os(iOS)
import CoreMotion
#endif
```

With the necessary framework imported, add this code just after your properties:

```
//Controls
#if os(iOS)
lazy var motionManager: CMMotionManager = {
  let motion = CMMotionManager()
  motion.accelerometerUpdateInterval = 1.0/10.0
  return motion
}()
#endif
var movement = CGPointZero
```

The motion manager will receive approximately 10 updates per second, which should be sufficient for this game.

Scroll down to `update(_:)` and find the gap between the delta time calculation and the updating of the components. Once you locate it, add the following code:

```
//Motion
#if os(iOS)
  if (motionManager.accelerometerData != nil) {
    movement = CGPointZero
    if motionManager.accelerometerData!.acceleration.x > 0.02 ||
      self.motionManager.accelerometerData!.acceleration.x <
-0.02 {

      movement.y =
        CGFloat(motionManager.accelerometerData!.acceleration.x)

    }
    if motionManager.accelerometerData!.acceleration.y > 0.02 ||
      self.motionManager.accelerometerData!.acceleration.y <
-0.02 {

      movement.x =

CGFloat((motionManager.accelerometerData!.acceleration.y) * -1)

    }
  }
#endif
```

If the accelerometer differs more than 0.02 in the x- or y-scale, then update the movement property accordingly. The x- and y-values relate to the device being in portrait position and don't automatically compensate for screen rotation.

Currently, this game only supports landscape orientation. When you set the movement property, you compensate by assigning the x-value to the y-value of the movement property, and the y-value to the x-value of the movement property. You also need to reverse the y-axis of the accelerometer data.

Now, add this code directly below the code you just added, after `#endif`:

```
//player controls
if let player = worldLayer.childNodeWithName("playerNode") as?
EntityNode,
  let playerEntity = player.entity as? PlayerEntity {
    if !(movement == CGPointZero) {
      playerEntity.moveComponent.movement = movement
    }
}
```

This updates the `movement` property on the player's movement component to the movement value you just calculated.

The last thing you need to do to get the character moving is tell the `motionManager` to begin receiving accelerometer updates.

Go to **GameState.swift** and insert this code below `levelScene.setupLevel()`:

```
#if os(iOS)
levelScene.motionManager.startAccelerometerUpdates()
#endif
```

Now, return to **GameScene.swift** and update the `componentSystem` instance variable as follows:

```
lazy var componentSystems: [GKComponentSystem] = {
  let animationSystem = GKComponentSystem(componentClass:
AnimationComponent.self)
  let playerMoveSystem = GKComponentSystem(componentClass:
PlayerMoveComponent.self)
  return [animationSystem, playerMoveSystem]
}()
```

Here, you add the component to the component system.

Excellent! Now build and run the game on your physical device. The character will move around the screen as you tilt the device.

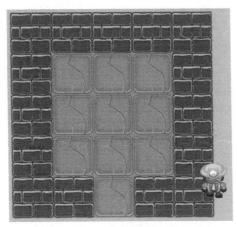

However, there are a few issues to address with the hero's movement:

- The animations don't update based on the movement speed and direction.

- The camera is static; it would be a lot better if the camera followed the hero wherever he went.

- The hero can walk through walls, or rather, over the top of them. Adding collisions will fix this problem.

Updating the animations

You could argue that it's possible to face the same direction no matter where you walk, but in practice, it wouldn't make a lot of sense.

For this fix, you'll need some more robust helpers.

In the root directory for this book, locate **SKTUtils** and drag the contents into your **Helpers** group in Xcode.

Navigate to **PlayerMoveComponent.swift** and in `updateWithDeltaTime(_:)`, add the following code below the code you added earlier:

```
switch movement.angle {
case 0:
  //Left empty on purpose to break switch if there is no angle
  break
case CGFloat(45).degreesToRadians() ..<
  CGFloat(135).degreesToRadians():
  animationComponent.requestedAnimationState = .Walk_Up
  lastDirection = .Up
  break
case CGFloat(-135).degreesToRadians() ..<
  CGFloat(-45).degreesToRadians():
  animationComponent.requestedAnimationState = .Walk_Down
  lastDirection = .Down
  break
case CGFloat(-45).degreesToRadians() ..<
  CGFloat(45).degreesToRadians():
  animationComponent.requestedAnimationState = .Walk_Right
  lastDirection = .Right
  break
case CGFloat(-180).degreesToRadians() ..<
  CGFloat(-135).degreesToRadians():
  animationComponent.requestedAnimationState = .Walk_Left
  lastDirection = .Left
  break
case CGFloat(135).degreesToRadians() ..<
  CGFloat(180).degreesToRadians():
  animationComponent.requestedAnimationState = .Walk_Left
  lastDirection = .Left
```

```
    break
 default:
    break
  }
```

An extension from `SKTUtils` lets you convert a `CGPoint` to an angle. Based on the angle of the movement, you assign a different animation by updating the `requestedAnimationState` property.

Also, include the idle animations by adding the following code, right below the code you just added:

```
if xMovement == 0 && yMovement == 0 {
  switch lastDirection {
  case .Up:
    animationComponent.requestedAnimationState = .Idle_Up
    break
  case .Down:
    animationComponent.requestedAnimationState = .Idle_Down
    break
  case .Right:
    animationComponent.requestedAnimationState = .Idle_Right
    break
  case .Left:
    animationComponent.requestedAnimationState = .Idle_Left
    break
  }
}
movement = CGPointZero
```

If the movement is zero, then you set an idle animation based on the last direction moved. Once you've set all the animations, you set the movement property back to zero.

Build and run your game, and enjoy fluid animations as you move the character around the screen by tilting the device.

Centering the camera on the hero

Open **GameScene.swift**, locate `createNodeOf(type:location:)` and *remove* this line:

```
  centerCameraOnPoint(location)
```

You originally added this line to move the camera to the location of the last tile added. Now, you want the camera to follow the hero.

Find `update(_:)` and add this code at the bottom of that function:

```
//Update player after components
if let player = worldLayer.childNodeWithName("playerNode") as?
EntityNode {
```

```
        centerCameraOnPoint(player.position)
    }
```

You add the code at the end of the function to make sure it executes *after* the component updates that cause the hero to move. Build and run the game to test the camera.

Adding collisions

Walls aren't very useful if the player can simply walk through them. You also need to think ahead about how game entities will interact and make contact with other entities —such as the hero picking up a health boost or getting trampled by a rock golem.

This chapter doesn't cover collisions, because Chapter 9, "Beginning Physics", as well as more advanced chapters, have already done so. If you're having trouble with collisions, please refer back to those chapters for more detail.

That having been said, open **GameSettings.swift** and add the following enum under the other enums:

```
enum ColliderType:UInt32 {
    case Player       = 0
    case Enemy        = 0b1
    case Wall         = 0b10
    case Projectile   = 0b100
    case Food         = 0b1000
    case EndLevel     = 0b10000
    case None         = 0b100000
}
```

Now, navigate to **PlayerEntity.swift** and add the following code to the initializer, just after where you add the components:

```
let physicsBody = SKPhysicsBody(circleOfRadius: 15)

physicsBody.dynamic = true
physicsBody.allowsRotation = false

physicsBody.categoryBitMask = ColliderType.Player.rawValue
physicsBody.collisionBitMask = ColliderType.Wall.rawValue
physicsBody.contactTestBitMask = ColliderType.Enemy.rawValue |
    ColliderType.Food.rawValue | ColliderType.EndLevel.rawValue

spriteComponent.node.physicsBody = physicsBody
```

You can set up the physics body anywhere, but remember—you must set it to the physics body property of your sprite component node.

That's all you need to do in your player entity.

Now, head back to **GameScene.swift** and scroll to the top of the file.

Replace the class declaration with the following:

```
class GameScene: SKScene, tileMapDelegate,
SKPhysicsContactDelegate {
```

In `didMoveToView(_:)`, add the following under `//Delegates`:

```
physicsWorld.contactDelegate = self
physicsWorld.gravity = CGVector.zero
```

You state that this class accepts the contact delegate protocol, and you set up the physics world. All that's left to do is assign a physics body to your walls.

Scroll to `createNodeOf(type:location:)` and update the `.tileWall` case as follows:

```
case .tileWall:
   let node = SKSpriteNode(texture:
atlasTiles.textureNamed("Wall1"))
   node.size = CGSize(width: 32, height: 32)
   node.position = location
   node.zPosition = 1
   node.physicsBody = SKPhysicsBody(edgeLoopFromRect:
CGRect(origin: CGPoint(x: -16, y: -16), size: CGSize(width: 32,
height: 32)))
   node.physicsBody?.categoryBitMask = ColliderType.Wall.rawValue
   node.name = "wall"
   worldLayer.addChild(node)
   break
```

Build and run, and watch as the walls stop the character dead in his tracks. Where's his trusty mining pick?

You've only just started building this game—there's plenty more to add! Proceed to the next chapter, where you'll be procedurally generating levels using GameplayKit's randomization. But first, if you've been itching to build a bigger tile map, the challenge below is for you.

Challenges

There's just one challenge for this level - and it's a chance for you to be creative!

As always, if you get stuck, you can find solutions in the resources for this chapter—but give it your best shot first!

Challenge 1: Your Custom Level

Your hero looks a little cramped in his room. Try building a bigger level that is ten rows and twenty columns in size.

Remember, the template variable isn't the only thing you need to update to make the level bigger. The `mapSize` property is also very important to avoid any overflow errors.

It can be tedious to update the template, but remember that you can always copy and paste rows to save time.

Make sure you post a screenshot of your design on the raywenderlich.com forums to show off your creativity!

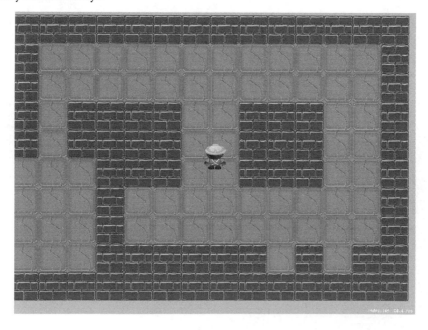

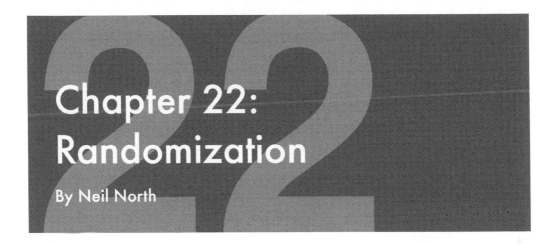

Chapter 22: Randomization

By Neil North

The first time you proceed into a game dungeon, your senses are alive with the feeling of adventure. But once you've thoroughly explored the landscape and learned the secrets of its environment—the thrill is gone, as they say. Along with some of the entertainment value. You know too much!

What if every time you went back, the layout and environment were completely different? There may be some familiar elements, but no matter how many times you went to the dungeon, you'd never learn the fastest or safest way to the end of the level. No online guide or tutorial could help you; the world would remain elusive—and random!

When you use the techniques of procedural level generation, you're no longer involved in building levels. Instead, you build the model, and the game uses that model to build the levels—dynamically.

The model contains information about how the level must be built. This can be as simple as requiring that the end of the level is reachable from the start of the level, or as complex as requiring that the rooms and pathways connect in a logical way.

To get a wide variety of results from your model, it's essential to use randomization. This isn't always as simple as picking a random number between 1 and 10. Thankfully, GameplayKit includes a lot of advanced randomization features that are well worth exploring.

In this chapter, you'll use GameplayKit's advanced randomization features to build the procedural level generator you will be using in Delve.

What does it mean to be random?

In the context of programming, the term **random** refers to a result that's perceived to be unpredictable. It sounds simple enough, right? But creating truly random numbers presents a series of challenges for software engineers.

In the real world, if you throw down some dice, you would call the result random, because you're unable to predict how the dice will land. This may be functionally true, but theoretically, if you could somehow measure every contributing factor—the way the dice were thrown, the velocity of the dice, the hardness of the surface—and apply the laws of physics, you could predict the result, and it would no longer be random.

Just like the real world, generating truly random numbers in a software environment is fundamentally flawed by the fact that we live in a world of cause and effect. Because computers require logical instructions, it becomes difficult to perform a calculation without knowing all of the components that go into the task and how they affect each other.

Confused? Try not to stress about it too much; instead, focus on the point that if you—or more importantly, the player—are unable to predict an outcome, then it's technically random.

With apps and games, though, true randomness can reek havoc. For example walls could spawn between you and the exit that make the level unable to be completed, or too many enemies could spawn in narrow spaces creating huge difficulty spikes.

The trick is finding a calculation that results in an acceptable number as far as the gameplay is concerned, as well as one the user is unable to predict. This means the results must be free of perceivable and predictable patterns.

Before iOS 9 introduced GameplayKit there were three ways to generate random numbers:

- **rand()**: A standard C function for generating random numbers. The `rand()` function uses an initial seed to start generating numbers. The default seed is 1, which menas every time you start using `rand()` you will have the same sequence of numbers unless a different seed is specified using `srand()`.

- **random()**: `random()` is the same as `rand()` in functionality. `random()` originates from the POSIX standard, more details can be found here: http://bit.ly/1GLS6NY

- **arc4random()**: This function originated from BSD and has been the most popular choice of the three functions in recent years. It doesn't require a seed in order to produce different patterns every time it is used and has a maximum range twice the size of the other two options, this also allows it to be "more random" and less likely to follow a pattern than the latter two.

As mentioned previously the software needs a seed to generate a number, the number is never truly random because if you know the seed then you know the resulting number too. `arc4random()` solves this dilemma by re-seeding itself regularly using a hardware subsystem.

The result will be unpredictable, and thus random—even if, in reality, that result was pre-determined.

Randomization with GameplayKit

GameplayKit comes with a lot of great tools to help you make better games. Its randomization features can assist you in two big ways:

- **Distributions**: A distribution is an array where numbers can be distributed in pattern or a specific lack of a pattern. A single number generated using the ARC4 method will be sufficiently random, but distributions allow you to link together sequential numbers in a series. Cryptography-based random numbers can exhibit patterns, distributions give you more control over what patterns and trends appear.

- **Sources**: These are the algorithms used to produce random numbers. The ARC4 random method is one source, but GameplayKit also includes the **Linear Congruential** and **Mersenne Twister** sources. These will be covered in detail after you look at the types of distributions available.

Randomization distributions

GameplayKit comes with three standard types of distributions from which you can choose:

- **Random**: As the name suggests, this distribution is designed to provide the most randomness and is least likely to follow a pattern.

- **Gaussian**: In this distribution, results are weighted towards the **mean**, or middle-most value, of the range of potential numbers. The distribution then uses **deviation** curves to distribute weighting to the other available numbers. Statistically, in a 1 to 10 range, a 5 or 6 might appear 50% of the time, while a 1 or 10 might only appear 5% of the time.

- **Shuffled**: Technically, a shuffled distribution works like an ordinary random distribution with one key difference. Once a number is returned, it won't be returned again until all of the other numbers have been returned, as well. For example, consider a range of numbers from 1 to 10; if the generator returns a 7, it won't return a 7 again until the nine remaining numbers have also been returned.

You can combine all three distributions with any of the three sources to provide a result.

To begin testing randomization, we've provided a playground named **random.playground** at **starter\Delve** in the resources for this chapter. Open it now.

First, add this code:

```
let randomFive = GKRandomDistribution(forDieWithSideCount: 5)
```

This will let you generate random numbers between 1 and 5, inclusive, using a random distribution. Think of it as simulating a five-sided die. The distribution itself does not represent a random number, it is the object that provides random numbers that comply to the rules of the distribution.

To check the range of the random distribution, add the following:

```
randomFive.lowestValue
randomFive.highestValue
randomFive.numberOfPossibleOutcomes
```

These return the results 1, 5 and 5, respectively. Each of these properties describes attributes of the distribution, the lowest value, the highest value and the total number of possabilities the distribution can yield.

Now, you're going to generate 10 random numbers based on a random distribution, using the default ARC4 random source. Add this code to your playground:

```
//1
var i = 0
var numbers:[Int] = []

//2
repeat {
  numbers.append(randomFive.nextInt())
    i++
} while i < 10

//3
print(numbers)
```

1. A variable to track the times your loop has been iterated and an array to store the results.

2. Loop the function ten times requesting the next integer from the distribution each time.

3. Display the random numbers between 1 and 5, inclusive, that were added to the array.

In the results sidebar, you'll see something like this: 3, 1, 5, 4, 1, 4, 1, 2, 1, 1 (your numbers may vary). The random distribution object acts as your generator where, upon request, you can obtain the next integer or the next Boolean value.

Now, modify the `randomFive` initialization like so:

```
let randomFive = GKGaussianDistribution(forDieWithSideCount: 5)
```

You have changed the `GKRandomDistribution` to a `GKGaussianDistribution` but left the initializer the same. The minimum, maximum values and number of possabilities do not change however the way the values are distributed does change.

The results sidebar will show a similar pattern to the following output: 2, 3, 4, 4, 4, 2, 3, 4, 3, 4 (again, your numbers may vary). Now, the result is weighted toward the middle of the range of numbers—which in this case is 3.

> **Note:** Even with a weighted distribution, it's entirely possible to generate an unlikely number ten or more times in a row. The likelihood of that happening might be close to that of winning the lottery, but it's always a possibility. Why do you think people continue to buy lottery tickets?

Finally, modify the initializer again. This time, change it like so:

```
let randomFive = GKShuffledDistribution(forDieWithSideCount: 5)
```

Now you are using a `GKShuffledDistribution` with the same initializer as previous, once again the only thing that changes is how the distribution is handled.

The results sidebar output will look something like this 4, 1, 2, 3, 5, 4, 2, 1, 3, 5 (again, your numbers may vary).

Notice how this result does *not* repeat a number until all the numbers have been returned. It's still possible to have two of the same number, side by side, at the beginning and end of cycles as all numbers are available again at the end of the cylcle.

The shuffled distribution becomes the most predictable of the distribution as you know the last number of the cycle will always be the number that hasn't appeared yet.

Randomization sources

So far, you've only used GameplayKit's default source, ARC4 random, but there are two other sources available:

- **Linear Congruential**: The algorithm is faster than ARC4 but also considered to be less random and more likely to follow a pattern. This source is recommended when you need to generate results quickly.

- **Mersenne Twister**: This is the slowest of the three but also the most random, when true unpredictability is important over speed this is the one to use.

The primary tradeoff to consider when choosing a source is between **randomness** and **performance**. To increase the randomness of a source, you have to perform extra computations, which negatively impact performance.

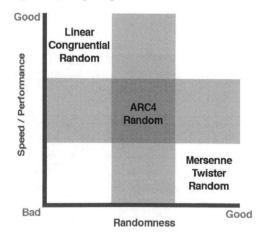

All three methods produce numbers that you're unlikely to predict—so technically, they're all sufficiently random, and definitely good enough for most games.

The deciding factor will be performance. Based on when a random value is generated, it may have an impact on the game loop. Perhaps you have an enemy you want to wander randomly around the level, the random direction is not important but how long it takes to decide which way to go is important.

Add the following code at the end of your playground to have a look at how you can implement different random sources:

```
//1
let randomSource = GKARC4RandomSource()
//2
let randomDist = GKRandomDistribution(randomSource:
randomSource, lowestValue: 1, highestValue: 5)

//3
i = 0
numbers = []

repeat {
  numbers.append(randomDist.nextInt())
    i++
} while i < 10

print(numbers)
```

1. First, you set your random source; in this example, you use the ARC4 random source. You can also try using `GKLinearCongruentialRandomSource()` and `GKMersenneTwisterRandomSource()` to see if you can spot the differences in their outputs.

2. In the previous examples, you initialized with a convenience method a dice of n number of sides. Here, you specify a `randomSource`, `lowestValue` and `highestValue`. If you intend to use ARC4 random, then you don't need to specify a random source because ARC4 random is the default source.

3. Using the same variables you assigned above, you loop through ten iterations of random numbers.

Can you tell the difference in randomness between each result? If you can't detect a pattern then it is safe to say each method is sufficiently random. The take away from this section is that the default of ARC4 random should be suitable in most situations unless performance is an issue.

The drunkard walk algorithm

In the last chapter, *you* created a level for your game. Now, it's time for *the game* to create its own levels. Of course, first you need to instruct it how to do that. :]

In particular, you'll be using the **drunkard walk algorithm**, for which you'll implement these steps:

1. First, you'll fill the tile map with wall tiles.

2. Next, you'll select a random spot on the tile map as the start point and mark it as a ground tile.

3. You'll randomly generate a cardinal direction: north, south, east or west.

4. Then, based on the direction, you'll select a point on the tile map next to the currently selected point, and mark it as a ground tile, if it isn't one already.

5. You'll repeat steps 3 and 4 until you've reached your desired number of ground tiles.

This algorithm has several advantages over other level generator algorithms:

*   **Plenty of possibilities**: Just like a drunk stumbling home after a night at the pub, this algorithm could take you anywhere.

*   **Simple to implement**: The procedure is quite straightforward and won't take you long to implement.

*   **Guaranteed path**: The procedure works by walking the path, so you can be sure the end of the level is reachable.

There are a few downsides to consider, too:

*   **Too random**: It's entirely possible that the end of the level could be on top of—or next to—the start of the level. You can attempt to manage this with different random distribution types, but ultimately, it could be a problem.

*   **Not consistent with real world patterns**: While this algorithm might work well for a cave level, it might not for other types of environments, and even though it's random, you'll run into a lot of the same level attributes.

But not to worry—the solutions to these problems will be covered in the next chapter, where you'll look at advanced procedural level generation. Before you can get there, though, you need to learn the basics.

Getting Started

It's time to pick up your dungeon crawler, **Delve**, from where you left off in the last chapter.

Before you get started implemementing the drunkard walk algorithm, there are two gameplay features you have to add to the game: a health bar for the player, and the ability to tap to start the game.

> **Note:** This is an optional section. If you'd like to build this yourself, keep reading. But if you'd like to get straight to the drunkard walk algorithm, feel free to skip to the next section, "Implementing the drunkard walk", where we will have a starter project ready for you.

First, open **GameScene.sks** and set the scene's background color to black:

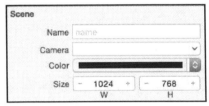

This will look better for areas that don't have any tiles, rather than the default gray.

Next open **GameSettings.swift** and add this new enumeration:

```swift
enum tapAction {
    case startGame
    case attack
    case dismissPause
    case nextLevel
    case doNothing
}


var gameDifficultyModifier = 1
var gameLoopPaused = true
```

Here you create an enumeration to keep track of what action a tap will currently perform. At the beginning of the game, you'll tap to start, but later a tap will attack, and so on.

You also add some variables to keep track of the current game difficulty, and if the game is paused.

Open **GameScene.swift** and add these two properties to the top of the class:

```
var health = 1000
var tapState = tapAction.startGame
```

Here you create a property to keep track of the player's health, and keep track of the current action a track will perform. To start, a tap will start the game, as mentioned earlier.

Next you'll add a basic GUI to the game to display the player's health. To do this you'll need some art, drag **GUI.xcassets** from the resources for this chapter into your **Resources** group in Xcode. Be sure to select **Copy items if needed**, **Create groups**, and the **Delve** target.

Now let's display the GUI. To do this, open **GameState.swift** and find `GameSceneInitialState`. Inside `didEnterWithPreviousState(_:)`, replace the line `levelScene.paused = false` with the following:

```
levelScene.paused = true
gameLoopPaused = true
levelScene.tapState = .startGame

let healthBackground = SKSpriteNode(imageNamed: "HealthUI")
healthBackground.zPosition = 999
healthBackground.position = CGPoint(x: 0,
  y: (levelScene.scene?.size.height)!*0.455)
healthBackground.alpha = 0.4
levelScene.guiLayer.addChild(healthBackground)

let healthLabel = SKLabelNode(fontNamed: "Avenir-Black")
healthLabel.position = CGPoint(
  x: (levelScene.scene?.size.width)!*0.01,
  y: (levelScene.scene?.size.height)!*0.449)
healthLabel.name = "healthLabel"
healthLabel.zPosition = 1000
levelScene.guiLayer.addChild(healthLabel)

let announce = SKSpriteNode(imageNamed: "TapToStart")
announce.size = CGSize(width: 2046, height: 116)
announce.xScale = 0.5
announce.yScale = 0.5
announce.position = CGPointZero
announce.zPosition = 120
announce.alpha = 0.6
levelScene.overlayLayer.addChild(announce)

let announcelevel = SKLabelNode(fontNamed: "Avenir-Black")
announcelevel.position = CGPoint(x: 0, y: -100)
announcelevel.color = SKColor.grayColor()
announcelevel.fontSize = 40
announcelevel.zPosition = 120
```

```
announcelevel.text = "Level \(gameDifficultyModifier)"
levelScene.overlayLayer.addChild(announcelevel)
```

This pauses the game through SKScene's built in `pause` property, and adds the GUI elements to the game. This should be review from previous chapters in this book.

Then add this new method:

```
override func willExitWithNextState(nextState: GKState) {
  for node in levelScene.overlayLayer.children {
    node.removeFromParent()
  }
}
```

This dismisses the temporary "Tap to Start" UI that you placed within the overlay layer when you leave this state.

In GameSceneActiveState, add this method:

```
override func didEnterWithPreviousState(previousState: GKState?)
{
  levelScene.paused = false
  gameLoopPaused = false
  levelScene.tapState = .attack
}
```

After the user taps, you will enter the active state. When you enter this state, you unpause the game and set the tap action to attack.

In GameScenePausedState, add this method:

```
override func didEnterWithPreviousState(previousState: GKState?)
{
  levelScene.paused = true
  gameLoopPaused = true
  levelScene.tapState = .dismissPause
}
```

Later you'll add the ability to pause the game. When you enter the pause game state, you pause the game and set the tap state to dismiss the pause.

In GameSceneLimboState, add this method:

```
override func didEnterWithPreviousState(previousState: GKState?)
{
  levelScene.tapState = .doNothing
  levelScene.health = levelScene.health + 30
}
```

This state may not make much sense just yet. This state allows the game to continue without any actions taking place, it will be used when the player completes the level to give them a moment to enjoy their victory before the victory state is called.

In `GameSceneWinState`, add these methods:

```
override func didEnterWithPreviousState(previousState: GKState?)
{
  levelScene.paused = true
  gameLoopPaused = true

  levelScene.tapState = .nextLevel

  let announce = SKLabelNode(fontNamed: "Avenir-Black")
  announce.position = CGPointZero
  announce.fontSize = 80
  announce.zPosition = 120
  announce.text = "You Won!!!"
  levelScene.overlayLayer.addChild(announce)
}

override func willExitWithNextState(nextState: GKState) {
  gameDifficultyModifier++
  for node in levelScene.overlayLayer.children {
    node.removeFromParent()
  }
}
```

When the player eventually finds the exit, you'll transition to this state. It displays a "You won" overlay, and increases the difficulty for next time.

In `GameSceneLoseState`, add these methods:

```
override func didEnterWithPreviousState(previousState: GKState?)
{
  levelScene.paused = true
  gameLoopPaused = true

  levelScene.tapState = .nextLevel

  let announce = SKLabelNode(fontNamed: "Avenir-Black")
  announce.position = CGPointZero
  announce.fontSize = 80
  announce.zPosition = 120
  announce.text = "You Died!"
  levelScene.overlayLayer.addChild(announce)
}

override func willExitWithNextState(nextState: GKState) {
  for node in levelScene.overlayLayer.children {
    node.removeFromParent()
  }
}
```

If the player runs out of health, you'll transition to this state. It displays a "You lose" overlay.

Return to **GameScene.swift** and add the following inside
`touchesBegan(_:withEvent:)`:

```swift
switch tapState {
case .startGame:
  stateMachine.enterState(GameSceneActiveState.self)
  break
case .attack:
  //To be added

  break
case .dismissPause:
  stateMachine.enterState(GameSceneActiveState.self)
  break
case .nextLevel:
  if let scene = GameScene(fileNamed:"GameScene") {
    scene.scaleMode = (self.scene?.scaleMode)!
    let transition = SKTransition.fadeWithDuration(0.6)
    view!.presentScene(scene, transition: transition)
  }
  break
default:

  break
}
```

Based on the tap state, you perform different actions here. Usually, you switch to a
different state in the state machine.

Then add this line to the top of `update(_:)`:

```swift
if gameLoopPaused { return }
```

This exists the update loop if the game is paused.

Finally, implement `didFinishUpdate()` as follows:

```swift
override func didFinishUpdate() {
  if let label = guiLayer.childNodeWithName("healthLabel") as?
SKLabelNode {
    label.text = "\(health)"
  }
}
```

This simply updates the health label to the player's current health after `update()` has
finished.

Finally, add the splash screen and icon for this app. To do this, delete **Assets.xcasset** from
your project and add the replacement I've created for you in the resources for this
chapter. Then, add an image view to your LaunchScreen.storyboard set up to display

DELVE-splashscreen2. If you forgot how to do this, refer to Chapter 1, "Sprites".

Build and run:

Implementing the drunkard walk

> Note: If you skippead ahead from earlier in this chapter, you can continue with the **starter\Delve_HealthBarAndStates** project in the resources for this chapter. This is the same as where you left off the game in the previous chapter, with the added features of a health bar and basic game states.

The first step to setting up your algorithm is to navigate to the **LevelHelper.swift** file and make the map square. Does it need to be square? Not at all but a square workspace works well for random walk paths as it gives you room to move in each direction. *Modify* this property like so:

```
var mapSize = CGPoint(x: 20, y: 20)
```

Next, you need a way to ensure the path stays within the bounds of the map to avoid overflow errors—after all, there's no telling where a drunk might end up.

To do this, add the following function below `tileMapSize()`; not within the function, but after it:

```
func isValidTile(position position:CGPoint) -> Bool {
  if ((position.x >= 1) && (position.x < (mapSize.x - 1)))
  && ((position.y >= 1) && (position.y < (mapSize.y - 1))) {
    return true
  } else {
    return false
  }
}
```

Based on the position provided in relation to the map size, this function returns `true` if the tile is within bounds, and `false` otherwise.

You also move the boundary in by a tile to avoid ending up with a ground tile next to "air", inadvertently letting the player walk outside the bounds of the map.

Updating the map generator

Proceed to `generateMap()`, remove its contents and replace them with this:

```
//1
var currentLocation = CGPoint(
    x: GKGaussianDistribution(
        lowestValue: 2,
        highestValue: Int(mapSize.x) - 2).nextInt(),
    y: GKGaussianDistribution(
        lowestValue: 2,
        highestValue: Int(mapSize.y) - 2).nextInt())
//2
let direction = GKRandomDistribution(forDieWithSideCount: 4)
```

1. You need a starting point along both the x- and y-axes. While anywhere within the bounds would be fine, using a Gaussian distribution ensures that most of the time, the start point will be toward the middle of the tile map.

2. There are four cardinal directions in which the generator can move; this random distribution will select from among them.

Since the current location will be your starting point, mark it as such by adding the following line right below the two variables you just added:

```
setTile(position: currentLocation, toValue: 4)
```

Build and run to see the result (ignore the warnings for now).

Note: Don't forget to tap to start the game—and see the map!

That's not the most exciting map—yet. However, at least you know procedural map generator is definitely capable of assigning a start point. :]

One problem you can see straight away is that there's no limit to where the character can move. You can fix this by changing the default tile type: The level generator requires them to be walls.

Head over to **GameScene.swift** and update `setupLevel()` by modifying the line that currently reads `worldGen.generateLevel(0)` to this:

```
worldGen.generateLevel(1)
```

Build and run again to see the results of this change. Now the character will be correctly imprisoned in a world of bricks.

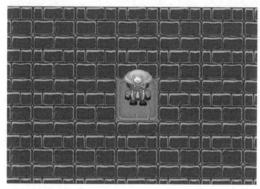

What a nightmare! And he doesn't even have his mining pick yet.

To give your miner more space, navigate back to **LevelHelper.swift** and add the following line at the end of `generateMap()`:

```
var i = 40
```

This will act as your count of how many tiles the procedure should move when creating the path. This number may not be perfect, but you'll be able to tweak it after you begin to see results.

Now, below that variable, add the following code:

```
//1
repeat {
  //2
  var newPosition = CGPointZero
  switch direction.nextInt() {
  case 1:
    newPosition = CGPoint(x: currentLocation.x, y:
currentLocation.y - 1)
  case 2:
```

```
    newPosition = CGPoint(x: currentLocation.x, y:
currentLocation.y + 1)
  case 3:
    newPosition = CGPoint(x: currentLocation.x - 1, y:
currentLocation.y)
  case 4:
    newPosition = CGPoint(x: currentLocation.x + 1, y:
currentLocation.y)
  default:
    break
  }
  //3
  if isValidTile(position: newPosition) {
    //4
    if getTile(position: newPosition) <= 3 {
      currentLocation = newPosition
      i--
      //5
      if i == 0 {
        setTile(position: currentLocation, toValue: 5)
      } else {
        setTile(position: currentLocation, toValue: 3)
      }
    }
  }
} while i > 0
```

1. The process will be repeated until i falls below 0.

2. You create a newPosition variable and assign it a location on the grid, based on the four cardinal directions in which you can move. It doesn't matter which number is which, as long as you cover all four directions.

3. You need to test if the new tile is within the acceptable bounds of the tile map, so you use the isValidTile(position:) function you created earlier.

4. You check if the tile is a wall type. This will make sure you aren't overwriting a start or end point.

5. If all checks pass, you set the tile as a ground tile. If the variable i has reached 0, then you set it to an end tile.

Great! Now build and run to see the magic.

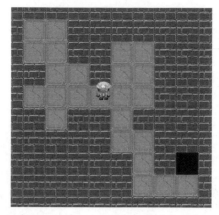

Once again, if all goes according to plan, yours should look completely different from mine. :]

Before you tweak the generator further, now would be a good time to take care of that black hole in your level where the end point should be.

Reaching the exit

Every game has to have a goal; in Delve, it will be going as deep into the dungeon as possible. But to make that possible for the player, your game needs a stairs tile and something to trigger the event of moving from one level to the next—once the hero reaches the tile, of course.

Create a new Swift file inside the **Entities** group and name it **LevelEndEntity.swift**. Replace the contents of the file with the following:

```
import Foundation
import UIKit
import SpriteKit
import GameplayKit

class LevelEndEntity: GKEntity {

  var spriteComponent: SpriteComponent!

  override init() {
    super.init()

    let texture = SKTexture(imageNamed: "Exit")
    spriteComponent = SpriteComponent(entity: self, texture:
texture, size: CGSize(width: 32, height: 32))
    addComponent(spriteComponent)

    let physicsBody = SKPhysicsBody(edgeLoopFromRect:
CGRect(origin: CGPoint(x: -16, y: -16), size: CGSize(width: 8,
```

```
  height: 8)))
      physicsBody.categoryBitMask = ColliderType.EndLevel.rawValue
      physicsBody.dynamic = true
      spriteComponent.node.physicsBody = physicsBody

  }
}
```

This entity is fairly standard. It handles a sprite component and a physics body to detect the touch between the hero and the stairs. It has no other components.

Go to **GameScene.swift**, locate createNodeOf(type: location:) and update the following case statement like so:

```
case .tileEnd:
  let levelEndEntity = LevelEndEntity()
  let levelEndNode = levelEndEntity.spriteComponent.node
  levelEndNode.name = "levelEnd"
  levelEndNode.position = location
  levelEndNode.zPosition = 1
  addEntity(levelEndEntity)
  break
```

Once again, this is very similar to the code you added for your other tiles.

Build and run to make sure the exit tile appears correctly.

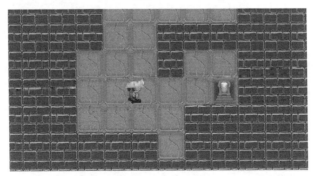

Now, you need to make the exit tile trigger the level change, and make the scene reload with a new level to explore.

Scroll to the bottom of **GameScene.swift** and include this code at the bottom:

```
//MARK: physics contact

func didBeginContact(contact: SKPhysicsContact) {
  let bodyA = contact.bodyA.node
  let bodyB = contact.bodyB.node

  if bodyA?.name == "levelEnd" && bodyB?.name == "playerNode" {
```

```
    stateMachine.enterState(GameSceneWinState.self)
    movement = CGPointZero
  }
}
```

In the previous chapter, you added the `SKPhysicsContactDelegate`, and this is one of the functions that goes with the protocol.

> **Note**: This is a very basic implementation of physics contacts. Under normal circumstances, you would have each node or entity handle the contact themselves. Check out Chapters 9, 10 and 11, "Beginning to Advanced Physics" to learn more about how you could implement this.

One last step. Locate `createNodeOf(type:location:)` and navigate to the `.tileStart` case. Add this code before the `break`:

```
centerCameraOnPoint(location)
```

Now when you build and run, it will look a lot neater as the camera will center on the start point. When you tap to start it will already be in the correct position.

Build and run, and you can now beat the level!

Making better levels

So far, you've had GameplayKit construct each level with a standard random distribution, which can lead to a variety of results.

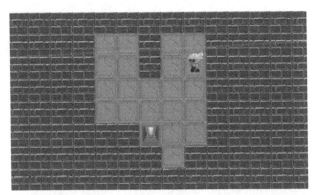

Some of these results aren't great, and if you want to add features to the game, such as enemies or health pick-ups, then there's no logical place to put them right now.

Now you will implement a few improvements to the level generator to create more interesting levels.

Go to your **LevelHelper.swift** file and find generateMap(). Update the direction variable as follows:

```
let direction = GKShuffledDistribution(forDieWithSideCount: 4)
```

In theory, the shuffled distribution will always produce rooms of various sizes and it would be impossible to create a straight corridor, since the generator will have to move in all four directions before it can move in the same direction again.

Build and run to confirm this theory.

As expected, the result is a small room with only small deviations.

Now try updating the direction variable to this:

```
let direction = GKGaussianDistribution(forDieWithSideCount: 4)
```

You would expect the result to still be random, but include corridors in the two directions in the middle of the range.

Build and run to see what sort of level you build.

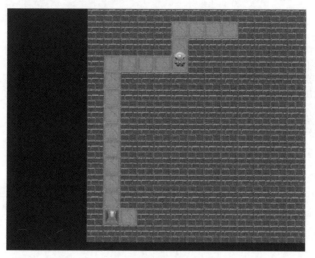

Since the Gaussian distribution doesn't follow strict rules, it's entirely possible that your level looks nothing like this. Also note that this level was built next to a bounding wall, so *down* may not have been the generator's first choice for the direction. That aside, there does seem to be a massive trend in at least two directions.

Combining distributions

You can draw some conclusions from the exercise you just completed:

- **Shuffled distributions** are great for making *rooms* with elements of randomness.
- **Gaussian distributions** are good for making *corridors* in the two most prominent directions.
- **Random distributions** follow no rules—they are "random".

Your challenge now is to create something more interesting by combining different distributions.

Empty the contents of generateMap(). Then begin by adding the following:

```
var currentLocation = CGPoint(
   x: GKGaussianDistribution(lowestValue: 2,
      highestValue: Int(mapSize.x) - 2).nextInt(),
   y: GKGaussianDistribution(lowestValue: 2,
      highestValue: Int(mapSize.y) - 2).nextInt())
setTile(position: currentLocation, toValue: 4)
```

No changes have been made to these lines from when you first implemented them. You select a start point weighted towards the middle of the map by using gaussian distribution then set the first tile as the start point.

Now, add this below the code above:

```
let generators = [GKGaussianDistribution(forDieWithSideCount:
4), GKShuffledDistribution(forDieWithSideCount: 4),
GKRandomDistribution(forDieWithSideCount: 4)]
let generatorPicker = GKRandomDistribution(forDieWithSideCount:
generators.count)
```

You add all distribution types to an array, and then you use an additional random distribution to pick a distribution from the array. Clever, right? :]

You could also cycle between Gaussian and shuffled to get a selection of rooms connected by corridors, but this should produce more interesting results.

Now, you need some rules:

```
let movementsPerSet = 35
let numberOfSets = 15
```

Each generator will run 35 times and then switch to the next generator, 15 times total. Once again, you can tweak this to your liking.

Now, add this:

```
//1
for (var i = numberOfSets; i >= 0; i--) {
  //2
  let currentGen = generators[generatorPicker.nextInt() - 1]
  //3
  for (var j = movementsPerSet; j >= 0; j--) {
    var newPosition = CGPointZero
    switch currentGen.nextInt() {
    case 1:
      newPosition = CGPoint(x: currentLocation.x, y:
        currentLocation.y - 1)
    case 2:
      newPosition = CGPoint(x: currentLocation.x, y:
        currentLocation.y + 1)
    case 3:
      newPosition = CGPoint(x: currentLocation.x - 1,
        y: currentLocation.y)
    case 4:
      newPosition = CGPoint(x: currentLocation.x + 1,
        y: currentLocation.y)
    default:
      break
    }
    if isValidTile(position: newPosition) {
      if getTile(position: newPosition) <= 3 {
        currentLocation = newPosition
        if i == 0 && j == 0 {
          setTile(position: currentLocation, toValue: 5)
        } else {
          setTile(position: currentLocation, toValue: 3)
        }
      }
    }
  }
}
```

Here's what you're doing:

1. You prepare a `for` loop for the number of sets.

2. You select a random distribution, at random. Tired of hearing the word random yet? :]

3. You prepare another `for` loop for the number of generations within each set.

Now, build and run to see your masterpiece of randomness!

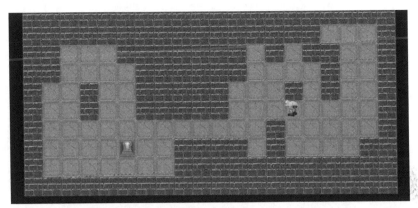

While the levels should be a lot more interesting, after you've generated a few, you'll notice a trend where the level path moves toward the bottom left of the screen.

This is the Gaussian distribution impacting the direction of movement.

It would be great if you could shuffle the directions for each set. It's a good thing you know all about shuffling numbers!

Right under the constants you set for movements per set and numbers of sets, add this:

```
let patternPicker = GKShuffledDistribution(forDieWithSideCount:
4)
```

Now, just inside the first `for` loop, under the `currentGen` constant, add the following:

```
let currentPattern = [patternPicker.nextInt(),
                      patternPicker.nextInt(),
                      patternPicker.nextInt(),
                      patternPicker.nextInt()]
```

Since you're using a shuffled distribution of four possible outcomes, you know the pattern will never contain more than one of each number.

Finally, add this constant above the `switch` and update the `switch` to this:

```
let direction = currentPattern[currentGen.nextInt() - 1]
switch direction {
```

This means that for the entire set, the directions will be based on the pattern. This provides some consistency to the set; however, it also means the next set will probably be completely different. That's exactly what you want, it allows for the possability of consistent hallways but doesn't allow them to always trend in the same direction.

Build and run to explore your new random world.

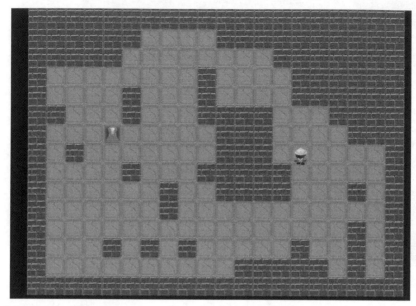

It doesn't have to end here—you can keep tweaking the randomness to your heart's content, as well as adjust the number and size of the sets.

In the real world, everything happens for a reason. The next chapter brings Delve closer to reality by using room/block/sector-based level design with a touch of randomness to make sure there's always variation in the gameplay. This is the same method that games like *Diablo III* and *Spelunky* use to generate their levels to be both functional and unpredictable.

It's also time to think about those rock golems. They're out there somewhere, lurking in the shadows. Don't worry, though—you have a weapon for that!

Challenges

There's just one challenge for this chapter, designed to give you a bit more practice with GameplayKit's randomization.

If you get stuck, you can find solutions in the resources for this chapter—but give this your best shot before you look!

Challenge 1: Random tiles

Doesn't the dungeon look just a tad too pristine to you?

If you were to walk into a thousand year-old dungeon, there's no way the tiles would all look the same. They would have different colorations, be in different conditions, some might have rock golem graffiti...

Lucky for you, there are eight different tile types in the **Tiles.atlas** folder for you to use.

You can add all of these tiles to an array of strings, and then use a random distribution to choose a tile based on the count of the array.

Don't forget, you could also randomize the ground below your player's feet at the start point as well.

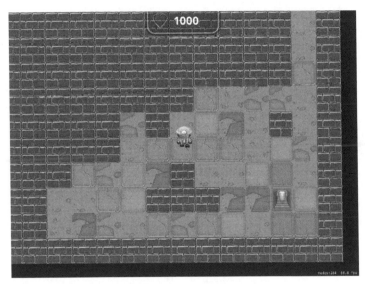

Chapter 23: Procedural Levels

By Neil North

In Chapter 21, "Tile Map Games", you created an entire level of a dungeon game by setting number codes in an array. Then, in Chapter 22, "Randomization", you used GameplayKit's randomization features to procedurally generate entire levels.

In this chapter, you'll use a combination of both techniques to procedurally generate levels in a more controlled manner—so you can make them more fun and interesting for your players while still benefiting from the automation provided by random generators.

As the levels layout become more logical, it also gives you more logical places to spawn game objects. For example, when you enter a kitchen in a new building, it may be completely different to any kitchen you have seen before but you would expect cupboards and benchtops against the walls, a window on at least one side, and that appliances and a sink be on the benchtops. If these expectations aren't met then the kitchen would not feel like a kitchen.

Your overall objective is to make levels that feel as if they were each handcrafted by a human being, not generated on the fly by a machine. Using **room-based procedures** is one of the most effective ways to achieve this. In simple terms, you prebuild a selection of *regions* or *rooms* which the game then stitches together in a random arrangement.

In this chapter, you will implement the new world generator and finish the core functionality of Delve.

Note: This chapter begins where the previous chapter's challenge left off. If you were unable to complete the challenge or skipped ahead from an earlier chapter, don't worry—simply open the starter project from this chapter to pick up in the right place.

Room-based procedural level design

Building levels with room-based procedures entails the following:

- You provide the game with a selection of pre-built rooms that it can place in different patterns.

- Each level is made up of these rooms, either in a grid arrangement, or placed at random within the space and joined by randomly generated corridors.

- While the rooms are pre-built, their arrangement within the grid, or in the level at large, is almost completely random.

- Some rooms can potentially block pathways or entrances to other rooms; however, the game must still have a path from beginning to end.

This technique has a number of advantages, including:

- **Structured and controllable**: The resulting level is still unpredictable, but you maintain a lot of control over the layout and structure of the level.

- **Human-built feel**: Each room is handcrafted by you, making the level feel more like a "real" dungeon.

- **Stability**: While you may not be able to test every permutation your level generator can create, you'll have a lot more confidence than you would in fully random methods.

What about the disadvantages, you ask?

One drawback is that it can be a lot of work to hand-craft enough rooms to keep the game interesting. But for a simple game like Delve, there isn't much to dislike about this method.

Building a better generator

In this update to your level generator, you'll use the grid-based approach to position your rooms. The first thing you need are the rooms to align to your grid.

To simplify the process of laying out the level, you'll make each room the same size: 10 tiles wide by 10 tiles high.

You're going to be procedurally distributing the rooms throughout the grid, but not in an entirely random fashion. So you need to think about any restrictions you might want to put on the positions of the different rooms in order to get a level design that suits your purposes. For example, you don't want to inadvertently leave any gaps in the walls that lead outside the bounds of the level.

Below is a sample level with slicing to show where each room is situated and what type of room it is.

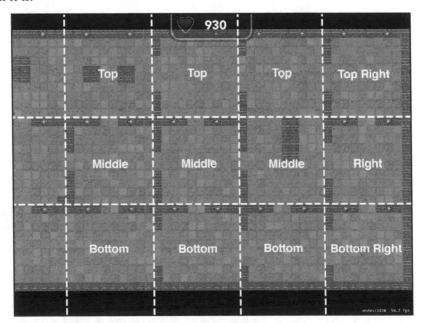

Take a look at each section and note its characteristics.

Each section contains wall pieces for the left side and top of the room only (with the exception of sections at the bottom and right sides of tile map). This makes it easier to create adjoining rooms, and helps you avoid walls of double thickness, which would cost you space.

Now that you've seen the layout, it's time to start building the rooms.

Building the rooms

Open your project from the last chapter, or if you didn't complete that chapter, open the starter project provided at **starter\Delve**.

There are a few different ways you can store your room data. One of the simplest and safest is using structs.

In the **Helpers** group, create a new file named **LevelComponents.swift**.

Replace the contents of the file with the following:

```swift
import Foundation

struct tileMapSection {
  struct sectionMiddle {

  }
  struct sectionTopLeft {

  }
  struct sectionTopRight {

  }
  struct sectionBottomLeft {

  }
  struct sectionBottomRight {

  }
  struct sectionLeft {

  }
  struct sectionRight {

  }
  struct sectionTop {

  }
  struct sectionBottom {

  }
}
```

Each section of the grid with have its own set of one or more rooms, each room with a different tile configuration.

Next comes the creative part: making the rooms. It can be quite confusing to work with a bunch of numbers, so I recommend keeping this reference somewhere handy:

```
Air          = 0
Wall         = 1
Wall Light   = 2
Ground       = 3
Start        = 4
Finish       = 5
Enemy Spawn  = 6
Food Spawn   = 7
```

To each section struct, add the following:

```
static let sections:[[[Int]]] = []
```

The `sections` constant contains a three-dimensional array. You're grouping your column and row data, again, by each room template.

To give you an example, update the `sectionMiddle` struct as follows:

```
static let sections:[[[Int]]] = [
    [
        [1,1,2,1,3,3,1,2,1,1],
        [1,3,3,3,3,3,3,3,3,3],
        [1,3,3,3,3,3,3,3,3,3],
        [1,3,3,3,3,6,6,3,3,3],
        [3,3,3,3,3,3,3,3,3,3],
        [3,3,3,3,3,6,6,3,3,3],
        [1,3,3,3,3,3,3,3,3,3],
        [1,3,3,3,3,3,3,3,3,3],
        [1,3,3,3,3,3,3,3,3,3],
        [1,3,3,3,3,3,3,3,3,3],
    ],
    [
        [1,1,2,1,3,3,1,2,1,1],
        [1,3,3,3,3,3,3,3,3,3],
        [3,3,3,3,3,3,3,3,3,3],
        [3,3,3,1,1,1,1,1,3,3],
        [1,3,3,1,3,3,3,1,3,3],
        [1,3,3,1,3,6,3,1,3,3],
        [3,3,3,1,3,3,3,1,3,3],
        [3,3,3,3,3,3,3,3,3,3],
        [1,3,3,3,3,3,3,3,3,3],
        [1,3,3,3,3,3,3,3,3,3],
    ]
]
```

Each section in the array is a ten by ten tile map room. In `sectionMiddle` the walls have been placed on the left and top sides. It can be daunting to look at a block of numbers but with some practice you will start to see each room like this:

Now, you'll need to create rooms for all the section types. How many rooms you create for each section depends on the level of variation you'd like.

If you aren't feeling creative or simply don't wish to make all of the rooms, you can find an already completed version of the **LevelComponents.swift** file located at **starter \Resources** for your convenience.

> **Note**: Having lots of physics bodies can present complicated calculations each frame, and the more of them you have, the more likely you are to experience a frame rate drop. Keep this in mind when adding wall tiles to your rooms.

Once you have at least one room for each section, you're ready to update the level generator. Feel free to add more than one room per section. I'm sure you realize by now that more is better!

Navigate to **LevelHelper.swift** and add these variables to your `tileMap` struct:

```
let sectionSize = CGPoint(x: 10, y: 10)
var sections = CGPoint(x: 5, y: 3)
```

The `sectionSize` constant sets the size of each room as 10 by 10 tiles. You also need to know how many rooms there will be on the grid; you handle this in the `sections` variable.

Now your `mapSize` variable is wrong. There's a quick and easy way to handle this problem. Update `mapSize` as follows:

```
var mapSize:CGPoint {
  get {
    return CGPoint(x: sections.x * sectionSize.x,
```

```
      y: sections.y * sectionSize.y)
  }
}
```

This code will calculate the map size every time you request it, based on the number of sections and the number of tiles within each section.

You need a simpler way to copy a room template to your tile map layer. Add this function under the level creation area of the level helper class:

```
mutating func setTilesByTemplate(template:
[[Int]],sectionIndex:CGPoint) {
  for (indexr, row) in template.enumerate() {
    for (indexc, cvalue) in row.enumerate() {
      setTile(position: CGPoint(
        x: (Int(sectionIndex.x * sectionSize.x) + indexc),
        y: (Int(sectionIndex.y * sectionSize.y) + indexr)),
        toValue: cvalue)
    }
  }
}
```

The function accepts the template, which is a two-dimensional array of tiles. It also accepts a section index, which lets you locate the position of each tile within its section.

Now you need a way to handle the layout of the rooms. Add this function below `generateMap()`:

```
mutating func setTemplateBy(rowIndex:Int,leftTiles:[[[Int]]],
  middleTiles:[[[Int]]], rightTiles:[[[Int]]]) {

  var randomSection = GKRandomDistribution()

  //Left Tiles
  randomSection = GKRandomDistribution(
    forDieWithSideCount: leftTiles.count)
  setTilesByTemplate(leftTiles[randomSection.nextInt() - 1],
    sectionIndex: CGPoint(x: 0, y: rowIndex))

  //Right Tiles
  randomSection = GKRandomDistribution(
    forDieWithSideCount: rightTiles.count)
  setTilesByTemplate(rightTiles[randomSection.nextInt() - 1],
    sectionIndex: CGPoint(x: Int(sections.x - 1), y: rowIndex))

  //Middle Tiles
  var i = 2
  randomSection = GKRandomDistribution(
    forDieWithSideCount: middleTiles.count)
  repeat {
    setTilesByTemplate(middleTiles[randomSection.nextInt() - 1],
```

```
      sectionIndex: CGPoint(x: i - 1, y: rowIndex))
    i++
  } while i < Int(sections.x)

}
```

When you run this function, you pass in the row index for the section, and the sections from which you wish to select rooms. For example, if you were adding the bottom row of the grid, then you'd pass in an index of the count of total rows minus one, and then the bottom-left, bottom-middle and bottom-right sections.

Locate `generateMap()` and replace its contents with the following:

```
//top Row
setTemplateBy(0,
  leftTiles: tileMapSection.sectionTopLeft.sections,
  middleTiles: tileMapSection.sectionTop.sections,
  rightTiles: tileMapSection.sectionTopRight.sections)

//Middle Row
var row = 2
repeat {
  setTemplateBy(row - 1,
    leftTiles: tileMapSection.sectionLeft.sections,
    middleTiles: tileMapSection.sectionMiddle.sections,
    rightTiles: tileMapSection.sectionRight.sections)
  row++
} while row < Int(sections.y)

//Bottom Row
setTemplateBy((Int(sections.y) - 1),
  leftTiles: tileMapSection.sectionBottomLeft.sections,
  middleTiles: tileMapSection.sectionBottom.sections,
  rightTiles: tileMapSection.sectionBottomRight.sections)
```

For each type of row, you run the function you just added. Since there can be more than one middle row, you repeat the function until you run out of middle rows.

You're passing in the section information from **LevelComponent.swift**, so you can add and remove rooms freely without touching this code.

Build and run to test your new procedural level generator.

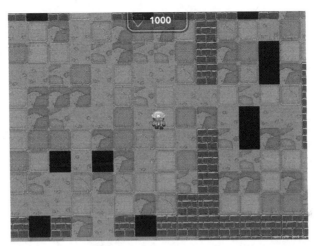

Even though our results are completely different, I can say with confidence that your dungeon looks great! Except for the black holes everywhere—it's time to fill them with content.

> **Note**: For the rest of this chapter, you're going to implement the remaining tiles and gameplay for Delve. It's pretty cool stuff, but if you only wanted to learn about procedural levels, feel free to skip to the next chapter, where you'll learn how to add support for game controllers.

Filling the dungeon

That has an ominous ring to it, doesn't it? Unless you're creating a game of pure exploration, your game won't be all that compelling without enemies, collectables and other objects.

First, no dungeon is complete without torches on the walls. Navigate to **GameScene.swift** and locate `createNodeOf(type:location:)`. You'll be creating a new wall, except this one will have a torch. It won't act any differently than a regular wall; it will simply look different.

Update the `.tileWallLit` case as follows:

```
case .tileWallLit:
  let node = SKSpriteNode(texture:
atlasTiles.textureNamed("Wall2"))
  node.size = CGSize(width: 32, height: 32)
  node.position = location
```

```
    node.zPosition = 1
    node.physicsBody = SKPhysicsBody(edgeLoopFromRect: CGRect(
      origin: CGPoint(x: -16, y: -16),
      size: CGSize(width: 32, height: 32)))
    node.physicsBody?.categoryBitMask = ColliderType.Wall.rawValue
    node.name = "wall"
    worldLayer.addChild(node)
    break
```

That's it. Build and run to make sure your wall tiles appear correctly and that your miner can't pass through any of them.

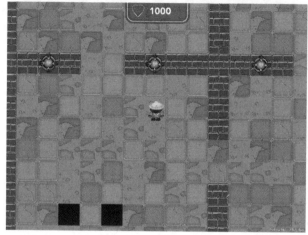

There are still some black spots. That's OK! You'll fill in those areas next.

Handling health

There isn't anything in the level that can harm you yet. The rock golems will emerge from the shadows soon, but in the meantime, you need something to give the character a sense of urgency to escape the level.

Dungeons aren't always the most healthy of environments, so the player's health will decline automatically over time.

In **GameScene.swift**, add this below your other instance variables:

```
//Timers
var lastHealthDrop: NSTimeInterval = 0
```

This will let you track the time between drops in health.

Proceed to the update(_:) loop and insert the following right above the **"Update all components"** comment:

```
//Periodically change health and report
//1
if currentTime > (lastHealthDrop + 2.0) {
  health = health - 5
  lastHealthDrop = currentTime
}

//2
if health < 1 {
  stateMachine.enterState(GameSceneLoseState.self)
}
```

There are a couple of steps here:

1. This makes the miner's health drop by five for every two seconds the game is running. All told, this gives the player about six and a half minutes to complete the level. That may seem like a lot, but when enemies are attacking, time will fly!

2. If health is below 1, then the hero has died, and you'll progress the game to the losing screen.

To make sure everything works as expected, build and run, and keep an eye on the health bar at the top of the screen.

Gameplay can feel rather bleak when all you seem to do is lose health. You can fix that by adding health boosts.

In your **Entities** group, add a new file named **FoodEntity.swift**. Replace the code inside with the following:

```
import Foundation
import UIKit
import SpriteKit
import GameplayKit

class FoodEntity: GKEntity {

  var spriteComponent: SpriteComponent {
    guard let spriteComponent =
componentForClass(SpriteComponent.self)
      else { fatalError("MobEntity must have a SpriteComponent") }
  }
    return spriteComponent
  }
```

```
    override init() {
      super.init()

      let texture = SKTexture(imageNamed: "Health")
      let spriteComponent = SpriteComponent(entity: self,
        texture: texture, size: CGSize(width: 32, height: 32))
      addComponent(spriteComponent)
      let physicsBody = SKPhysicsBody(rectangleOfSize:
        CGSize(width: 25, height: 25))
      physicsBody.categoryBitMask = ColliderType.Food.rawValue
      physicsBody.collisionBitMask = ColliderType.None.rawValue
      physicsBody.contactTestBitMask =
ColliderType.Player.rawValue
      physicsBody.allowsRotation = false

      spriteComponent.node.physicsBody = physicsBody
    }
}
```

This entity is very straightforward: It's a non-animated sprite node with which the hero can make contact.

To implement the entity, go to **GameScene.swift** and locate the `.tileFood` case in `createNodeOf(type:location:)`. Once you find it, update it with this:

```
case .tileFood:
   //1
   let node = SKSpriteNode(texture:
atlasTiles.textureNamed(textureStrings[randomFloorTile.nextInt()
 - 1]))
   node.size = CGSize(width: 32, height: 32)
   node.position = location
   node.zPosition = 1
   worldLayer.addChild(node)
   //2
   let food = FoodEntity()
   food.spriteComponent.node.name = "foodNode"
   food.spriteComponent.node.position = location
   food.spriteComponent.node.zPosition = 5
   addEntity(food)
   break
```

Have a look at what this code is doing:

1. Since the food will be collectable, you need to add a ground tile underneath it.

2. Add the food to the scene, and remember to name it correctly, as you'll be using the name for the contact delegate.

Build and run to make sure the food appears correctly in your scene.

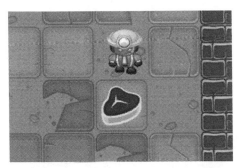

While it looks tasty, nothing happens when you make contact with it. Scroll down to `didBeginContact(_:)` and add this `if` statement at the bottom:

```
if bodyA?.name == "foodNode" {
  if bodyB?.name == "playerNode" {
    bodyA?.removeFromParent()
    health = health + 40
  }
}
```

When a node named **"playerNode"** makes contact with a node named **"foodNode"**, you remove the food node from the scene and increase the hero's health by 40 points.

Build and run to test the health boost.

> **Note:** You still want the player to feel under pressure, so don't set the health boost too high. It should be enough to make it worth picking up, but not essential to completing the level successfully.

Bring in the rock golems

You've stirred up quite a fuss by delving into the dungeons of the rock golems. Now, they're coming to get you!

A texture atlas has been provided for you at **starter\Resources** with the name **enemy.atlas**. Drag the texture atlas into the **Resources** group in your project.

You'll need a new entity to support your enemy characters. In your **Entities** group, add a new file named **EnemyEntity.swift**.

Replace the contents of the file with this:

```
import Foundation
import UIKit
import SpriteKit
import GameplayKit

class EnemyEntity: GKEntity {

  var spriteComponent: SpriteComponent!
  var animationComponent: AnimationComponent!
  var enemyHealth:CGFloat = 1.0

}
```

You provide a link to the sprite and animation components and a variable for the enemies' health. They're made from stone and some sort of magic, so you would expect they could take a hit or two, right?

Under your variables, add the following override initializer:

```
override init() {
  super.init()

  let atlas = SKTextureAtlas(named: "enemy")
  let texture = atlas.textureNamed("EnemyWalk_0_00.png")
  let textureSize = CGSize(width: 40, height: 42)
  spriteComponent = SpriteComponent(entity: self, texture:
texture, size: textureSize)
  addComponent(spriteComponent)
  let moveComponent = EnemyMoveComponent(entity: self)
  addComponent(moveComponent)
  animationComponent = AnimationComponent(node:
spriteComponent.node, textureSize: textureSize, animations:
loadAnimations())
  addComponent(animationComponent)

  let physicsBody = SKPhysicsBody(rectangleOfSize: CGSize(width:
32, height: 32))

  physicsBody.categoryBitMask = ColliderType.Enemy.rawValue
  physicsBody.collisionBitMask = ColliderType.Wall.rawValue
  physicsBody.contactTestBitMask = ColliderType.Player.rawValue
  physicsBody.allowsRotation = false

  spriteComponent.node.physicsBody = physicsBody
```

```
    }
```

You'll notice two errors at this point:

- You don't currently have a movement component for enemies. You'll be adding this soon.

- There's no `loadAnimations()`. You'll add that right now!

Under the initializer, add this function:

```
func loadAnimations() -> [AnimationState: Animation] {
  let textureAtlas = SKTextureAtlas(named: "enemy")
  var animations = [AnimationState: Animation]()
  //1
  animations[.Walk_Down] =
    AnimationComponent.animationFromAtlas(textureAtlas,
    withImageIdentifier: AnimationState.Walk_Down.rawValue,
    forAnimationState: .Walk_Down)
  animations[.Walk_Up] =
    AnimationComponent.animationFromAtlas(textureAtlas,
    withImageIdentifier: AnimationState.Walk_Up.rawValue,
    forAnimationState: .Walk_Up)
  animations[.Walk_Left] =
    AnimationComponent.animationFromAtlas(textureAtlas,
    withImageIdentifier: AnimationState.Walk_Left.rawValue,
    forAnimationState: .Walk_Left)
  animations[.Walk_Right] =
    AnimationComponent.animationFromAtlas(textureAtlas,
    withImageIdentifier: AnimationState.Walk_Right.rawValue,
    forAnimationState: .Walk_Right)
  //2
  animations[.Die_Down] =
    AnimationComponent.animationFromAtlas(textureAtlas,
    withImageIdentifier: AnimationState.Die_Down.rawValue,
    forAnimationState: .Die_Down,repeatTexturesForever: false)

  return animations
}
```

It looks like a lot of code, but it's pretty straightforward:

1. If the golem is onscreen, you'd expect it to be walking toward you, so it doesn't need an idle state. Make sure you have animations for all four directions.

2. You'll be doing your best to fight back against the golems, so if you have any intention of winning the battle, you definitely need to give them a death state.

The entity is almost ready, but you're still missing a movement component. In the **Components** group, add a new file named **EnemyMoveComponent.swift**.

Replace the contents of the file with this:

```
import SpriteKit
import GameplayKit
```

Before you add the component, it's important to consider that it will work a little differently than the other updatable components.

This component will require the position of the hero character for every update; it will check if the hero is within the follow range, and if so, attempt to follow him.

There are a few ways you could handle this, but one of the most efficient would be to modify the component's system. It already sends an update command every frame, so it may as well provide the location of the hero, too.

> **Note**: Another good way to do this would be to use GameplayKit's Agents, Goals, and Behaviors, as you learned in Chapter 20, "Agents, Goals and Behaviors." For this chapter, you will roll your own simple movement component, but if you want more advanced movement behavior, definitely look into that.

Add the following code under the imports:

```
class EnemyMoveComponentSystem: GKComponentSystem {

    func updateWithDeltaTime(seconds: NSTimeInterval,
  playerPosition: CGPoint) {
      for component in components {
        if let enemyComp = component as? EnemyMoveComponent {
          enemyComp.updateWithDeltaTime(seconds, playerPosition:
  playerPosition)
        }
      }
    }

}
```

A component system normally has a function to update all of its components; this one now has a function to do that and pass in the `playerPosition` as well.

Directly below this class, add another class declaration:

```
class EnemyMoveComponent: GKComponent {

}
```

The movement component will need access to the sprite to alter its location, and access to the animation to change the animation that's currently running. Add this code inside the new class you just created:

```
var isAttacking = false

var spriteComponent: SpriteComponent {
  guard let spriteComponent =
entity?.componentForClass(SpriteComponent.self) else
{ fatalError("A MovementComponent's entity must have a
SpriteComponent") }
  return spriteComponent
}

var animationComponent: AnimationComponent {
  guard let animationComponent =
entity?.componentForClass(AnimationComponent.self) else
{ fatalError("A MovementComponent's entity must have an
AnimationComponent") }
  return animationComponent
}

init(entity: GKEntity) {

}
```

You've also added an `isAttacking` variable, so that once an enemy is activated, it will follow you and not stop until it's dead!

Before you add the update loop, there's some additional information you'll need about how the enemies move and acquire their targets.

Go to **GameSettings.swift** and add the following inside the `playerSettings` struct:

```
//Enemy
static let enemyMoveSpeed: CGFloat = 70.0
static let enemySenseRadius: CGFloat = 300.0
static let enemyDamagePerHit: CGFloat = 0.55
```

You can adjust the speed and target acquisition radius as required. The health property you added above is equal to 1.0; if each attack does 0.55 damage, then it will take two hits to kill an enemy.

Return to **EnemyMoveComponent.swift** and add this function below your initializer:

```
func updateWithDeltaTime(seconds: NSTimeInterval,
playerPosition: CGPoint) {
  super.updateWithDeltaTime(seconds)
}
```

Now, your component implements the update function described by your component system.

The first thing you'll need to decide is if the enemy should start attacking. Add this code within the braces:

```
if spriteComponent.node.position.distanceTo(playerPosition) <
  playerSettings.enemySenseRadius {
    isAttacking = true
}
```

Using an SKTUtils extension named distanceTo(_:), and the game setting you added above, you check if the hero is within range. If the hero's close enough, you send the enemy on the attack.

If isAttacking is true, then you'll need to move the enemy. Add this right below the code you just added:

```
if isAttacking {
  //1
  var direction = (playerPosition -
spriteComponent.node.position)
  direction.normalize()
  direction = CGPoint(x: direction.x * (CGFloat(seconds) *
playerSettings.enemyMoveSpeed), y: direction.y *
(CGFloat(seconds) * playerSettings.enemyMoveSpeed))
  //2
  spriteComponent.node.position += direction
  //3
  switch direction.angle {
  case CGFloat(45).degreesToRadians() ..<
CGFloat(135).degreesToRadians():
    animationComponent.requestedAnimationState = .Walk_Up
    break
  case CGFloat(-135).degreesToRadians() ..<
CGFloat(-45).degreesToRadians():
    animationComponent.requestedAnimationState = .Walk_Down
    break
  case CGFloat(-45).degreesToRadians() ..<
CGFloat(45).degreesToRadians():
```

```
    animationComponent.requestedAnimationState = .Walk_Right
    break
  default:
    animationComponent.requestedAnimationState = .Walk_Left
    break
  }
}
```

Take a closer look at what this code is doing:

1. You find the direction from the enemy to the player by subtracting the enemy position from the player position. Then, using the `SKTUtils` normalize function, you reduce the distance to a common peak. Then, you work out how far to move the hero by using the delta time, the new direction and the enemy speed.

2. You update the sprite node's position by adding the direction. Once again, this isn't standard functionality and requires `SKTUtils`.

3. Just as the hero required, you'll need to calculate the angle of the enemy's walk. Unlike the hero, there's no idle state, so you don't need to handle a zero angle.

Those are all the components your enemy needs! But before you can preview it, you need to add the character to the scene.

Proceed to **GameScene.swift** and scroll to the Entity-Component system instance variables at the top of the file. Your new component system is a little different from the ones in the array, so add it separately, underneath the variables:

```
let enemyMoveSystem = EnemyMoveComponentSystem(componentClass:
EnemyMoveComponent.self)
```

Scroll down to `update(_:)` and replace the code just below the **"Update player after components"** comment with this:

```
if let player = worldLayer.childNodeWithName("playerNode") as?
EntityNode,
  let playerEntity = player.entity as? PlayerEntity {
  //1
  enemyMoveSystem.updateWithDeltaTime(deltaTime,
    playerPosition: player.position)
  //2
  centerCameraOnPoint(player.position)
  //3
  if (lastHurt > 1.2) {
    playerEntity.animationComponent.node.shader = nil
  } else {
    lastHurt = lastHurt + deltaTime
  }
}
```

You can break it down into three steps:

1. If the player exists, then you tell the enemy movement system the player's current location and the delta time.

2. You center the camera on the player.

3. You haven't yet implemented what happens when the player takes damage. When you get to this stage, this code will remove the shader applied to your character when he takes damage.

Since you haven't implemented the lastHurt timer, go to your class properties again and add this under the lastDeltaTime property:

```
var lastHurt: CFTimeInterval = 5.0
```

Now, you can finally add the enemy to the scene. Go to createNodeOf(type: location:) and update the .tileEnemy as follows:

```
case .tileEnemy:
  let node = SKSpriteNode(texture:
atlasTiles.textureNamed(textureStrings[randomFloorTile.nextInt()
- 1]))
  node.size = CGSize(width: 32, height: 32)
  node.position = location
  node.zPosition = 1
  worldLayer.addChild(node)

  let enemyEntity = EnemyEntity()
  let enemyNode = enemyEntity.spriteComponent.node
  enemyNode.position = location
  enemyNode.name = "enemySprite"
  enemyNode.zPosition = 55
  enemyEntity.spriteComponent.node.name = "enemyNode"
  enemyEntity.animationComponent.requestedAnimationState
= .Walk_Down
  addEntity(enemyEntity)
  break
```

To make sure you've added the enemy to the right layer, go to addEntity(_:) and replace what's currently there with this:

```
entities.insert(entity)

for componentSystem in self.componentSystems {
  componentSystem.addComponentWithEntity(entity)
}
enemyMoveSystem.addComponentWithEntity(entity)

if let spriteNode =
entity.componentForClass(SpriteComponent.self)?.node {
```

```
    if spriteNode.name == "enemyNode" {
      enemyLayer.addChild(spriteNode)
    } else {
      worldLayer.addChild(spriteNode)
    }
  }
```

Build and run to see your enemies in action!

They flock toward the hero just as you want, but they don't do anything when they make contact with him.

Go to `didBeginContact(_:)` and add the following just above the `foodNode` if statement:

```
if bodyA?.name == "enemyNode" {
  if bodyB?.name == "playerNode" {
    //1
    bodyA?.removeFromParent()
    //2
    health = health - 50
    if let player = worldLayer.childNodeWithName("playerNode")
      as? EntityNode,

      let playerEntity = player.entity as? PlayerEntity {


playerEntity.spriteComponent.node.removeActionForKey("flash")

playerEntity.spriteComponent.node.runAction(SKAction.sequence([
        SKAction.colorizeWithColor(SKColor.redColor(),
          colorBlendFactor: 1.0, duration: 0.5),
        SKAction.colorizeWithColor(SKColor.whiteColor(),
          colorBlendFactor: 1.0, duration: 0.5),
      ]), withKey: "flash")
      lastHurt = 0.0

    }
  }
}
```

Look at each step in turn:

1. Upon impact with a player, you destroy the rock golem. It's harsh, but if they want to protect the dungeon, sacrifices must be made.

2. You reduce the player's health by 50, which means that even if you're a fast runner, you can't really afford to take too many hits.

3. In all of the chaos, it can be hard to tell if you're taking damage. You signal this quite clearly by adding a simple sequence of actions that makes the hero flash red when hit.

Build and run, and test the contacts.

It works as you intended. But it's a little rough: one miner against hordes of rock golems, with no way to defend himself. Now you're going to tip the scales.

Creating a projectile

Armed with an unlimited supply of mining picks, the hero will be prepared to fight off the hordes of rock golems.

All movement in the game happens via the accelerometer, so the screen itself is completely free to accept inputs that affect the gameplay.

Thanks to the camera, the hero remains at the center of the screen. A tap to the left of the hero will throw the projectile left, while a tap to the right will throw right, and so forth all the way around the circle. You'll be able to throw the projectile from all 360 degrees around the hero, based on the tap location.

To make the gameplay more fluid and ease the player's frenzied hands, when the player taps a direction, the hero should continue throwing in that direction until the player taps a different direction. You'll also need to make sure the hero can't throw the weapon too frequently.

Go to your properties in **GameScene.swift** and locate the timers. Add this to the timers:

```
var lastThrow: NSTimeInterval = 0
```

Also, in your properties, there's a section for controls. Add the following in that section:

```
var playerAttack = CGPointZero
```

This is where you'll the store angle of the attack until the player selects a new angle.

Now, scroll down to touchesBegan(_:) and find the .attack case; update it as follows:

```
case .attack:
  for touch in touches {
    let location = touch.locationInNode(self)
    if let player = worldLayer.childNodeWithName("playerNode") {
      playerAttack = location - player.position
    }
  }
  break
```

Based on the location of the tap in relation to the hero's position, you update the playerAttack instance variable.

Now, navigate to update(_:), which is where you'll be telling the hero to throw his weapon. At the bottom of the function, add this code:

```
    if playerAttack != CGPointZero {
      if lastUpdateTimeInterval > (lastThrow + 0.3) {
        if let player = worldLayer.childNodeWithName("playerNode")
{
          let atlasTiles = SKTextureAtlas(named: "Tiles")
          let node = SKSpriteNode(texture:
atlasTiles.textureNamed("Projectile"))
          node.size = CGSize(width: 18, height: 24)
          node.zPosition = 65
          let projEntity = ProjectileEntity(withNode: node,
origin: player.position, direction: playerAttack)
          addEntity(projEntity)
          lastThrow = lastUpdateTimeInterval
        }
      }
    }
```

To recap, you've already set up the controls for selecting the direction of the throw, and with this code, you implement the throwing action itself.

> **Note**: If you don't want the player to auto-throw the weapon, you can set
> `playerAttack` back to `CGPointZero` at the end of the `if` statement, and it won't
> fire again until the next tap.

You'll get an error at this point, because you haven't created the projectile entity yet.
Now would be a great time to add it. :]

In the **Entities** group, create a new file named **ProjectileEntity.swift** and replace its
contents with the following:

```
import Foundation
import UIKit
import SpriteKit
import GameplayKit

class ProjectileEntity: GKEntity {

}
```

Now in the **Components** group, create another new file named
ProjMoveComponent.swift and replace its contents with the following:

```
import SpriteKit
import GameplayKit

class ProjMoveComponent: GKComponent {
  //1
  var node = EntityNode()
  var nodeDirection = CGPointZero
  //2
  let projSpeed = CGFloat(235.5)
  let projRotationSpeed = CGFloat(15.5)
  //3
  init(entity: GKEntity, origin:CGPoint, direction:CGPoint) {

    node.entity = entity
    node.position = origin
    nodeDirection = direction
    //4
    nodeDirection.normalize()
  }

  override func updateWithDeltaTime(seconds: NSTimeInterval) {
    super.updateWithDeltaTime(seconds)
    //5
    node.zRotation = node.zRotation + (CGFloat(seconds) *
projRotationSpeed)
    //6
    node.position = CGPoint(x: (node.position.x +
```

```
(nodeDirection.x * (projSpeed * CGFloat(seconds))))), y:
(node.position.y + (nodeDirection.y * (projSpeed *
CGFloat(seconds))))))
    }
}
```

Let's move step by step through this class definition:

1. Since there are no animations, there's no reason why this component can't have its own sprite instead of using a sprite component.

2. You can tweak the speed and rotation until you feel comfortable with the results.

3. This initializer is a little different, since the entity already knows its behavior at the point node creation.

4. Remember to normalize to remove increases or decreases in speed, based on how close or how far away the tap is from the hero.

5. You set the rotation of the node based on the speed, delta time and current rotation.

6. You set a new position for the node based on the direction, speed and delta time.

Now, go back to **ProjectileEntity.swift** to finish implementing the entity.

Add this code in your entity class:

```
var projComponent: ProjMoveComponent!

init(withNode node: SKSpriteNode, origin: CGPoint, direction:
CGPoint) {
  super.init()

  projComponent = ProjMoveComponent(entity: self, origin:origin,
  direction:direction)
  addComponent(projComponent)

  let physicsBody = SKPhysicsBody(rectangleOfSize: CGSize(width:
10, height: 20))

  node.position = CGPointZero

  physicsBody.categoryBitMask = ColliderType.Projectile.rawValue
  physicsBody.collisionBitMask = ColliderType.None.rawValue
  physicsBody.contactTestBitMask = ColliderType.Wall.rawValue |
ColliderType.Enemy.rawValue

  physicsBody.dynamic = true

  projComponent.node.physicsBody = physicsBody
  projComponent.node.name = "projectile"
  projComponent.node.addChild(node)
}
```

This is very similar to your other entities, but take note that each initializer must know the node, the origin point of the throw and the direction of the throw.

Go back to **GameScene.swift** and locate `addEntity(_:)`. Have a look at its structure.

The function adds nodes on the assumption that they belong to a `SpriteComponent`. Since this component is a little different, add the following code at the end of the function:

```
if let projNode =
entity.componentForClass(ProjMoveComponent.self)?.node {
  worldLayer.addChild(projNode)
}
```

There's one last thing: You need to implement the component system for the projectile move component—unless you want to leave a trail of pick axes behind you, that is.

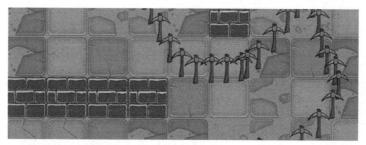

In your instance variables for **GameScene.swift**, update the component system to be as follows:

```
lazy var componentSystems: [GKComponentSystem] = {
  let animationSystem = GKComponentSystem(componentClass:
AnimationComponent.self)
  let projMoveSystem = GKComponentSystem(componentClass:
ProjMoveComponent.self)
  let playerMoveSystem = GKComponentSystem(componentClass:
PlayerMoveComponent.self)
  return [animationSystem, projMoveSystem, playerMoveSystem]
}()
```

Now you can build and run to make sure the projectile works as intended.

The weapon works, but you still need to configure its contacts. If the projectile hits an enemy, you need to inflict damage on that enemy and destroy the projectile.

You should also destroy the projectile if it hits a wall. You don't want the hero to be able to kill enemies through the walls.

At the bottom of the GameScene class, add this function:

```
func damageEnemy(projectile:SKNode, enemyNode:SKNode) {
  //1
  projectile.removeFromParent()
  if let enemy = enemyNode as? EntityNode,
    let enemyEnt = enemy.entity as? EnemyEntity {
      //2 Enemy takes damange
      enemyEnt.enemyHealth = enemyEnt.enemyHealth -
        playerSettings.enemyDamagePerHit
      //3 Kill enemy if damage is significant
      if enemyEnt.enemyHealth <= 0.0 {
        enemyMoveSystem.removeComponentWithEntity(enemyEnt)
        enemyEnt.animationComponent.requestedAnimationState
= .Die_Down
        //4
        enemy.runAction(SKAction.sequence([
          SKAction.runBlock({ () -> Void in
            enemy.physicsBody = nil
          }),SKAction.waitForDuration(2.5),
            SKAction.fadeOutWithDuration(0.5),
            SKAction.removeFromParent()]))
      } else {
        //Damaged but not killed
      }
    }
}
```

Here's what you're doing in this function:

1. You destroy the projectile on impact and remove it from the scene.

2. You inflict the standard damage on the enemy from your playerSettings.

3. If the enemy's health is equal to or below 0.0, you kill the enemy. This includes setting its animation to the death state and removing its move component.

4. To stop the miner from taking damage as he walks over the body, you remove the enemy's physics body. After a short period of time, you fade the alpha channel of the enemy to 0.0 and remove the enemy from the scene.

This gives you a very smooth way to handle enemy deaths.

Scroll up to didBeginContact(_:) and add the following:

```
//1
if bodyA?.name == "wall" {
  if bodyB?.name == "projectile" {
    bodyB?.removeFromParent()
  }
}

//2
```

```
if bodyA?.name == "projectile" {
  if bodyB?.name == "enemyNode" {
    damageEnemy(bodyA!, enemyNode: bodyB!)
  }
}

if bodyA?.name == "enemyNode" {
  if bodyB?.name == "projectile" {
    damageEnemy(bodyB!, enemyNode: bodyA!)
  }
}
```

1. If the projectile makes contact with the wall, you destroy the projectile.

2. If either the projectile or the enemy makes contact with each other, then you run the function you created in the last code block.

Build and run to show those rock golems who's boss!

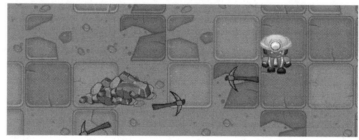

You've now implemented the core mechanics and given your levels structure. This is the point at which you can have some fun trying different grid sizes and room layouts.

But there's still a lot of great functionality to cover. Once you're ready, proceed to the next and final chapter for Delve, where you'll add a lot of important polish to take this game from beta to production quality. You'll also prepare Delve to run on the new Apple TV with tvOS, and give it production-quality resources.

Dungeon crawlers like Delve feel great when played with a video game controller. You'll be adding support for controllers in both iOS and tvOS environments, using a class that's easy to port to any iOS or tvOS game!

Challenges

In addition to procedurally generating levels, you can increase the game's difficulty procedurally too. Your challenge is to give that a shot!

As always, you can find the solution among the chapter's resources—but give it your best shot first.

Challenge 1: Difficulty

As you complete each level, the level counter goes up, but the difficulty doesn't change at all. Can you think of a way to make the game incrementally more difficult as the player delves deeper into the dungeon?

In **GameSettings.swift**, there's already a variable by the name of `gameDifficultyModifer` that represents the current level's number. You can use this variable to alter the difficulty. **GameState.swift** would be the best place to implement most changes, as the game runs the initial state every time the level loads. One easy thing to do would to set the player's initial health (`levelScene.health`) to a lower value based on difficulty.

Chapter 24: Game Controllers

By Neil North

Ever since the earliest video game consoles, the controller has been synonymous with gaming: It's hard to think of one without the other.

When you consider how much technology and trends have changed, it's truly amazing how similar the controllers of today look to the earlier models. It shows just how well they were designed, even in their infancy.

The only thing that's come close to knocking the controller down a notch has been the rise of touchscreen devices with accelerometers. The number of phones and tablets available can't be ignored, and developers have changed the way they make games in order to keep up with the emerging market.

In iOS 7, Apple announced support for MFI game controllers and provided developers with a framework to tap into them—either via lightning connector or Bluetooth.

If the vast majority of modern phone and tablet games are designed for touchscreens and accelerometers, why should you care about game controllers? Here's why:

- **First person genre**: Powerful engines like Unity and Unreal Engine have made it possible for developers to bring the first person experience to mobile. You can use virtual controls onscreen, but they are nowhere near as precise or comfortable as a controller.

- **Strong niche market**: There aren't a massive number of games supporting controllers —even now, two major iOS releases later. If you support controllers, and make it known that you do, it gives you access to a powerful audience. If they're willing to spend money on peripherals, and you provide an excellent implementation of that peripheral, they will likely be willing to spend a lot more for your product.

- **Precision and comfort**: Onscreen thumbsticks have reached their peak, and quite often don't offer the precision of real thumbsticks. It's also nice to sit with the tablet in front of you and get into a comfy position rather than having to sit looking down at it.

- **No screen obstructions**: When you're touching the screen, you're also blocking your view of the game environment.

- **The new Apple TV**: You can support MFI controllers for the Apple TV with almost exactly the same code.

There are a few downsides, as well:

- **Not every genre makes sense**: Can you imagine playing a match-three-style game with a controller? Some modern touchscreen games simply don't work with a controller.

- **The rules**: Apple wants to maintain an App Store where any game available can be played entirely without a controller. This makes perfect sense, but it also creates a few challenges for developers—especially developers who want to release tvOS games meant to be played with a regular game controller due to the limited inputs of the Apple TV remote.

- **Market is still niche**: This is both a good and a bad thing. While controllers are generally not too hard to implement, there might not be enough positives to support it in some cases.

In this chapter, you'll implement support for MFI game controllers in Delve. Then you will add a target for tvOS and add controller support for tvOS as well including using the Apple TV Remote as a controller.

Controller formats

There are a number of different controllers on the market, but don't worry, you don't have to support all of them, individually. There are two standard layouts that can be supported:

- **Standard gamepad**: The standard gamepad has a D-pad, two shoulder buttons, a pause button and four action buttons.

- **Extended gamepad**: In addition to the standard controls, there are two thumbsticks that don't have a click action, and two additional shoulder buttons. If you have a Playstation or Xbox controller, this is the layout they follow.

With the addition of the Apple TV and tvOS, there's a third gamepad type available:

- **Micro gamepad**: This gamepad really is micro. It allows for a software D-pad that uses a touch surface, two action buttons—one located under the D-pad touch area—and a motion accelerometer. So far, the only remote in this format is the Apple TV remote.

Here are some common examples of each gamepad:

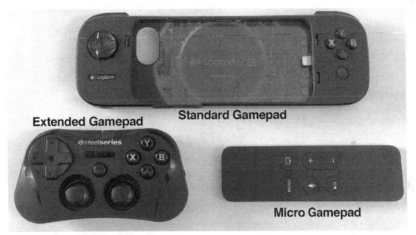

For a more exhaustive list of available game controllers, have a look at this website: https://mficontrollers.afterpad.com

Getting Started

Before you begin working with game controllers, there's one big improvement you should make to Delve.

Currently, the game is pretty quiet. It's time to add some music and sound effects!

> **Note:** This section is optional, and review of material found earlier in this book. If you'd like to dive right into game controllers, feel free to skip ahead to the "Creating the controller manager" section, where we'll have a starter project ready for you.
>
> But if you'd like to continue building the entire game yourself, keep reading!

Make sure you have Delve open from where you left it off after the previous chapter's challenge. If you didn't complete the previous chapter's challenge, you can find a starter project in **starter\Delve**.

First, drag the **Sounds** folder from the resources of this chapter into your project.

Next, open **GameState.swift** and find GameSceneInitialState. Add this to the top of didEnterWithPreviousState(_:):

```
SKTAudio.sharedInstance().playBackgroundMusic("delve_bg.mp3")
SKTAudio.sharedInstance().backgroundMusicPlayer?.volume = 0.4
```

This starts the background music playing.

Next open **GameScene.swift** and add some actions for the sounds:

```
//Sounds
let sndEnergy = SKAction.playSoundFileNamed("delve_energy",
waitForCompletion: false)
let sndHit = SKAction.playSoundFileNamed("delve_hit",
waitForCompletion: false)
let sndKill = SKAction.playSoundFileNamed("delve_kill",
waitForCompletion: false)
let sndShoot = SKAction.playSoundFileNamed("delve_shoot",
waitForCompletion: false)
let sndDamage = SKAction.playSoundFileNamed("delve_take_damage",
waitForCompletion: false)
let sndWin = SKAction.playSoundFileNamed("delve_win",
waitForCompletion: false)
```

Now you just need to play the sound effects at the appropriate times. Start by finding didBeginContact(_:), and add replace the code that handles the collision between "levelEnd" and "playerNode" with this:

```
if bodyA?.name == "levelEnd" && bodyB?.name == "playerNode" {
  stateMachine.enterState(GameSceneLimboState.self)
  movement = CGPointZero

  for enemyNode in enemyLayer.children {
    if let enemy = enemyNode as? EntityNode,
      let enemyEnt = enemy.entity as? EnemyEntity {
        enemyMoveSystem.removeComponentWithEntity(enemyEnt)
        enemyEnt.animationComponent.requestedAnimationState
= .Die_Down
        enemy.physicsBody = nil
    }
  }

  SKTAudio.sharedInstance().pauseBackgroundMusic()

  self.runAction(SKAction.sequence([sndWin,SKAction.waitForDuratio
```

```
n(2),SKAction.runBlock({ () -> Void in
    SKTAudio.sharedInstance().resumeBackgroundMusic()
    self.stateMachine.enterState(GameSceneWinState.self)
  })]))
}
```

Now rather than entering the `.GameSceneWinState` directly, you enter a new `GameSceneLimboState` that gives the player time to enjoy the game over sound effect and register that they lost before tapping to restart.

Next, play the damage sound effect in the collision between "enemyNode" and "playerNode", right after decreasing the player's health:

```
runAction(sndDamage)
```

Play the energy sound effect in the collision between "foodNode" and "playerNode", right after increasing the player's health:

```
runAction(sndEnergy)
```

Inside `damageEnemy(_:enemyNode:)`, play the kill sound effect in the case where `enemyEnt.enemyHealth` is less than 0:

```
runAction(sndKill)
```

In the else case of the same if statement, play the hit sound effect:

```
runAction(sndHit)
```

In `update(_:)`, play the shoot sound effect right after `addEntity(projEntity)`:

```
runAction(sndShoot)
```

And that's it - build and run to enjoy some groovy tunes!

Creating the controller manager

> **Note**: If you skipped ahead from earlier in this chapter, you can pick up with the **starter\Delve_Sounds** project in the resources of this chapter. This is the same as where you left off the game in the previous chapter's challenge, but with sound effects and music added.

Your game controller functionality is unlikely to differ greatly from game to game. The class you'll build will be designed to make it very easy to move between games, with minimal effort to implement.

In your project's **Helpers** group, add a new Swift file named **SKTGameController.swift** and replace its contents with this:

```
import SpriteKit
import GameController
```

The GameController framework has the same name for both iOS and tvOS.

Note: Game controllers don't work with OS X, despite being able to connect via Bluetooth.

You need a way to let actions from the controller update your game scene. In this implementation, you'll use delegation. Add this protocol under the imports:

```
protocol SKTGameControllerDelegate: class {
  func buttonEvent(event:String,velocity:Float,pushedOn:Bool)
  func stickEvent(event:String,point:CGPoint)
}
```

Button presses and thumbstick movements have their own separate functions.

Each button on an MFI controller is pressurized, so when you press a button, it will give you a velocity reading between 0.0 and 1.0.

It's important to note that every time the velocity changes, the function will be called again. You can handle the on/off state of buttons by watching the pushedOn Boolean value.

Now, add this code below the code you just added:

```
enum controllerType {
  case micro
  case standard
  case extended
}

class SKTGameController {

}
```

This code contains a simple enum to determine what type of controller is connected, and the class declaration for your game controller class.

To let the game controller class retain information about the controller between changing scenes, you'll use the singleton design pattern.

Add this code above the class declaration:

```
let GameControllerSharedInstance = SKTGameController()
```

This creates a constant for the instance of `SKTGameController`.

Now, add these instance variables inside the class declaration:

```
//1
weak var delegate: SKTGameControllerDelegate?

//2
var gameControllerConnected: Bool = false
var gameController: GCController = GCController()
var gameControllerType: controllerType?
var gamePaused: Bool = false

//3
class var sharedInstance:SKTGameController {
  return GameControllerSharedInstance
}
```

You declare a number of variables here:

1. This delegate is your link to the current scene that adopts the protocol.

2. The first variable tracks if a game controller is currently connected; the second is a link to the game controller itself; the third stores the type of controller based on the enum you added; and the last is a pause toggle.

3. This is a variable that returns the current singleton instance of the class.

Next, add the following code below your instance variables:

```
//1
init() {
  NSNotificationCenter.defaultCenter().addObserver(self,
    selector: "controllerStateChanged:",
    name: GCControllerDidConnectNotification,
    object: nil)
  NSNotificationCenter.defaultCenter().addObserver(self,
    selector: "controllerStateChanged:",
    name: GCControllerDidDisconnectNotification,
    object: nil)


  GCController.startWirelessControllerDiscoveryWithCompletionHandl
  er() {
      self.controllerStateChanged(NSNotification(name: "", object:
  nil))
    }
    self.controllerStateChanged(NSNotification(name: "", object:
  nil))
```

```
    }

    //2
    deinit {
      NSNotificationCenter.defaultCenter().removeObserver(self,
          name: GCControllerDidConnectNotification, object: nil)
        NSNotificationCenter.defaultCenter().removeObserver(self,
          name: GCControllerDidDisconnectNotification, object: nil)
    }
```

Take a closer look at the initializer:

1. When the class is initialized, it registers an observer for controller connections and disconnections. When one or the other happens, the observer notices the state has changed and calls the function named `controllerStateChanged(_:)` will be called.

2. When the class is released, it also needs to remove the observers.

Now that you've included calls to `controllerStateChanged(_:)`, implement it below the previous functions:

```
@objc func controllerStateChanged(notification: NSNotification)
{

  if GCController.controllers().count > 0 {
    gameControllerConnected = true
    gameController = GCController.controllers()[0] as
GCController
    //More code to be added here
    controllerAdded()
  } else {
    gameControllerConnected = false
    controllerRemoved()
  }

}
```

This function sets up the instance variables you added earlier.

If the count of controllers is greater than zero, you change the `gameControllerConnected` variable to `true`. You then add the game controller at index zero to the `gameController` variable.

The code above uses two functions that you haven't implemented yet: `controllerAdded()` and `controllerRemoved()`.

Before you can call `controllerAdded()`, you need to specify what sort of controller is connected.

Add the following code in place of the `//More code to be added here` comment:

```
#if os(iOS)
  if (gameController.extendedGamepad != nil) {
    gameControllerType = .extended
  } else {
    gameControllerType = .standard
  }
#elseif os(tvOS)
  if (gameController.extendedGamepad != nil) {
    gameControllerType = .extended
  } else if (gameController.microGamepad != nil) {
    gameControllerType = .micro
  } else {
    gameControllerType = .standard
  }
#endif
```

On the iOS platform, you check to see if the current game controller adopts the extended gamepad method; if it doesn't, it must be a standard controller. Supporting tvOS is similar, but you need to account for micro controllers, as well.

Now you've covered all possible official MFI controllers, with minimal effort!

Its time to implement `controllerAdded()` and `ControllerRemoved()`, so add them below the function you just added:

```
func controllerAdded() {
  if (gameControllerConnected) {
    //Add code here
  }
}

func controllerRemoved() {
  gameControllerConnected = false
  gameControllerType = nil
}
```

There are a few ways you could pass the information from the controller to the scene. You could:

- **Read the value of each control manually**: You would generally do this via the game loop. It's one of the simpler solutions, but it also means a lot of additional heavy lifting for something that may not have changed every time you try to read it.

- **Use a value change handler**: Your value change handler would execute a preset action every time the value of an input button or thumbstick changed. This is the method you'll implement for this game, as it has the least impact on game performance and works well using a protocol.

- **Use a pressed change handler**: This would work similarly to the value change handler, but would call the preset action when a button is pressed or depressed, instead of with every change in pressure. Using a pressed change handler has no impact on sensitivity as any value greater than 0.0 is considered to be "pressed", it doesn't have to reach 1.0.

Assigning Controls

For this game, you'll use directional movement and weapon firing, and you'll use the A button to pass through menu screens.

Each controller has its own limitations, so you'll need to plan accordingly:

- **Extended gamepad**: This is the most versatile controller, but note that most extended controllers lack motion support.

- **Standard gamepad**: Losing two thumbsticks isn't a big deal for a game that only involves the left thumbstick, because you can simply move that functionality to the D-pad. In Delve, you'd normally want two thumbsticks, so you'll need to decide on an alternative.

- **Micro gamepad**: This is where you really need to get creative. Luckily, you only need one button; however, the single D-pad is still a problem. The micro controllers all have motion, but it doesn't allow for the accuracy required for attacking.

Your biggest issue is needing two controls that support 360-degree movement (one for movement, and one for firing). You could handle this in a few ways:

- **Substitution**: The player will only want to attack when there's an enemy nearby. You could create a basic AI to find the closest enemy, and if it's within a certain range, auto-attack in its direction.

- **Stacking**: You could assume that the hero will be attacking in the same direction as he's walking, and combine the controls. This doesn't always work as you intend, though, as more likely than not, your hero will be running away from an enemy onslaught.

- **Toggling**: You could set the D-pad to move the player, but use it for attacking if the user holds down another button.

- **Cooperation**: Standard controllers are connected to the device directly, so while the D-pad takes over movement, you could let the device motion from the accelerometer control the direction of the attack.

Each option has its pros and cons, and you may want to use a different option for each controller type, or let players choose what they prefer.

Standard gamepad

The standard gamepad will use the cooperation approach.

Add the following to `controllerAdded()` in place of the `//Add code here` comment:

```
if gameControllerType! == .standard,
   let pad:GCGamepad = gameController.gamepad {

}
```

If the current controller is of the standard type, you access the gamepad property and assign it to `pad`.

Inside the `if` statement, add this code:

```
pad.buttonA.valueChangedHandler = { button, value, pressed in
   if self.delegate != nil {
     self.delegate!.buttonEvent("buttonA", velocity: value,
pushedOn: pressed)
   }
}
```

Here, you register an action to be performed whenever the platform detects a different value coming from `pad.buttonA`.

The change handler provides three variables to the action: a `button` property; a `value` between 0.0 and 1.0 that represents how much pressure the user is placing on the button; and `pressed`, a Boolean value representing whether or not the button is in a state of being pressed.

Then, if a delegate is available, you call the `buttonEvent(_:velocity:pushedOn:)` function specified in the protocol.

Directly below this code, within the same `if` statement, add the following to cover the D-pad:

```
pad.dpad.up.valueChangedHandler = { button, value, pressed in
   if self.delegate != nil {
     self.delegate!.buttonEvent("dpad_up", velocity: value,
pushedOn: pressed)
   }
}
pad.dpad.down.valueChangedHandler = { button, value, pressed in
   if self.delegate != nil {
     self.delegate!.buttonEvent("dpad_down", velocity: value,
pushedOn: pressed)
   }
}
pad.dpad.left.valueChangedHandler = { button, value, pressed in
   if self.delegate != nil {
```

```
        self.delegate!.buttonEvent("dpad_left", velocity: value,
    pushedOn: pressed)
      }
    }
    pad.dpad.right.valueChangedHandler = { button, value, pressed in
      if self.delegate != nil {
        self.delegate!.buttonEvent("dpad_right", velocity: value,
    pushedOn: pressed)
      }
    }
```

This covers all of the controls found on the standard controller. Now you need to tell the game scene what to do with this information.

Using the controller commands

It's time to implement the delegate in your game's scene.

Go to **GameScene.swift** and update the class declaration as follows:

```
class GameScene: SKScene, tileMapDelegate,
SKPhysicsContactDelegate, SKTGameControllerDelegate {
```

Notice that you've added the SKTGameControllerDelegate. Now, you need to include the two functions from the protocol.

Include the following code in didMoveToView(_:), at the bottom:

```
//Game Controllers
SKTGameController.sharedInstance.delegate = self
```

This sets the game controller delegate to the current scene.

Add this code at the bottom of your game scene class:

```
//MARK: SKTGameController Delegate

func buttonEvent(event:String,velocity:Float,pushedOn:Bool) {

}

func stickEvent(event:String,point:CGPoint) {

}
```

The tapState property introduced in the previous chapter let you have different interactions for different states when the player is touching the screen. You can use this same property to define how to handle button interactions.

Add this code to buttonEvent(_:velocity:pushedOn:):

```
switch tapState {
case .startGame:
  if event == "buttonA" {
    stateMachine.enterState(GameSceneActiveState.self)
  }
  break
case .dismissPause:
  if event == "buttonA" {
    stateMachine.enterState(GameSceneActiveState.self)
  }
  break
case .nextLevel:
  if event == "buttonA" {
    if let scene = GameScene(fileNamed:"GameScene") {
      scene.scaleMode = (self.scene?.scaleMode)!
      let transition = SKTransition.fadeWithDuration(0.6)
      view!.presentScene(scene, transition: transition)
    }
  }
  break
case .attack:

  break
default:
  break
}
```

This code is almost exactly like the code in touchesBegan(_:withEvent:). The big change is that you've wrapped each event in an if statement that tests if the player is pressing button A.

If you own a standard format controller, you can build and run the game to make sure the A button dismisses the start-up screen and any game over scenes.

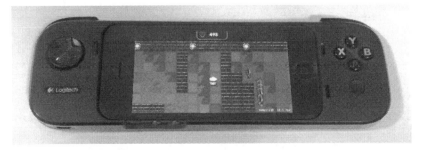

Note: A lot of standard format controllers use USB connectivity instead of Bluetooth, like the one pictured above. Keep in mind, if you want to test your game using this sort of controller, you'll have to build and run with the cable connected directly to your Mac, then unplug it and place the phone in the controller.

This workflow could get rather frustrating, which is why we recommend you use an extended controller with Bluetooth for testing.

Movement controls

The cooperation approach is going to work well here, but you're going to need the game to make decisions based on which controller is connected.

Begin by updating the `.attack` case in `buttonEvent(_:velocity:pushedOn:)` to the following:

```
case .attack:
  if event == "dpad_up" {
    movement.y = CGFloat(velocity)
  }
  if event == "dpad_down" {
    movement.y = CGFloat(velocity) * -1
  }
  if event == "dpad_left" {
    movement.x = CGFloat(velocity) * -1
  }
  if event == "dpad_right" {
    movement.x = CGFloat(velocity)
  }
break
```

The velocity measure isn't just for buttons; it can also be used on the d-pad. Using the velocity will give the player refined movement control, making the game feel smoother.

Now, scroll to `update(_:)` and update the motion section as follows:

```
  //Motion
#if os(iOS)
if (self.motionManager.accelerometerData != nil) {
  //1
  var motion = CGPointZero
  if self.motionManager.accelerometerData!.acceleration.x > 0.02
||
    self.motionManager.accelerometerData!.acceleration.x < -0.02
{
  motion.y =
```

```
CGFloat(self.motionManager.accelerometerData!.acceleration.x)
  }
  if self.motionManager.accelerometerData!.acceleration.y > 0.02
||
    self.motionManager.accelerometerData!.acceleration.y < -0.02
{
    motion.x =
CGFloat((self.motionManager.accelerometerData!.acceleration.y) *
-1)
  }
  //2
  if (SKTGameController.sharedInstance.gameControllerConnected
== true) {
    //3
    if (SKTGameController.sharedInstance.gameControllerType ==
      .standard) {
      self.playerAttack = motion
    }
  } else {
    self.movement = motion
  }
}
#endif
```

1. Instead of setting the motion directly to the movement property, you assign a motion variable.

2. If a controller is connected, you configure for the controller. If you don't find a controller, you assign the motion to the movement property.

3. If the controller type is standard, you use the motion to aim the weapon. If the controller type is extended, then you don't need to use motion—instead, the extra thumbstick will do nicely.

There's an added advantage to checking the controller status every time the game loop is called: You can easily and seamlessly switch between available controller types.

Build and run, and you can now move the player via the D-pad, use the motion from the device to define the attack direction, and dismiss menu screens using the A button.

Extended gamepad

The extended controller type has plenty of controls available, so no tricks are required to get great results.

Return to **SKTGameController.swift** and add this code below the `if` statement for the standard controller type in `controllerAdded()`:

```
if gameControllerType! == .extended,
   let extendedPad:GCExtendedGamepad =
gameController.extendedGamepad {

}
```

Same as with the standard controller, you first check the type, and then access the relevant property from the game controller based on its type.

Now, inside the `if` statement, add this code:

```
//1
extendedPad.buttonA.valueChangedHandler = { button, value,
pressed in
   if self.delegate != nil {
     self.delegate!.buttonEvent("buttonA", velocity: value,
pushedOn: pressed)
   }
}
//2
extendedPad.leftThumbstick.valueChangedHandler = { dpad, xValue,
yValue in
   if self.delegate != nil {
     self.delegate!.stickEvent("leftstick", point:CGPoint(x:
CGFloat(xValue),y: CGFloat(yValue)))
   }
}
extendedPad.rightThumbstick.valueChangedHandler = { dpad,
xValue, yValue in
   if self.delegate != nil {
     self.delegate!.stickEvent("rightstick", point:CGPoint(x:
CGFloat(xValue),y: CGFloat(yValue)))
   }
}
```

1. You implement the A button in the same way you did the standard controller.

2. The thumbsticks are a little different. They pass in x- and y-values that you can use to create a `CGPoint` to represent the character's movement. Each value ranges from -1.0 to 1.0, with 0 being stationary.

Back in **GameScene.swift**, scroll to `stickEvent(_:point:)` and add this code:

```
switch tapState {
  case .attack:
    if event == "leftstick" {
      movement = point
    }
    if event == "rightstick" {
```

```
        playerAttack = point
      }
    break
default:
   break
  }
```

That's it! Connect an extended controller if you have one available, and build and run to try it out.

You can move the hero with the left stick, attack with the right stick in whichever direction you move it, and dismiss menu screens with the A button.

Next, you've going to implement the micro controller. But because the micro controller only works on the Apple TV, you'll need to support that first.

Adding the tvOS target

From the menu bar in Xcode, select **File**, then **New**, and finally **Target...** to begin adding your tvOS target.

In the template selector, choose **tvOS/Application** from the left menu and then **Game**.

Click **Next**.

In the options, give the target a **Product Name** of **DelveTV**, make sure the **Language** is set to **Swift** and the **Game Technology** to **SpriteKit**. Click **Finish**.

At this point, build and run the **DelveTV** target on your Apple TV or tvOS simulator.

You'll see the normal sample project, complete with spinning spaceships if you tap or click the touchpad on the remote.

But you're headed underground, not into space! Locate the **DelveTV** folder, **rename** it **TV Controller** and **delete** the following files:

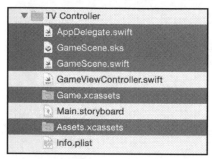

Now, locate the resource files at **starter\Resources** and drag the folder named **Assets.xcassets** into this same group.

Make sure when you select the target, you only select **DelveTV**:

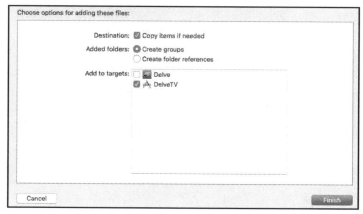

Click **Finish**.

This assets file contains Delve's app icons, top shelf images and launch images.

While you're in the **TV Controller** target folder, access **Info.plist** and change the **Bundle name** to **Delve** to override the target name.

Each file within each group of the **Delve** group must now have its target relationships updated to both available targets.

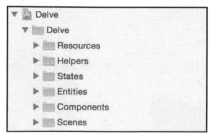

Work through each file and select both targets from the Utilities panel:

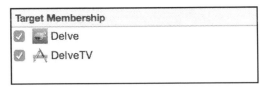

Add the **iOS Controller\AppDelegate.swift** to the tvOS target as well.

When you're done, build and run the game to make sure it doesn't crash - that will verify that you've set all of the proper targets.

After the launch screen, you'll get a blank screen for no apparent reason. Before you start flipping tables, have a look at **GameViewController.swift** inside the **TV Controller** group. Notice how the scene is created a little differently? The default **GameViewController.swift** that is generated with the new target needs a small change.

Update the scene declaration to this:

```
if let scene = GameScene(fileNamed: "GameScene") {
```

Build and run to see the results.

> **Note**: Want to know how to find unknown errors like this? It was clear the scene hadn't been loaded, as the background was the default gray.
>
> The scene declaration is an `if-let`, which means that if the line fails for whatever reason, it won't be run and won't produce an error. That's how you know this is the point of failure.

Now the scene will load, but you have a few other problems with your GUI that need attention:

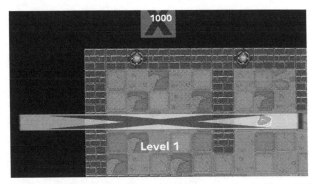

Go to your **GUI.xcassets** folder, select one of the images from the middle-left menu and have a look at the devices in the Attributes Inspector.

Check the **Apple TV** box in addition to the Universal option, because the Universal option doesn't include tvOS.

Now, navigate to the folder **projects\starter\Resources\tvOS GUI**, where you'll find each of your GUI components; drag and drop each one into its appropriate spot in the **GUI.xcassets** folder:

Build and run again, and everything will look perfect! You aren't quite there yet, though —you still need to implement game controller support.

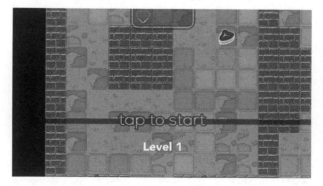

Supporting controllers on tvOS

By default, the Apple TV remote can interact with many standard iOS functions, such as `touchesBegan(_:)`. If you intend to set up the Apple TV remote as a custom micro controller, then you don't want this standard functionality to mess with it.

Apple has provided a simple way to control these interactions.

Access the tvOS-targeted **GameViewController.swift** and update the imports to include the GameController framework:

```
import GameController
```

Now, update the class declaration as follows:

```
class GameViewController: GCEventViewController {
```

The GameController framework includes `GCEventViewController` for the specific purpose of allowing control over the way the view controller responds to the Apple TV remote.

In `viewDidLoad()`, add this right before you instantiate the game scene:

```
controllerUserInteractionEnabled = false
```

This disables the standard functionality of the controller—so, for example, a game controller's B button won't exit the game.

When a game controller is connected, `GCControllers.controllers()` will return two controllers. In early beta builds, the game controller would automatically take index 0, allowing for seamless transfer between remote and game controller. In the latest beta build, this isn't the case, so you'll have to check the index yourself.

Go to **SKTGameController.swift** and update `controllerStateChanged(_:)` by adding these lines at the top of the `#elseif os(tvOS)` statement:

```
if gameController.vendorName == "Remote" &&
  GCController.controllers().count > 1 {
    gameController = GCController.controllers()[1] as
GCController
}
```

If the controller at the first index has the name `"Remote"`, and there is more than one controller connected, then you change the current controller to the controller at index 1.

Connecting a controller

The extended controller you set up earlier will also work on tvOS, now that you've done this preliminary setup.

On your Apple TV, go to **Settings/Remotes and Devices/Bluetooth** and pair your controller. Don't forget to unpair with your iOS device first, since a controller can only be paired with one device at a time.

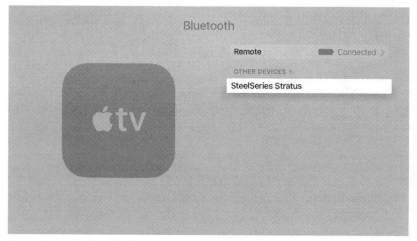

Build and run. The remote still won't work as intended, as you haven't set up the micro controller. However, a connected game controller will work with the same controls as in the iOS version.

Micro gamepad

Just like the standard and extended gamepads, you need to set up value handlers for the micro gamepad controls.

It should be noted that the Apple TV Remote functions a little differently when enabled as a game controller. The play/pause button becomes known as the X button, the Menu button becomes the pause button and the screen button becomes the home button.

You'll use the toggling approach to handle the control problem presented by the micro controller. When the player holds the X button down, the D-pad will change the direction of attack.

In **SKTGameController.swift**, add this new property:

```
var lastShootPoint = CGPoint.zero
```

Then add this code to `controllerStateChanged(_:)`, right after the two `if os(...)` blocks:

```
#if os(tvOS)
if gameControllerType! == .micro,
  let microPad:GCMicroGamepad = gameController.microGamepad {

  //1
    microPad.buttonA.valueChangedHandler = { button, value,
pressed in
      if self.delegate != nil {
```

```
            self.delegate!.buttonEvent("buttonA", velocity: value,
    pushedOn: pressed)
            }
        }

        //2
        microPad.allowsRotation = true
        //3
        microPad.reportsAbsoluteDpadValues = true
        //4
        microPad.dpad.valueChangedHandler = { dpad, xValue, yValue
    in
            if self.delegate != nil && !microPad.buttonX.pressed {
                self.delegate!.stickEvent("leftstick", point:CGPoint(x:
    CGFloat(xValue),y: CGFloat(yValue)))
            }
            if self.delegate != nil && microPad.buttonX.pressed {
                // 5
                let curShootPoint = CGPoint(x: CGFloat(xValue),y:
    CGFloat(yValue))
                self.lastShootPoint = self.lastShootPoint * 0.9 +
    curShootPoint * 0.1
                self.delegate!.stickEvent("rightstick",
    point:self.lastShootPoint)
                self.delegate!.stickEvent("leftstick", point:CGPoint(x:
    0.0,y: 0.0))
            }
        }
    }
    #endif
```

There's a lot going on here, so take a look at the breakdown:

1. This handles the standard A button functionality.

> **Note**: The A button on the Apple TV remote is the same as the click on the D-pad touch area.

2. When you hold the remote in the portrait position, the D-pad functions as expected; if you turn the remote to landscape, and expect it to change the orientation of the D-pad controls, then this value needs to be `true`.

3. Absolute values consider the center of the touch area to be the center of the D-pad, while non-absolute values consider the first point of touch to be the center of the D-pad, and adjust accordingly with every new touch.

4. The micro controller provides different events, depending on the state of button X.

5. You don't want to use the direct input of the right stick because the user may start

moving their finger on the trackpad intending to move fractions of a second before they release the play/pause button. If you used direct input, this would cause them to shoot in the direction they intended to move, resulting in a frustrating experience. Instead, here you blend the shoot input based on previous shoot input to more accurately reflect the player's intention.

There's one last thing. Remember that on tvOS, your touch handlers are still called, and you don't want to do anything in the attack state on tvOS. So in touchesBegan(_:withEvent:), wrap the content inside the case .attack: state with an ifdef:

```
case .attack:
  #if (iOS)
  for touch in touches {
    let location = touch.locationInNode(self)
    if let player = worldLayer.childNodeWithName("playerNode") {
      playerAttack = location - player.position
    }
  }
  #endif
  break
```

Go to your tvOS settings menu and disconnect your controller if you did earlier, so only the remote is connected. Build and run. Move around with the D-pad and hold the play/pause button to stop and fire in the direction you're pressing on the D-pad. Make sure you hold your controller in a landscape position.

Right now, the controls feel a little fast on both of the controllers and the remote. The accelerometer controls felt OK, so you need to make sure you don't affect the speed of the accelerometer controls when you fix the other controllers.

> **Note**: Remember that the tvOS remote has an accelerometer, as well! While you won't work with it in this chapter, with the right game, the remote's accelerometer could enhance your gameplay and make up for the limited controls on the Apple TV.

Tightening up the controls

The standard controller D-pad and default accelerometer controls move the character at what feels like a reasonable pace.

The extended controller and Apple TV remote seem to exhibit excessive acceleration, and movement doesn't feel natural. Both of these controller types use stickEvent(_:point:) in **GameScene.swift**; go there now and update it as follows:

```
//1
func stickEvent(event:String,var point:CGPoint) {
  switch tapState {
  case .attack:
    if event == "leftstick" {
      //2
      movement = point.normalize() * 0.5
    }
    if event == "rightstick" {
      playerAttack = point
    }
    break
  default:
    break
  }
}
```

With this code, you simply do the following:

1. You update the function declaration with `var` to make the `point` value mutable.

2. You normalize the movement to remove any excess acceleration, and then halve it again to bring the max speed in line with the other controls.

That's it! Build and run your game. You are now successfully supporting three control formats on iOS: device, standard gamepad and extended gamepad; and two control formats on the Apple TV: the remote and the extended gamepad.

At this point, you've used GameplayKit's fantastic features to create tile map games that you can easily scale and improve. You've covered powerful methods of procedural generation that you can use with more complex algorithms to create truly original levels. Your toolkit to make impressive procedural tile map games is complete!

Challenges

There's just one short challenge for this chapter, to give you a little more experience with controllers.

As always, if you get stuck you can find the solution in the resources for this chapter, but give it your best shot first!

Challenge 1: Pause game

Apple's *Human Interface Guidelines* make it mandatory to implement a pause button for all controllers.

Using what you've learned about the game state and change handlers, implement a pause button for Delve for all controller layouts.

Once you've implemented change handlers, you'll need to call the scene delegate to change the scene's state.

Section VI: Bonus Chapters

To thank you for purchasing this book, we've included some bonus chapters for you!

These bonus chapters come as an optional PDF download, which you can download for free here:

- www.raywenderlich.com/store/2d-ios-tvos-games-by-tutorials/bonus-chapters

In these bonus chapters, you'll learn about some APIs other than Sprite Kit that are good to know when making games for iOS. In particular, you will learn how add Game Center leaderboards and achievements into your game, use the new iOS 9 ReplayKit API, and add iAds into your game.

In the process, you will integrate these APIs into a top-down racing game called Circuit Racer, where you take the role of an elite racecar driver out to set a world record. It would be no problem if it weren't for the debris on the track!

Conclusion

We hope that you have enjoyed your adventure through this book. If you followed along the entire way, you have made five complete iOS and tvOS games with Sprite Kit and Swift from scratch – spanning everything from zombies to cats to rampaging dinosaurs.

You now have all the knowledge it takes to make a hit game, so why not go for it?

Come up with a great idea, prototype a game, get people to play it, watch them for feedback and keep iterating and polishing your game based on all you have learned. Be sure to set aside time in your schedule to add juice to your game, and make sure you have killer art and sound effects, following the advice in the book.

We can't wait to see what you come up with! Be sure to stop by our forums and share your progress at www.raywenderlich.com/forums.

You might also be interested to know that we have a monthly blog post where we review games written by fellow readers like you. If you'd like to be considered for this column, please visit this page after you release your game: www.raywenderlich.com/reviews

We have one final question for you: Did we succeed in our goal to write the best book on game programming you've ever read? Please email us anytime at ray@raywenderlich.com to let us know either way.

Thank you again for purchasing this book. Your continued support is what makes the tutorials, books and other things we do at raywenderlich.com possible. We truly appreciate it.

Best of luck in all your iOS adventures,

— Mike, Michael, Ali, Neil, Toby, Rod, Marin, Tammy, B.C., Vinnie, Ray and Vicki

The *2D iOS & tvOS Games by Tutorials* Team

Made in the USA
Charleston, SC
30 October 2015